Liberals under Autocracy

Liberals under Autocracy

*Modernization and Civil Society
in Russia, 1866–1904*

Anton A. Fedyashin

THE UNIVERSITY OF WISCONSIN PRESS

Publication of this volume has been made possible, in part, through support from the Andrew W. Mellon Foundation.

The University of Wisconsin Press
1930 Monroe Street, 3rd Floor
Madison, Wisconsin 53711-2059
uwpress.wisc.edu

3 Henrietta Street
London WCE 8LU, England
eurospanbookstore.com

Library of Congress Cataloging-in-Publication Data
Fedyashin, Anton A.
Liberals under autocracy : modernization and civil society in Russia,
1866–1904 / Anton A. Fedyashin.
p. cm.
Includes bibliographical references and index.
ISBN 978-0-299-28434-3 (pbk. : alk. paper) — ISBN 978-0-299-28433-6 (e-book)
1. Viestnik Evropy (Saint Petersburg, Russia). 2. Russia—Intellectual life—
1801–1917. 3. Russia—Politics and government—1801-1917. 4. Liberalism—
Russia—History—19th century. I. Title.
DK189.2.F44 2012
947.08'2—dc23
2011042001

*To the two
most important women in my life:*

MY MOTHER IRINA
AND
MY WIFE ANITA

Contents

Acknowledgments

I would like to thank my dissertation committee members—my advisor Catherine Evtuhov, the late Richard Stites, and Harley Balzer—who made possible the metamorphosis of a graduate project into a book. James Shedel's class on Central European politics subconsciously triggered this project.

My parents, Irina and Andrei, were at the source of it all as they retracted the Iron Curtain and allowed me to grow intellectually by exposing me to the best of what both sides of the Cold War world had to offer. To my mother, Irina, I owe my love of knowledge and passion for inquiry. From my father, I inherited the joie de vivre that is the fuel of intellectual persistence. My grandparents on both sides of the family created a warm and joyous childhood such as those I have read descriptions of in the best Russian novels. This book would never have seen the light of day had it not been for my wife Anita who inspired, cajoled, and forced the speedy and successful completion of this project. By creating every imaginable material and intellectual condition for my work, she bore the greatest responsibility for its completion. In the process, she has become an intellectual companion and a co-traveler for life. I could not have been luckier. I owe the greatest debt to Ray and Christina Hanna for creating a home in Washington and the Shenandoah Valley. Evan Jenkins unfortunately did not live to see the completion of this project, which he would have welcomed joyously. A dear friend, he greatly extended my intellectual horizons, musical tastes, and sommelier experience.

I am in debt to Alexander Martin, Randall Poole, Alfred J. Rieber, and David McDonald for their priceless advice on the manuscript. Gwen Walker of the University of Wisconsin Press has been the best guide for a first book project that I could ever have imagined. The History Department at American University, where I completed the book while teaching, became an academic family that stimulated and encouraged me. I am especially grateful to Eric Lohr, Pamela Nadell, Peter Kuznick, Richard Breitman, Allan Lichtman, Alan Kraut, Max Friedman, Katharina Vester, and the late Bob Griffith for their support and advice. I have also received crucial intellectual sustenance from the Washington, DC, Russian History Seminar. The project of writing a dissertation and then turning it into a book would have been more tedious were it not for the delightful combination of intellect and good spirits at Martin's Tavern in Georgetown, including Peter Dunkley, Claus Westmeier, Amy Leonard, Howard Spendelow, and the lynchpin of it all—the late Richard Stites. I would also like to thank the staffs of the European Reading Room at the Library of Congress, the Pushkin House Archive in Saint Petersburg, and the Russian State Library in my native and beloved city of Moscow. The launch of the Initiative for Russian Culture at American University in September 2011 made me realize even further the value of this project. I am profoundly grateful to the three people whose vision inspired the Initiative: Susan Lehrman, Peter Starr, and His Excellency Sergey I. Kislyak, Ambassador of the Russian Federation to the United States.

As each intellectual product is the result of a person's entire mental experience, the friends who have intellectually accompanied me have become companions for life: William Aaron, Andrea Despot, James Keidel, Damon Kovelsky, Kirill Orekhov, and Brandon "Carlos" Schneider. Having written about a journal as an institution, perhaps the greatest lesson I have learned is that no scholar stands alone.

Liberals under Autocracy

Introduction

THIS BOOK GREW OUT OF a keen interest in the political culture of contemporary Russia, whose post-Soviet transition made current many issues from the late imperial era. The long nineteenth century now speaks directly to the present and parallels between the late tsarist and post-Soviet periods abound despite the obvious differences. One of the most provocative questions that reemerged after the collapse of the Soviet Union is liberalism's viability as a political force. During the 1990s, reformers who referred to themselves as liberals misjudged the effects of economic shock therapy that they implemented according to a Western "liberal" model, which reemerged in the late twentieth century as a conservative agenda in its classical laissez-faire sense. Because of these mismanaged economic reforms, liberalism became a term of abuse in Russia synonymous with reckless socio-economic experimentation, rapacious capitalism, rampant corruption, and political chaos.

None of this was true about Russia's prerevolutionary liberalism, which deserves closer examination that is sure to enrich the current debate about liberalism's future by exploring the nuances of previous socio-economic transformations in Russia. This work will attempt to salvage liberal values by analyzing the liberal development program that evolved in the late Romanov Empire during a period of similarly destabilizing socio-economic transformations brought on by the relentless economic development that characterized the Western world as a whole in the nineteenth century. By the 1860s, several states in the new and old worlds had to transform estate-based administrative systems into participatory ones, which resulted in the War of Reform in Mexico, the Civil War in the United States, the *Ausgleich* out of which Austria-Hungary emerged, the unifications of Italy and Germany, and the Third Republic in France. Russia became part of this wave of reformism after the embarrassing defeat in the Crimean War (1853–1856) uncovered the Romanov Empire's socio-economic backwardness. Tsar Alexander II (1855–1881) launched the Great Reforms with the emancipation of the serfs in 1861 and then restructured the courts, the administrative system, and the military.

As part of the administrative reform, the Russian state created a network of local self-government units known as *zemstvos* in 1864.[1] Set up on the district and provincial levels, they tended to local socio-economic needs such as schools, clinics, infrastructure, veterinary care, and insurance, but were explicitly forbidden to involve themselves in political affairs. Popularly elected and bringing together landowners and peasants, the zemstvos became the first officially sanctioned experiments in inclusive self-administration.[2] In combination with the other reforms of Alexander II, the zemstvos stimulated the growth of professions as they soaked up doctors, teachers, agronomists, architects, lawyers, and many other specialists. As a middle class began to develop, the disparate professional groups sought mutual contact and a framework through which to articulate their aspirations independently of the state.[3] Professional and academic organizations sprang up all over the Russian Empire.[4] Such organizations, together with the zemstvo network and a renaissance of journalism, became the building blocks of a vibrant extraparliamentary civil society.[5]

The 1860s also spawned a powerful radical revolutionary movement whose members considered the Great Reforms a diversionary tactic due to their incomplete nature: the peasants did not receive land into private ownership, the zemstvo network did not culminate with a proto-parliamentary imperial zemstvo institution, censorship was eased but not abolished, and the police system remained intact. The Romanov Empire entered a volatile period as the state navigated the treacherous current of reforms. Challenges came not only from revolutionaries, but also from an increasingly influential liberal component of civil society that saw the Great Reforms as unfinished, but stopped short of calling for the overthrow of the government. The subject of this book is this loyal opposition to the state.

The story's central characters are the thick monthly journal the *Herald of Europe* (*Vestnik Evropy*, 1866–1918) and the remarkable constellation of intellectuals who ran it between 1866 and 1904 when this flagship of Russian liberalism became the most influential social and intellectual journalistic institution in an empire where literary culture wielded unparalleled influence.

At the height of its popularity in the 1880s and 1890s, the *Herald of Europe* sold around eight thousand monthly copies, but this number does not reflect family members who read it and access to public library copies. For comparison's sake, the most popular thick journal in Russia, *Notes of the Fatherland* (*Otechestvennye zapiski*, 1818–1884), peaked at around ten thousand subscribers before being shut down in 1884, while the most popular newspaper, Aleksei Suvorin's *New Time* (*Novoe vremia*, 1868–1917), printed about fifty thousand daily copies in the 1890s.[6] The circulation figures, however, should not eclipse an understanding of the journal's influence.

By the mid-nineteenth century in Russia, literary or "thick" journals had become the main instruments through which society explored and contextualized itself. Virtually every major nineteenth-century Russian novel first appeared in serialized form. As a result, "collected works" became popular, lucrative, and painstaking projects that brought together scattered publications. There were other cultural and intellectual institutions in Russia, such as the imperial court, the schools and universities, salons, discussion groups ("circles"), academies of arts and sciences, and theaters, but among these, the thick journal became a unique cultural nexus because of its breadth. It recorded, analyzed, and coordinated social, economic, and literary developments in Russia (and abroad) and then delivered this cultural synthesis to the reader. In addition to creating reader communities, journals also became focal points around which intellectuals structured their social and literary identities. Proximity bred intellectual kinship as contributors exchanged ideas about books they read as well as lectures and events they attended. Close personal, artistic, political, and financial support networks fostered the intellectual survival and growth of several generations of writers.

In Russia, the "community of journals" created a particularly tight and structured literary world.[7] Historian Timofei Granovskii wrote to a friend in 1844: "With a journal one can do much good, more than with a whole library of scholarly works which no one reads."[8] Much as they had done with the genre of the novel, Russians took the European journal tradition and imparted to it greater cultural influence. Russia's political system forbade parliamentary activity and social participation in planning reforms and, as a result, the public's constrained intellectual energy flowed with greater vigor into the journals. Literary critic Vissarion Belinskii wrote: "The world of the journals is the political world in miniature."[9] By the 1880s, the *Herald of Europe* had become the champion of liberal issues and without its examination the history of Russian liberalism remains woefully incomplete.

Headed by four Petersburg intellectuals—Mikhail Stasiulevich, Aleksandr Pypin, Konstantin Arsen'ev, and Leonid Slonimskii—the *Herald of Europe* and its salon constituted a major constellation on the Romanov Empire's intellectual firmament, attracting such luminaries as Ivan Turgenev, Aleksei Tolstoy, Ivan Goncharov, Vladimir Solovyov, Anton Chekhov, Maksim Gorky, and even Émile Zola, among many others. The journal became a communications network with strings that ran far into the provinces and cultivated the public sphere despite the taboo on public discussion of politics, not to mention public participation. Although Stasiulevich, Arsen'ev, and Pypin have attracted scattered attention, no historian has ever examined the *Herald of Europe* as a conceptual nexus, although its popularity and influence made a crucial contribution to the emergence of a public sphere in Russia. The journal became an essential component of a thriving extraparliamentary civil society and its editors were members of zemstvos as well as numerous professional and academic associations.

At an average length of 350 pages, each issue of the *Herald* published original literary works by Russian and foreign authors and explored literary issues, diplomatic affairs, artistic trends, the latest scientific discoveries, emerging sociological and economic theories, and fresh historical research. Most importantly, however, the *Herald*'s extensive network of contributors made it possible to present highly detailed snapshots of local conditions in the Russian Empire. The journal produced a system of values based neither on a mode of production, nor a class, neither on the peasant commune, nor *Homo economicus*, but on the enlightened individual drawing energy and meaning from the zemstvo. The journal thereby articulated a moral economy based on values that grew out of specific local conditions. The *Herald* offered a point of contact to Russia's professional groups and articulated a vocabulary of self-definition in relation to the state and the peasantry. The journal itself offered a coordinate plane of liberal loyalties during the period of post-emancipation socio-economic flux by legitimizing individual initiative via the zemstvos, which middle-class bourgeois identity by itself had consistently failed to do in Russia. Published in the capital and bearing "Europe" in its title, the journal thus functioned more like a liberal mirror of Russia than a window to the West.

The *Herald of Europe* story offers an alternative picture of the late imperial intellectual field, which historians have traditionally portrayed as a battleground between irreconcilable extremes of radicalism and autocracy. Furthermore, it demonstrates the viability of prerevolutionary liberalism and avoids the narrative pitfall that describes Russian history as moving inexorably towards the collapse of liberal values in the maelstrom of 1917. Too many historians have portrayed Russian liberalism as intellectually weak and politically impotent—an inaccurate and unfair evaluation that this book challenges.[10] Far from being ineffectual and moribund, Russian liberalism was a dynamic force that affected the economic, social, and cultural aspects of the Romanov Empire until its collapse. This book contributes to an overdue but growing historiographical trend that explores the Romanov Empire's non-radical political history.

One of the earliest and most persistent characterizations of Russian liberalism by Western historians was that it was statist in its belief that the government was the only civilizing agent in Russia, which distracted Russian liberals from issues of individual freedom and administrative non-intervention.[11] The *Herald* group, on the other hand, believed that society needed to negotiate its rights with the state. Many Western scholars have argued that Russian liberalism "developed in relation to Western European theories" and was "a process of Westernization."[12] Just like its Austrian and German relatives, Russian liberalism also became a victim of the exceptionalist *Sonderweg* stigma, a misconception that several scholars of Central Europe have already challenged.[13] This book aims to do the same for Russia. The *Herald of Europe*'s history therefore emphasizes the normality of Russia's late imperial experience (without losing sight of its uniqueness) and challenges Russian exceptionalism and the supposedly inherent anti-liberal component in Russian society and among the intelligentsia.[14]

Many generalizations and oversimplified judgments have resulted from equating liberalism with parliamentary democracy and full civil rights and then projecting this external and idealized model back onto late imperial Russia. Such a present-based standard of mature liberal democracy has obscured more than it has explained about Russia's late imperial civil society. Indeed, although the *Herald* closely followed European cultural, political, philosophical, and economic trends, it did not measure Russia with a Western yardstick, nor did it argue for grafting Western liberal ideals onto Russia. The *Herald* looked to Russia's unique local self-government institutions as the seedbeds of a liberal society.

Many Western scholars have rightly associated Russian liberalism with the zemstvo movement, but have differed in their evaluation of this symbiosis. George Fischer argued that Russia's "opposition liberalism" was inconsistent and weak in its vacillations between "small deeds" within the zemstvos and "crazy dreams" of social justice.[15] Richard Pipes argued that Russia had no effective liberal movement between 1885 and 1900, and that liberalism was only born with "the zemstvo movement's loss of its apoliticism."[16] The *Herald* materials demonstrate that instead of "apoliticism," it would be more accurate to speak of an "extra-parliamentarism" that did not completely subvert liberal values. They also qualify Pipes's (and Max Weber's) assertion that Russian liberalism was a movement of ideas instead of socioeconomic interests. Indeed, the *Herald of Europe* analyzed Russia's evolving economic conditions and articulated alternative development strategies. The volume and depth of economic analysis on the *Herald*'s pages demonstrates that its contributors understood what Theodore Von Laue maintained the Russian liberals had little sense of—"the problems confronting men in charge of governing the Russian Empire in a competitive world order."[17]

Another important historiographic trend has focused on the legal aspects of liberal thinking. Viktor Leontovitsch's *Geschichte des Liberalismus in Russland* remained for many years an isolated pioneer in the field. An émigré trained as a lawyer, Leontovitsch focused on how the presence or absence of legal norms of civic liberty and property ownership conditioned the political, ideological, and economic developments from the time of Catherine II until 1917.[18] Tracing the evolution of non-political rights, he included Sergei Witte and Pyotr Stolypin in the liberal lineup. Interest in the legal aspects of Russian liberalism reemerged in the 1990s with Andrzej Walicki's examination of legal neo-Kantians and Gary Hamburg's biography of Boris Chicherin, but both books paid little attention to the economic and administrative components of liberal thinking that the *Herald* liberals championed.[19]

Some Western historians have focused on the religious roots of fin-de-siècle Russian liberalism, but the *Herald* group did not belong to this tradition.[20] Indeed, the *Herald* group never developed a tendency toward what some historians considered the three predominant currents of non-Marxist thought in early twentieth-century Russia: new religious consciousness, Christian socialism, and idealistic liberalism.[21]

Both Russian and Western scholars have also explored the experience of the liberal Constitutional Democratic (Kadet) Party and its leaders during Russia's parliamentary period of 1905–1917. In the process of describing the Kadet leaders, Terence Emmons outlined the generational fault line of Russia's future liberals between the doldrums of the 1880s and the activism of the 1890s, but this temporal distinction did not hold for the *Herald* contributors, who remained consistent in their basic outlook throughout the last quarter of the nineteenth century.[22] Melissa Stockdale's characterization of Pavel Miliukov as a "sociological liberal" who classified liberty as a contingent by-product of social change, instead of an inherent right of individuals, echoes what the *Herald* group had already articulated in the 1880s.[23] Unfortunately, the tendency to project constitutional aspirations and Kadet politics onto Russian liberalism before 1905 has tended to eclipse its more prominent components. For example, Vladimir Kitaev attempted to read constitutionalism into the *Herald of Europe* although in reality it was a minor issue.[24] The *Herald* group did not consider constitutionalism to be the foundation of liberalism in Russia, although it certainly did not oppose it.

Finally, the socio-economic component of liberalism has produced the most confusion, which is where Western and Soviet historiography have echoed each other most often. Daniel Balmuth's definition of Russian liberalism as a carrier of general humanistic values and a supra-class phenomenon with "arbitrary" values, as Soviet scholars Pavel Zyrianov and Valentin Shelokhaev argued, hypnotized Western historiography until the 1970s.[25] Gary Hamburg maintained that the Russian nobility's "politics of structural political change" gave way to a "politics of economic interest" in the quarter century before 1905.[26] Unfortunately, Hamburg did not include the *Herald of Europe* in his excellent study, although the journal acted as a reconciler of peasant and landed interests and a common platform for joint action. Leopold Haimson argued that the Russian liberals failed to accommodate the "dual polarization" of state/society and town/country in Russian society after 1905.[27] The *Herald* materials suggest, however, that the journal's socio-economic program could have bridged the gulf between state and society on the local level had the revolution of 1905 not redirected public opinion toward high politics.

In the Soviet Union, Marxist ideology created anomalies in evaluations of prerevolutionary liberalism. The demarcation that Lenin had drawn between liberalism and revolutionary democracy continued with minor variations as Soviet historians pigeon-holed liberalism into the class-based matrix—most often "gentry" versus "bourgeois."[28] From the 1970s on, however, a number of works began to explore late imperial social movements in their greater socio-cultural complexity.[29] Nataliia Pirumova's pioneering but cautious attempt to examine the movement outside the usual Marxist framework and within the context of the zemstvos started this trend.[30] Nonetheless, the "two liberalisms" tradition endured into the late 1970s.[31] Almost simultaneously, Vera Leikina-Svirskaia extended the term intelligentsia to include non-radical professionals and social activists.[32] Predictably, the debate about whether the urban bourgeoisie, the intelligentsia, the liberal landed gentry, or industrial magnates were the real shapers of liberal values reached no conclusive results. Pirumova updated her study in 1986 by focusing on the intelligentsia's role in articulating liberal values.[33] She moved even further away from the Marxist framework, but relegated the *Herald* to a minor supporting role in what she interpreted as a phenomenon centered on personal interaction through correspondence, informal meetings, and salons.

The 1990s witnessed the collapse of ideological constraints and caused a resurgence of interest in Russian liberalism. Some Russian scholars suggested that Russian liberalism became a "system of values" in the beginning of the twentieth century with the emergence of a "new generation of the Russian intelligentsia."[34] But the *Herald* materials demonstrate that liberalism reached its conceptual critical mass at least a decade before the proposed date. Early post-Soviet efforts to grapple with the liberal legacy have produced portrait galleries of Russian liberals with minimal analytical synthesis.[35] Later attempts used the lives of liberalism's chief proponents to avoid treating it in abstract and theoretical terms, but have also urged further research into the details of Russian liberalism before attempting to synthesize them.[36]

Beginning in the 1990s, numerous conferences have brought together Russian and Western scholars to reexamine the liberal legacy.[37] One resulting collection of essays overreached in its attempt to find an overarching and inclusive definition of liberalism from the eighteenth to the early twentieth century.[38] All of the contributors agreed vaguely that the primacy of the individual was at the center of liberal values, but the legal, social, economic, and political repercussions presented a minefield. Another collection tentatively emphasized a "family of liberalisms" that existed in Europe, which is closer to the truth in that different political and historical experiences bred different liberal programs. Liberalism's rich journalistic roots and legacy remain a fallow field, however—something that Russian scholar Boris Itenberg has consistently urged scholars to examine more closely.[39] And the *Herald of Europe* is the obvious starting point for such an inquiry.

The interaction between liberalism and journalism not only needs much more work, but also requires reinterpretation. Without fail, Soviet scholars treated the *Herald of Europe* as a "liberal bourgeois" publication, and although short articles about it appeared in every Soviet volume dedicated to prerevolutionary journalism, they focused on the standard Soviet fare of "revolutionary waves" and the "liberation movement" in a most tendentious way (although some of the factual information therein is useful).[40] Louise McReynolds's pioneering work in the field of Russian journalism emphasized the archaic values and attitudes of the Russian intelligentsia and characterized the process of creating a new public space as "the paradox of integration and escapism."[41] However, unlike McReynolds's journalistic liberals, the *Herald* group was suspicious neither of European liberties, nor of the inherent inequalities of European capitalism. Instead, the journal blamed the state's sluggishness in legislative modernization and socio-economic decentralization for producing inequalities. Only Daniel Balmuth's *The Russian Bulletin, 1863–1917: A Liberal Voice in Tsarist Russia* has examined a specific publication in depth and explored its effects on civil society.[42] Unlike the *Herald*, however, the "professors' newspaper" was Populist in its leanings and sympathetic to socialism.

A general definition of liberalism in Russia would have to include championing freedom of the press, constitutionalism, and the rule of law, but such a definition is too broad, although it reflects what the *Herald* group also championed. A basic problem that unifies much of the historiography of Russian liberalism on both sides of the Atlantic is the tendency to treat liberal theory and liberal practice independently. The *Herald* story brings them together. Covering the "to the people" movement, the Russo-Turkish War of 1877–1878, the assassination of Tsar Alexander II, the counter-reforms of Alexander III, and many other historical milestones, the *Herald of Europe* became a liberal lens that refracted the major events of the late imperial era. Although the *Herald* liberals steered clear of high politics, they nevertheless refused to treat the state as an antithesis of the civil society in which they were all actively involved.

Three works exploring the world of the *Herald of Europe* appeared in the 1990s—Viktor Kel'ner's short biography of Mikhail Stasiulevich, Dmitrii Balykin's exploration of Aleksandr Pypin's scholarship, and Anatolii Alafaev's exploration of *Herald* reformism in the late 1870s and early 1880s. Although interesting, both biographies explored their subjects in isolation from each other and contextualized them poorly within Russia's liberal movement, while Alafaev examined *Herald* liberalism through the outdated prism of Marxist categories.[43]

An examination of the *Herald of Europe* as an institution in a non-radical environment actually enriches our understanding of Russian social philosophy. The journal articulated its program in reaction to two powerful intellectual trends—on the one hand, Populism with its idealization of agrarian relations and opposition to capitalism, and on the other, Marxism with its tendency to idealize industrialization and the working class. The Populists and Marxists engaged in a fascinating debate about Russia's development alternatives in the 1890s, which historians have covered.[44] As the *Herald* consistently argued, however, socio-economic modernization could only succeed if society participated in it through the zemstvos, which the Populists considered a tool of the gentry and the Marxists ignored altogether. The Marxist-Populist fireworks thus obscured the liberal point of view, which was actually more pragmatic in many ways. Indeed, the *Herald* bridged the gulf between bourgeois and democratic liberalism by championing local issues. Borrowing from both Populists and Marxists, the journal articulated a vision of socio-economic development that made *Herald* liberalism unique.

The *Herald* liberals recognized that they had common origins with the Populists in the humanistic tradition of Russian literature. Like the Populists, the *Herald* liberals were concerned with the peasantry's interests, but instead of focusing on distributive justice, the *Herald* championed the peasants' legal status, civil liberties, and greater representation within the zemstvos. The *Herald* treated the rural population neither as a collective messiah, nor a helpless throng, but argued instead for direct local economic empowerment. Arguing that they had inherited the Populist legacy, the *Herald* liberals updated it to fit global socio-economic realities and did not believe that Russia should remain an agrarian society. The journal accepted capitalism as an inevitable global process and entertained no utopian schemes to avoid it.

Through its polemics with the Marxists, the journal criticized finance minister Sergei Witte's industrialization program and exposed its costs. Although the *Herald* accepted capitalism's growing pains, it nevertheless refused to see modernization as a Procrustean bed for the peasantry. Unlike Witte, the *Herald* liberals refused to treat the economic sphere as a means to achieve long-term foreign policy interests. On the contrary, the idea of self-government and responsibility—versus economic efficiency or *raison d'état*—stood at the center of the *Herald*'s economic views. Through the zemstvo network, the journal not only focused on the human beings behind modernization's statistics, but also advocated the acquisition of civic responsibilities through local self-government instead of the leap of an inexperienced population into mass politics. Local socio-economic concerns thus acted as the catalyst of civic consciousness. The story of the *Herald* demonstrates that the central debate during the 1890s concerned not abstract theories, but the relationship between local self-government institutions and the state during economic modernization. Moreover, at a time when Russia was the world's largest emerging market, the *Herald* articulated an economic development model without the convergent development assumption that all societies must evolve toward a Western socio-economic and political model.

To sum up, the *Herald of Europe* avoided the reference points upon which many Russian liberals (and their biographers) focused: Western models, natural rights theories, neo-Kantian idealism, Christianity, socialism, and Marxism. The journal's reference frame was neither an estate, nor a class, but instead the extensive zemstvo network, which distinguished Russian liberalism from its European relatives and is the working definition of liberalism in this book. The journal evaluated socio-economic progress from the local point of view, which gave *Herald* liberalism a specifically Russian flavor, not that of a foreign import.[45] Indeed, the *Herald*'s lifespan mirrored that of the zemstvos'—it appeared in 1866, two years after the zemstvos did, and ceased to exist when the Bolsheviks sealed their fate too in 1918.

There are valuable lessons here for twenty-first century developing economies and societies in transition. Doubts about liberalism's viability in post-Soviet Russia appeared because the "liberals" of the 1990s implemented a libertarian model of economic reforms that led to popular bewilderment—hence the visceral aversion to "liberal" values among Russians today.[46] As a result, social indifference became the price of "liberal" pragmatism. *Liberals under Autocracy* aims to clarify the differences between late imperial liberal values and post-Soviet libertarianism.

The book draws on three source bases. The journal articles constitute the primary sources, which the book's narrative analyzes and places into the context of the intellectual trends of the time. Second, archival research, memoirs, and published correspondence provide the journal's history and explain the relationship between its contributors as well as their personal involvement in local affairs. Memoirs, daily newspapers, other thick journals, and the economic literature of the period constitute the third component, which provides the context of the development debate that unfolded on the *Herald*'s pages. The narrative recreates the intellectual world into which the journal brought the reader and dissolves many artificial boundaries in the evolution of Russian intellectual history.

The book is divided into three parts of three chapters each. Part 1 will integrate the biographies of the *Herald*'s main contributors—founder and chief editor Mikhail Stasiulevich, de facto counsel and legal specialist Konstantin Arsen'ev, historian and literary scholar Aleksandr Pypin, and foreign policy and economics specialist Leonid Slonimskii. The first three chapters will explain why these men became liberals, what circumstances brought them together, and how the era in which they matured shaped their views. Part 2 will explore how the journal was founded and why it deserves to be examined as an institution. The chapters will cover the *Herald*'s initial conceptual affinity with Populism, the evolution of its views on the peasantry, its reaction to Russian radicalism, and its eventual separation from Populism—all of which happened in the context of Russia's rich nineteenth-century literary tradition. Part 3 will explore the journal's program of economic decentralization through the extension of the rights and responsibilities of local self-government and the part that this would play in ameliorating modernization's effects. The last chapter will analyze the *Herald*'s criticism of Marxist ideology and late imperial modernization and explore the journal's blueprint for a humane form of modernization, which resulted in a new definition of a moral economy that evaluated modernization based on its effects on the local level.

PART I

The Men of the *Herald of Europe*

Look unto the rock whence ye are hewn.

—ISAIAH, 51:1

1

Born under the Iron Tsar

Family and School

No THOROUGH TREATMENT of the *Herald of Europe* can ignore the biographies of its founders—their family milieu, childhood, and formative years. The value of exploring the men's social backgrounds, the emotional atmosphere in which they grew up, and the intellectual guidance they received lies not in anticipating adult opinions, but in providing fuller portraits that, on the one hand, capture the drag of emotional wounds and social handicaps and, on the other, point out the advantages of family support and intellectual precocity.

The only common factor that Mikhail Stasiulevich, Aleksandr Pypin, Konstantin Arsen'ev, and Leonid Slonimskii shared was growing up in middling social milieus that combined upward mobility with status-consciousness and anxiety. The differences resided in specific circumstances. For example, Stasiulevich's childhood was unhappy, while Pypin's was the opposite. Stasiulevich's early days left few clues to indicate that he would become a prominent intellectual, while Pypin's natural curiosity and his family's encouragement of reading gave him an early start. Nevertheless, Pypin followed a fundamentally different social philosophy than his famous radical cousin Nikolai Chernyshevskii, although the boys grew up in the same household. Arsen'ev's father was a prominent Saint Petersburg bureaucrat and professor and this opened many doors for his son, yet later in life, Arsen'ev envied Stasiulevich's academic achievements, although they paled in comparison to Pypin's. Slonimskii also grew up in an enlightened family, but he felt that his Jewish roots formed an insurmountable obstacle to professional achievement and he renounced them eventually. Pypin, Arsen'ev, and Slonimskii also had in common the presence of strong and positive role models, while Stasiulevich had none.

From a historical point of view, the *Herald* liberals' backgrounds also shed light on the oases of enlightenment that existed during a period unjustly condemned for its regressive policies and stifling control of public opinion. Their family backgrounds also challenge the artificial "state versus society" characterization of Nicholas's era inherited from intellectuals such as Belinskii and Aleksandr Herzen, who oversimplified a rapidly evolving socio-intellectual environment. The Decembrist Uprising and its wake thus constituted an exception to an otherwise self-confident empire where liberal ideals seemed foreign indeed and where literature—long considered the barometer of public opinion in Russia—dealt primarily with two issues: defining an individual sphere and articulating a national ideology. Neither had direct bearing on the liberal and constitutional values that many people from the West of later periods projected back onto Russia under Tsar Nicholas I.

Mikhail Stasiulevich:
Imperial Capital, Humble Beginnings, 1826–1843

Mikhail Matveevich Stasiulevich was born in Saint Petersburg on August 28, 1826, and was baptized at the Church of the Ascension in the Admiralty district, a wealthy enclave of the nobility that included the Winter Palace and many ministries. Eight months before Mikhail's birth, the unexpected death of Tsar Alexander I had created the opportunity for the Decembrist Uprising. Idealistic but logistically unprepared, the young officers who led it did not stand a chance when the new tsar, Nicholas I, ordered the mutiny crushed on Senate Square. By the summer of 1826, over a hundred participants were sentenced to exile in Siberia and on July 13, the five leaders of the uprising were hanged. Nicholas's accession ushered in a conservative age and Saint Petersburg became a prominent symbol of the era's contradictions.

A city of 440,000 inhabitants when Mikhail was born, Saint Petersburg's administrative and cultural center extended from the embankment of Vasil'evskii Island to the Fontanka Canal and along Nevskii Prospekt.[1] As one scholar has eloquently put it, beyond "the enchanted circle and sometimes living among it, another population toiled and served—a universe of merchants, lower officials, free and unfree servants, ordinary townspeople, and the denizens of the lowest depths of crime, beggary, and prostitution."[2]

From its foundation, Peter's city symbolized enforced enlightenment where the forces of progress and conservatism, freethinking and censorship, education and ignorance were locked in struggle. The evolution of Russia's consciousness in the first half of the nineteenth century manifested itself in Saint Petersburg's cultural richness. In the process of pursuing Napoleon into Europe in 1813 and 1814, young Russian officers absorbed the culture of European capitals, but returned to find Tsar Alexander's government increasingly wary of reforms. "Now it is unbearable to look upon Petersburg's empty life and to listen to the chatter of old men who praise everything old and condemn any movement forward," wrote future Decembrist Ivan Iakushkin after returning from Europe.[3] These attitudes did not go unnoticed by the authorities. The state had jealously guarded the education of its subjects since Peter the Great and in the 1820s tried to stem the tide of European ideas. When Saint Petersburg University opened in 1819, its mission was to inculcate "morality, good service, [and] effort." In 1821, humanities professors were accused of paying insufficient attention to Holy Scripture, undermining public morality with natural law theory, and teaching that only the natural sciences explain "how things really are."[4] The consequent purges sparked the search for new means of expression, which the legacy of the Enlightenment, tenuous and socially limited as it was, had already prepared by the 1820s. Nevertheless, the daily change of the palace guard, the frequent military parades and maneuvers, and the enormous open spaces that they required became part of Petersburg's neoclassical aura and symbolized a stable autocracy that most expected to last for centuries.

Like his predecessor, but to a greater degree, Nicholas I interpreted Russia's victory over Napoleonic France as the triumph of autocratic stability over the destructiveness of the French Revolution and its liberal ideals. Petersburg's architecture reflected this triumphalism. The Stock Exchange and the famous columns on the point of Vasil'evskii Island were completed in 1816, the Admiralty Building in 1823, and the building of the general staff in 1829. Saint Isaac's Cathedral was under construction and the Senate and Synod buildings were completed in 1834, which was also when the famous monumental column to Alexander I appeared on Palace Square. Between 1825 and 1832, neoclassical ensembles defined the boundaries of Mikhailovskii and Theater Squares.[5] In other words, Mikhail Stasiulevich grew up among the architectural symbols of autocracy.

After the Decembrists' failure, Russia's "window on Europe" became the home of the "continental gendarme" who continued the pace of the Congress System that prevented revolutionary eruptions all over the continent. Nevertheless, the impact of German philosophy and Romanticism during the 1820s and 1830s encouraged creative forces that gained strength in proportion to

the pressure they experienced from Russian censorship and police surveillance. Private studies, dining rooms, and salons became the epicenters of intellectual debates in which Petersburg's "second builder" and Russia's greatest poet Aleksandr Pushkin also participated.[6] In the year of Stasiulevich's
birth, he was working on *Eugene Onegin* (finished in 1831) and composed
"The Confession," "The Winter Journey," "The Prophet," "Deep in Siberian
mines," and the following stanza on Nicholas's accession:[7]

> He was made emperor, and right then,
> Displayed his flair and drive,
> Sent to Siberia a hundred-twenty men
> And strung up five.[8]

The decade in which Mikhail was born was bursting with creative potential as Russia's educated society matured intellectually. A few months before
his death in 1826, writer and historian Nikolai Karamzin confided to a
friend: "Without false pride about my profession as a writer, I see myself,
without embarrassment, among our generals and ministers."[9] Karamzin,
who never donned a military or state uniform, was the first to recognize that
literature was a form of service to one's country. He thereby reinforced a
trend that had already started under Catherine the Great with such writers
as Gavriil Derzhavin, Nikolai Novikov, Aleksandr Radishchev, and Pushkin himself, who personified Russia's transition from the Enlightenment to
Romanticism and symbolized Russian individuality in an age of neoclassical
universalism. In 1828, Pushkin voiced his ambivalence towards Petersburg's
Euclidean perfection and surface gloss:

> Capital of pomp and squalor,
> Stately jail of souls unfree,
> Firmament of greenish pallor,
> Frost, and stone, and misery.[10]

Mikhail's childhood coincided with the first golden age of Russian literature when the search for Russianness inspired young minds to move away
from imitating Western examples, culminating in the works of Nikolai Gogol,
Mikhail Lermontov, and, once again, Pushkin. Karamzin published Russia's
first accessible and popular history in twelve volumes between 1816 and 1829.
Until then, even highly educated Russians knew very little about their history.

Karamzin was also a leading proponent of purging the literary language of Slavonic archaisms and bringing Russian closer to its spoken form, an endeavor which Pushkin's poetry perfected. The novel was emerging as the leading literary genre in Europe and three great Russian novelists were Stasiulevich's contemporaries: Ivan Turgenev was born in 1818, Fyodor Dostoevsky in 1821, and Leo Tolstoy in 1828.

Stasiulevich's childhood experience, however, was not one of sparkling salons, theater nights, and extravagant balls. Instead it resembled Dostoevsky's in that both boys' fathers were military doctors. Matvei Stasiulevich was a noble with Polish roots, but neither he, nor his wife Nadezhda, owned any landed property. As a biographer of Dostoevsky has put it, "medicine was an honorable, but not very honorific profession in Russia" and most army doctors, if they could manage it, kept a private practice on the side to make ends meet.[11] In December 1826, Matvei resigned his commission and became a district doctor in the small town of Luga south of Saint Petersburg, but soon abandoned his family forever by moving to the Caucasus. In a letter to a friend, Stasiulevich admitted many years later that he had experienced much pain from "what serves as a source of happiness for others—family."[12] His fragile health precluding a military career, Mikhail entered the Larin Gymnasium in 1837 in Saint Petersburg, which offered him a scholarship due to "his mother's extreme poverty."[13]

The Larin Gymnasium was an experimental institution and the brainchild of Count Sergei Uvarov, who was Tsar Nicholas's minister of education. Located on Vasil'evskii Island, which was Saint Petersburg's business district, the gymnasium opened in 1836 and accepted not only children of the nobility and bureaucrats, but also those of Russian and foreign merchants, a first for a gymnasium in the capital. Another departure from the norm was that students could choose to specialize in commercial affairs instead of taking classical languages, although Mikhail pursued the classical path. The school's charter gave priority to the acquisition of Russian over ancient Greek and Latin and mandated German and French lessons "for practical purposes, without any grammatical theory, except for some rules for structuring ordinary phrases." The curriculum was demanding and meticulously structured from reveille at five a.m. until evening prayer at nine p.m. Tsar Nicholas had allocated additional funds for the gymnasium and visited it annually to meet students and professors.[14] As one scholar put it, the Larin Gymnasium became proof of Uvarov's success in "the herculean feat of putting the Russian gymnasia on a par with the best of Europe."[15]

Mikhail's seven-year education, which he completed with distinction in 1843, planted him squarely in Saint Petersburg. While his mother remained in Luga province until her death, Mikhail eventually gained access to the capital's "enchanted circle" as a prominent intellectual, successful publisher, and distinguished member of the city duma. A self-made man, he rose from humble beginnings and a failed family—circumstances quite different from his future colleague Aleksandr Pypin.

ALEKSANDR PYPIN: TALENT IN THE PROVINCES, 1833–1849

Aleksandr Nikolaevich Pypin was born on April 6, 1833, in Saratov, a provincial town on the Volga River that was the cultural center of the Volga Germans, whom Catherine the Great had settled in this region. Initially a military and commercial outpost, by the nineteenth century Saratov had become a bustling river port located midway between Astrakhan and Kazan. The town stood on a scenic bluff on the western side of a bend in the river, and the economy of the region developed so rapidly that by the 1830s Saratov and its hinterland resembled the developed Russian heartland.[16] Nikolai Chernyshevskii once compared his hometown's administrative structure with "multilayered Europe" with its "autocratic monarchies, constitutional monarchies with parliaments, aristocratic and democratic republics."[17]

In his memoirs, Aleksandr (Sasha) Pypin wrote that he grew up in an extended family composed of the Pypin and Chernyshevskii households. Pypin's maternal grandmother Pelageia Golubeva, "a severe woman of the old school," arranged both of her daughter's marriages. Her husband, Sasha's maternal grandfather, had been the archpriest of Saratov's Sergiev Church and his death left the family in dire straits. In order to retain the privileged position that her husband's post had guaranteed, Pelageia immediately announced through the local bishop that her late husband's position was open to a talented student from the Penza seminary with the condition that he marry her eldest daughter Evgeniia. The most promising contender was Gavriil Chernyshevskii, who soon became part of the family. Pelageia's second goal was to secure serfs, so she married her second daughter Aleksandra to petty nobleman Nikolai Pypin, who owned one soul in the village of Itkarka about ninety miles from Saratov. The marriage allowed Aleksandra to purchase nineteen more souls and the tiny village became the supplier of the household's basic needs. The family did not have much money and yet, as Nikolai Chernyshevskii put it, "it had everything it needed," even though the Pypins alone had eight children.[18] By luck or great wisdom, Pelageia judged well the character of her sons-in-law because by all accounts the new household coexisted happily.

Born in 1828, Nikolai Chernyshevskii was five years Pypin's senior, but despite the difference in age, the cousins played together and Sasha looked up to Nikolai as to an older brother. Later in life, Nikolai Chernyshevskii wrote of the household:

> In our family during my childhood, there were five mature adult members: my grandmother, two of her daughters, and the daughters' husbands . . . It was a pure Switzerland composed of five cantons. Nobody asserted authority over any of the other four. Nobody consulted any of the other four when they did not need their cooperation and did not want their advice. But because of the closeness of interests and mutual feelings, nobody undertook anything important without voluntary consultation with everybody else.[19]

The adults often left the children to themselves and allowed them to fashion their lives after the models of sound industry that the parents provided. Gavriil homeschooled Nikolai, gave Sasha lessons in French, and hired a Volga German to teach both boys his native language while Gavriil taught Russian to the German tutor in order to save money. The mothers loved books and the families often read together. The central source of knowledge was Gavriil's home library, which the boys used at their discretion. Pypin recalled that its contents ranged from old religious texts and church and secular histories, including Karamzin's magnum opus, to the recent works of Pushkin and Gogol. In the 1840s, Gavriil subscribed to newspapers and thick journals such as *Notes of the Fatherland* (*Otechestvennye zapiski*, 1818–1884), which contained articles by social and literary critics Aleksandr Herzen and Vissarion Belinskii. The library even attracted the attention of the historian Nikolai Kostomarov, who would become one of the *Herald of Europe*'s earliest contributors during his exile to Saratov in 1848.[20]

Pypin's father Nikolai was an official in the Saratov Civil Chamber. A petty noble from Penza province, he grew up in a village and knew the peasant life well. Although Sasha's two peasant nannies exposed him to fairytales, he came to know the real peasant world during the summer harvest seasons when he and his father traveled to Itkarka. Sasha recalled that his father treated his serfs very well and the peasants loved and trusted their owner. After Emancipation, they still asked Nikolai Pypin for advice, "but did not

always follow it," and when they came to Saratov they "made themselves at
home" in the family house.

This idyll notwithstanding, serfdom was the fundamental matrix of socio-
economic relations in Russia and its abuses formed an inescapable backdrop
in Saratov. With a population of fifty thousand by the 1840s, the town offered
"frequent examples of the arbitrary use of authority, of class injustice, unbridled privilege, and the terrible cruelties of recruitment for twenty-five years
of degrading military service."[21] Sasha was not ignorant of this darker side
of patriarchal Russia. When they traveled to Itkarka, Nikolai Pypin pointed
out to his son the houses of landlords who had been murdered by their peasants. The boy witnessed punishment by the knout as well as military recruitment and the drunken orgies that preceded the soldiers' departure. One of
serfdom's side effects was the popularity among the peasants of wild stories
about freedom in far-off lands of milk and honey.[22] The landowners and
police tried to debunk these myths in vain. Sasha witnessed peasant families
departing individually and en masse for the Caucasus or "Odesta" (Odessa)
only to be forcibly returned to their villages by the police.[23]

Unlike Stasiulevich's, Pypin's home became a haven from this grim reality and gave him a secure and even privileged start in life. A biographer wrote
of Nikolai Chernyshevskii that he "grew up with knowledge of two avenues
of service which, as performed by his father and uncle, possessed integrity
and dedication."[24] The same applied to Sasha. Indeed, father Chernyshevskii
and local official (and landowner) Pypin were role models quite unlike the
ones that Gogol described in *Dead Souls*, which was published in 1842—the
year that Sasha enrolled in the Saratov Gymnasium where those who specialized in the classics, as Sasha did, automatically received the fourteenth
rank when they entered state service. Of the forty students who started with
him, only eight graduated. Unlike his cousin Nikolai, Pypin actually attended
classes, but complained in his memoirs of apathetic teachers, stifling discipline, and boring classical language sessions. Similar experiences discouraged
so many children that few continued their education at universities, especially
given the impediments of the cost and the journey, but Sasha persevered.

Nikolai Chernyshevskii left Saratov to study in Saint Petersburg in 1849
and composed his first epistle to his cousin on the road. "Your mind is developing," he wrote, "and that is why new interests appear everywhere."[25]
In June 1846, eighteen-year-old Nikolai asked his thirteen-year-old cousin
for help with a geometry problem involving the Pythagorean theorem,
which he copiously illustrated in his correspondence.[26] In other letters, he

introduced Sasha to the dilemma of Buridan's Ass and sent him a class schedule; urged him to study German and French; sent him Latin phrases and poems to translate and return for an evaluation; and copied Lermontov's poems for him.[27]

From his letters to family members, it is clear that Nikolai Chernyshevskii noticed the glaring class differences in Saint Petersburg, where his provincial roots counted for nothing in the eyes of the capital's elite. As one biographer has put it, "the plunge from a socially sheltered and comfortable childhood into the socially frigid real world of the capital was Chernyshevskii's first experience of the cruelty and injustice of the old Russian class system."[28] This is a slight exaggeration since Nikolai had already witnessed this in Saratov, but being on the receiving end of condescension makes a big difference, especially for a precocious teenager. He shared his feelings with Sasha. Petersburg also brought his country's backwardness to Nikolai's attention. In August 1846, he complained to Sasha that learning had insufficiently rooted itself in Russia. "Half the members of the Academy of Sciences are foreigners," he wrote. Europe had already produced René Descartes, Sir Isaac Newton, and Gottfried Leibniz, while Russia had nothing to show for her enlightenment beyond an army of 1.5 million soldiers that "threatened Europe as the Huns and Mongols had done in the Middle Ages." Chernyshevskii ended the letter with a plea to his younger cousin:

> Let us firmly resolve, with all the strength of our soul, to work together with others to put an end to this epoch in which learning has been foreign to our spiritual life, that it may cease to be a borrowed caftan, a sorrowful impersonal aping for us. Let Russia also contribute what it should to the spiritual life of the world, as it has contributed and contributes to political life, to enter powerfully, independently, in the role of a savior for humanity in another great arena of life—learning, as it has already done in the arena of state and political life. And may this great event be achieved through us, even if only in part. Then we will not have lived in vain in this world; we may calmly look down upon our earthly life and peacefully enter life beyond the grave. To contribute not to the temporary, but to the eternal glory of our state and of humanity—what can be higher and more desirable than this? Let us ask God that he allocate this fate to us.[29]

Chernyshevskii's biographers have often quoted this passage as the future revolutionary's credo but ignored its thirteen-year-old addressee—Nikolai would not have composed these lines if he did not believe that they would resonate with his cousin. Ironically, the younger Pypin's career would contribute much more to Russian learning than Chernyshevskii's. In 1848, Sasha won a prize for his essay "On the Influence of the Varangians on the Everyday Life of the Slavs," which the district educational committee considered the best of his peers in "thoughts, expression, detail, and effort."[30] Convinced of Sasha's brilliance, Nikolai started an epistolary crusade with requests to enroll him in Saint Petersburg University. Meanwhile, Nikolai's long letters introduced his young protégé to Saint Petersburg years before Sasha actually arrived there in the summer of 1850 to take his entrance exams.

KONSTANTIN ARSEN'EV:
THE SILVER SPOON OF STATE SERVICE, 1837–1849

The third member of the *Herald* group needed no vicarious introduction to the imperial capital. Konstantin Konstantinovich Arsen'ev was born in Saint Petersburg on January 21, 1837, six days before Aleksandr Pushkin sustained the injuries that would kill him. Unlike his future colleagues, Konstantin came from a well-established Petersburg family. His father Konstantin Ivanovich Arsen'ev was taught Latin and geography at the Saint Petersburg Pedagogical Institute. Due to its clarity and readability, his *Concise General Geography* (1817) became a standard textbook for the next thirty years, notwithstanding the bad press it received for mentioning Maximilien Robespierre in connection with his hometown of Arras. Arsen'ev's *Statistical Description of the Russian Empire* (1819) was even more controversial.[31]

The elder Arsen'ev was a proponent of Smithian statistics, a trend that explored a nation's quality of life and productivity instead of enumerating facts, as the cameralist school had done. His *Description* therefore became the first statistical examination of Russia based on theory. He divided classes into economically productive (the peasantry) and unproductive (clergy, gentry, and bureaucrats) and argued that "the enserfment of the peasants is a major obstacle to the improvement of agriculture" because the "freedom of the producer and of trade is the most secure guarantee of the increase of individual and social wealth." Arsen'ev even attacked the military recruitment system because it diminished the productive labor pool. In a novel approach, he used statistics to criticize state policies. As a recent scholar has put it, for Arsen'ev, a statistician "was a rational human being capable of interpreting nature with or without the state's approval."[32]

In the process of purging Saint Petersburg University of independent and critically minded faculty, obscurantist university curator Dmitrii Runich found in Arsen'ev's books and his students' notes traces of "godlessness and revolutionary ideas" as well as disclosures "of state secrets" (in the form of financial statistics), which caused his dismissal.[33] Under the protections of Grand Duke Nikolai Pavlovich (the future Nicholas I), however, Arsen'ev dedicated his energy to the Imperial School of Engineering, Fyodor Dosto- evsky's alma mater.[34]

When his most influential patron became tsar in 1826, Arsen'ev's career blossomed. Already a member of the Codification Commission under the talented Mikhail Speranskii, in 1828 Arsen'ev was made tutor in geography and statistics to Grand Duke Alexander (the future Alexander II), which not only brought Arsen'ev into the inner sanctum of the imperial court, but also granted him unprecedented access to state archives (upon which he drew for his lectures) and resulted in a long fact-finding trip through the Russian provinces. He worked closely with Russian poet Vasilii Zhukovskii (also a tutor) and the editor of the prominent literary journal *The Contem- porary* (*Sovremennik*, 1837–1868), Pyotr Pletnev, who would play an impor- tant role in the creation of the *Herald of Europe*. Contrary to Tsar Nicholas's reputation for being anti-liberal, he gathered a remarkable group of progres- sively minded men to educate his son, which played a large part in paving the way for the Great Reforms.[35]

The 1830s witnessed a swell of enthusiasm for statistics all over the Western world as the Belgian, British, French, and American governments organized statistics departments.[36] Tsar Nicholas also understood the administrative value of knowledge and welcomed this trend in Russia. It was time, he be- lieved, to organize an efficient government that was no longer a hostage to circumstances and forced to rely on ad hoc committees to deal with prob- lems as they appeared.[37] This explains why Nicholas appointed Arsen'ev to tutor the future "tsar liberator." By the time the statistics craze peaked, Arsen'ev was already a champion of policy-oriented quantification. In 1834, Tsar Nicholas appointed him to the Council of the Minister of Internal Affairs and he became a member of the Statistical Division, which collected data, analyzed it, and made policy recommendations. Arsen'ev was in the right place at the right time as the ministry quickly rose to political promi- nence due to the ability of those in power to recognize and utilize the talents of young career officials. An epicenter of reformism, the ministry's first move was to restructure "provincial administration and strengthen its connection to the central government."[38] This gargantuan task required the services of talented statisticians, and Arsen'ev was instrumental in establishing the provincial statistics committees in 1834.

Arsen'ev hoped that through statistics "the nation and its population would become known to itself and to the government," and this belief was part of his overall commitment to glasnost—the open publication and discussion of what had previously been a state secret.[39] As Grand Duke Alexander's formal education was reaching its conclusion in 1837, Zhukovskii and Arsen'ev convinced Tsar Nicholas to send the heir-apparent on a seven-month tour of his future realm as a necessary introduction to the local diversity of Russia. Upon returning, Arsen'ev was no longer needed at court and could dedicate his time to family matters and his infant son Konstantin, although he also continued his geographical and statistical work in the Provisional Statistical Committee from 1845 to 1854. He also published multiple articles and books on eighteenth-century Russian history, including short histories of the reigns of Catherine I and Peter II.[40]

In 1845, the elder Arsen'ev played a central role in founding the Russian Geographical Society, which united people who actively supported peasant reform.[41] As one scholar has argued, the society became "a major instrument for advancing economic, demographic, and social studies of regions destined to be touched most directly by the Great Reforms."[42] Arsen'ev's magnum opus, the *Statistical Essays on Russia*, appeared in 1848. He dedicated it to Grand Duke Alexander with the following words: "To love Russia is the sacred duty of every Russian, but we can love her consciously and with conviction only when we know her, when we have studied her past and present, and when we have adequately assessed the people's strength, advantages, and shortfalls." He also added that he remembered with what dedication Alexander loved his country and regretted "the various impediments to the free development of a new and better life for the people." Arsen'ev's thinly disguised references to serfdom did not pass the censor's muster and he ordered the dedication removed from copies intended for sale to the public.[43]

The younger Konstantin Arsen'ev thus grew up in a household where discussion of statistics, geography, and history was a daily affair. Men of state and prominent intellectuals visited his father, as his correspondence attests.[44] However, Arsen'ev *fils* published nothing about his childhood, although he admitted that he had "a developed interest in historical reading" when he entered the School of Jurisprudence in Saint Petersburg, while Arsen'ev's memoirs point to this period of his life (1849–1855)—not his childhood—as a crucial formative period.[45] Nevertheless, his family background proved to be a great advantage in terms of access to the best educational facilities that Russia had to offer and, unlike Stasiulevich and Pypin, he was in the position to follow an easy career path into the highest ranks of state service.

LEONID SLONIMSKII:
ENLIGHTENMENT IN THE JEWISH PALE, 1850–1868

The same did not hold for the youngest member of the *Herald of Europe* group, Leonid-Ludwig Zinov'evich Slonimskii, who was born in 1850 in Zhitomir within the Pale of Settlement, beyond which Russian Jews did not have the right to live. His father Haim Zelig (Zinovii Iakovlevich) Slonimskii (1810–1904) was a perpetually indigent Jewish intellectual, mathematician, and inventor whose biography, like the elder Arsen'ev's, provides important insights into the environment in which Leonid grew up. Indeed, Haim ended up patriarch of a remarkable family that produced a long line of intellectuals: Soviet literary scholar Aleksandr Slonimskii (1881–1964), American composer and musicologist Nicolas Slonimsky (1894–1995), Soviet writer and Maxim Gorky's secretary Mikhail Slonimskii (1897–1972), and Polish poet Antoni Słonimski (1895–1976) were Haim's grandsons; Soviet (now Russian) composer Sergei Slonimskii (b. 1932) was his great-grandson.[46]

As a recent scholar has put it, "across the nineteenth century, the Russian Jews' physical concentration in the Pale [of Settlement] sustained, and was sustained by, a distinctive way of life considerably more removed from that of the surrounding population than was then the case with Jews in Western Europe."[47] Officially sanctioned legal discrimination preserved Judaism as a religion as well as a distinct social order in Russia. Late twentieth-century scholarship has emphasized the leap from "medieval" conditions to the secular and revolutionary ideologies that circumstances forced upon Russian Jews. While the European Jews emancipated themselves by integrating, the argument went, Russian Jews not only remained outsiders in their own countries, but were also alienated from their European counterparts who moved along a different historical trajectory.[48] More recent scholars have challenged this oversimplified schema, but none has yet paid attention to Haim Slonimskii, a prominent member of the Russian Jewish Enlightenment, or Haskalah.

Born in the Polish town of Białystok in 1810, Haim grew up in a conservative Jewish family. Many years later, he wrote about his childhood experience: "The Russian language is so foreign to a Jew that he can only learn it with the help of another Jew who translates it for him using patois. Having learned this language, the Jew finds nothing in it about himself or his religion, if you do not count hostile insinuations."[49] Dedicated to enlightening his fellow Jews, Haim published all of his books in Hebrew. In 1835, he wrote *The Foundations of Wisdom*. After Halley's Comet appeared in 1835, he published an astronomy primer entitled *The Comet*. In 1838, he finished *The Annals of the Heavens*. And in subsequent books, he introduced his readers to Copernicus, Newton, Kepler, and other scientific giants.

Haim was also a talented inventor. In 1845, the Saint Petersburg Academy of Sciences awarded him the prestigious Demidov Prize worth 2,500 rubles for a prototype of a calculating machine. In the 1950s, Soviet authorities claimed that Haim's 1859 paper on duplex telegraph communications (simultaneous messages in both directions) proved that the Russians were pioneers in the field.[50] Soviet writer Mikhail Slonimskii remembered his grandfather as a "mathematician, astronomer, engineer, polyglot, speaker of almost twenty foreign languages," but added that his "hopeless impracticality set him apart."[51] Indeed, Haim repeatedly failed to patent his inventions or to publish his findings. Judging by the frequency with which his son Leonid moved his family from one apartment to another, he seems to have inherited his father's disregard for financial and practical affairs.[52]

By the 1860s, Haim became a prominent figure of the Haskalah, which promoted "the values of enlightened religious tolerance, the importance of learning the language of the land and earning the trust of the state."[53] The new Jewish social elite to which the Haskalah gave birth intervened and negotiated between the state and the community. In Berlin and Warsaw, Haim published the popular-scientific weekly newspaper *Ha-Tsefirah* (*Dawn*, 1862 and 1874–1931), which covered politics, literature, and the sciences.[54] He contributed many articles on scientific topics and, in 1874, one of these proposed what has become known as the date-meridian, a line that fixes the Sabbath and the holy days for Jews all over the world in reference to Jerusalem instead of Greenwich.[55]

Emerging from such an enlightened, albeit financially precarious household, Leonid began his gymnasium education in Warsaw, but when in 1862 Haim became the headmaster of the Zhitomir rabbinical seminary and the censor of Jewish books and newspapers, he brought his son with him and Leonid completed his education at the Zhitomir Gymnasium. The Zhitomir rabbinical seminary was one of Tsar Nicholas's state-sanctioned tools directed against religious and cultural isolationism. Confident that the Jews could acculturate to Russian society, Haim argued in 1865 that although the "state rabbis" were "not strong enough to spread enlightenment, they were at least able to check the spread of fanaticism, the first step in preparing enlightenment."[56] According to a contemporary, the seminary under Slonimskii became famous among enlightened Jews and Zhitomir eclipsed Vilna as "a Mecca" for learning.[57] Devoted to the cause of the Haskalah, Haim became one of the twenty-one "patrons and dignitaries" of the Society for Promoting Enlightenment among Jews in Russia, which was established in 1863 to provide "material support" for "worthy" intellectual projects.[58]

In Zhitomir, where Leonid grew up, Jews made up nearly half of the population, and yet local authorities prohibited Jewish residences and businesses in certain areas of town even though the state imposed certain forms of Jewish integration. Haim attempted to acculturate his children and, in a household infused with the values of the Haskalah where "the exact sciences were greatly revered," his three sons slowly distanced themselves from their traditions.[59] In her memoirs, Leonid's mother-in-law, Polina Vengerova, wrote: "Two things, my mother used to say, I know with absolute certainty: my generation will certainly live and die as Jews should; our grandchildren will live and die as non-Jews. But I cannot foretell what will happen to our children."[60] Russian Jews faced a difficult choice between acculturation and assimilation by the mid-nineteenth century. The elder Vengerova was right about her own grandchildren's fate—Leonid and his wife eventually converted to Orthodoxy.

CONCLUSION

The family backgrounds and childhoods of the *Herald* group demonstrate that Russian liberals emerged from a variety of social and psychological backgrounds, which imparted to each individual a certain potential whose outcome would be determined by future experiences. Stasiulevich's poverty and broken family became obstacles that he decided to overcome by the time he entered the gymnasium to which his noble background granted him access. Pypin's happy childhood among educated role models promised intellectual success without determining the path to it. Paradoxically, the familial intimacy that reigned in the household would also act as an obstacle to establishing close relationships with acquaintances in the future. Arsen'ev grew up in a household saturated with academic achievements. Would he adopt his father's interests or reject them? And would he follow a secure and successful career in state service? Leonid grew up in an enlightened Jewish family acutely aware of its otherness but willing to acculturate. He could either use this awareness as a source of creativity or become its victim.

The family backgrounds and childhood experiences of the future *Herald* liberals also offer an alternative vision of Russia under Tsar Nicholas I. "It was characteristic of the Nicholaian system that the police were to educate the public and the schools to discipline them," a scholar of educational institutions has written.[61] While the young men's backgrounds challenge this assessment of Nicholas's era, their university experiences thoroughly contradict such an excessively bleak oversimplification.

2

Formative Years
The Birth of Ideas

W HILE FAMILY BACKGROUND and childhood provided the raw
material for the *Herald* personalities, secondary education guided
their formation by taking them away from the primary social-
izing institutions, which were their homes, and exposing them to peers. The
university years produced a leap in their character formation as the clashing
forces of conformity and competition formed the young men's emotional
temper, personality traits, habits of mind, and social attitudes. The first similarities between the *Herald* liberals began to appear at this stage of their lives.

Stasiulevich, Pypin, and Arsen'ev studied in Saint Petersburg in the 1840s
and 1850s, a period when Russia was developing an original and humane
literary tradition. Although French socialism and German idealism constituted the bulk of the youths' reading at the time, none of the *Herald* liberals
became Hegelians or socialists. Stasiulevich and Pypin studied history a few
years apart at Saint Petersburg University, while Arsen'ev pursued a legal education at the elite School of Jurisprudence where the curriculum and rules of
conduct intentionally shielded the students from the outside world.

The young men's experiences also demonstrate that it is an oversimplification to call the period of Nicolaevan reaction in the wake of 1848 the "seven
dismal years." The intellectual currents were much more varied and complex
than is suggested by the philosophical fireworks, socialist dreams, and proto-
revolutionary tendencies that historians regularly associate with the names of
Nikolai Stankevich, Mikhail Petrashevskii, Belinskii, and Herzen. Indeed,
most educated Russians appreciated the expansion of the education system,
new bureaucratic posts within the state, the beautification of cities, and the
flourishing intellectual life. British industrial towns and France's barricaded

cities did not appeal to the majority of the educated public. The Russian Empire seemed to have reached the height of domestic stability and international influence, which is why the loss in the Crimean War would become such a shock.

Instead of discussing Proudhon, Cabet, Fourier, Leroux, Feuerbach, or Hegel, Stasiulevich and Pypin immersed themselves in purely academic pursuits, while Arsen'ev's personality evolved in a boarding-school bubble. The intellectual storms that raged around such prominent figures as Belinskii and Herzen barely affected Stasiulevich. More au courant of these men's writings, Pypin recoiled from some of their opinions and, although he lived with Chernyshevskii, he disagreed with his cousin's views as they became increasingly politicized in the 1850s. Surprisingly, Arsen'ev, who attended an elite institution and faced the brightest career prospects, became the most disillusioned with the quality of his education. Coming from a younger generation, Leonid Slonimskii studied at the Juridical Department of Kiev University between 1868 and 1872, an even more intellectually stormy period among students. Nevertheless, his education taught him to approach political economy, the most divisive subject of his day, dispassionately and analytically.

Indeed, since none of the *Herald* liberals felt alienated from society, none sought an escape in small revolutionary circles of soul-mates and none rejected Russian culture in favor of anything foreign. Despite different experiences, the *Herald* men were fairly typical, normal, and well-adjusted members of Russian educated society, which also points to the native roots of *Herald* liberalism.[1]

MIKHAIL STASIULEVICH: AN ACADEMIC IN THE MAKING, 1843–1852

When in August 1843 Mikhail Stasiulevich entered the historical-philological division of the Philosophy Department at Saint Petersburg University, he became a witness to the renaissance of Russia's universities under education minister Sergei Uvarov. Describing the academic atmosphere of the time, one historian has written that "a new crop of public-spirited professors forged closer ties with their surrounding communities through 'circles,' consulting work, and the public lectures that Uvarov mandated as regular features of university life."[2] The lectures not only fueled debates, but also turned professors into prominent figures and popular guests in salons. University enrollments more than doubled between 1833 and 1848 as Uvarov navigated between his goal of creating an enlightened bureaucracy and Tsar Nicholas's mistrust of universities as breeding grounds of revolution.

Uvarov convinced the fiscally conservative finance minister Egor Kankrin to increase the Education Ministry's budget threefold and used it to raise salaries and expand university facilities, laboratories, libraries, and presses.[3] Uvarov zealously patronized the Academy of Sciences in its work of unearthing and publishing Russia's archives, and he supported the growing interest in "scientific" history based on the study of original documents, believing that this was safer than researching contemporary affairs. He defended his policies in articles that he commissioned for the *Journal of the Ministry of National Enlightenment* (*Zhurnal ministerstva narodnogo prosveshcheniia*, 1834–1917), which he founded in 1834. Turning the page on the persecutions of faculty of the 1820s, Uvarov encouraged new course offerings. For example, beginning in 1837, the director of the Larin Gymnasium, Adam Fischer, began to lecture on psychology, logic, metaphysics, epistemology, and ethical philosophy at the university.[4] In defense of this curriculum, Uvarov and Fischer reminded their overly patriotic critics that an education in tune with Orthodox values did not require the negation of all European ideas.

Beyond the university's walls, Russian literature experienced the "remarkable decade" (1838–1848). In Moscow, Uvarov allowed historian Timofei Granovskii to give a series of public lectures in 1843–1844, which became a sensation. As one biographer put it, Granovskii preached justice toward one's fellow man, intellectual freedom, and a "sense of principle and legalism in government"—a contemporary called the lectures a "political event."[5] Despite Uvarov's cautious direction—for example, Granovskii was forbidden to mention Hegel—the universities nevertheless became the least constrained venues for debate.

Throughout the 1840s, Uvarov even supported the publication of the journals *Notes of the Fatherland* and *The Contemporary* and defended them from conservative attacks. He believed that both publications were "beneficial to literature" and represented "the best examples of Russian journalism."[6] He also believed that they were useful safety valves for criticism of the state's reluctance to reform. The editor of *The Contemporary*, Pyotr Pletnev, even joined the faculty of Saint Petersburg University in 1832 as a professor of Russian literature and language and became dean in 1840—a post he retained until 1861—contributing greatly to its reputation as a center of learning.

As Pletnev put it in a speech commemorating the university's twenty-fifth anniversary in 1844—a year after Stasiulevich enrolled—it had finally "won over the respect of parents from all estates, so that even the highest state officials have decided, with full confidence, to educate their children here."[7] This definition of success reflects the importance that Uvarov placed on university education as a prerequisite for state service. The university responded to state requests for specially trained personnel as different ministries sponsored university departments.[8] Although Uvarov coordinated university enrollments with the needs of the state, this measure was in harmony with western European practices in a conservative age. Stasiulevich entered an expanding and confident institution with a highly professional, relatively young, and progressively minded faculty.

He specialized in classical literature and languages under the renowned specialist on ancient Greece Mikhail Kutorga, who had traveled to leading European universities in the 1830s to acquaint himself with the latest achievements in classical studies. Kutorga emphasized original sources, trained his students in historical methods, and rigorously examined the historiography of his field. To further his students' training, he organized seminars in his home.[9] Under Kutorga's guidance, Stasiulevich argued in his senior thesis that Homer was a "collective persona" and that the language and the organization of the *Iliad* and *Odyssey* proved that their original composition predated written language in Greece. For this first academic effort, he received a silver medal.[10] Two years later, he defended his master's thesis, "The Athenian Hegemony," which he published in 1849.[11] His meticulous, disciplined, and balanced approach to historical documents demonstrated that he had acquired the habits of intellectual restraint and thorough examination that were essential to a successful academic career.

Stasiulevich acquired these skills at an auspicious time. In the wake of the European Revolutions of 1848, the Russian state intensified censorship and surveillance. The university authorities ordered professors to omit "superfluous information" from their lectures, which meant that politically sensitive phrases and words could damage careers. In 1849, Tsar Nicholas appointed the more conservative Prince Platon Shirinskii-Shikhmatov in Uvarov's place. The new education minister raised tuition, reduced the student body in all universities, limited enrollment strictly to members of the gentry, and curtailed the universities' autonomy. In January 1849, Stasiulevich began to teach history at the Larin Gymnasium while supplementing his income with private lessons.

In an environment of growing suspicion and surveillance, Stasiulevich chose a safe classical subject for his master's thesis, but his participation in an affair involving professor Granovskii exposed him to the complicated way in which historical research and writing intertwined with politics after 1848. An admirer of liberal reforms and institutional history, Granovskii had submitted his doctoral dissertation, titled "The Communes in France," to Moscow University in 1847. Although the subject dealt with the Middle Ages, by 1849 the title had become unacceptable, so Granovskii shifted his work's emphasis from the struggles of the communes for independence to the French monarchy's centralization policies in the twelfth century. As a result, the monarchy's chief theorist, Abbot Suger of Saint Denis, became the center of Granovskii's work.

The public defense went well, but the ensuing debate over his sources and non-academic writing style spilled into the press. In May 1850, Stasiulevich published an article in the popular journal *Muscovite* (*Moskvitianin*, 1841–1856) accusing Granovskii of being insufficiently scholarly because he had not worked with primary sources. "Abbot Suger," as the thesis was renamed, did not fulfill "those demands that scholarship makes of specialized, scholarly compositions," wrote Stasiulevich.[12] Granovskii's students sprang to his defense and a debate continued for two years until Stasiulevich admitted that he had misunderstood Granovskii's real intention—to make history accessible to the public. After realizing his mistake, Stasiulevich became especially respectful of Granovskii and sent him copies of all his published works.

The crux of the debate concerned, of course, the role of history and the function of the historian in Russian society. Stasiulevich initially missed the bigger picture that Granovskii (thirteen years his senior) had grasped and after the debate became "undoubtedly more engaged over the question of the nature and function of history, and by implication, the role of the historian."[13] As one scholar has put it, Granovskii did to history what others were doing to imaginative literature and literary criticism by turning them "into a channel for the expression of independent thought and enlightened values."[14] When Stasiulevich became a professor and gave public lectures himself, he followed Granovskii's example and became a popular public figure in his own right. Stasiulevich's ideas about history had come even closer to Granovskii's by the time he defended his doctoral dissertation, "Lycurgus of Athens," in 1852, in which he argued that emancipating historical characters from the narrow constraints of philology and treating them in "simple human terms would show their relevance to readers and make classical history accessible to a wider audience."[15]

In 1852, Stasiulevich quit the Larin Gymnasium and became a senior lecturer (*dotsent*) in the history of the Middle Ages at Saint Petersburg University. Beyond the university, state suspicions of public opinion sometimes reached absurd levels. When Nikolai Gogol died in 1852, the local authorities forbade Turgenev to place an obituary in the Saint Petersburg press. When he succeeded in sneaking it past the censors in Moscow, he was arrested and eventually exiled. Stasiulevich, however, steered clear of scandal. By 1853, he was an adjunct professor with three independent publications and a solid scholarly reputation. Although the academic community was hypersensitive to the social and intellectual turmoil during the last years of Nicholas's reign, Stasiulevich's student life and early professional success unfolded in the quiet academic sphere that evolved independently of the philosophical storms that raged in the capital's salons during the 1840s and 1850s. Stasiulevich's conduct demonstrated a penetrating, but reserved and disciplined worldview independent of peer pressure and the storm and stress of the intelligentsia's first philosophical experiments, although the lessons he carried away from the Granovskii affair would soon bear fruit.

The Granovskii affair taught Stasiulevich another valuable lesson. "Our journals," he admitted to a friend at the time, "are not worth participating in. All scholarly arguments are settled depending on the editor's personal relationship to the authors."[16] Instead, Stasiulevich dedicated himself fully to his studies. The rest, he wrote, was "vanitas vanitatum et omnia vanitas [vanity of vanities and all is vanity]."[17] Nonetheless, negotiating the treacherous waters of academia became an exercise in both diplomacy and restraint—two qualities that would serve the future editor well—as Stasiulevich immersed himself in research and teaching between 1853 and 1856. His experience reflected a general Russian trend under Tsar Nicholas I of academia acting as an alternative to politics, fertile soil for the evolution of civil society, and the root of the *Herald*'s moderate tone. With Nikolai Chernyshevskii showing increasing interest in intellectual currents beyond the university and exposing his cousin to them, Aleksandr Pypin's student years unfolded more dramatically than Stasiulevich's.

ALEXANDER PYPIN:
AN INDEPENDENT STATE OF MIND, 1849–1857

Sasha Pypin completed his education at the Saratov Gymnasium in the inauspicious year of 1849, just when the Ministry of Education curtailed university enrollments, so his parents decided that it was best to send Sasha to Kazan University, instead of Saint Petersburg. In 1849, the university had only 309 students, but Pypin admitted in his memoirs that it resembled "a veritable temple of learning" to a provincial boy.[18] The Kazan educational district included the enormous territory from Perm and Viatka in the north to Astrakhan in the south, and the entire Urals region. Students from the Caucasus and Siberia also attended. Leo Tolstoy finished his studies there the year that Pypin arrived and the famous Russian mathematician Nikolai Lobachevskii was assistant district superintendent.

Like Stasiulevich in Saint Petersburg, Sasha joined the Historical-Philological Department where famous Slavist Viktor Grigorovich taught. His stimulating lectures attracted Sasha to the subject and since the university library was still small at the time, Grigorovich granted his students access to his personal collection. His enthusiasm was infectious and his knowledge of the subject was first-hand thanks to Uvarov's policy of sending professors abroad.[19] Grigorovich had spent two and a half years traveling in "European Turkey" (the Balkans) and learning Slavic languages and customs, of which he later published an account. After Grigorovich died in 1877, Pypin described him as a learned humanist and idealist trapped among administrators and pseudo-specialists.[20] In the 1840s, however, the field of Slavic studies was in its infancy and Pypin struggled to find his way in the absence of introductory courses and published materials.

The philosophical parting of ways with his cousin began as a result of Pypin's interest in this uncharted territory. In a letter to his parents, Chernyshevskii was wildly enthusiastic about new additions to the curriculum of Kazan University:

> It is wonderful that they have added political economy because along with history . . . it stands in the forefront of all the sciences. Without political economy it is impossible to take a single step in the academic world. And this is not just a fad, as some say; no, political-economic questions are now at the forefront of theory as well as practice, in other words in the sciences and in affairs of state.[21]

His cousin's enthusiasm notwithstanding, Sasha showed little interest in political economy and took instead the history of the Church, world history, French and German, the history of world literature, philosophy, and Slavic languages.[22]

While Sasha studied in Kazan, Nikolai Chernyshevskii continued to bombard the family with letters urging them to transfer Sasha to the capital. Having completed his first year at Kazan, Pypin spent the summer of 1850 on the road with his father traveling through Ukrainian colonies along the Volga. For the first time, Sasha became conscious of the differences between the Great and Little Russians—the Ukrainians seemed to possess more self-esteem, he noticed, and behaved more freely and were cleaner in their appearance.[23] At the end of the summer, Chernyshevskii and Pypin traveled to Kazan to complete the transfer paperwork. They took a boat to Nizhnii Novgorod where they attended the annual trade fair, then traveled to Moscow, and from there made their way to Petersburg atop a postal coach where the seats were cheaper.

In the fall of 1850, Sasha was one of four second-year philology students at Saint Petersburg University. In his memoirs, he described how Uvarovian classicism came under attack for exposing students to Homer, Thucydides, and Sophocles. Instead, Shirinskii-Shikhmatov encouraged the study of the Church Fathers while "republican ideas and pagan mythology were removed during the teaching of the Greek language."[24] The university administration canceled all philosophy classes, split the Philosophy Department into History-Philology and Physics-Mathematics, and sent observers into classrooms to monitor the content of lectures. Mikhail Kutorga, Stasiulevich's mentor, had a reputation for harboring liberal views, so when Pypin attended his lectures, the superintendent of the Saint Petersburg educational district personally sat in and occasionally walked up to Kutorga during his lectures and stared at him, to the latter's great annoyance.[25] As usually happens, Pypin remembered, censorship attracted even greater attention to European affairs among the students.

Pypin arrived in Saint Petersburg after the police had arrested and sentenced members of the Petrashevtsy group, an informal discussion circle of idealistic youths that included Fyodor Dostoevsky. Large gatherings in private apartments ceased, but liberal views remained popular among the students and peddlers continued to sell banned literature, which they carried around in canvas bags. When Chernyshevskii introduced his cousin to the works of French utopian socialist Charles Fourier, Pypin found in them too much "arbitrary fantasy" for his taste. He preferred the "firm and decisive logic" of Ludwig Feuerbach to the "fantasy of the French socialists."[26]

Pypin found the field of Russian literary studies in its infancy, which forced the students to explore it with minimal guidance. When in 1853 Pypin decided to write his senior thesis on late eighteenth-century Russian comedy, he had to use as his guides Kutorga's critical approach to original sources and the exegetic expertise that he had gleaned from seminars on classical philosophy. His thesis met with the highest approval in the form of a gold medal.

In the process of conducting research, Pypin concluded that Russian literature in the late eighteenth century was an unjustly overlooked contribution to Russian culture. Aesthetically clumsy, it nevertheless demonstrated "the consistent upbringing of eighteenth-century society to the acceptance of science, literature, and social interests." The period was essential to understanding the history of "social attitudes and tastes," he wrote, and argued further that Belinskii was wrong in condemning this literary period for its failure to champion the cause of social justice. Pypin's interest in Russian culture became a lifelong project of ground-breaking exploration. Belinskii had died in 1848 largely ignorant of the history of Russia's social movements, so a "new group of researchers," Pypin wrote in his memoirs, took up the task of exploring them.[27] As he joined these pioneers during the "seven dismal years," bibliographies and biographical dictionaries were in demand and became safe forms of academic research that avoided political issues. Pypin became part of Russia's first group of literary historians, which also included Aleksandr Afanas'ev, Orest Miller, Nikolai Tikhonravov, and Pyotr Pekarskii.[28]

After they arrived in the capital, Nikolai Chernyshevskii introduced his cousin to literary historian Irinarkh Vvedenskii, also a native of Saratov, whose salon had converted Chernyshevskii to Belinskii and Herzen.[29] Unlike his cousin, however, Pypin remained critical of both men's views, while debates about socialism left him uninterested. He preferred the literary angle of the discussions and described the salon's atmosphere as "liberal" but different from the philosophical circles of the 1830s and 1840s with their heated debates about Hegelian philosophy and socialist ideals. The members gossiped about the latest literary news, joked about the government's attempts to control public life, and "waited for the outcome" of society's depressed "intellectual and moral state."[30] While Chernyshevskii clarified his revolutionary ideas under the influence of these gatherings, Pypin saw in them an opportunity to network with the capital's intelligentsia, and at one of these evenings he met the military doctor Gavriil Gorodkov, whose wife's sister he would marry several years later.

Pypin's research into the literatures of the Slavic peoples reinforced his belief in the value of ethnic self-expression. In his memoirs, he disagreed with Belinskii's condemnation of Ukrainian literature for its petty provincial plots that ignored the more important social problems.[31] In Pypin's opinion, any form of literary creativity stimulated national consciousness and contributed to enlightenment, so he welcomed all manifestations of literary experimentation regardless of their origins.

In October 1853, the Russo-Turkish War broke out and Russia's initial military and naval successes forced France and England to join forces with the Ottoman Empire by 1854, launching the Crimean War. When the British fleet blockaded Russian ships outside the island fortress of Kronstadt, Pypin joined the droves of onlookers who traveled there to catch a glimpse of the British ships in the distance. Pypin's recollections of this period echo hundreds of others. The glaring inconsistencies between official reports and the reality described by eyewitnesses undermined public confidence in the government. The appalling conditions at the front and logistical incompetence, wrote Pypin, "led to the bankruptcy of the old administrative system," which had disregarded "public opinion" while sticking to "political principles that constituted the real calamity of national life."[32] Pypin remembered how a friend informed him of Sevastopol's fall with mixed emotions: sadness about the military defeat and joy about the blow to the autocracy's reputation.

The Crimean War opened a floodgate of "illegal" literature in the form of draft proposals and manuscripts, as well as the famous *Voices from Russia* anthologies that emanated from Herzen's free press in London. The pamphlets addressed everything from government structure to abuses of power by local authorities in distant regions of the empire, and the authors included prominent figures such as Mikhail Pogodin, Timofei Granovskii, Boris Chicherin, and Konstantin Kavelin. Belinskii's famous letter to Gogol "resurfaced" in hand-written copies. As "an anxious attitude and anxious expectations" gripped Russian society during the war, Pypin entered the world of Russia's leading thick journals, *The Contemporary* and *Notes of the Fatherland*.

In a letter to his parents, Pypin described his weekly salon itinerary: Saturdays at Slavist Izmail Sreznevskii's first and then at Roman historian Nikolai Blagoveshchenskii's; Fridays at literary historian Aleksandr Nikitenko's with Nikolai Chernyshevskii; Thursdays at *Notes of the Fatherland* editor Andrei Kraevskii's; and frequent visits to *Contemporary* editors Nikolai Nekrasov and Ivan Panaev.[33] The *Contemporary* network introduced Pypin to writers Ivan Goncharov, Ivan Turgenev, Leo Tolstoy, and Dmitrii Grigorovich, literary critic Aleksandr Druzhinin, and playwright Aleksandr Ostrovskii.

Pypin's "bibliographic" friends suggested that he publish his thesis on eighteenth-century comedy in *Notes of the Fatherland*, but he refused because he thought it too specialized for a general audience. Instead, in 1853 he contributed an article about an obscure eighteenth-century playwright Vladimir Lukin and from then on contributed more pieces on topics that included medieval Russian translations of stories from *A Thousand and One Nights*, traces of Alexander the Great in Russian folklore, Russian fairytales discovered in medieval manuscripts, and apocryphal biblical tales.[34] Chernyshevskii informed his aunt and uncle in 1853 that their son's articles had become topics of conversation in Nikitenko's salon.[35]

On Sundays, Chernyshevskii and his young wife Olga hosted a salon of their own and Pypin, who had moved in with them, was often present at these gatherings, where he met famous literary critic and radical Nikolai Dobroliubov in 1856. Meanwhile, Chernyshevskii reported to his aunt and uncle that "Sashenka continues to earn his rights to academic celebrity."[36] Pypin read Dobroliubov's articles on the works of Turgenev, Ostrovskii, Dostoevsky, and Goncharov and appreciated how the critic "immersed himself in these literary paintings; he believed in them, like reality."[37] However, Pypin disagreed with Dobroliubov's demand that writers combat social wrongs. Pypin witnessed the split between the purely artistic and socially oriented directions in Russian literature that appeared in the 1850s with Turgenev, Druzhinin, and Vasilii Botkin defending the artistic tendency and Dobroliubov and Chernyshevskii defending the social one.[38] In his memoirs, Pypin maintained that he belonged to neither camp and argued that "both 'directions' were closely and organically linked to each other" and that "the key to Russian literature lay in this organic connection."[39] Simultaneously, he defended the popularizers of history, such as Nikolai Blagoveshchenskii, who made the classical past accessible to a wider audience. Pypin believed that this was the only way to overcome popular aversion to state-enforced classicism, which he nonetheless considered essential to a well-rounded education, believing that knowledge of ancient history "could become an important tool of social consciousness."[40]

By 1855, Pypin was recommending older scholars, such as his colleague, the literary historian Pekarskii, to the editors of *The Contemporary*.[41] In 1856, at the age of twenty-three, Pypin became a corresponding member of the Imperial Russian Archaeological Society and a full member of the Imperial Geographic Society. In 1857, he asked the censors for permission to translate Friedrich Schlosser's *History of the Eighteenth Century and of the Nineteenth until the Overthrow of the French Empire*, which was part of a joint project with Chernyshevskii under the auspices of *The Contemporary*, and aimed to introduce the Russian public to world history by translating and publishing the most popular Western works on the subject.[42] At the same time, Pypin defended his master's thesis, "A Sketch of the Literary History of Old Russian Novels and Fairytales," and received half of the prestigious Demidov Prize, which resulted in a position as lecturer in European literature at Saint Petersburg University. However, since the ministry had not yet allocated the funds for the new Department of Western European Literature, it decided to send Pypin abroad to acquaint him with the latest scholarship and visit the eastern European regions in whose literatures he would specialize. Chernyshevskii wrote to his parents: "Sashenka sees his dream of going abroad materialize and can consider his career made."[43]

During his years at the university, Pypin demonstrated an intellectual reserve, scholarly dedication, and academic ambition similar to Stasiulevich's. Indeed, Chernyshevskii, who corresponded regularly with the Saratov household, repeatedly made excuses for his cousin's poor penmanship due to his workload and poor sleeping habits.[44] Although Pypin was engaged in the capital's intellectual circles, he nonetheless remained aloof. One biographer has even described him as a "reserved, 'closed' person, [who] opened up completely neither to those close to him, nor to his colleagues."[45] Although his memoirs contain interesting descriptions of his peers, they demonstrate emotional connections neither to them nor even to Chernyshevskii, who remained his closest friend. Pypin became a scholar who placed method above conclusions, which allowed him to maintain a healthy distance from the subject matter and to minimize the literary and historical preconceptions that must have pressed in from all sides under the influence of the Slavophile-Westernizer debate that continued into the 1850s. Parallel to this abstract debate, the evolution of the field of Slavic literatures and languages played a crucial role in the formation of Russia's national self-consciousness, with Pypin on the cutting edge of the new discipline. In the process, Pypin developed a cool academic approach to matters of national consciousness while at the same time believing them to be crucial to a healthy liberal world view. This same attitude would become a defining characteristic of the *Herald of Europe* message, while intellectual engagement combined with emotional sangfroid would serve Pypin well as the journal's editor.

KONSTANTIN ARSEN'EV: INTEGRATING INTO THE ELITE, 1849–1855

Konstantin Arsen'ev's education, unlike Stasiulevich's and Pypin's, followed a state-oriented path. At twelve years of age, he entered one of Russia's two institutions that supplied personnel directly for higher civil service—the School of Jurisprudence, where famous Russian composer Pyotr Tchaikovsky was three years his junior.[46] The school's founder, Prince Pyotr Ol'denburgskii, was Tsar Nicholas's nephew, and had convinced the tsar in 1835 that "the dearth of educated and informed officials in the chancelleries of the judicial offices constitutes one of the most important inconveniences that prevent this part [of the administration] from being brought to the level to which the emperor would like to raise the entire government."[47] In other words, the School of Jurisprudence aimed to promote legality and formal procedure in a bureaucracy otherwise dominated by informal relationships and local patronage networks.

The school's 1838 statute articulated its central goal "to train noble youth for service in the state judiciary" and its graduation list "read like the *Who's Who* of the Russian civil administration," as one historian has put it. During 106 years of existence, it produced twenty-four ministers or their equivalent, thirty-five appointed and eleven elected members of the State Council, and seventy-three senators.[48] Distinguished lawyer and future contributor to the *Herald* Vladimir Stasov graduated in 1843. Arsen'ev studied in distinguished company.

The school offered a seven-year program with a specialization in law that prepared students for service in the Ministry of Justice. Enrollment heavily favored the gentry so that between 1835 and 1885 only six percent of the graduates came from other estates. The strictly supervised boarding-school environment socialized the students by limiting their exposure to the outside world and since the school was located in the capital, permission to leave campus was limited and a strict code of conduct applied when students did so. Parents worked hard to enroll their children although tuition was ten to fifteen times what universities cost. The school's classes averaged between 230 and 240 members annually and the best students graduated with the eleventh state rank automatically and went on salary immediately whether they had a job or not. This set them apart from their university colleagues and acted as an effective reward mechanism and a persuasive disciplinary tool since grades for behavior affected a student's overall standing.

The demanding curriculum regimented the days from six a.m. until ten p.m. The school favored a practical education. In Russian language classes, the students read official proclamations. Greek was not an option, but Latin was a prerequisite for juridical courses. Since foreign languages were essential to jurists in a country that took much from Western examples, French and German took up one quarter of overall class time. The last three years offered a broad spectrum of law and related courses, including forensic medicine and political economy. Although less demanding than university law courses, the variety was greater. In addition, the jurists worked with documents from ministry archives, took procedure courses from professional bureaucrats, and attended special lectures on contemporary legal problems.

The school pampered its students to compensate for its disciplinary demands. For example, the jurists' three-course lunch and two-course dinner humbled the average university diet. Frequent music concerts, physical activity clubs, and the beautifully kept campus compensated for the strictly controlled environment. Prince Ol'denburgskii was immensely popular. He frequently inspected the school, visited the infirmary, entertained the students lavishly, and even gave them spending money anonymously. The school invited successful alumni to meet the students and speak to them regularly and the graduation ceremonies always attracted high state dignitaries and members of the imperial family.[49]

The school combined character formation with professional training, but the tie that was supposed to bind the students together was the inculcation of moral values, which aimed to make of the graduates loyal, efficient, diligent, and honest bureaucrats. This training encouraged a strong feeling of corporate loyalty to the school and, as one student remembered, the hazing of the newcomers forced them "to create such bonds with their classmates that they would never require outside help."[50] *Égalité* and *fraternité* characterized the relations between the students, although the school's authorities often tested this loyalty with internal investigations and punishments.[51] As each group of graduates entered the ranks of the bureaucracy simultaneously, their loyalty spread across state institutions, but was especially strong within the Ministry of Justice. In all this, the school was no different from elite educational institutions elsewhere in Europe.

Unfortunately, when Arsen'ev entered the school in 1849, its director, Major-General A. P. Iazykov, was in the process of implementing military discipline, part of which came in the form of marching classes. A purge replaced foreign personnel as well as "civilian" Russian professors with officers, most of whom lacked educational credentials. The sterner regulations came after it was discovered that one of the members of the Petrashevtsy group, Vasilii Golovinskii, was a jurist. The state need not have worried, however. In his memoirs, Arsen'ev argued that his classmates were much less interested in Saint-Simon and Fourier than the students of the Tsarskoe Selo Lyceum, a more radically minded institution.

According to Arsen'ev, the greatest threat to discipline was smoking, which proves that politics did not penetrate the campus. Although the younger students experienced corporal punishment regularly, the administration threatened the upperclassmen only verbally. Arsen'ev's class was the first to protest this abuse by refusing to visit the director and inspectors on the eve of graduation in 1855, but this was a few months after Alexander II became tsar and a thaw was already in the air. According to Arsen'ev, whatever moral fiber the students acquired came despite the school's disciplinary policies, not because of them.[52]

Arsen'ev's low opinion of its academic standards reflected the school's emphasis on obedience and service to the detriment of natural curiosity and originality of thought. Arsen'ev's class left the general education stage (the first four years) with "a poor knowledge of the Latin language, history, and geography and almost total ignorance of mathematics, physics, and natural history." What modern languages the students knew they had picked up at home, he maintained. "We were treated like boys and we studied like boys, not like students," Arsen'ev remembered. Even in the upper classes, there was little personal communication between the professors and students and little intellectual guidance. Arsen'ev made an exception for Russian language and literature professor Nikolai Vyshnegradskii who taught Turgenev's *Huntsman's Sketches*, published in 1847, in which Vyshnegradskii saw a condemnation of serfdom. The majority of the legal courses, however, were boring and incomprehensible, with the exception of forensic medicine and criminal law, taught by the renowned Saint Petersburg University professor Pyotr Kalmykov. From these courses, Arsen'ev wrote, the students emerged with "the heavy feeling of something being wrong with the world around us."[53]

The seduction of automatic rank upon graduation forced the students to preserve the appearance of effort. Arsen'ev's peers rarely read newspapers and did not learn about Belinskii until after graduation. The isolation severely limited their world and confined their goals to state service. Even the Crimean War made a negligible impact on the students' lives. "Russia's power was for us an axiom beyond any argument," wrote Arsen'ev. The topic for the final exam in German was to compare the year 1853 with 1453 and aimed "clearly to encourage chauvinistic excitement." The students left the school completely ignorant of the political situation in the empire and the significance of Tsar Alexander's accession.

It did not surprise Arsen'ev that the School of Jurisprudence produced so few legal scholars, with the exception of the notoriously reactionary Konstantin Pobedonostsev. Few successful lawyers and no notable zemstvo personalities emerged from its halls. Indeed, another graduate wrote: "From the School of Jurisprudence we carry away nothing but rank, a diploma listing all of our courses, and a meaningful medal that reads 'respice finem' [Give thought to the goal]."[54] The feeling of corporate loyalty remained on the "schoolboy level" and was "artificial" and "false," wrote Arsen'ev thirty years later. His class quickly lost its cohesion after graduation. "The state of our spirits at the time of graduation," Arsen'ev complained, "resembled most closely a blank sheet of paper upon which our future life would have to write one thing or another."[55] Unlike his colleagues Stasiulevich and Pypin, Arsen'ev ended his student years without the experience necessary for running and contributing to a journal, although he would make up for this during his professional career as a lawyer. Compensating for what he saw as Russia's under-developed legal culture and worldview would become Arsen'ev's job at the *Herald of Europe*.

LEONID SLONIMSKII:

FROM LAWYER TO ECONOMIST, 1868–1872

Unlike Konstantin Arsen'ev, Leonid Slonimskii received an excellent legal education at the Juridical Department of Saint Vladimir University in Kiev from which he graduated in 1872. Unfortunately, he left no recollections of his experiences and was reticent about that period of his life. Even his son Nicolas wrote, "I knew little about my father's youth and education, except that he graduated from the University of Kiev."[56] Nevertheless, a reconstruction of his environment strongly suggests that the roots of Slonimskii's interest in economics go back to the men under whom he studied in Kiev, especially professor Nikolai Bunge (minister of finance, 1881–1887), from whom Slonimskii borrowed the core economic concepts that he developed further on the pages of the *Herald of Europe*.

When the Juridical Department opened in 1835, its faculty was predominantly Russian and the curriculum emphasized Russian law. By 1840, the faculty had become one of the strongest in the empire due in part to the influx of former members of the Second Department of His Majesty's Chancellery, which was responsible for codifying Russian law under Mikhail Speranskii's guidance.[57] When Leonid arrived in Kiev in 1868, its population was in the process of doubling from 68,000 in 1863 to 127,000 in 1874. The recovery of the beet sugar industry after Emancipation and the construction of the Southwestern railroad through town—the train station was completed

in 1870—attracted laborers and settlers. Self-government and business opportunities constantly distracted the juridical faculty, about which the students complained bitterly.[58] Having been expelled by Nicholas I in 1827, Jews
returned to Kiev under Alexander II and by 1874 the Jewish population had
reached fourteen thousand.[59]

In the wake of the Great Reforms, the Haskalah movement faced a
dilemma. On the one hand, Russian Jews could enter universities more freely.
On the other, the Haskalah tried to reinvigorate its own institutions of higher
learning, the yeshivas, although the trend among Jewish youths was not in
their favor and Leonid followed the majority who entered Russian universities.[60] When Leonid enrolled in 1868, Saint Vladimir University was enjoying the blessings of the 1863 University Charter that granted a degree of
self-government to the faculty who elected the rector and the deans. As one
scholar has noted, the university received "three of the choicest gifts in the
bestowal of the autocracy: academic freedom, professional self-government,
and social authority."[61] According to one account, the university administration under Rector Nikolai Bunge treated the students "genially and benevo-
lently, without formalism and bureaucratic subordination" and most students
completed their studies without problems.[62]

There were about nine hundred students at the university in the late
1860s, and the atmosphere was much more democratic than in Saint Petersburg when Stasiulevich and Pypin studied there. The juridical and medical
departments were the most popular.[63] Leonid's university years came in
the wake of the Great Reforms, which turned young minds away from the
"philosophical and aesthetic idealism" of the 1840s and 1850s and towards
"socio-cultural and scientific ideals," as a fellow student put it. Lectures on
political economy became very popular in the 1860s, and the student body
was split between the "radicals," mostly medical students and science majors,
and the "liberal-progressives," mostly students of law, history, and mathematics. The two groups regularly organized debates in the university cafe-
teria.[64] The academic year lasted seven months and the university authorities
complained that the students attended an average of only ten lectures during
this period.[65] In other words, university law students—unlike those at the
School of Jurisprudence—had plenty of free time to pursue extracurricular
interests.

By the time Leonid enrolled, the faculty included luminaries such as criminal law specialist Aleksandr Kistiakovskii and political economist Nikolai
Ziber.[66] Only Bunge and Kistiakovskii insisted on monitoring their students'

progress personally, which earned them great respect.[67] Since political economy was one of the two non-juridical required courses that the University Statute of 1842 mandated—the other was forensic medicine—the law students immersed themselves in the relevant texts.[68] While the generation to which Stasiulevich, Pypin, and Arsen'ev belonged read literature, German philosophy, literary criticism, and the French socialists, Slonimskii's peers devoured Adam Smith, David Ricardo, and Karl Marx, among many others.

Slonimskii's experience at Saint Vladimir University was that of assimilation. The Jewish students in the late 1860s and early 1870s did not distinguish themselves from their Ukrainian or Russian counterparts. Jewish students generally kept their distance from Jewish communities in university towns and rarely set foot in synagogues, while the first self-organized Jewish student groups did not appear until the end of the nineteenth century, long after the Ukrainians and Poles had organized their own.[69] Instead, during the 1860s Jewish students in Kiev were more likely to belong to the *zemliachestva*, an informal association of students from the same locality, which was the dominant form of association life at the time.[70]

The greatest influence on Leonid was Nikolai Bunge, who joined the law faculty in 1850 and became full professor of administrative law (*politseiskoe pravo*) in 1869 when Slonimskii was in the second year of his studies. Bunge also lectured on statistics, which he approached as a policy tool in the manner of the elder Arsen'ev, and a recent biographer has even argued that Bunge was the "pioneer of the sociological direction in Russian statistics."[71] He always introduced his courses on administrative law and statistics with several lectures on political economy that became so popular that even medical students attended them.[72] Bunge believed that monarchy was a suitable form of government for Russia only as long as it was founded on "legality, glasnost, and local elections." Glasnost did not mean a free press, but less intrusive censorship and the right to criticize state policies. Much like Mikhail Katkov and Konstantin Kavelin, Bunge was an Anglophile who believedthat British institutions of local self-government had prevented the revolutionary wave from crossing the channel in 1848. Therefore, "self-government of the community constitutes the real stronghold of monarchies," he wrote, and by the 1860s, he had become the "leader of the university's progressive party."[73]

Bunge did not limit his expertise to the lecture hall. He had been a member of the Rostovtsev (later Panin) Commission that worked out the emancipation of the serfs. Bunge was also the first Russian economist to examine the peasant question in connection with credit institutions, taxation, passport laws, and migration. He believed, for example, that since the peasant commune was an established and tested institution, it should be allowed to outlive its utility, but should not be artificially preserved. As a way to pay for Emancipation, Bunge supported an income tax, an idea ahead of its time and one that the *Herald* would champion beginning in the 1870s. In 1862, Bunge established the Kiev branch of the State Bank, which he temporarily headed in 1866, and in 1868 he helped establish the City of Kiev Mutual Credit Company and the Kiev Private Commercial Bank, Russia's first provincial joint-stock bank. A year later, the Kiev Stock Exchange opened with his support and in 1871 he helped found the Kiev Industrial Bank. In addition, Bunge served as a member of the municipal duma, but refused to become head because of his academic responsibilities.[74]

Bunge incorporated his understanding of finances and Russian business conditions into his lectures. He urged his students to avoid generalizations unsupported by facts and to analyze economic dogmas carefully. One of his students wrote that in a time when grand reform plans carried away youthful minds, "his merciless logic destroyed these seductive constructions, and they fell to our feet like the broken toys of children." He appreciated Adam Smith's penetrating insights into universal economic laws, but criticized him for underestimating historical and geographic details. Bunge taught his students to approach economics historically and to deal with concrete facts.

As Slonimskii was attending his lectures, Bunge was in the process of moderating his free-trade opinions, which had become popular among Russian liberals in the mid-1850s. He now admitted that moderate state involvement in the market produced a healthy and stable economy. His views evolved in reaction to the financial crisis of the 1870s: the economic boom of the late 1860s had been a result of short-term low- and no-interest state credits, but by the early 1870s many banks and joint stock enterprises folded as the investment bubble burst. After the 1873 European recession, Bunge supported state-sponsored reforms that prevented mass impoverishment, eased socio-economic tensions, and thereby deprived socialism of its most convincing arguments.[75] When Leonid Slonimskii began to publish in the *Herald of Europe* in the late 1870s, his drew on Bunge's views. Indeed, this non-radical and historically conscious "economism" would become the hallmark of the *Herald*'s message.

Conclusion

It would be an overstatement to identify these formative years as the first steps that the future *Herald* members took towards each other. However, their experiences made it more likely that they would find a common language when they did meet. The university years set a certain rhythm and imparted a tone to their intellectual evolution upon which further experiences would produce no more than variations.

The men of the *Herald* developed their first character traits at this stage. While Stasiulevich demonstrated great dedication to his academic calling and persistence in analyzing classical texts, Pypin took a greater risk when he entered the fledgling field of Slavic and Russian literatures through which he had to feel his own way. Nevertheless, both men demonstrated intellectual discipline and scholarly balance—no abrupt changes of course, no extreme ideological commitments and animosities, and no fanatical enthusiasms. By the 1850s, they seemed firmly set on the academic path to scholarly, not revolutionary, achievements that would come in the form of persuasion and proof, not zealous pamphleteering. The ability to discern shades of gray, which the pursuit of academic careers encouraged, would become essential to their editorial duties.

Arsen'ev and Slonimskii took the juridical path at drastically different institutions. The boarding school environment at the School of Jurisprudence prepared civil servants and inculcated obedience to authority and corporate loyalty. The Juridical Department of Saint Vladimir University granted plenty of freedom to explore the world of ideas. Although Arsen'ev graduated with a guaranteed job at the Ministry of Justice, thirty years later, he sounded bitter and disappointed about his education, which fell short of his literary aspirations. Slonimskii, on the other hand, left no accounts of Saint Vladimir University, but the courses in political economy that he attended there formed the foundation upon which he developed his ideas.

As Stasiulevich, Pypin, and Arsen'ev entered their respective professions in the 1850s, the Russian Empire was undergoing the dramatic economic, social, and cultural changes brought on by the Great Reforms. Ironically, the personal experiences that led to the foundation of the *Herald of Europe* had much less to do with the general optimism of the era than with career obstacles and disappointment with the course of Tsar Alexander's liberal experiments.

3

No Place for Talent

Academia and State Service

AFTER GRADUATING, Stasiulevich, Pypin, and Arsen'ev entered the professional world during the thaw that followed the death of Tsar Nicholas I in 1855. All three entered promising fields during the Reform era, but all became disappointed with the rate and extent of the changes. Stasiulevich and Pypin formed their views in Europe and articulated them from the lectern after returning to Russia. Although both respected European learning, they interpreted their experiences differently. While Stasiulevich embraced European intellectual sensibilities wholeheartedly and advocated them in Russia, Pypin became aware of the difference in levels of national consciousness in western and central Europe and returned to Russia with the intent of raising its own. Both, however, became convinced that history was more than an academic endeavor—it could be a socially important and intellectually emancipating activity. State service suffocated Arsen'ev's intellectual energy, although he found an outlet for it in the legal profession that the Judicial Reform of 1864 created. Nevertheless, journalistic writing weaned him from the courtroom, although his experience therein proved to be a great asset in the world of journalism. Leonid Slonimskii's Jewish background barred his intellectual talents from the lecture hall and state service. Uninterested in the legal profession, he turned to journalism to express his opinions.

Circumstances interwove the fates of Stasiulevich, Pypin, and Arsen'ev with the brilliant canvas of the Great Reform era as a backdrop. In the second half of the 1850s, imaginative literature in Russia blossomed with remarkable vitality. Ivan Turgenev published *Rudin* (1856), *A Nest of Gentry* (1859), and *On the Eve* (1860). The young Leo Tolstoy completed the *Sevastopol Stories*

(1855–1856), while Goncharov finished *Oblomov* (1859) and Dostoevsky completed *Notes from the House of the Dead* (1860). The journal *Notes of the Fatherland* published an unprecedented four thousand copies a month at the time, while journals such as *Library for Reading* (*Biblioteka dlia chteniia*, 1834–1865) and the *Russian Herald* (*Russkii vestnik*, 1856–1906) also tried to keep up with the public's thirst for cultural and social material. While Chernyshevskii and the poet Nikolai Nekrasov imparted to the *Contemporary* an increasingly radical and utilitarian character in the late 1850s, literary critic and Anglophile Aleksandr Druzhinin attracted less politicized readers to the *Library for Reading*, which he intended to act as an arena for dispassionate literary criticism. The leading moderate journal of the time was Mikhail Katkov's *Russian Herald*.

The 1850s witnessed the first fissures between the relatively affluent gentry "fathers" of liberalism, such as Timofei Granovskii and Pavel Annenkov, and the more radical "sons" who belonged to other estates and became known as the *raznochintsy* or "men of different ranks."[1] Turgenev addressed the divide in his famous *Fathers and Children* (often mistranslated as "Fathers and Sons"), which he published in 1862. Chernyshevskii became the most outspoken representative of this group and under his guidance, many Russian youths followed materialism and determinism, glorified biology and physiology, and embraced utilitarian ethics. Ardent champions of social justice, the younger minds began to comprise the "intelligentsia" and displace the older and more dispassionate intellectuals.

Liberalism was in its statist phase, which was symbolized by Konstantin Kavelin's "Memorandum on the Emancipation of the Peasants in Russia," which championed a benevolent monarchy that stood immeasurably higher than all sectional interests and would remain stable as long as the tsar did not abuse his power. For Kavelin, the state was the main agent of progress and the instrument of rational social organization—therefore progressive members of society could do little more than wait for reformer tsars, but meanwhile support the liberal bureaucrats that they admired. Chernyshevskii published the "Memorandum" in 1858 in *The Contemporary*, but even Kavelin's moderate approach incurred royal displeasure and precipitated the author's fall from court favor. The censors called editor Ivan Panaev to account for the publication and threatened the journal with closure, which dashed Kavelin's hope that the intelligentsia could work with the autocracy in the interests of reform.[2]

By the 1860s, when the radical intelligentsia began to split from the more moderate liberals, Nikolai Dobroliubov identified liberalism with *oblomov-shchina*—a term denoting a do-nothing approach to life modeled on Goncharov's main character Oblomov. A radical "dictionary" of the early 1860s defined a liberal as a "man loving freedom, usually a boyar [who enjoys the] freedom to look through a window without doing anything, then go for a walk, to the theater, or a ball."[3] Herzen wrote to a friend about the older generation: "[Such] people are frightened by the responsibility of independence; their love of moral freedom is satisfied by eternal waiting, eternal aspiration."[4] Such was the ebullient but polarized social world that the future *Herald* members entered in the second half of the 1850s.

STASIULEVICH AND PYPIN: TO EUROPE AND BACK, 1852–1866

In May of 1856, Stasiulevich received permission to travel to Europe in order to acquaint himself with the "methods and course of history teaching in Italy, France, England, and Germany."[5] It was nothing short of a grand tour with the added pleasure of attending lectures at major universities in Switzerland, Italy, France, Great Britain, and of course the German states. For example, in Paris Stasiulevich attended the lectures of renowned French historian Jules Michelet at the Collège de France.

While exploring the Rhine Valley around Kreutznach in the summer of 1857, Stasiulevich ran into Isaak Utin, a rich baptized Jewish merchant from Saint Petersburg, who had brought his six sons and daughter to Germany. Stasiulevich already knew Nikolai Utin, who had been his student. Stasiulevich helped Liuba, the daughter, study for her entrance exams, paving the way for marriage. In Kreuznach he also met D. E. Bernaki, a Russian merchant, thanks to whose subscription to Aleksandr Herzen's *Polar Star* (*Poliarnaia zvezda*, 1855–1868) and *The Bell* (*Kolokol*, 1857–1867) (both illegal in Russia) Stasiulevich could read about the bureaucratic arbitrariness and abuse of power that both publications exposed on a regular basis. Under the combined effect of Germany's politicized lecture halls, Bernaki's opinions, and Herzen's publications, Stasiulevich decided to prepare a course on the "modern historical method" that would allow him to touch on contemporary affairs. "The historical method or the art of *writing* history are closely connected to the art of *making* history, i.e. to living politically," he wrote to a friend. In Heidelberg in late 1857, Stasiulevich learned that Saint Petersburg University had hired and was also sending abroad Aleksandr Pypin, who had attended some of Stasiulevich's lectures.

In his memoirs, Pypin remembered happily the post-Crimean thaw and its welcome penetration of the universities, which coincided with his appointment to a yet non-existent Department of Western European Literatures. His two-year stint in Europe was a result of the university's inability to pay him in 1858, and he gladly joined the flood of Russians going abroad. Between 1855 and 1860, the number of Russians traveling to Europe increased from 2,355 to 70,044.[6] Young Russian academics, Pypin would write later, formed "a special group" whose interests brought them together.[7] Nikolai Karamzin's *Letters of a Russian Traveler* was particularly popular among the youth who sought exposure to the countries they knew only from books, and many experienced cultural shock upon discovering the real thing. The interest was genuine, however, and Europe at the time was awash in Russian student-tourists.

In the spring of 1858, Stasiulevich met Pypin and his fellow graduate Boris Utin in Berlin and the three traveled through the German states together until they split in Paris. In May 1858, Pypin and Utin crossed the channel to make their pilgrimage to Aleksandr Herzen's house in Putney just outside the British capital, which was a Mecca for progressively minded Russian visitors. When Pypin returned to London a year later, he met literary critics Pavel Annenkov and Vasilii Botkin as well as Ivan Turgenev in Herzen's house. Pypin described the host as "hospitable, kind, like a spoiled Russian *barin* [kind landowner]," fluent in many languages and with a great sense of humor.[8] Pypin admitted his great respect for Herzen's *Bell*, which he believed demonstrated Herzen's "deep love for his motherland."[9] According to Chernyshevskii, Pypin was completely happy with his European experience in general and especially about the extension of his stay in 1859.[10]

In Heidelberg later that year, Pypin met historian Friedrich Christoph Schlosser, the Russian translation of whose *History of the Eighteenth Century* Pypin and Chernyshevskii had completed together in Petersburg. Pypin brought a copy of it as a gift for the author. Instead of a simple outcome of events, Pypin wrote in his memoirs, history was for Schlosser a "moral lesson and trial of the just and the unjust, a verdict against evil, and a sermon of elevated, humane demands." In Schlosser, Pypin wrote, "German history achieved both high academic standards and social principles."[11] Pypin's views were converging with Stasiulevich's—history could be more than an academic endeavor.

In the fall of 1859, Pypin arrived in Prague where he spent several months befriending the Czech intelligentsia, which was gathering its strength in the wake of the 1848 defeat. Former Pan-Slavist, professor of Slavonic languages at the University of Prague, and librarian of the Czech Museum, Vaclav Hanka, took the young Russian scholar under his wing and introduced him to the "Czech Conversation" group, which included Slovene philologist Franc Miklošič, poet Pavel Šafárik, historian and politician František Palacký, and writer Karel Jaromir Erben. Pypin found the atmosphere "very modest, very provincial and patriarchal."[12] The men discussed literature and history over beer and Wiener schnitzel and were dedicated to cultivating Czech national consciousness through literature, journalism, and education. Hanka insisted that Pypin attend performances at the "Czech" theater, which took place during the day in Prague's main German theater, given the absence of a national stage at the time. The plays were mainly comedies, but the troupe would occasionally perform dramas based on episodes from national history. Pypin realized, however, that Pan-Slavism would come to nothing when he found out that the young Czechs "did not have a clue about contemporary Russian literature."[13]

Pypin returned to Russia in January of 1860. His European experience may not have made a Westernizer of him, but it certainly discredited the remnants of his Slavophilic notions and undermined any chance for the emergence of isolationist sensibilities in the young scholar. He wrote: "The [Russian] people, the vast majority of whom was still enserfed, was materially great, but vague in content, uncultured, unclear, and without rights, and so to make it the carrier of an elevated 'national idea' required a great deal of faith, i.e. a peculiar sort of enthusiasm."[14] He had seen the people up close in his youth and entertained no illusory notions about its messianic promise. The disillusionment with Slavophilism and Pan-Slavism turned Pypin's attention to Russia's cultural past. Later in life, he would express gratitude to his literature professors—"the real romantics of the Slavic Renaissance"—who sought the "national soul" through academic analysis, which often went against the Slavophiles' views.[15] While learning from European examples, Russian society would do even better by exploring its own history, Pypin concluded, and this attitude would become one of the pillars of *Herald* liberalism.

While Stasiulevich and Pypin were in Europe, the turmoil of German and Italian unifications blended cultural nationalism with political ferment and contributed to the politicization of historical discourse in the universities. At home, Nikolai Chernyshevskii published a landmark series of articles in 1858 and 1859 in *The Contemporary*, which explored French politics under

Napoleon III and listed the average liberal's "predictable responses" and hopes: gradual reform from above; social and political stability through conciliation and compromise; fear of radical measures and revolutionary zeal; toleration of opposing opinions; respect for the dignity of the individual; and a belief in the power of enlightened men to exercise influence on social development. Most importantly, the liberal understood freedom in a very narrow and purely formal sense as "an abstract right" and "permission on paper," failing to see that a legal right had value only to persons with the material means to enjoy it. The absence of such means among the overwhelming majority of the Russian population therefore relegated liberal values to a small group of people, deprived them of popular support, and doomed them to impotence. Chernyshevskii's articles set the tone with which radicals would criticize liberalism for being half-hearted, ineffectual, and hypocritical.[16] Compared to Pypin's European experiences, his cousin's writings emphasized the deepening intellectual rift within the ranks of Russian educated society.

Meanwhile, Stasiulevich married into a family whose members would become prominent in Russia's revolutionary movement and would eventually attract the gendarmerie's attention to Stasiulevich himself. Having studied under his guidance in Europe and in Petersburg, Liuba fell in love and agreed to marry Stasiulevich.[17] Soon after the wedding in April 1859, the young couple moved into one of Utin's properties on 20 Galernaia Street behind the Senate and Synod buildings, which would eventually become the head office of the *Herald*.[18] Nikolai Utin organized Russia's section in the First International and corresponded with Karl Marx. Together with his brothers Boris and Evgenii, he would also contribute articles to the *Herald of Europe*.

Stasiulevich returned from Europe with the firm belief that Russia had to develop along European lines. Contemporaries recalled that his university lectures "covered the latest achievements of European scholarship, and the audience heard them with great attention and interest, and with each lecture the number of students increased."[19] Stasiulevich also gave public lectures full of "hints about the true contemporary state of Russia" in Petersburg's Passazh, a commercial arcade on Nevskii Prospekt.[20] Fellow Petersburg University professor P. V. Ostrogorskii called Stasiulevich a "brilliant lecturer-popularizer" who "showed us for the first time history's significance and explained the profound meaning of civilization."[21] Literary critic Aleksandr Skabichevskii confirmed Stasiulevich as a "talented popularizer" who "behaved himself like a European," used the language of contemporary scholarship, and knew his subject well.[22] What Herzen wrote of his own professors applied to Stasiulevich as well: "They took their stand in the lecture-room not as mere professional savants, but as missionaries of the religion of humanity."[23]

Although Stasiulevich and Pypin came to similar conclusions about Russia's future during their European trip, they expressed them in different ways. Upon returning to Saint Petersburg in 1860, Pypin moved into a new apartment with Chernyshevskii and his wife next to the university on the Vasil'evskii Island.[24] According to contemporaries, Pypin's lectures were straightforward and scientific without superfluous flourishes or catchy phrases.[25] Nothing about his professional career attracted suspicion. Stasiulevich, on the other hand, had already attracted the attention of the authorities in 1855 as one of the suspected authors of Nikolai Dobroliubov's acerbic attack on the late Nikolai Grech, a conservative journalist, philologist, and pedagogue.[26] In 1860, the police received reports about the excited popular reactions that Stasiulevich's unorthodox views on social change and political sensibilities in Europe elicited, so the Ministry of Interior began to limit his public appearances. Meanwhile, Pypin reentered the capital's salon culture and expanded his connections. He began to visit historian Nikolai Kostomarov's apartment on Tuesdays, spent Thursdays and Saturdays in the company of Chernyshevskii's friends, and on Sundays was a guest at Konstantin Kavelin's.[27]

The university atmosphere into which Stasiulevich and Pypin returned became increasingly radical as the Great Reforms unfolded. As one scholar has put it, the student movement acquired "fundamental importance in Russian politics" at the very time that Stasiulevich and Pypin began to teach.[28] In order to curb nihilist influences on the student body, the tsarist government implemented new university regulations in 1861 that restricted the enrollment of *raznochintsy*, banned unauthorized student assemblies, and placed student self-help societies under strict supervision. What started as a protest against these measures soon turned into street demonstrations demanding political liberties and social justice. Sympathetic to the students' cause, but cautious about how they proceeded, Konstantin Kavelin, legal scholar Vladimir Spasovich, Boris Utin, Pypin, and Stasiulevich tried to democratize the academic atmosphere of Saint Petersburg University.[29] When education minister Evfimii Putiatin established a special peer-elected commission to create new university rules, its members Pypin, Utin, and Stasiulevich tried their best to retain as much corporate independence for the student body as possible, but Putiatin, who favored centralized control, personally oversaw the new university charter and blocked their initiatives. When the new statute was ready in September 1861, Pypin became one of fifteen faculty members who refused to distribute it.

Professors Stasiulevich and Boris Utin found themselves on the opposite side of the academic barricade from Evgenii and Nikolai Utin, both of whom took an active part in the student demonstrations. "Precocious, brilliant, and ambitious," Nikolai became the most prominent advocate of political demands among the students, forming what became known as "Utin's party." Agitated by inflammatory leaflets, to which he contributed, and by his speeches, the students of Saint Petersburg University took to the streets on September 26 and 27, 1861. Aided by troops, the police dispersed the crowds and arrested almost three hundred young men, Nikolai and Evgenii Utin among them. Nikolai spent a month in the Peter and Paul Fortress and then embarked on a revolutionary career that included the Central Committee of the Land and Freedom organization and close cooperation withthe Polish insurrectionists in 1863, which forced him to flee to London and earned him a death sentence in absentia. In Switzerland, however, Nikolai would oppose the anarchist extremism and populist maximalism of Mikhail Bakunin, who despised the influence of Marx's "army of German Jews" led by the "little Russian Jew Utin."[30] The family connection did not bode well for Stasiulevich.

When the student disturbances took place, Stasiulevich refused to support them, believing that any opposition outside the application and petition system was likely to prove counterproductive. He was equally appalled, however, when the authorities meted out excessive punishments and temporarily closed the university in the fall of 1861. When it became clear that all hopes for further reform and democratization were illusory, Stasiulevich resigned along with Kavelin, Spasovich, Boris Utin, and Pypin—although they did so separately to prevent it from appearing as a collective political statement.[31] Pypin justified his decision as a refusal to become an administrator under Putiatin's new system.[32] Stasiulevich explained his motives in a letter to his wife: "Only a strong reaction can maintain order under present conditions; that is why I do not want to become an executioner, and even if I wanted to, I could not."[33] One student called the resignation a "courageous civil act" to which "public opinion reacted favorably."[34]

When Stasiulevich then tried to join the Military Academy's history faculty, Grand Duke Nikolai Mikhailovich, the academy's head, turned him away.[35] Remarkably, his only academic activity remained to lecture Crown Prince Nikolai Aleksandrovich on ancient and medieval history. Stasiulevich dedicated the rest of his time to writing *The History of the Middle Ages through Its Writers and the Latest Research* (1863–1865), which covered its subject matter through chronologically arranged excerpts from original documents and renowned historians' commentaries in Stasiulevich's translation.

Meanwhile, the government prohibited Pypin from reading public lectures. Before resigning, he had intended to give a series of talks on "medieval Russian literature and false books." The proposal bounced around state offices, but none could find any fault with it until the Holy Synod justified its prohibition by pointing to the "broad nature" of Pypin's proposal, which made it "impossible to judge its merits."[36] Pypin soon found himself in financial straits from which he could only emerge by working more closely with *The Contemporary*, though he was wary of its increasingly radical tone. Beginning in 1861, the police placed Pypin under surveillance for being "especially close" to Chernyshevskii and "facilitating Herzen's correspondence."[37] While the Education Ministry sent Pypin on another eight-month European tour to gather information about Western educational systems, the police opened his correspondence with Chernyshevskii in which Russia's educational and political systems were compared unfavorably to those of Germany.[38] When Chernyshevskii wrote *What Is To Be Done?* between December 1862 and April 1863 in his cell at the Peter and Paul Fortress, he sent Pypin the manuscript in parts after the censors perused them. Pypin oversaw the novel's publication on the pages of *The Contemporary* and delivered books and cigars to his cousin in prison.[39]

Pypin had alternative areas of activity after his resignation. In 1859, he had been one of the founding members of the Literary Fund, created to support financially struggling writers and their families, and became a committee member in 1863.[40] He worked closely with writers Nikolai Nekrasov and Mikhail Saltykov-Shchedrin on *The Contemporary*'s editorial board, although the latter left due to disagreements with Pypin's excessively liberal political views.[41] Between 1863 and 1864, Pypin and Vladimir Spasovich edited and published the *Survey of the History of Slavic Literatures* (1865) for which Pypin received the prestigious Uvarov Prize.[42] Throughout this period, he made numerous appeals to the authorities on his cousin's behalf, but in vain. On February 5, 1864, Chernyshevskii was stripped of his title and property and condemned to fourteen years of forced labor and permanent exile in Siberia. In March, he sold his father's house to Pypin, who then took upon himself the care and education of his cousin's children.[43] The responsibility proved to be a burden because Chernyshevskii's wife Olga could not get along with the Pypin family.[44] Organizing the publication of Chernyshevskii's works to bring his family some income, Pypin became increasingly suspect in the eyes of the police and even some of his literary colleagues.[45]

In 1866, Nekrasov made Pypin the deputy chief editor of *The Contemporary*. According to the more liberal censorship statute of 1865, select thick journals, *The Contemporary* among them, could publish without submitting prior survey copies to the censor's office. However, in the event that the contents were found to be offensive, the chief editor and deputy editors were held criminally responsible and the journal received an official warning.[46] Nekrasov and Pypin had an agreement that when one of them went abroad, the other took over responsibility for the journal.[47] Pypin was in charge when the censorship bureau ordered the presses to stop in April 1866 as a result of economist Iulii Zhukovskii's criticism of the landed nobility in his article "The Question of the Young Generation," which appeared in the March issue. The state accused Pypin and Zhukovskii of damaging the "honor and reputation of the gentry."[48] The accused hired Konstantin Arsen'ev as counsel, who gladly took the case on behalf of people who, as he put it, "faced a completely groundless accusation."[49] In Pypin's view, Arsen'ev was the reason that they won their case initially, although a subsequent trial jailed them for three weeks.[50] Years later, Arsen'ev referred to this case as an example of state "persecution of the radical press," but it proved to be a blessing in disguise because it introduced him to the members of the future *Herald* group.[51]

From their European travels, Stasiulevich and Pypin gathered impressions of what civil society in the West offered that Russia could emulate. Both were taken in by the thriving university cultures where politics and academia mixed. Moreover, the lack of cultural interchange among the Slavic peoples reinforced Pypin's determination to become a pioneer in this field. Both men encountered obstacles to realizing their visions in Russia during the Great Reforms, however, because academia's institutional structure proved unable to accommodate their goals and thus redirected both to journalism, which demonstrated its importance as a medium of loyal opposition to the state at this time.

KONSTANTIN ARSEN'EV:
DISAPPOINTMENT AMID HOPE, 1855–1869

Legal education and legal consciousness in Russia were underdeveloped faculties in the 1860s.[52] As one contemporary argued, the sources of legislation were "shrouded in strict chancellery mystery"—the state never justified its judicial legislation and the press provided no insight into the workings of the legislative process. However, this began to change in the late 1850s as Tsar Alexander's government prepared the judicial reform that aimed to open up an estate-specific system and allow greater transparency of the judicial process. During the preparation of the reform, the state actually encouraged the press to react to its proposals. The School of Jurisprudence from which Arsen'ev graduated in 1855 gave its graduates a temporary advantage as the judicial reform created the legal profession that Russia's educational institutions failed to accommodate in the short term. Although after 1864 enrollments in newly created university law departments increased significantly, Arsen'ev's generation filled the temporary gap.[53]

Arsen'ev joined the Justice Ministry in 1858 when discussion of the judicial reform was in full swing. His introduction to publishing occurred in 1859, when he became assistant editor of the *Justice Ministry Journal* (*Zhurnal Ministerstva iustitsii*, 1859–1868), which covered the reform debate in depth. His passion for bureaucratic work rapidly ebbed, however, when his reformist enthusiasm ran up against entrenched bureaucratic interests. As a result, he became increasingly interested in literary criticism, some of which he published in Katkov's *Russian Herald*, but broke with the journal in 1861 as it drifted to the right and placed itself in the conservative camp.[54] Instead, Arsen'ev began to publish in *Notes of the Fatherland* and in the same year joined a salon of lawyers who discussed judicial reforms. Chief Procurator and distinguished lawyer Dmitrii Stasov headed this small salon, which also included Konstantin Kavelin, Vladimir Spasovich, and Boris Utin.[55]

The student disturbances of September 1861 marked a turning point in Arsen'ev's life just as they did for Stasiulevich and Pypin. When Stasov asked his colleagues at the Justice Ministry to sign a petition asking the tsar to mitigate the punishments, Arsen'ev did so eagerly, but after rumors of the petition reached the authorities, the police arrested Stasov and threatened all signatories with dismissal. Stasov was eventually released, but lost his position only to rise to the top of Russia's new legal profession. Arsen'ev was demoted and this convinced him further of the futility of state service, which ignored and often discouraged intellectual talent and initiative. He wrote in his diary that despite the spirit of the Great Reforms, many "old bureaucratic and police tactics remained: unregulated suspicion, the tendency to arrest first and investigate second, and intolerance of social activism's slightest tendencies."[56] Increasingly disillusioned with his ministerial post, in 1862 Arsen'ev began to share editorial duties at *Notes of the Fatherland* with established journalists Andrei Kraevskii and Stepan Dudyshkin and oversaw the journal's political news section.[57] He published a series of articles in favor of British constitutionalism and then took over the foreign news section. Disappointed with the bureaucratic routine at the ministry, Arsen'ev left state service at the end of 1862 after journalist and literary historian Valentin Korsh offered to put him in charge of the foreign section at the *Saint Petersburg News* (*Sankt-Peterburgskie vedomosti*, 1728–1914).

As all progressively minded people, Arsen'ev welcomed the judicial reform of 1864. A new hierarchy of independent courts open to all citizens replaced the old estate courts under gubernatorial control. The reform also modernized court procedure, shed its purely inquisitorial role, and introduced the adversarial element into court procedure—thereby creating the legal profession which Arsen'ev joined.[58] By 1866, he became a member of the Saint Petersburg Council of Jurors in which he remained until 1872.[59]

Arsen'ev made a successful legal career specializing in censorship cases including Pypin and Zhukovskii's 1866 trial. Arsen'ev also defended publisher Aleksei Suvorin against accusations that his book of essays entitled *All Sorts* took a dangerous political stand on criminal law and expressed sympathy for state criminals.[60] In 1869, Arseniev defended F. F. Pavlenkov—publisher of some of Dmitrii Pisarev's posthumous works—against the charge of disrupting the basic principles of government and confidence in the dignity of the emperor.[61] That year Arsen'ev gave a cautiously optimistic assessment of censorship in the Russian Empire:

> The abolition of preliminary censorship, by lessening press dependence on arbitrary circumstances and personal whim, made possible the discussion of subjects that were previously banned for literature. Analysis of government policies is even now not easy and not without risk, but several years ago the press could not even consider it. Tutelage over the press exists, of course, but it has lost its trivial, capricious character: it ponders content but does not hang on each separate word.[62]

The shifting of the censorship from bureaucrats to the courts was part of Russia's modernization. Although it came with certain drawbacks, the censorship statute of 1865 allowed the expansion of the publishing industry whose powerful representatives began to negotiate with the state for greater concessions.[63] Russian publishing blossomed during the thaw of the 1860s

and Stasiulevich's *Herald of Europe* would be one of the newcomers. However, the torrents of spring hid dangerous terrain and Arsen'ev's advice
became priceless to the *Herald*'s editor-in-chief.

The clash between Arsen'ev's expectation of progressive state policies and
the institutional structure that limited rapid reform within the Justice Ministry reflected Stasiulevich's and Pypin's experience in academia. Once again,
a liberal was born through frustration with a government that had launched
reforms, but vacillated on their extent. Arsen'ev's background as a trial lawyer
made him an attractive candidate for the *Herald of Europe* and explained
why he so carefully expressed himself on its pages.

LEONID SLONIMSKII:
JOURNALISM AS HAVEN, 1872–1882

Russian Jews found it impossible to pursue academic careers and very difficult to enter state service in the late imperial era. The legal profession offered
an outlet, but although Russian papers complained in the 1870s that Jews
made up a disproportionate number of lawyers, this was not the path that
Slonimskii decided to take. He was an academic at heart who "read Tacitus in
the original Latin before going to bed, so that his mind was far away from the
daily concerns of life."[64] Barred from the lecture hall and uninterested in the
legal profession, he decided to educate through journalism and moved to Saint
Petersburg in the 1870s, which his university education permitted him to do.

In the capital, he began to publish in the newly created specialized legal
press such as *The Court News* (*Sudebnyi vestnik*), *The Court Journal* (*Sudebnyi zhurnal*), and *The Journal of Civil and Criminal Justice* (*Zhurnal grazhdanskogo i ugolovnogo prava*, 1871–1894). Between 1875 and 1879, he wrote
the political survey section of the conservative *Russian World* (*Russkii mir*,
1871–1880) and became its deputy editor in 1879. In 1880, he also edited the
journal *Word* (*Slovo*). In 1878, Slonimskii published his first article, entitled
"About Forgotten Economists," in the *Herald of Europe*, in which he criticized
Marx's economic theories. He joined the *Herald* group through Stasiulevich's
short-lived newspaper *Order* (*Poriadok*) whose political section Slonimskii
wrote from 1881 until 1882 when the paper folded.

Although Slonimskii's first decade after graduation in 1872 was profes-
sionally nomadic, it was personally rewarding. Coming from a distinguished
intellectual background himself, in 1880 he married Faina Vengerova (Wengeroff), who came from an assimilationist family as remarkable as his own.

Her father Afanasii Vengerov was a prominent banker in Minsk and her mother Polina (Pauline) left a remarkable record of her life in *Rememberings: The World of a Russian-Jewish Woman in the Nineteenth Century*. Polina had several children who became accomplished in their own right. Faina's brother Semyon Vengerov became a noted literary scholar who corresponded with Turgenev and Tolstoy, edited the collected works of Pushkin, Shakespeare, and Schiller, and authored the *Critico-Biographic Dictionary of Writers*. In 1875, Semyon published one of the first literary biographies of Turgenev. Faina's sister Zinaida became a well-known translator of English, French, German, and Italian literature and a literary scholar in her own right whose work appeared on the pages of the *Herald of Europe* and other thick journals. Isabelle Vengerova became a celebrated piano teacher in the United States and taught Leonard Bernstein and Samuel Barber.[65]

Pauline Wengeroff—as her name is rendered in the West—complained of the generation to which her daughter and son-in-law belonged.

> And there came the third generation, afraid of neither God nor the Devil. Above all, they worshipped their own will and deified it. They burned incense, erected altars and, without embarrassment, without consideration, burned offerings to this deity, their own will. It was the tragic fate of this youth to have been raised without tradition. Our children carried no trace of the memories of an historic, independent Jewish people. They were strangers to the dirges of *Tisho be-Av*—strangers to the site of the grandeur of their past, expressed thrice daily in the prayers of longing for Zion. They were strangers to the rhythm of the Jewish holy days, with a joyous festival always following a day of sadness. This generation found no inspiration anywhere. They became atheists.[66]

Indeed, Faina joined the droves of Russian Jewish students who enrolled in the newly opened Saint Petersburg College for Women to study medicine, a subject that especially attracted females in the 1870s.[67] According to her son, Faina entertained revolutionary beliefs: "The outward indication of her radicalism was that she wore her hair short, which was regarded as a sign of 'nihilism'." However, her medical career was cut short when she fainted after seeing a cadaver, which also brought on the epileptic fits that stayed with her for life.[68]

Leonid and Faina Slonimskii raised their children in the Russian Ortho-dox faith, which they officially adopted after the birth in 1881 of their first son Mikhail, who found out that he was of Jewish background only at the age of twelve. The children grew up eating pork. Nicolas confirmed suspicions about his background in 1910 when he consulted his father's biography in the *Brockhaus and Efron Encyclopedia*. The article on Leonid Slonimskii referred him back to Haim Zelig Slonimskii and when Nicolas confronted his mother on the issue, "she became furious. 'It is not true!' She cried. 'I am a Ukrainian, and your father is a Russian Pole.'" "We were racially Jewish," wrote Nicolas, "but were baptized at birth to safeguard us from the humiliation that persons of the Jewish faith had to suffer in Czarist Russia. I grew up with the belief that Jews were an extinct race."[69]

The marriage, the birth of his first son Mikhail, and Leonid's joining the *Herald of Europe* coincided with a dark period in the history of the Russian Jews. In the wake of Tsar Alexander's assassination on March 1, 1881, a wave of pogroms that originated in the Ukrainian town of Elizavetgrad in April 1881 spread to the rest of the empire and violence continued in places well into 1883. According to the memoirs of Genrikh Sliozberg, a prominent Jewish lawyer, even the liberal daily press became helpless in the face of the approaching "dark storm cloud of Jewish oppression." This helps explain the lengths to which Leonid and Faina went to protect their children. Sliozberg wrote: "The liberal voice lived on, however, in the monthly journals, especially the *Herald of Europe*. But its sound became a squeak. The fear of [censors'] warnings and violent death shackled mouths, froze the ink, and dulled the quills."[70] The *Herald* must have appeared to Slonimskii as a safe harbor during the first months of Alexander III's reign. Moreover, Slonimskii's choice of journalism as a career is another reminder that it was the primary form of progressive self-expression and a central institution in the formation of a civil society in Russia.

CONCLUSION

By 1866, the stars had come into alignment for the creation of the *Herald of Europe*. Three of its four chief editors had become intellectual nomads seeking a platform from which they could articulate their ideas about Russia's future. Barred from the lectern, Stasiulevich would create an alternative dais that reached beyond universities and public lecture halls. Pypin would use the journal's pages to answer the eternal question "whither Russia?" But unlike the Slavophiles, he placed his bet neither on religion, nor the peasantry. He chose culture instead and turned the *Herald of Europe* into a tool for Russia to explore its historical and cultural identity. Arsen'ev would analyze the

Great Reforms with the meticulous attention to detail that lawyers were trained to wield. At the same time, the journal would also allow him to indulge his literary fancies. Slonimskii would eventually turn his intellectual creativity to the burning question of socio-economic development.

Remarkably, unlike the older liberals of the 1830s and 1840s, all four members of the *Herald* group would demonstrate no sentimentality about their subjects. There would be few traces of hidden polemics with the Slavophiles, but also no veneration of Peter the Great. There would be no love for chivalry and quixoticism and no debates about the individual's struggle against the historical dialectic. The *Herald* liberals had considered and outgrown these issues during their formative years. The journal spoke with the calm and yet authoritative voice of adults while it balanced academic integrity with popular appeal. As the radical message in Russia became louder and increasingly impatient, Stasiulevich, Pypin, and Arsen'ev preached moderation and gradual reform in the 1860s and formed an island of intellectual discipline and patience that placed long-term achievements above immediate wish fulfillment.

PART II

The *Herald of Europe* as the Flagship of Russian Liberalism

It is a strange thing: there is no political life in Russia whatsoever, and yet you feel yourself bound by politics.

> —M. STASIULEVICH to VLADIMIR GER'E, 9 April 1878
> (quoted in V. A. Kitaev, *Liberal'naia mysl' v Rossii, 1860–1880 gg.*)

4

Birth Pangs Full of Promise
The Literary Engine of Success

The culture of thick journals was not unique to Russia in the nineteenth century. Studies of British literature and journalism have examined how temporal features of serialization created a Victorian ideological tendency towards conceptions of sequential and progressive development.[1] The publication format and the responses of contemporary reviewers contributed to the "anti-closural" Victorian conception of human institutions, such as marriage and politics. The reader's sense of "long middles" in serialized novels favored "processual" thinking over termination.[2] Works published in installments, be they literary, critical, or scientific, created a special interpretive space that gave readers a greater sense of writing as a process and lessened the distance between the ongoing experiences of their lives and the fictional processes that they witnessed on the journals' pages. While the conventional novel conjured up images of the solitary reader absorbed in a book, magazine novels were frequently read aloud, while serialization meant that at any given time readers were at the same point in the novel. In Europe and the United States, the serialized novel engaged in, rather than retreated from, the great civic questions of the day.[3]

Russian journals fulfilled a similar role, but the absence of a political sphere magnified their influence. After Nicholas I died in 1855 and the Buturlin Censorship Committee ceased to exist, Russian literary journals proliferated. The newspaper business also flourished. Between 1851 and 1855, only thirty new periodicals appeared, but between 1856 and 1860, the number increased five-fold.[4] When Stasiulevich's *Herald of Europe* appeared in 1866, it was a newcomer among equally promising beginners and several well-established veterans. The literary giants were the highly popular *Contemporary* and *Notes of the Fatherland* both under Andrei Kraevskii's direction. In 1856, the *Russian Herald* started out as a moderate publication, but within a decade became the quintessential "establishment" journal under the guidance of its conservative and nationalist editor Mikhail Katkov. Because of his ties to officialdom, Katkov enjoyed protection and could outbid his competitors for the leading literary talents of the age: Leo Tolstoy, Fyodor Dostoevsky, Mikhail Saltykov-Shchedrin, Ivan Turgenev, Aleksei Pisemskii, and Nikolai Leskov, among others. Katkov's journal stood on the right of the political spectrum, while Kraevskii's *Contemporary* and *Notes of the Fatherland* appealed to the left and also boasted great literary talents such as Tolstoy, Turgenev, Afanasii Fet, Fyodor Tiutchev, and Apollon Maikov. In London, Aleksandr Herzen was still publishing the *Bell* in which he defined his own strain of liberalism. His correspondence with Nikolai Ogarev, however, demonstrates that they had subscriptions to the *Herald of Europe* and followed the articles closely, although they disagreed with the journal's overly moderate tone.[5]

New specialized journals also appeared in the wake of the Great Reforms. While Pyotr Bartenev's *Russian Archive* (*Russkii arkhiv*, 1863–1918) reflected the "establishment" approach in selecting and interpreting historical documents, Mikhail Semevskii founded *Russian Antiquity* (*Russkaia starina*, 1870–1918) to compete with *Archive* by publishing 'unsanctioned' literary materials from the eighteenth century on, especially works that never saw the light of day due to censorship restrictions. In 1866, Grigorii Blagosvetlov, former editor of the radical *Russian Word* (*Russkoe slovo*, 1859–1866), founded *The Cause* (*Delo*, 1866–1888), which became the most notable platform for radical Populism after Dmitrii Pisarev's death. It published writer Gleb Uspenskii and radical social critics Pyotr Tkachev and Pyotr Lavrov, among others.

The field was full of wrecks and hopeful newcomers when Stasiulevich decided to try his hand at publishing. His attempt, however, proved to be no ordinary undertaking. The result was a new gravitational force in Russia's intellectual field. It was a testament to its founder that in a crowded field of journals, the *Herald of Europe* became Russian liberalism's flagship and a nucleus around which a dense constellation of intellectuals revolved, from the eminent writers of the Golden Age to provincial statisticians. However, the road to prominence was not easy.

Filling the Liberal Niche

The 1860s was a difficult time for the Utin family. As soon as Nikolai emigrated for his safety, the police began monitoring his correspondence with

Stasiulevich, causing the latter to write presciently amid the euphoria of the Great Reform era: "I will try to arrange my affairs in such a way that I am ready for anything. To experience the stick from above and jabs from below, I agree, is very uncomfortable. It appears that a time of reaction has begun; the only question is how long it will last; I am afraid that there will be enough for our time. They consider us retrogrades, almost scoundrels from below, and from above they look upon us as instigators. Decent people—the so-called party of temperance—who nowadays find themselves between two fanaticisms will no doubt move aside and comprise."[6] Stasiulevich was not the only one searching for non-radical avenues of action during the 1860s, but it was still too early for critics of the state to organize themselves even informally. A common denominator was missing. Before agreeing on any platform, the moderate intelligentsia needed a medium through which to engage all of its members by focusing and channeling their debates. Filling this niche became Stasiulevich's life project and the central role of the *Herald of Europe*.

Stasiulevich credited Vladimir Spasovich with the idea of founding a journal, but before moving ahead, he consulted close friends Konstantin Kavelin and Boris Utin.[7] He also relied heavily on the advice of his mentor and friend Pyotr Pletnev, to whom Gogol and Zhukovskii had turned for advice about publishing. Pletnev wholeheartedly supported Stasiulevich's journal idea, but warned him that publishing was not only unprofitable, but also time-consuming and stressful. In November 1865, Stasiulevich informed Pletnev that he had submitted an application to the Chief Department on Press Affairs for permission to publish a "historical-political" quarterly. He decided to call it the *Herald of Europe* in honor of famous writer, critic, and court historian Nikolai Karamzin, who would have turned one hundred in 1866.[8] Karamzin had founded his *Herald of Europe* in 1802 as a historical and literary journal that would appeal to and unite Russia's best minds in the pursuit of enlightenment and public education. The journal explored intellectual and political trends in Europe and published prose and poems in translation. Yet Karamzin also criticized the Russian elite's proclivity to ape all things European and warned against remaining in a state of tutelage for too long. The journal was short-lived—Karamzin stopped publishing it in 1804 and devoted himself fully to writing the *History of the Russian State*.[9] Sixty years later, however, Stasiulevich decided to resurrect a journal that looked west with a curious but analytical eye.

Expecting the Interior Ministry to balk at the proposal, however, Stasiulevich decided wisely to emphasize the journal's historical nature and convinced accomplished historian Nikolai Kostomarov—who maintained that the title was his idea—to join the editorial board.[10] Meanwhile, through his connections Pletnev won over the chairman of the Petersburg Censorship Committee for Foreign Materials, the poet Fyodor Tiutchev, who interceded with interior minister Pyotr Valuev. The latter had owed his successful career to masterly navigating the razor's edge between reform and autocracy.[11] During a personal meeting with Stasiulevich, Valuev informed him that he had nothing personal against the journal, but that negative rumors circulated about the editor himself. Referring to the widespread rumors about Valuev's own professional indiscretions and abuses of power, Stasiulevich's answer was diplomatically insubordinate: "Who cares what bad things are said about people, Your Highness? They are not only said about me."[12]

The London *Daily Telegraph* correspondent E. J. Dillon, who had spent decades in Russia and came to know its official (and unofficial) intricacies well, left a colorful description of what was in store for Stasiulevich:

> On no profession in Russia does the nightmare of the Censure inveigh so heavily as upon journalism; an editor's life in one of the mushroom cities of the Far West, who is one day short of the letters 1 and v, another day short of money, and a few days later on is hurled into eternity by a pistol-shot, is tame in comparison with the checkered life of some Russian journalists. To foreigners it is a mystery how a capitalist can risk his money in such a precarious investment as a newspaper. Russian journals, however, require but a small capital to start them, and even that seldom belongs to the editor, who generally begins his journalistic career with credits, continues it in debt, and frequently ends it in bankruptcy. So trained are the editors of the latter class of periodicals that they cut and mutilate the contributions destined for their journals with the same unerring judgment, the same unbending vigor as the paid official.[13]

On December 12, 1865, Stasiulevich received permission to publish a journal that was initially to have five sections: critical historical research, analysis of new books and documents, a survey of historical literature and historical society proceedings, pedagogical literature, and historical chronology. Kostomarov supervised all materials related to history, while the editorial office could request foreign publications in unlimited quantities for purposes of review. In 1867, Stasiulevich received permission to add two more sections: a survey of foreign literature and a "chronicle of jurisprudence."[14]

After the government closed *The Contemporary* in 1866, Aleksandr Pypin found himself without a source of steady income while being responsible for

supporting his own family as well as Chernyshevskii's. He refused Nekrasov's offer to work for *Notes of the Fatherland* because Zhukovskii had also
declined it. Pypin then joined the short-lived *Contemporary Review* (*Sovremennoe obozrenie*, 1868), whose program was to "spread serious positivist
knowledge" and encourage "the self-education of man" by exploring "nature,
the history of culture, social development, and the sciences."[15] However,
differences with the editor led to a parting of ways. Pletnev had already recommended him to Stasiulevich and in 1867 and Pypin published a series
of articles on the Russian Freemasons in the *Herald*. Stasiulevich became
ecstatic about hiring an experienced editor and writer who had gone through
the "school of the *Contemporary*" and wrote to his wife that whatever salary
Pypin demanded "the journal would make up for in sales."[16] When she expressed concern about Pypin's association with Chernyshevskii, Stasiulevich
assured her that he would not let Pypin determine the journal's "political
tone."[17] Although Stasiulevich came to depend heavily on Pypin—and always
left him in charge while traveling abroad—Pypin wrote to Saltykov-Shchedrin
in 1871 that he was kept away from the day-to-day editorial work, which
Stasiulevich held entirely in his own hands.[18] Stasiulevich even paid Pypin a
very profitable one hundred rubles per printer's sheet, which provided him
with the steady income that he desperately needed and allowed him to continue his academic research, which he published on the *Herald*'s pages. Until
his election to the Academy of Sciences in 1897, Pypin earned his livelihood
from the journal, eventually becoming its resident historian—a role that Stasiulevich had originally envisaged for Kostomarov.[19]

At first, the *Herald*'s financial situation was shaky. In 1866, it had only
twenty-six subscriptions and in 1867—forty-three. To stay afloat, Stasiulevich
sold some of his personal belongings and reduced his own salary to fifty rubles
per month in 1867. Yet he chose to look on the bright side, and as subscriptions grew steadily he decided to expand the journal and turn it into a literary and political monthly.[20] Stasiulevich redesigned the journal cover into
its signature orange, while the December 1867 issue redefined the *Herald*'s
mission as the "gradual change and betterment of the social order by way of
perfecting and developing the individual personality, by way of enriching
the people and educating its thoughts." "Labor, Effort, Knowledge" became
the journal's motto.[21] Stasiulevich's gamble produced the desired results—by
March 1868, subscriptions reached 3,500.[22]

Meanwhile, Stasiulevich organized financial support from the Gintsburg
banking family.[23] While making his fortune through a state grant on sales of

alcohol, Isaak Utin became close with Osip Gintsburg, who had made his fortune through a monopoly on gold extraction. Utin built an apartment building in which Osip's son Goratsii rented a flat. The building is still standing at 20 Galernaia Street, behind the Senate and Synod buildings in the heart of Saint Petersburg. Liuba and Stasiulevich moved into the building after their marriage and Stasiulevich also maintained his office there. A prominent Jewish philanthropist who loved playing the role of a liberal, Goratsii soon became an integral part of Stasiulevich's circle. By the late 1860s, the *Herald* had become the mouthpiece of the loyal opposition that staunchly defended the Great Reforms and opposed any retreat from their accomplishments. Unlike the members of the radical intelligentsia, however, Stasiulevich believed in convincing instead of judging the public and encouraging instead of threatening the autocracy. Encouraging the emergence of a public sphere, however, would prove to be a time-consuming affair that required patience and careful cultivation, a demanding combination, as Stasiulevich would find out in the increasingly polarized intellectual atmosphere of the 1860s.

THE POLITICS OF NATIONALISM:
THE POLISH QUESTION

So politicized were the 1860s that the *Herald* had to articulate its position on an event that took place before Stasiulevich even founded the journal. The Polish Uprising of 1863 forced the Russian liberals to choose between their political convictions and their patriotism. For example, Katkov, the erstwhile moderate, became aggressively nationalistic:

> Let us remember the year 1612, let us also remember that one hundred years later there was 1812. . . . The conqueror before whom all Europe fell, directed all of his forces against us. Poland opened the way for him into our land; it fought against us under his eagles, and together with him was present at the burning of Moscow.[24]

The "Polish Question" played an important role in the *Herald*'s early success. In 1868, Katkov denounced Stasiulevich's journal as a "Masonic brotherhood" that not only "inspires and encourages the political significance of various nationalities" but also acts as a representative of Russia's "enemies from within."[25] In his personal correspondence, Stasiulevich admitted that the 1863 uprising was most untimely as it interrupted the "organic connection" of Poland and Russia. Indeed, all the members of the *Herald* group considered the uprising counterproductive.[26]

Five years after the rebellion, the epithet "Polish" remained an accusation, while most of the people associated with the *Herald* in its early days were in one way or another tinged with "Polishness."[27] Stasiulevich's surname betrayed Polish roots. Contributors Leonid Polonskii, Spasovich, and Pypin were Polonophiles, and only Kostomarov, a Ukrainian, had earned a reputation for hating the Poles. His articles about the Time of Troubles, Cossack hetman Bogdan Khmel'nitskii, and the decline of the Polish state in the *Herald*'s early issues were highly critical of the Poles and not only contributed to the journal's popularity, but also protected it from accusations of pro-Polish attitudes at a time when these were liabilities.[28]

The Polish Question resurfaced on the pages of the *Herald* in the early 1870s when education minister Tolstoi began to implement Russification policies in Polish education and Stasiulevich saw an opportunity to continue his educational crusade by defending the schools.[29] However, Stasiulevich's enthusiasm for the Prussian system ended when Bismarck launched his *Kulturkampf* in the early 1870s and the journal began to publish articles by historian Mikhail Dragomanov in support of Polish rights against both Prussian and Russian encroachments.[30] Nevertheless, Dragomanov condemned both the Polish rebels and Herzen for supporting them in 1863, while Spasovich published pro-Polish pieces under his own name, instead of "V. D."[31] Distinguishing between nationality and ethnicity (*narodnost'*), Polonskii argued that only the Finns could rightly claim the status of nationality, which justified their separate statehood within the empire. The Poles were only an ethnicity and their attempts to establish a separate state threatened the empire's existence directly. Polonskii and Stasiulevich believed that local self-government and language rights were sufficient to satisfy Polish national yearnings and the *Herald* therefore agitated for an educational and judicial reform as well as the introduction of zemstvos into the western provinces as rapidly as possible.[32] Neither in their articles, nor in their personal correspondence, however, did any of the *Herald* men support full Polish independence and they believed that administrative exclusivity bred separatism.

Stasiulevich hired journalist L. G. Lopatinskii to contribute "Polish letters" to the journal, while Warsaw joined Berlin, Florence, and Paris in having a staff correspondent. Lopatinskii drew the readers' attention to a group of moderate Poles—the organicists—who argued for reconciliation with Russia, rejected romantic nationalism and revolutionary conspiracies, and focused their attention on their country's economic and cultural reconstruction. This moderate party coalesced around the *Przegląd Tygodniowy* (*Weekly Review*, 1865–1904) that appeared in 1865 and based itself on "the principles of contemporary scientific positivism."[33] Stasiulevich even published a few articles by prominent "Polish pragmatists" in the early 1870s.[34] Lopatinskii meanwhile argued for an alliance between the young Polish positivists and the Russian liberals, but a second official warning in 1873 and Stasiulevich's caution prevented this from happening and he opened the journal once again to Kostomarov's Polonophobic articles.[35]

The Polish Question posed a dilemma for the *Herald* group, as conservative journalists accused its strain of liberalism of being foreign, even Polish, and therefore particularly subversive. The *Herald* group's resignation from Petersburg University paralleled their Polish colleagues' inability to find teaching positions during Tolstoi's Russification campaign. Both liberal groups had to prove their patriotism to radical opponents and both were suspected by the state. However, the respective pro-Russian or pro-Polish stigmas they carried prevented an alliance, which demonstrated the increasing influence of public opinion and nationalist sentiment. Pressuring the state was out of the question, while directing public opinion would demand popularity and time. Nevertheless, a censor wrote of the *Herald* in 1878 that a "delicate bouquet of Polonism" accompanied its Europeanism.[36]

THE POLITICS OF LITERATURE: THE EMERGENCE OF NIHILISM

Nihilism emerged as a world view in the 1850s when the positivist tradition escaped from the laboratories and lecture halls and became wedded to political sentiments by youths who projected positivist values onto human relations. Nihilism preached radical skepticism towards all forms of human activity—religious beliefs, political values, family loyalties, and sexual behavior. Anything that could not withstand scientific proof was targeted as regressive. Although its proponents rarely examined nihilism on its own terms, it became a crucial catalyst for radical political activity. So influential did this attitude become by the 1860s that it forced writers to take a stand and further politicized the journal culture. Stasiulevich took a hard line against nihilism, which he saw as incompatible with the evolution of civil society.

Although the *Herald of Europe* became Russia's leading popular historical journal by 1868, Stasiulevich understood that literature was the real engine of success, and in this field, the journal had to compete with heavyweights.

Nikolai Nekrasov and Mikhail Saltykov-Shchedrin published their works in *Notes of the Fatherland*. Dostoevsky and Tolstoy wrote for Katkov's *Russian Herald*. In order to attract contributors, therefore, Stasiulevich began to attend Saint Petersburg's salons.

He became a regular at Vladimir Bezobrazov's weekly "economic dinners," during which the guests debated modernization issues.[37] Of his friend and education minister Aleksandr Golovnin's salon, Stasiulevich wrote that he was the only one in attendance who was not a member of the State Council.[38] At one of these evenings in 1868, Stasiulevich met the poet and playwright Aleksei Tolstoi, whom he lured away from Katkov's journal with the promise of greater profits—five hundred rubles per printer's sheet, an enormous sum for the time, but one that Stasiulevich was convinced would pay off.[39] Tolstoi was himself the host of a popular salon where Stasiulevich made the acquaintance of writers Ivan Goncharov and Grigorii Danilevskii, poets Fyodor Tiutchev and Iakov Polonskii, and literary critic Aleksandr Nikitenko.[40] When, in 1868, Tolstoi found himself in tough negotiations with a publisher, Stasiulevich gladly took over the process and defrayed the costs of publication in exchange for part of the profits. He thereby gained in Tolstoi a cooperative contributor to the *Herald*.[41] Although they disagreed on politics, Tolstoi published in the *Herald* while at the same time criticizing Stasiulevich for transforming it into a political platform.[42]

Ivan Turgenev became an early convert to the *Herald*'s cause. In 1866, he wrote to his friend the poet Aleksandr Fet that the "reappearance of the *Herald of Europe* is the most pleasant phenomenon yet."[43] In July of the following year, he accepted enthusiastically Stasiulevich's offer to publish on its pages. He was happy to distance himself from Katkov's journal, although he admitted to Herzen that the *Russian Herald* was the most popular publication with the Russian public and it paid well.[44] The business arrangement turned into a lifelong friendship between them. After Turgenev died in Paris on August 22, 1883, Stasiulevich accompanied his body back to Russia and organized the funeral. The Russian authorities created so many problems that Stasiulevich wrote to his wife in exasperation: "You would think I am bringing back the body of Nightingale the Robber [*solovei-razboinik* was an epic robber from medieval Russian tales]! A nightingale—yes! A bandit—no!"[45] He also prepared and edited Turgenev's posthumous collection of works.

The *Herald*'s prominence brought new risks as Stasiulevich had to navigate carefully between profit and the nihilist controversy that erupted in the

1860s. Dmitrii Karakozov's assassination attempt on Tsar Alexander II on April 4, 1866, cast a long shadow on the progressive movement. Katkov declared that "Karakozov's shot cleared the air" and from that point on his conservative journal's influence increased rapidly.[46] Kavelin's *On Nihilism and Necessary Measures Against It*, which he submitted to Tsar Alexander in May 1866, defended the reforms and the liberal nobility as their most loyal implementers. Kavelin referred to Chernyshevskii's *What Is To Be Done?* as the "nihilists' cherished reading."[47] The radical revolutionaries were breaking away from the progressive intellectuals, forcing the thick journals to take a stand, which they often did through the literary works they published.

Although Stasiulevich went out of his way to attract literary talent, he ignored writers who had "compromised themselves" as conservatives, such as Nikolai Leskov and Vasilii Avenarius, whose *Plague* Stasiulevich refused to publish because of its overt anti-nihilism.[48] Aleksei Tolstoi invited Stasiulevich to his house on several occasions to hear Goncharov reading chapters of his new novel the *Precipice*. Although it was also anti-nihilist in its criticism of the "new generation" in the character of Mark Volokhov, Stasiulevich found it "a delightful thing of the highest caliber. What a great talent! One scene is better than the next!" and saw in it a love story that would attract a wide audience.[49] He fought hard to convince Goncharov to publish his novel in the *Herald*, which came out in five installments in 1869. Stasiulevich was convinced of the novel's success and spared neither money nor time in his efforts to win Goncharov over from *Notes of the Fatherland*. He even had to push the author to finish his work because Goncharov himself became alarmed at the reaction to Turgenev's, Leskov's, and Pisemskii's works by the so-called "unofficial, radical" censorship.[50]

Writing the novel in Bad Kissingen in 1868, Goncharov went through emotional vicissitudes and only Stasiulevich's aggressive epistolary encouragement kept the writer at work. Goncharov admitted to a friend that Stasiulevich "knows how to inspire creativity and very delicately influences [my] self-esteem with his intelligent, sober, honest criticism."[51] Stasiulevich and his wife even met Goncharov in Bad Schwalbach in August 1868 to collect the first chapters in person.[52] So nervous was Goncharov about the novel's reception that he asked Stasiulevich for permission to print an article defending it before it even appeared, but Stasiulevich refused. "I am completely dejected," Goncharov wrote to Stasiulevich in late 1868, "and of course I deeply regret deciding to publish it. How happy I would be if circumstances forced you to close the journal and turn away the *Precipice*! I am afraid that

I will become very sick and even worse! Sometimes I just want to abandon everything and run away!"[53]

After the novel appeared, the *Herald* published Evgenii Utin's critique of it, in which the author respectfully defended the younger generation and advanced the thesis that a clique of reactionaries was using the honorable writers of the older generation to discredit the Russian youth.[54] Goncharov was nobody's puppet, of course, and his criticism of the nihilists evolved as he was working on the novel. By presenting both sides of the story in the *Herald*, however, Stasiulevich was hedging his bets, but the public reaction proved his acumen once again—the *Precipice* caused a tremendous boost in circulation.[55] Utin's article displeased Goncharov, who complained to Stasiulevich about it, reminding him that people were "tearing the journal out of each others' hands" to read his novel's installments anyway.[56] Some scholars have even suggested that Goncharov's moderate anti-nihilism, which reflected the *Herald*'s position on the subject, was the point of departure for *Demons* on which Dostoevsky started work in 1870.[57]

Goncharov's novel caused a furor. Turgenev found it too long and too outdated. Vasilii Botkin described it as a "wordy rhapsody that is nauseatingly boring." The *Saint Petersburg News* welcomed the novel's final installment because it was already too long. *Notes of the Fatherland* accused Goncharov of obscurantism. Some declared Goncharov's career over. *The Cause* published a review entitled "Talented Talentlessness," which read: "The novel, which does not inspire in the reader progressive thought and progressive conclusions, could only have been written by a retarded and weak-minded individual. Never has an intelligent person written a stupid work after ten years of effort." Another reviewer of the same paper argued that *Precipice* reflected the outdated liberal ideals of the 1840s. *The Dawn* (*Zaria*, 1869–1872) argued that "the poverty of his world view and paleness of ideals" made Goncharov a second-rate writer. In a second review, *Notes of the Fatherland* condemned the "bile and blind rage, proud conceit and inhumane arrogance" that inspired the author to denounce "everything that was enlightened in human beings."[58]

Stasiulevich's gamble paid off handsomely. According to writer Pyotr Boborykin, "all literate Russia" attacked the novel, but the negative attention contributed to the *Herald*'s popularity.[59] The *Herald* published the *Precipice* from January to May. In the spring of 1869, the journal had 3,700 subscribers, which by April increased to 5,000—the "Pillars of Hercules" in the Russian publishing business, as Stasiulevich put it—and by May 1 subscriptions reached 5,200.[60] Stasiulevich boasted to Goncharov that on the first of every month people lined up to buy the new issue as if to queue for bread.[61] Despite a short falling-out over Utin's article, Stasiulevich and Goncharov remained friends for life and Goncharov made him one of the executors of his will. According to one contemporary, Stasiulevich was the only person to whom the "anchorite" Goncharov remained close.[62] Members of Stasiulevich's salon remembered it as the only place where Goncharov felt perfectly at home until his last days.[63] Tolstoi's and Goncharov's contributions significantly enhanced the journal's reputation and attracted the playwright Aleksandr Ostrovskii, poet Iakov Polonskii, and writers Nadezhda Khvoshchinskaia-Zaionchkovskaia (who published under the name V. Krestovskii), Aleksandr Levitov, and Nikolai Uspenskii.

Although literature was the *Herald*'s "investment policy," Stasiulevich also attracted talented political analysts. Leonid Polonskii, Evgenii Utin, and historian Nil Koliupanov became regular contributors. When Nikolai Kruze was dismissed from his job as a censor in the 1850s, Petersburg's literati organized a conspicuous farewell to this social activist and liberal.[64] He would go on to serve on the Petersburg provincial zemstvo board until Tsar Alexander II dissolved it for insubordination, but Stasiulevich also hired Kruze as the journal's specialist on zemstvo questions. On the other hand, writer Mariia Tsebrikova, who explored women's rights, only published one article in 1871 because she proved too radical for Stasiulevich's taste.[65] In the 1870s, historian Vladimir Ger'e, linguist Iakov Grot, military historian Modest Bogdanovich, historian of literature Aleksandr Veselovskii, and renowned historian Sergei Solovyov also published in the *Herald of Europe*.

A descendant of Karamzin, historian Mikhail Pogodin also contributed in the 1860s, but severed his ties with the journal due to suspicions about Stasiulevich's radicalism. Pogodin wrote: "The reappearance of the same disgusting [political] thoughts makes me suspect that you may have lost your mind on some issues."[66] Although the *Herald* continued Karamzin's legacy, the journal also criticized his political theories. In 1870, Pypin roundly condemned Karamzin's *Memoir of Ancient and Modern Russia* (1810–1811) as the product of "stubborn" and "angry" conservatism that unjustly supported "state absolutism" and opposed emancipation and the freedom of Poland. Writers Nikolai Strakhov and Fyodor Dostoevsky came to the defense of the conservative cause, but Pypin continued to argue that the *Memoir* was an exception to Karamzin's Enlightenment-informed world view.[67] That same year, Stasiulevich published an obituary for Aleksandr Herzen, which defended him from conservative slander and agreed with Herzen's criticism of the Russian autocracy.[68] Herzen's acquaintances and regular correspondents, Evgenii and Nikolai Utin, had kept Stasiulevich informed of the great exile's life in Great Britain. Between Pypin's work and Stasiulevich's obituary, the journal was clearly expressing a liberal attitude.

Stasiulevich himself wrote little for the journal and mostly under pseudonyms. His contributions focused on the debate about secondary education— professional vs. classical schools.[69] He argued that the government should introduce the Prussian *Realschulen* curriculum with its stress on modern languages and the sciences into Russian secondary schools in order to educate Russian students in the manner of their European counterparts and thereby broaden the social base of the universities. Looking to the Prussian model, Stasiulevich sought "to introduce a new system of European life" into Russia.[70] However, in 1871, conservative education minister Dmitrii Tolstoi forced through a classical program meant to reinforce Orthodox values and prevent the penetration of Western ideas into Russia. The state discouraged further debate on the issue and Stasiulevich abandoned his crusade.

For many years, Stasiulevich corresponded with Populist philosopher Pyotr Lavrov, who also knew Pypin from the Petersburg Chess Club of which both were founding members.[71] By the late 1860s, however, Lavrov came to believe that certain articles and novels placed the journal into the conservative camp along with Katkov's *Russian Herald* and Mikhail Pogodin's *Dawn*. He voiced the general Populist criticism of the *Herald* as a champion of bourgeois, "Western" values that disparaged the legacy of the 1860s.[72] Saltykov-Shchedrin also criticized the *Herald* for its materialism and Western values.[73] When economics professor Illarion Kaufman published "The Viewpoint of Karl Marx's Politico-Economic Criticism" in the May 1872 issue, economist Nikolai Danielson—the first translator of *Das Kapital* into Russian—mailed it to Marx who used *Herald* articles extensively for research purposes.[74]

In the late 1860s, the *Herald* group organized its own salon, which became known in Petersburg as the "round table." Every Monday, Stasiulevich and his wife hosted guests in their home, but by the 1890s, the *jour fixe* moved to Saturdays. According to distinguished lawyer Anatolii Koni, a regular contributor to the journal, Stasiulevich's salon became one of Petersburg's cultural nuclei at which guests discussed the most important literary, social, and political questions, criticized the autocracy, and defended civil rights and popular education.[75] Such openness could only take place in the private sphere.

No publication was free from tsarist censorship and all unofficial criticism had to be muted or veiled.

Navigating Success

By 1870, the *Herald* had become the capital's most coveted journalistic employer. It paid well and the atmosphere in the editorial offices was creative and friendly.[76] From the very beginning, Stasiulevich retained the right of final approval, but collegiality reigned as he relied heavily on his editors' input. It greatly helped that Stasiulevich had two "highly placed" friends. Dmitrii Sol'skii, a friend from younger days, became State Comptroller in 1873, state council member and chairman of the Legal Department in 1889, chairman of the National Economy Department in 1893, and eventually state council chairman between 1904 and 1906.[77] Stasiulevich's more important insider contact was Aleksandr Golovnin, former liberal education minister and state council member. As early as 1866, he warned Stasiulevich that education minister Tolstoi considered the *Herald* suspicious. In 1871, he wrote Stasiulevich that "strong enemies were gathering against the journal."[78]

The relationship was symbiotic. In November of 1868, Golovnin appealed to Stasiulevich to defend the zemstvos against attacks from conservatives who demanded greater administrative control over the local councils. The *Herald*'s December issue came out strongly in defense of zemstvo rights.[79] In 1871, Golovnin asked Stasiulevich for information on the state of the Russian publishing business to be included in a report for the State Council, which then argued that there was no need to implement extraordinary measures to control the press.[80]

The *Herald* experience demonstrated the tortuous way in which Russian liberals began to articulate their ideas and define their loyalties by explaining what they *did not* support or believe. This literary process was bound to take time and demonstrated how intimately cultural and political sensibilities became intertwined during the Great Reform era. In the competition for influence over public opinion, the *Herald* emerged as a bastion of liberal reformism opposed to the radical "nihilist" and the conservative camps.

By the early 1870s, the *Herald* had experienced a burst of popularity. A censor's report read: "The *Herald of Europe* has a large number of readers among educated members of society and the professional class."[81] Sober business sense and publishing acumen were behind this success, but Stasiulevich understood that it was too early to celebrate. He had navigated the journal through its rough formative period, but he also knew that prominence brought unwelcome attention from the authorities. Although an optimist by nature, Stasiulevich was anything but naïve. As Russia moved along its tortuous reform path, he would have to navigate increasingly turbulent waters. In this, Pypin and Arsen'ev became invaluable first officers. Navigating the treacherous waters of censorship and politics even strained Stasiulevich's close relationship with Pypin sometimes. According to Pypin's daughter, in the early 1870s Stasiulevich wanted to cut down on specialized scholarly articles as the *Herald* became more popular, but Pypin argued that the journal owed its readers an "unofficial" interpretation of the Russian past. However, Stasiulevich remained wary of adopting a political cause openly.[82]

5

Publishing as Philanthropy
Printing and Politics

THE BLESSINGS OF CENSORSHIP

While the *Herald of Europe* laid the responsibility for Russia's growing radicalism on government policies, the journal attempted to explore the origins of civil society through literary and historical studies. The state's reaction demonstrated that even the reformist tsar's government had trouble distinguishing between a loyal and radical opposition. Ironically, state censorship propelled the moderate *Herald* to the height of its popularity. Meanwhile, the journal became increasingly popular in the provinces, which demonstrated the rapid spread of public interest in a non-radical and yet critical interpretation of Russia's past and present beyond the capitals.

Editorial caution notwithstanding, storm clouds began to gather over the *Herald* in its fifth year. In December 1870, the Moscow City Duma sent Alexander II a note expressing anxiety about rollbacks of the Great Reforms. Alexander reacted with anger. The Censorship Bureau received an order to increase its vigilance and turned its attention to the *Herald of Europe*. Warnings about impending action came from all quarters, including Nekrasov and Saltykov-Shchedrin. In 1870, the *Herald* began to publish chapters of Pypin's *Notes on the Social Movement under Alexander I*, from which the censors cut out ten pages that included Nikolai Novosil'tsev's constitutional project of 1819. While the censors found Pypin guilty of searching for liberal strains of thought among state officials, he believed that the time had come for Russian historians to "justify" the "men of the 1820s."[1] Stasiulevich, however, became nervous and admitted in a letter to Pypin that he had lost the "censor's scent."[2] When Arsen'ev sent him the manuscript of "The Outcome of the Court Reform," he asked Stasiulevich to "pay special attention to it and to submit it to [self-] censorship," but even this could not protect a "marked journal."[3]

Pypin's research indirectly articulated the *Herald*'s moderate political views by clothing them in the language of literary research that barely concealed the hope that spontaneous social initiative would lead Russia out of "darkness, stagnation, and ignorance." In search of intellectual progress, Pypin explored the Decembrists, the Petrashevskii Circle, the Slavophiles, Westernizers, and Populists. He paid special attention to Herzen and Chernyshevskii. Infused with positivist optimism, Pypin believed that nations developed in relation to each other and that the historian's job was to trace these tangled trajectories and extract moral lessons from them. Most importantly, he believed that the study of literature was essential to historical understanding. For example, Pypin considered Pan-Slavism premature given the level of ignorance among Russians of the history of other Slavic cultures. He used literature to gauge a people's psychology and its intellectual progress. Using a non-specialized and accessible narrative, Pypin paid special attention to the development of social consciousness, which made him suspect in the eyes of the authorities.[4]

In 1871, the Academy of Sciences decided to make Pypin an adjunct in the field of Russian philology and history. However, because the *Herald* group strongly opposed Count Tolstoi's "pseudo-classicism," he and Chief of Gendarmes Pavel Shuvalov opposed Pypin's candidacy.[5] Conscious of the overwhelming current against him, Pypin decided to avoid controversy—Alexander II had already appointed a commission to consider the appointment—and declined the honor.[6]

Meanwhile, Spasovich, Evgenii Utin, and Arsen'ev took part in the infamous 1870–1871 Nechaev trial, the latter as a defense lawyer for the eighty-seven individuals accused of involvement in Sergei Nechaev's radical terrorist group known as The People's Revenge, which stood accused of murdering its member Ivan Ivanov in 1869. Nechaev himself had escaped abroad leaving his comrades to face the court. Stasiulevich believed that the *Herald* owed it to society to comment on the court proceedings. After careful consideration of its contents, Arsen'ev published "The Political Trial of 1869–1871" in the November 1871 issue.

Arsen'ev argued in his article that political persecution drove the opposition underground while at the same time encouraging its "gradual subdivision and degradation." The socialism of the 1860s emerged as a collective attitude in response to this disunity and appealed to all people who were sympathetic to the sufferings of others. Arsen'ev also argued that trials would not stifle this natural empathy and that only eliminating the causes that encouraged radical acts could stem the revolutionary tide. By blocking off legal paths for helping the downtrodden and then reacting inadequately to clandestine attempts to do so, the state alienated the youth and made it susceptible to radical propaganda.[7] The censors considered the article sufficiently provocative to submit a report about it to interior minister Aleksandr Timashev, who forwarded his concerns to Tsar Alexander.

The result was the *Herald*'s first official warning in November 1871, which Stasiulevich considered a badge of honor. Kavelin wrote to him: "I think it will only increase the number of your subscribers."[8] He was right. In 1870, the printer sent out 6,997 copies of the journal and in 1872 that number rose to 8,003. Petersburg had the most subscriptions—between 1,500 and 1,800.[9] Moscow consistently brought in about 500. The provincial orders steadily grew from 4,915 in 1870 to 5,552 in 1872. Kherson, Kiev, and Kharkov provinces in Ukraine became the undisputed leaders. Yet the *Herald* never made Stasiulevich a fortune and his name never appeared among those of distinguished Russian philanthropists.

The journal's administrative office was located at 30 Nevskii Prospekt by the Kazan Bridge on the same block where the Evropa Hotel currently stands. The editorial offices were in Utin's building on Galernaia Street where Stasiulevich kept appointments every Wednesday. Most of the people who met him described Stasiulevich as a simple, straightforward, and warm person who treated novice writers with respect and conducted his correspondence in a timely fashion.[10]

STASIULEVICH'S ENLIGHTENMENT PROJECT

As an extension of the *Herald*'s mission of enlightening through public discourse, Stasiulevich decided to organize his own printing shop and gain independence from his six-year relationship with printer F. S. Sushinskii. Located at number seven on the Second Line of Vasil'evskii Island, where Shevchenko Square is now located, Stasiulevich's would become one of Petersburg's largest and best printing companies. Opened in November 1872, by the end of 1873 it broke even and became profitable the next year. Moreover, Stasiulevich's enterprise weathered serious competition from Aleksei Suvorin's publishing house, which appeared in 1876.

E. J. Dillon's description of censorship in the Russian Empire provides valuable insight into what Stasiulevich had to endure in the process of establishing and running his company. The efficacy of the censorship laws depended largely on the state's exclusive control over printing offices, type foundries, booksellers' shops, circulating libraries, and all cognate trades and callings. None of these establishments could open without special authorization. An in-depth inquiry pried into the applicant's antecedents, "the sins and backslidings of fathers being visited upon sons and daughters and the imprudence of the children recoiling upon their parents." The rest deserves to be quoted in full:

> Every new printing machine, every set of type bought, sold or repaired, every book or pamphlet destined to be printed, must be first announced to the authorities, verified by them, next entered in detail in a number of books, and then sent to the Censure for examination. If a printer gets one of his presses altered and neglects to notify the fact to the authorities, he is fined five hundred rubles, besides being visited with other and more serious pains and penalties. If a journal, having been read by the Censure, is sanctioned for publication, but the written authorization should happen to be delayed, the printer who dared to set it up in type and publish it, would be fined three hundred rubles and imprisoned for three months. A person who sells type, printing presses, hectographs, etc., is in duty bound to look upon the intending purchasers as against the State, and must, in his own interests, turn them away, unless he knows them personally, and is in possession of their real names and address. Nor is this acquaintance considered sufficient to allow of business relations: he can deal only with authorized printers, and he is exposing himself to a heavy punishment if he parts with a set of type without having first seen, with his own eyes, the authorization to the buyers to purchase and keep a printing press. Permission to open a bookshop, a circulating library or a reading-room is more difficult to obtain than a railway concession.[11]

With his first major project, Stasiulevich intended to emphasize not only his business's profitability, but also the progressive education ideology behind the whole endeavor. In the *Herald*'s April 1874 issue, Stasiulevich printed a "Plan of Publication for the 'Russian Library'"—cheap volumes containing the works of Russia's greatest writers and poets: Pushkin, Lermontov, Gogol, and others. Prominent literary scholars and writers took part in the in the preparations: Pypin, bibliographer and biographer Pyotr Efremov, and writers Nekrasov, Goncharov, Turgenev, Saltykov-Shchedrin, and Pavel Annenkov.[12] Once again, Stasiulevich's enterprise anticipated and successfully competed with Suvorin's "Inexpensive Library."

The Russian Library was not a commercial enterprise. Stasiulevich intended it to be affordable. He set the price at seventy-five kopecks per volume, regardless of how much effort it took to negotiate the copyrights and each volume's cost of production. The advertisement for the new series read that it intended to "share the wealth of our literature with those who have been condemned by lack of funds to nourish their minds with literature of suspect quality."[13] The first widely accessible volume of Pushkin's work appeared in ten thousand copies in March 1874 and profits from it went for hunger relief in Samara province.[14] The second volume of Lermontov's works appeared on bookshelves in May 1874; Gogol in November of the same year; Zhukovskii in the winter of 1875; and Griboedov in June 1875. Altogether, 18,484 volumes sold in twenty months, which Turgenev considered a great success, especially for a start-up business.[15] Yet he wrote of Stasiulevich in a letter to Annenkov: "His affairs in Russia, as usual, hang by a hair, yet the hair does not break."[16] The first five volumes completed the first Russian Library series. Stasiulevich followed through with a second series: the best of Turgenev's work appeared in early 1876, Nekrasov's in April 1877, Saltykov-Shchedrin's in May 1878, and Leo Tolstoy's in December 1878. Every volume, except for Pushkin, came out in five thousand copies, which Stasiulevich believed would fulfill public demand for literary works at the time.

Although the Russian Library brought Stasiulevich little profit, the publishing business became a form of enlightenment philanthropy. Kavelin published *The Goals of Psychology* (1872) through Stasiulevich's shop. In 1874, Pypin and Nekrasov bankrolled the second edition of John Stuart Mill's *Principles of Political Economy*, translated, edited, and with commentary by Chernyshevskii, for whom this publication was the only source of income at the time. In 1875, Stasiulevich printed Herbert Spencer's *Principles of Sociology*, which was later banned from public libraries. Many books dealing with communal landholding came out of Stasiulevich's shop: A. I. Vasilchikov's *Land Ownership and Agriculture in Russia and Other European States* (2 volumes, 1876) and Iulii Ianson's *Statistical Research into Peasant Allotments and Payments* (1877). Both books found their way into Karl Marx's library.[17]

THE TURGENEV FACTOR

Although Stasiulevich's publishing business grew and prospered in the 1870s, the *Herald of Europe* remained at the forefront of his vision. And one of the reasons for the journal's success during this decade was Ivan Turgenev's involvement in it, which proved yet again how tightly socio-political sensibilities intertwined with literature in Russia. In the absence of a political sphere, civil society articulated and negotiated its attitudes through literary characters, which made the choice of publication venue more than a purely financial and aesthetic consideration for many writers. So polarized became public opinion that association with certain journals could tarnish a writer's reputation regardless of the quality of his work.

Beginning in 1870, Turgenev published almost exclusively on the pages of the *Herald*, which boosted its popularity. As a marketing strategy, Stasiulevich usually published Turgenev's novels in January issues as New Year's presents for his readers and an encouragement to subscribe.[18] When Stasiulevich announced the serial publication of *The Torrents of Spring* in the autumn of 1871, subscription reached its high point of just over six thousand. Turgenev's *Huntsman's Sketches* (1871), which had been banned in the 1850s, and *Virgin Soil* (1877) helped maintain the *Herald*'s popularity. In the latter, Turgenev portrayed the members of the "going to the people" movement of 1874–1875 as altruistic but misguided youths, instead of the infernal and criminal elements that the official press depicted in its coverage of their court trials. Although the novel belonged in the anti-nihilist and anti-socialist tradition, the censorship committee argued about whether to publish its second half because Turgenev had only demonstrated that socialist uprisings were premature, but not impossible. The censors who decided in favor of publication maintained that stopping the presses would only incite public anger and attract increased interest. Interior minister Timashev sided with the latter group and the novel's conclusion appeared as planned in February 1877.[19] The *Herald* attracted the same criticism for publishing *Virgin Soil* as conservative critics directed at Turgenev for being an "isolated Westerner." Simultaneously, the Russian radicals saw in him a well-off intellectual guilty of excessive "liberalism" and "aristocratism."

Turgenev spent most of his time in Paris in the 1870s where he became friends with George Sand, Prosper Mérimée, Alphonse Lamartine, and Gustave Flaubert, whose works he translated and published in the *Herald of Europe*. After the Franco-Prussian War (1870–1871), Flaubert gathered around him the young talents Émile Zola, Alphonse Daudet, Edmont de Goncourt, and Guy de Maupassant, and Turgenev became part of this circle.[20] Before he had made a name for himself in literature, Zola published literary reviews and criticism, but began to have trouble placing them in the late 1860s when French editors accused his pen of being "too violent" and his reviews of carrying "revolutionary methods into literary discussion."[21] When in 1875 Turgenev suggested to his young colleague that he publish in the *Herald*, Zola jumped at the opportunity.[22] The Russian censors had trouble finding fault with his interpretation of French politics.[23]

Stasiulevich hired Zola as the *Herald*'s Paris "correspondent" to inform Russian readers of French literary, artistic, and social events.[24] As his friends described it, from May 1875 until November 1880, Zola "organized his professional life around two calendars, the Gregorian and the Julian," always bearing in mind Petersburg's twelve-day lag.[25] As one biographer put it, the "fine commission for a great Russian newspaper" allowed the young writer to "move into better quarters, begin to fatten out, and gain weight wonderfully."[26] Altogether Zola contributed sixty-four "Lettres de Paris" to the *Herald of Europe*. The contract also stipulated that all of his literary works would appear in France only after the *Herald* had published their Russian translations, the first of which, *Abbé Mouret's Transgression* (the fifth installment of the "Rougon-Macquarts" cycles), appeared in the spring of 1875.[27] The novel combined theology and physiology, the doctrine of natural sin and the idea of hereditary doom, in the story of a young priest torn between his instincts and his education. Zola described the plot as "the story of a man neutered by his early education who recovers his manhood at twenty-five through the solicitations of nature but fatally sinks back into an impotent state."[28] Zola's anticlericalism enraged Russian conservative and religious critics, but found great favor with readers. *Scenes of Political Life under the Second Empire*, which began to appear in the *Herald*'s January 1875 issue, aimed to expose the kitsch and broad farce of political life during the Second Republic, but also introduced Russian readers to a more open political system.

The *Herald* became so popular when Zola wrote for it that Stasiulevich published *His Excellency Eugène Rougon* and *Lettres de Paris* as books, which sold out immediately.[29] Zola was exceptionally grateful to Stasiulevich and, through the *Herald*, to the Russian reading public for giving him the opportunity to speak his mind when French critics reviled him.[30] Stasiulevich hired Anna Engelgardt, Aleksandr Engelgardt's wife and one of the first and most prominent members of the Russian women's rights movement, to translate

Zola's work.[31] She stayed on as the journal's translator until her death in 1903. By 1880, however, when he became sufficiently famous to make a living by publishing in his own country, Zola separated from the *Herald*. His views on literature drew criticism from, among others, Populist philosopher Nikolai Mikhailovskii who wrote in *Notes of the Fatherland* that Zola had substituted "the science of man" for "strictly defined moral and political ideals."[32] As a counterweight to Zola's "self-propagandizing," as Polonskii described it, Arsen'ev began to publish the *Herald*'s "Literary Survey" in 1880.

BETWEEN RADICALS AND CONSERVATIVES

By the 1870s, the *Herald of Europe* was firmly in the loyal opposition camp, but despite its moderate tone, it continued to run afoul of the authorities throughout the decade. The censors forbid at least one article and one book from the print shop every year. Meetings with the censors, conducted during the last four days of each month, became vital to the journal's existence. According to Boborykin, a regular contributor since 1873, Stasiulevich took the censorship threat so seriously that he refused to accept serialized literary submissions unless he could read the entire text up front.[33] Simultaneously, the *Herald* began to articulate its liberal values in opposition to those of the increasingly radical Populist movement.

Despite Stasiulevich's caution, in July 1873 the journal received its second official warning for Pypin's "Characteristics of Literary Opinions from the 20s to the 50s"—the first article to examine the work of Petrashevskii since the authorities banned his name from appearing in print (hence the article's broad title). Because Pypin concluded that state policies had encouraged revolutionary organizations such as the Petrashevtsy, the censors accused him of justifying "the conspirators of 1848."[34] In the same article, Pypin also compared Belinskii's fate to Chernyshevskii's, which drew criticism from Turgenev, who saw no connection between the men of the 1840s and those of the 1860s.[35] In 1875, Pypin's articles on Belinskii became the first attempt to write his biography. Arsen'ev's article "Transformation of the Legal Statutes" was critical of the state's encroachments on the jury system and the censors accused it of "undermining trust in the government."[36] Stasiulevich admitted to his wife that he was at a loss to explain how these articles crossed "the vague line of sedition."[37] Pressure from the censors reached such a degree that in 1873 Turgenev wrote sarcastically to Fet: "You will be happy when this honest, moderate, monarchical publication is closed on charges of radicalism and revolutionism."[38]

After receiving the second warning, Stasiulevich became even more circumspect and examined every line of text to make sure that nothing could arouse the censors' suspicions. Working from eight in the morning until midnight, Stasiulevich dedicated his life to the journal.[39] Even while abroad, he received daily correspondence and piles of manuscripts. Of censorship's arbitrariness, E. J. Dillon wrote: "It is, perhaps, superfluous to remark that the principles by which Censors are guided in forbidding or permitting leading articles, stories, etc., are as difficult to discover as those which determined Buridan's ass to choose one haystack in preference to the other."[40] Luckily, the amnesty of 1877 wiped the slate clean of warnings.[41]

Members of the radical intelligentsia also treated the *Herald* with suspicion. When in 1874 news reached socialist Pyotr Lavrov in London that his friends tried to arrange for his articles to appear in the journal to help him make ends meet, he was outraged. "We upbraid the constitutionalists," he wrote, "and suddenly everyone finds out that I am asking them for work: they will tell everyone, and it will be a scandal."[42] At the time, Lavrov was editor of the most important Russian émigré socialist periodical, *Forward!* (*Vpered!*, 1873–1877). Its doctrine of "preparationism," however, was not the same as the *Herald*'s, although both targeted "critically thinking individuals." Lavrov's book *Historical Letters*, published in 1869, had offered progressively thinking Russians an alternative to nihilism and conspiratorial duplicity, but his fatalistic sense of duty to the masses reinforced by gnawing guilt eventually forced him into the vanguard of revolutionary socialism, separating him from the moderate opponents of the tsarist regime, such as the *Herald* group.

Lavrov and Pypin clashed in 1876 over the publication of Chernyshevskii's revolutionary *Prologue* in *Forward!* As soon as Pypin found out about Lavrov's intentions, he sent him an angry letter emphasizing the primacy of family relations over revolutionary interests—Pypin feared that the publication of this work would further damage Chernyshevskii even in Siberian exile. However, Lavrov argued that he had to publish Chernyshevskii's work before the younger generation forgot about him completely. Such a contribution to the revolutionary movement in Russia would be much more effective, Lavrov added acrimoniously, than Pypin's publication of *Prologue* as a "literary rarity" twenty years after its composition.[43]

The *Herald* condemned radical terrorism openly. On December 6, 1876, members of the radical Land and Freedom group conducted a demonstration next to Kazan Cathedral in Saint Petersburg. By condemning the event, Stasiulevich carefully expressed part of the *Herald*'s political program. He had received a letter from Golovnin in which the former education minister explained the futility of such demonstrations. Stasiulevich published part of this correspondence in the January 1877 issue.[44] Golovnin had argued that in Russia, revolution, reforms, and progress came only from above. Referring to the failed "to the people" movement, Golovnin argued that even when the revolutionaries preached directly to the downtrodden *muzhik*, that same *muzhik* reported them to the police. Impatient revolutionaries only delayed reforms, which the state was constantly considering and implementing.[45] According to Osip Aptekman, one of the leaders of Land and Freedom, the radical Populists found the *Herald* attitude both insulting and unfair.[46]

Fighting a battle on two fronts, the journal defended the zemstvos against conservative projects to place them under the landed nobility's supervision, which Sergei Witte's uncle Rostislav Fadeev proposed doing in his popular book *Russian Society in the Present and the Future (What Should We Become?)* (1874). Polonskii proposed instead to unite the zemstvos, the bureaucracy, and the peasant affairs committees (*prisutstvie po krest'ianskim delam*) on the district and provincial levels into one institution. He furthermore suggested that the provincial zemstvos elect three candidates, of which the tsar would choose one to join the State Council. The latter idea resembled Pyotr Valuev's plan and Dmitrii Miliutin's 1879 administrative reform project. Nevertheless, the censors forbid the *Herald* to publish Polonskii's article.[47] Nothing came of the ministers' project either, because foreign affairs distracted attention from domestic reforms in the late 1870s.

THE BALKANS

The Russo-Turkish War of 1877–1878 became the first conflict in the runup to which public opinion played a decisive role in Russia. The strongest impulse to expansion into southeast Europe was Pan-Slavism, which championed the creation of a federation of Slavic states under Russian guidance and attracted mostly conservative thinkers. Through its critique of Pan-Slavism, the *Herald* further articulated a socio-economic message that preferred cultural to political influence and domestic reforms to foreign adventures. Pypin argued that without cultural Pan-Slavism, political aspirations would come to naught.

On the eve of the war, when Pan-Slavic passions ran high and became synonymous with patriotism, Stasiulevich decided to publish historian Sergei Solovyov's *Russia and Europe in the First Half of Alexander I's Reign* (1877), which ran counter to the prevalent public opinion in support of Russian involvement in the Balkans. Solovyov even joked that since the book was clearly not in the Pan-Slavist camp, Stasiulevich would have to put a picture of the author without his head on the cover in order to sell the volume. In fact, it became so popular that it sold out immediately and a German translation appeared a few months later.[48]

The Russian press meticulously covered the uprisings against Ottoman rule in Bosnia-Herzegovina, Bulgaria, and Serbia in the 1870s. Kraevskii's *Voice* (*Golos*, 1863–1883) was highly critical of Russia's involvement in the Slavic uprisings, but it was an exception. Suvorin's *New Time* and V. V. Komarov's *Russian World*—where Leonid Slonimskii worked at the time—supported General Mikhail Cherniaev's leadership of the lackluster Serbian army and defended Russia's Pan-Slavic goals. By describing the gory details of Ottoman atrocities, *New Time* became instrumental in creating a public mood that the tsar could not ignore without losing face.[49]

Members of the *Herald* group were skeptical about Russia's involvement in Balkan affairs. Kavelin argued in a letter to Stasiulevich that the government would do better by improving the lot of the peasantry than concerning itself with the Balkan Slavs. Annenkov considered comical the state's justification of involvement because of the pressure of public opinion: "All this noise is no more than the madness of a chained dog that rattles its chain only as far as its owner has allowed it." The journal's "Domestic Survey" for September 1876 criticized the involvement of the Russian public in foreign policy issues and its appeal to "religious brotherhood," which the author believed could become an excuse for Russian Muslims to support the Turks. Having read Polonskii's article, Dostoevsky responded to it in his *Diary of a Writer*. The Russian people knew "nothing above Orthodoxy," he argued, and therefore attempts to stop the "elemental and organic" movement threatened the very essence of the Russian nation. The *Herald*, however, refused to engage in a debate with a writer who "does not argue, but only crosses himself."[50]

In November 1876, Polonskii published his programmatic "The Russian Question in the Southeast of Europe," wherein he argued that should Russia annex any Balkan Christian population, it would turn from "a distant brother into an internal enemy." Pan-Slavism was not a solution to Russia's pressing internal problems. Furthermore, aggressive policies toward the Ottoman Empire would alienate Russia from her European neighbors and undermine the "common European ideals" that Russia shared.[51]

Against his ministers' advice, Alexander II declared war on the Ottoman Empire in April 1877 and even suspended Kraevskii's *Voice* for forty days because of its opposition to military actions. Newspapers played such an important role during the war that this led to the appearance of Russia's first great journalistic talents—Vasilii Nemirovich-Danchenko, Grigorii Gradov-skii, and Vladimir Giliarovskii.[52] Mindful of the fate of the *Voice*, the *Herald* came out with a lukewarm endorsement of the war in May 1877 by arguing that the success of the reforms by 1877 meant that Russia was entering the conflict in better shape than in 1828 or 1853.

Although the *Herald* supported the Russian army and the overall effort to force the Ottoman government to implement agricultural reforms on its territories, the journal stopped short of endorsing Pan-Slavic dreams and focused instead on the tax burden that the war imposed on the Russian peasantry and the cultural barriers still separating the Russians from their Slavic brethren. From the moment that war broke out, Pypin took up the issue of Pan-Slavism and argued that before leading the Slavs, Russia had to undergo her own "renovation." Separating political from cultural Pan-Slavism, he maintained that cultural understanding and religious tolerance needed to precede the political unification of the Slavic peoples, which was a goal for "future historical periods." He condemned the "stupid chauvinism" of what he called "ultraslavophilism," which rested on three demands—the primacy of Russia, the Russian language, and Orthodoxy. He also refused to see Slavic unity as a counterbalance to European civilization—Russia could best help the Slavs by "putting her own affairs in order." Pypin specifically targeted the works of historian Vladimir Lamanskii, whom he considered a Pan-Slavist extremist.[53] In the late 1870s, Pypin was willing to accept Slavic unity only as a process of socio-cultural exploration.

In December 1879, Pypin became a senior member of the Imperial Russian Geographical Society and his first presentation to the ethnographic division focused on the southern Slavs.[54] Pypin had even prepared a field expedition to the region, but the political tension in the wake of the war undermined the trip. Instead, Pypin channeled all of his energy into the *History of Slavic Literatures* (1879–1881), which Stasiulevich published. The conservative press condemned the work as overly critical of Pan-Slavism, while the censor's bureau cut fourteen pages on constitutional projects out of the manuscript, but this did not diminish the book's popularity with the reading public, while German, French, and Czech translations appeared within three years.[55]

By 1881, Stasiulevich's printing company was the third largest in Russia after the Academy of Sciences and "Social Aid" ("Obshchestvennaia pomoshch'"). The *Herald* was the third most popular thick journal in the country after *Notes of the Fatherland* and *The Deed*. Monthly subscriptions in the late 1870s stabilized at about six thousand.[56] Stasiulevich's bookstore, which abutted the printing shop, sold thousands of Russian books and western European titles in translation. Despite the difference in social views between Stasiulevich and Nekrasov, the poet published his major works through Stasiulevich's shop: *Who Lives Well In Russia, Complete Collection of Poems* (in one volume) and *Nekrasov for Russian Children*. After Nekrasov's death in 1878, Stasiulevich took upon himself the first posthumous collection of works, which came out in four volumes in 1879.

Stasiulevich's printing business attracted the progressive intelligentsia in increasing numbers. As usual, however, the steady increase in popularity also attracted the censors' attention. A Ministry of Interior memorandum from 1879 accused the *Herald* of two principal faults: first, dwelling on the advantages of a constitutional form of government and supporting further reforms, and second, criticizing excessive centralization and Russification in Poland and Ukraine for contributing to ill feeling towards the government and the Russian nationality. The *Herald* formulated its defense of local autonomy and initiative, the keystone of its political program, in administrative as well as ethnic terms. "Russia, in its civilization's infantile condition, should not take upon itself the role of organizing new states," wrote Stasiulevich.[57]

THE LORIS-MELIKOV "THAW"

Stasiulevich welcomed the new interior minister Mikhail Loris-Melikov in 1880, but adopted a wait-and-see attitude regarding the thaw that he initiated, which involved the liberalization of press laws, attempts to negotiate with the social elite, and willingness to consider public opinion. Between January and May 1880, the *Herald* published Pavel Annenkov's memoir "Extraordinary Decade," which once again brought up the names of Herzen and Belinskii. On the one hand, the work described the ideological controversies that had raged among the Russian intelligentsia since the 1840s. On the other, Annenkov described the rift between radicals Belinskii and Herzen on the one side and moderate liberals such as himself on the other. The appearance of the memoirs therefore reinforced the *Herald*'s separation from radical Populism in the late 1870s, which could not have come at a better time on the eve of the regicide. Although Annenkov referred to Herzen only by the first letter of the Russian spelling of his last name "G," the censors still took issue with the author's exploration of Russian and European socialism. The memoirs appeared thanks to Annenkov's personal friendship with the minister of state domains, Mikhail Ostrovskii, who was a friend of Loris-Melikov's predecessor Lev Makov. Still, Stasiulevich and Pypin decided not to follow up with Annenkov's biography of Herzen's close friend Nikolai Ogarev (who had died in 1877) in order not to provoke the censors further.[58]

Arsen'ev welcomed the Loris-Melikov thaw and immediately proposed that the government create locally elected consultative councils to aid the governors. He also believed that the zemstvos should elect "experts" to offer consultation to the State Council on reform projects. Furthermore, he insisted that peasants participate in electing these "well-informed persons." The work that lay ahead, Arsen'ev argued, must not only benefit the rural population, but must involve it too.[59]

Loris-Melikov's attempt to split the opposition to the state by favoring its moderate wing resulted in the creation of the Valuev Commission in November 1880, which attempted to re-codify the publishing laws. The Interior Ministry encouraged Russia's most prominent publishers to participate in some of the meetings, but, understandably, men who had lived in fear of the censors' arbitrary rules were skeptical of the invitation. In the end, however, influential liberals such as Stasiulevich, Arsen'ev, Anatolii Koni, historian Vasilii Kliuchevskii, and several Justice Ministry officials participated.[60] Koni described one of these meetings in his memoirs: "The newspaper and journal editors of the Valuev Commission behaved themselves without dignity and pusillanimously. Only Stasiulevich spoke and he spoke to the point."[61] Stasiulevich's address to the Commission boiled down to two central theses. First, he argued, Russia's educated society realized that the press was under strict supervision and when it intentionally avoided important topics, readers assumed that the government was covering something up. This "absence of glasnost" contributed to the mutual alienation between the state and its subjects. Second, in order to avoid this situation, the press demanded nothing more than for the state to treat it "by means of laws and courts, and to eliminate administrative arbitrariness."[62] In his diary, Valuev noted that Stasiulevich's speech was "long and dry," but that it found favor with the commission members.[63]

Reserved in his judgments, Stasiulevich evaluated all new legislation in its relation to the freedom of the press. When in 1880 Loris-Melikov abolished the Third Section (the political gendarmerie), Stasiulevich wrote to Pypin: "I do not know how Arsen'ev will welcome this day, but he already knows what I think—'Beware of the Greeks bearing gifts'."[64] In another letter to Pypin he wrote: "Our own censorship forces us to approach western civilization like lackeys, that is, to eavesdrop by western civilization's door, and to refrain from discussing what we have heard."[65] The only freedom that the Russian press enjoyed in the 1870s and 1880s, he believed, was to criticize the domestic and foreign policies of foreign governments but not its own.[66] Stasiulevich understood that criticism of his journal in the conservative press found favor among state officials, some of whom even commissioned these articles.

More credulous than Stasiulevich of the Interior Ministry's liberal tendencies, or perhaps just more optimistic, Konstantin Kavelin saw in Loris-Melikov's thaw the promise of a general change of course. He wrote to Stasiulevich in 1880: "The time of false silence and false alliances has passed even for us. It is time for each to express his opinion openly, honestly, and boldly."[67] Kavelin had published a series of articles on the peasant question and state power in the *Herald*, which Stasiulevich collected into individual volumes. More skeptical of the state's promises, however, he chose to print *Political Ghosts: State Power and Administrative Arbitrariness, One of the Contemporary Russian Questions* (1878) and *A Conversation with a Socialist-Revolutionary* (1880) in Behr's publishing company in Berlin—beyond the censors' reach.

Stasiulevich's skepticism notwithstanding, one of the positive outcomes of Loris-Melikov's tenure was permission to publish the daily newspaper *Order*, which, although short-lived, became another liberal hub. The editors were economist Vladimir Bezobrazov, positivist philosopher Evgenii de Roberti, Kavelin, and Valentin Korsh. By this time, the young economist Leonid Slonimskii was already a contributor to the *Herald*. After Korsh left *Order*, Slonimskii took over as editor of its foreign section.[68] Prominent lawyer Sergei Muromtsev, Moscow's de facto liberal opposition leader, was the daily's Moscow correspondent.[69] Legal writers Vasilii Sobolevskii, Ivan Durnovo, and Sergei Priklonskii as well as statistician and economist Vasilii Pokrovskii also contributed articles. Russian philosopher Gregorii Vyrubov was the Paris correspondent. Ivan Ianzhul and Nikolai Ziber covered British intellectual life. Émigré revolutionaries S. M. Stepniak-Kravchinskii, N. I. Dobrovolskii, and S. L. Kliachko were regular contributors too. Turgenev helped Guy de Maupassant to publish some of his early short stories, such as

"A Portrait," in *Order*.[70] Circulation reached five thousand by the end of 1881. It is a compliment to *Order* that its very existence irritated Pobedonostsev.[71] Meanwhile, the police monitored the meetings of the editors at Stasiulevich's home by recruiting one of his servants.[72]

Through *Order*, Stasiulevich came face to face with anti-Semitism. Aleksei Suvorin and literary critic Viktor Burenin, both of whom had themselves contributed to the *Herald* in the 1860s and early 1870s, catered to pedestrian tastes by explaining social ills in simplistic terms that instigated witch-hunts. For example, Suvorin repeatedly reminded his readers that the Gintsburg banking family was behind Stasiulevich's business and Burenin pointed out that Stasiulevich's wife was Jewish. Neither of the critics mentioned the fact that Suvorin had himself acquired *New Time* with the help of Jewish bankers from Warsaw.

In this atmosphere, an experienced legal mind was a welcome addition to the editorial staff of the *Herald*, which Konstantin Arsen'ev had officially joined in the spring of 1878. Already a regular contributor, in 1880 he began the monthly "Domestic Survey," which "set the standard for permissible criticism of the regime."[73] He was the opposite of his predecessor, Leonid Polonskii—much less self-consciously European and not at all an Anglophile. Stasiulevich never had to restrain Arsen'ev on the issue of liberalization in Russia and he was much better suited to the stricter censorship conditions that lay ahead. Nevertheless, Arsen'ev consistently condemned the regime's encroachments on zemstvo and municipal duma rights. He protested Chief Procurator of the Holy Synod Konstantin Pobedonostsev's heavy-handed treatment of religious minorities such as the Old Believers, Catholics, and Lutherans. He also warned against "the increasing danger of clericalism that threatens Russia."

Arsen'ev brought with him a breadth of interests and experiences. In 1874, he became a member of the Shakespeare Society where fellow players, members of the *Herald* circle among them, read critical essays on literary topics. This increased his literary interests and he began to contribute reviews to the journal, which Pypin gladly encouraged him to do. Between 1866 and 1874, Arsen'ev maintained his successful law practice and was among those who made the new courtroom procedures function. His work as a trial lawyer gave him first-hand exposure to Russia's social ills. Between 1878 and 1884, he lived with his family on an estate half a day's journey from Petersburg, where he was closely involved in rural and peasant affairs as a member of the zemstvo.[74]

Arsen'ev was one of the defense lawyers in the famous 1877 "Trial of the 193," during which members of Land and Freedom answered for establishing revolutionary peasant "colonies," agitating among religious sectarians, and fomenting "agrarian terrorism." Most of the public defenders involved in this case were also Stasiulevich's friends. The jury acquitted eighty-eight of the accused and the rest received light sentences. The Ministry of Interior published the proceedings in its weekly *Government Herald* (*Pravitel'stvennyi vestnik*, 1869–1917), from which other publications could reprint the information. However, Arsen'ev and the other lawyers hired their own stenographers to record every word of the proceedings, including the speeches of the accused. Stasiulevich understood, of course, that publishing these in the journal would lead to certain disaster, but even his publishing house failed to pull it off. Before the ink dried on *The Stenographic Report of the Case of the Revolutionary Propaganda*, the censorship bureau forwarded a copy directly to interior minister Timashev, who ordered the printing to stop and the police to confiscate all existing copies. The authorities banned and destroyed the book in the autumn of 1878, but Stasiulevich managed to salvage a few unofficial copies. State Comptroller Dmitrii Sol'skii, who received one of them as a present, wrote to Stasiulevich: "I sincerely thank you, dear friend Mikhail Matveevich, for sending [me] a non-existent book. Only you can perform such tricks."[75]

Having made a career in the government, Arsen'ev used his extensive contacts among reform-minded bureaucrats to keep the "Domestic Survey" as current as possible. Intending to cover the twenty-fifth anniversary of Tsar Alexander II's rule in 1880, he described to Stasiulevich how he wanted to approach the event: "My initial thought was the following: not to praise, but to show that everything that has been done up to now has only prepared and facilitated further steps forward."[76] This attitude set the tone of the *Herald*'s political sensibilities.

Restraint in an Age of Terrorism

In the late 1870s, the Land and Freedom terrorist group unleashed a massive campaign of assassinations in Russia that aimed to inspire the masses to overthrow the government by demonstrating the state's vulnerability. Russian Populists embraced the agrarian socialist theory that identified the peasantry, not the working class, as the engine of revolution. Recognizing some similarities between Populist and liberal grievances, the *Herald* liberals nonetheless argued that no common ground could exist between the two world views because Populism's essentialist, anti-urban, and peasant-centered ideology ran counter to the interests of civil society as the *Herald* envisioned it.

The *Herald* unequivocally condemned Vera Zasulich's assassination attempt on the life of Saint Petersburg Governor Fyodor Trepov that took place on January 24, 1878. However, the *Herald* did not condemn the jury's acquittal of Zasulich on March 31 of the same year. The "Domestic Survey" separated the "act" from the "person" and refused to treat the assassination attempt itself as a dangerous precedent. In his correspondence, Stasiulevich even admitted that there was no greater risk for the journal than to sound as if it in any way condoned "Trepov's acts." However, Sergei Kravchinskii's murder of Chief of the Gendarmerie and Chief of the Third Department Nikolai Mezentsov on August 4, 1878, shocked Stasiulevich. He wrote to a friend that Russia's "head cold" had turned into a form of "typhus" with "severe complications." This time, the journal took a firm stand on terrorism and denounced the appearance of "political fanaticism" in the ranks of the radical movement.[77]

When the journal condemned Kravchinskii's act, it became the first publication to engage an illegal organization in an open debate. The underground publication *Land and Freedom* (*Zemlia i volia*, 1878–1879), which appeared in 1878, answered the *Herald*'s condemnation: "These press writers, in exchange for the reduction of censorship, are ready to become the state's political policemen and detectives," the article read.[78] Leonid Polonskii blamed the "savage, indecent, and immoral" assassinations on their perpetrators' disturbed psychological states.[79] In response, editor of *Land and Freedom* Dmitrii Klements suggested that his liberal colleague attend a performance of Rossini's *William Tell* or Serov's *Judith* in order to understand the passion to achieve freedom that inspired the Populist terrorists against insurmountable odds.[80] In turn, Polonskii sarcastically reminded Klements that Tell had fought against a foreign occupation and Judith saved a city from a siege—neither pursued political and social reforms. Furthermore, Polonskii argued, history provided many examples of political assassinations stymieing the progress of freedom and order. Every self-respecting European writer, "even [German Social Democratic leaders] Liebknecht or Bebel," would have condemned the murders, argued Polonskii.[81] Klements asked in turn whether the Russian Populists had any other courses of action: "Instead of bread, the state gives society a stone, instead of a fish—a serpent!" William

Tell's legendary status was proof of his act's nobility. As an example of a successful assassination, Klements used Emperor Paul I, whose death inspired "general exultation."[82]

The Populist revolutionaries were not unanimous on the issue of assassinations. Klements himself would later condemn terrorist tactics, and Land and Freedom split into the People's Will and the Black Repartition in the summer of 1879 over the question of terrorism. The radical People's Will group took up the revolver and the bomb as its tools, and its most outspoken theorist, Nikolai Morozov, justified these methods using the example of Giuseppe Mazzini's brigades.[83] The Populist radicals saw the Russian autocracy as an occupying force and their goal as national liberation. According to *Land and Freedom*, there was no time to lose, the bourgeoisie was weak and before its constitution enslaved the people further even than "gentry monarchism" already had, a political coup d'état had to liberate "the working democracy."[84]

After the explosion in the Winter Palace on February 5, 1880, Arsen'ev continued Polonskii's condemnation of political terrorism by examining the results of assassination attempts from the time of Julius Caesar. He noted that most attempts had failed and that the ones that succeeded often proved counterproductive. An individual ruler rarely guided historical evolution, Arsen'ev argued, so eliminating someone even as important as the tsar would not change the status quo. Echoing Edmund Burke, Arsen'ev argued that "the order of things has been created over centuries and rests on too many foundations, which makes it impossible to destroy all of them simultaneously, even if the most important one is struck."[85] Arsen'ev was particularly suspicious of agrarian socialism, the goals and impatience of which, he thought, would do more harm than good.

Socialism was not a newcomer to Russia in the 1870s. Herzen had already explored its potential, but the debate that began in 1878 after the collapse of the "to the people" movement had an impatient feel to it. Polonskii wrote an article supporting Bismarck's policy of "state socialism," which eliminated the destabilizing danger that came from the desire to abolish private property and enforce common ownership. Members of Land and Freedom, on the other hand, looked to such popular "proto-socialist" heroes as Pugachev and Razin. Polonskii reminded the Populists that Pugachev claimed to be descended from the tsars and reserved for himself autocratic powers. Even German Socialist Ferdinand Lassalle, he argued, had described peasant uprisings in Germany as inherently reactionary. Russian agrarian socialism pursued vague aims, Polonskii concluded, that "demanded senseless sacrifices from the youth for the sake of an unattainable Arcadia."[86]

Instead, Polonskii offered an alternative genealogy of liberty and reformism. He traced Russia's liberal tradition back to the era of Peter the Great and, more specifically, to economist Ivan Pososhkov (1670–1726) and publisher Nikolai Novikov (1744–1818), both of whom maintained that the first step towards social progress was the abolition of serfdom. Since then, Russian liberals correctly argued for slow but consistent reforms, Polonskii wrote. Meanwhile, "twelfth hour" upstarts such as the Populists had the gall to accuse the liberals of supporting the autocracy while waiting for reforms to trickle down from the top with "mouths agape." To discredit the socialists, Polonskii pointed to the internecine conflict within the First International between them and the anarchists. In order to demonstrate the validity of their brand of socialism, Russian Populists argued that their ideals had been latent in the masses for centuries and that it would take only a spark to ignite this discontent. According to Polonskii, however, Russia's peasant culture, commune and all, was inherently opposed to social leveling and egalitarianism and instead encouraged in its members profoundly "statist" views.[87]

Responding to Polonskii's article, *Land and Freedom* accused the liberals of applying a double standard—welcoming the progress of human rights in the West but supporting greater police controls in Russia.[88] Klements, who was also a famous ethnographer (one of many revolutionaries who, having been exiled to Siberia, traveled widely and published works on native Siberian tribes[89]), chose the following quotation for his response article: "Woe to you lawyers! For you have taken away the key of knowledge; you did not enter in yourselves, and those who were entering in, you hindered" (Luke 11:52). Klements argued that the Russian peasants owed the Emancipation Act to Chernyshevskii and Dobroliubov, both of whom despised moderate liberals. The Russian people were inherently anarchic, according to Klements, and this explained the recurring disturbances in the country. Pugachev may not have been a socialist, but Polonskii's suggestion that Bismarck was, cast serious doubt on his understanding of socialism. Klements also accused the *Herald* of vacillating on Marxism because the journal published articles both for and against it.[90] Where did it really stand? The *Herald* was thus forced to choose a position on Marxism at least a decade before its "official" debate with the legal Marxists began during the 1890s.

Stasiulevich's choice of novels to publish contributed to the debate with the Populists. Polonskii published his short story "You Have to Survive" in

December 1878 under the pseudonym L. Lukianov. The plot involved the relationship between a corrupt bureaucrat by the name of Sakhanin, his student son who is desperate to change things but knows not how to proceed, and the son's university friend, Gorlitsyn, a radical Populist. During a conversation between the students, the junior Sakhanin argues that in order to achieve Populist ideals certain conditions have to be met, such as the transformation of a semi-feudal autocracy into a constitutional monarchy. He proposes that the friends make this their initial goal to which Gorlitsyn answers as if reciting the party catechism: "You are bourgeois to the marrow of your bones. . . . But we have no care for the bourgeoisie's interests and its settling of accounts with anyone."[91] When the police arrest the young Sakhanin because of a suspicious package he carries—it turns out to be class notes on chemistry—he writes a note to his father from the detention cell: "Do not worry, I have not done anything yet; but we can no longer live this way."[92] Polonskii's short story described not only the rift between fathers and sons, but between the sons themselves, and it depicted the basic split between the radical Populists and the more doubtful and cautious liberal colleagues, each one a Hamlet. They had similar sources of discontent, but used different strategies to rectify them, and yet they developed with reference to each other. The plot accurately reflected the actual relationship between Russian liberals and Populists.

Polonskii believed that broadening social participation could gradually de-escalate the standoff between the authorities and society and eventually eliminate the radical opposition. He simultaneously urged the authorities to avoid punishing the loyal opposition because such indiscriminate demonstrations of force would only encourage underground forms of opposition. The censors, however, considered even this cautious call for gradual reform too radical and cut out the mutinous lines.[93] In an attempt at a rapprochement, Polonskii credited the "fanatical and savage" radicals for calling "things by their real names."[94] Meanwhile, he wrote, the conservatives, into whose camp the radicals unjustly placed the liberals, were no better in publishing "outrageous lies that deny everything that is true about Russia," namely a passion for social justice among both the people and the intelligentsia.[95] Polonskii thus tried to situate the liberals between the radicals and conservatives, which worked well on paper, but not in the real world.

Arsen'ev echoed Polonskii's thoughts when he criticized the Serbian socialists' new weekly *The Guard*. In a sterling example of Aesopian language, Arsen'ev considered the pursuit of socialist goals premature for Serbia. "Capital," against which the Serbian socialists struggled in defense of "labor" was, in reality, labor's closest ally in the struggle for political rights: "In semi-free and unfree countries, the first, elementary question is the achievement of political rights through self-government."[96] A more fruitful approach than socialist romanticism and mythology, Arsen'ev argued, would be to focus on the Serbian people's immediate material needs and intellectual enlightenment. In this, the Serbian socialists would find many willing colleagues among the Serbian liberals. Although the article covered "foreign affairs," its basic argument applied to Russia.

In his diaries, however, Arsen'ev admitted that although he was "almost antagonistic" towards socialism, he sympathized with Chernyshevskii's arguments and Louis Blanc's historical works.[97] Many liberals felt sympathetic towards Populist aspirations, and yet their methods and extremist tendencies created too many obstacles. Stasiulevich wrote to Ger'e that the jury's acquittal of Zasulich surprised him, but that he would never criticize it openly at the risk of appearing to defend Trepov's behavior.[98] From their side, Populist thinkers such as Nikolai Mikhailovskii also vacillated. In 1879, Mikhailovskii claimed that "the hateful yoke of the bourgeoisie" was "already upon Russia,"[99] but a year later suggested that "in the practical struggle, it is insane not to benefit from alliances, be they accidental and temporary."[100]

According to Populist Nikolai Morozov, some Russian liberals sympathized with the underground organizations and were even ready to support their political—but not social—aims because the common goal was to undermine the autocracy.[101] In the late 1870s, some zemstvo liberals and radical Populists even talked of uniting against the state, but this could only happen if the Populists ceased and condemned terrorist activity. As revolutionary Populist Vladimir Debogorii-Mokrievich wrote in his memoirs, "the terrorists refused this condition and the negotiations produced no results."[102] A. K. Solovyov's attempt on Alexander's life on April 2, 1879, buried the issue. The second point of contention was capitalism, which was somewhat ironic since both camps recognized its deleterious effects on the countryside, yet the debate about which specific aspects of capitalism were to blame created an unbridgeable chasm. The Populists criticized state policies for encouraging private rapacity that inevitably found its way into the village. The liberals believed that the state's industrial subsidies undermined cottage industry and stifled its competitiveness, but accepted capitalism as a long-term boon. Even after the People's Will (Narodnaia volia, 1879–1885) admitted that the "achievement of the [Populist] aim by the act of 1 March 1881" had failed, the Populists still considered capitalism tantamount to the plague.[103]

Thus, on the eve of the regicide, the *Herald* was firmly ensconced as the mouthpiece of the loyal opposition to the state. A brief list of regular contributors illustrates the microcosm that Stasiulevich had created around the journal by 1880. Stasiulevich stood at the center. In the first circle around him were Pypin and Arsen'ev. In the next were cultural critic Vladimir Stasov, literary historian and critic Semyon Vengerov, Evgenii Utin, and writer Aleksandr Stankevich, who contributed important political analysis and literary criticism. Historians Konstantin Kavelin, Aleksandr Gradovskii, legal theorist Fyodor Voroponov, and literary critics Viktor Gol'tsev and Valentin Korsh covered social, literary, and historical issues. Physiologist Igor Sechenov, botanist Andrei Beketov, embryologist Il'ia Mechnikov, economist Nikolai Ziber, and sociologist Maksim Kovalevskii contributed their research and covered the latest scientific developments abroad. By the early 1880s, the *Herald* published just over six thousand monthly copies.[104] Well-established, the journal would need all of its editors' creativity and contacts to weather the period of counter-reforms, which began with Tsar Alexander III.

The Regicide and Its Aftermath

Arsen'ev called the seventh, and successful, attempt on Tsar Alexander's life on March 1, 1881, a "catastrophe" and reiterated his earlier emphasis on the insignificance of isolated terrorist actions against individual targets. "An order of things that has a thousand roots and foundations cannot be undermined or detonated—it can be transformed only by consistent and energetic work of many forces that take into account all the existing conditions and that the popular masses support, at least passively."[105] Arsen'ev praised Alexander's reforms, although he was critical of the "reaction" that consistently waxed and waned between 1862 and 1881. He also argued that repressive measures could not stamp out terrorism. Every succeeding attempt proved that terror from above was ineffectual against terror from below. In response to the *Herald* and other liberal journals, the *People's Will* wrote: "Caught off guard by the unexpected confusion, [the liberals] started howling in unison with the conservatives, but they did not know against whom."[106]

The *Herald* group interpreted March 1881 as a catastrophic setback for Russia's political development. In an anonymous pamphlet sarcastically entitled *The Black Repartition of Alexander II's Reforms*, Mikhail Stasiulevich referred to the new conservative clique—Chief Procurator of the Holy Synod Konstantin Pobedonostsev, publisher Mikhail Katkov, interior minister Count

Nikolai Ignat'ev, and education minister Dmitrii Tolstoi.[107] Arsen'ev wrote in January 1882: "The catastrophe of 1 March put an end to a short, but brilliant, period of our modern history, and its consequences are still too apparent."[108] Nevertheless, he also hoped that the "insanity of a negligible minority" would not obstruct the "development of an entire people."[109] Anatolii Koni wrote in his biography of Count Loris-Melikov: "That fateful day—March 1, 1881— delayed by a quarter century the peaceful realization of a constitution."[110]

Whatever temporary liberties the *Herald* may have enjoyed under Loris-Melikov, they disappeared after the regicide. By August 1881, an Interior Ministry memorandum accused the *Herald* of "aiming to replace insufficient forms of political expression with an increased freedom of the press" and of encouraging "the dissolution of social support for the state."[111] The conservative head of the Press Department (1883–1896), Evgenii Feoktistov, remembered that the unruliness of the press had rarely achieved such a scale as it did in the early 1880s and that "the leading role in this belonged to the 'Herald of Europe' of Stasiulevich."[112] The publishing house also ventured perilously close to trouble. Ianson's *Statistical Research into Peasant Allotments and Payments* rapidly became a banner for intellectuals critical of the conditions of Emancipation.[113]

The Censorship Bureau added to the conservative barrage, which forced Stasiulevich to make weekly trips there to defend his paper *Order*. Loris-Melikov's dismissal from the Interior Ministry after the regicide brought in N. P. Ignat'ev, who was closer to Pobedonostsev in outlook, and by the summer of 1881, the press began to feel the weight of increased oversight. Stasiulevich wrote to Pypin: "[It is like] an uninterrupted series of unbearable tortures: the feeling makes me want to resort to the bludgeon, not the court."[114] In January 1882, Ignat'ev closed the paper for forty-five days and wrote to Pobedonostsev: "I have banned 'Order' for a month and a half. Are you finally satisfied with me?"[115] The prohibition came at the worst possible time: *Order* had just completed a subscription (3,865) for the next year, but as soon as news of the ban spread, many subscribers demanded their money back. By month's end, Stasiulevich announced the paper's closing. When Vladimir Lenin wrote condescendingly of the Russian liberals' "smart attempts to lead the monarch over the desired line, so that he would not notice it himself," he was referring to liberal newspapers, such as *Order*.[116]

By March of 1882, Arsen'ev was remarking on the depth of the chasm that had opened between the state and society.[117] Nonetheless, some liberals saw something infernally noble in the Populist acts. Sixteen years old at the time of Tsar Alexander's assassination, Pypin's daughter wrote that the "heroes of the First of March grew into grand, light figures." Pypin himself was "especially somber" that day, but, she surmised, empathized with the revolutionaries because they had killed his cousin's "personal enemy." Twenty-five years later, the *Herald* published the 1882–1884 correspondence between Count Dmitrii Miliutin and Konstantin Kavelin, who wrote: "As pointless, aimless, and criminal as are the Populist revolutionaries' acts, you cannot deny them character, energy, and inventiveness in the pursuit of their goal. Whatever you may say, there lives in them a profound discontent that saturates all of Russian society more or less."[118] Although liberal expectations of state reformism crumbled, liberal arguments acquired weight as arrests thinned out the radical ranks and encouraged increasing numbers of "scientific" Populist treatises in the 1880s. With practical options for reform blocked, statisticians returned in increasing numbers to the fields and villages, while Populist and liberal theoreticians made themselves comfortable behind their desks. Ironically, the journalistic debate about to begin would only deepen the chasm between Populist and liberal.

6

A Parting of Ways

The *Herald of Europe* and Populism

FROM UTOPIA TO COOPERATION

The *Herald* group saw no promise for agrarian socialism in Russia and treated the peasant commune as an economic necessity during the transition to capitalism, instead of a model of socialist relations as the Populists believed. Instead of utopian revolution, the liberals championed micro-credit and colonization programs that would involve the zemstvos and allow the state to cooperate with civil society. In other words, the *Herald* shared with the Populists their concern for the peasantry, but condemned their radical means of solving Russia's agrarian problems, of which land shortage had become the most serious by the 1880s.[1]

In February 1881, Pypin had sent Alexander II his famous "Memorandum on the N. G. Chernyshevskii Case," which argued that the accusations against his cousin were unsubstantiated. The memorandum was highly critical of socialists, whom Pypin called "idealistic fanatics made up of excited youths who had found no place for themselves in the complex and tense relations of the contemporary world." He accused their leaders of unjustly co-opting Chernyshevskii's name to rationalize their actions and referred to Mikhail Bakunin as a "windbag" and Lavrov as a "crazed philosopher."[2] After the regicide, Pypin published an article in *Order* in which he called the murder "a tragic historical event that has shocked the minds of the people." He simultaneously defended liberalism against Pan-Slavist Ivan Aksakov who equated it with nihilism. Pypin also argued that the liberal press expected the state to "continue reforms, extend self-government, and defend the freedom of the press."[3] Pypin's position was not revisionism in the face of a national tragedy. It was rather a natural extension of the *Herald*'s economic approach to rural problems, which the journal had already begun to articulate in the 1870s. *Herald* liberalism evolved through debates about the causes of land shortage and rural differentiation, peasant resettlement policies, and the redistribution of the tax burden—concerns that it shared with Populists. No one could have predicted that these debates would eventually lead to a break between liberalism and Populism in Russia, but this was the first step in a slowly unfolding process.

The agrarian question first appeared in the periodical press as a debate about the shortage of arable land in the 1870s. In 1877, Professor Iulii Ianson of Saint Petersburg University published his *Statistical Researches of Peasant Allotments and Payments* through Stasiulevich's printing shop, in which he argued that Emancipation had left the peasantry with too little land while saddling it with overwhelming redemption payments. Not accusatory in its tone, the book nevertheless polarized the intelligentsia. The *Voice* argued that Ianson's findings were "scientific, accurate, and correct."[4] On the other hand, Slavophile Dmitrii Samarin wrote in 1880: "We deny the theory regarding the shortage of land as a principle that is [. . .] completely false and alien to our way of life."[5] Samarin argued that intensive agricultural methods, cottage industry, rented plots, and trade would alleviate the poverty that Ianson had unjustly blamed on insufficient plot sizes.[6] The conservative paper *Rus* referred to the book as "our liberals' famous Koran."[7]

The *Herald* reacted rapidly against what its editors saw as Slavophilic oversimplifications. Fyodor Voroponov—a justice of the peace, chair of several local agricultural committees, and a member of the board of the Peasant Bank—accused the Slavophiles of grossly underestimating a serious socioeconomic problem that affected millions of peasants. Samarin's "blank shot," argued Voroponov, only confirmed the gravity of the situation and the need for "decisive measures."[8] Famous Siberian archaeologist Nikolai Iadrintsev maintained that "shortage of land, which is evident in different provinces of European Russia, with all its unfortunate consequences, is a widely acknowledged fact."[9] Iadrintsev wrote as an expert on colonization, the causes of which he linked directly to land hunger west of the Urals. The *Herald* group also found evidence of the agrarian crisis in social statistics. Voroponov made a direct link between increasing peasant death rates and land shortage.[10] Arsen'ev found that recruitment commission findings demonstrated alarming increases in peasants unfit for military service due to sickliness and a general "degeneration of the tribe."[11] Critic and bibliographer Arsenii Vvedenskii noted that 80 percent of the empire's population experienced "physical and moral degradation."[12]

Both the liberals and Populists believed that Emancipation was unfinished and that the state's balancing act between intransigence and indecision made matters worse. However, the liberals and Populists parted company when it came to methods of redress. *The People's Will* and *Land and Freedom* identified the state and its officials as agents of backwardness and described the Russian government as an "iron colossus with clay feet."[13] The *Herald* group, on the other hand, detected more shades in the gloomy picture of Russia's agricultural conditions and developed an increasingly sophisticated interpretation of them. For example, Arsen'ev added problems of soil depletion and taxes to the negative effects of land hunger.[14] Many writers who published in the *Herald* were involved in commissions and boards that dealt with local problems. For example, in 1880–1881, Arsen'ev participated in a senatorial revision of Samara and Saratov provinces, which found increasing socioeconomic differentiation in the villages.[15] Kavelin's "Travel Letters" described the displacement of the poor peasants by kulaks.[16]

The poor harvest of 1880 brought the agrarian question to the attention of the reading public. The paradox of Europe's breadbasket experiencing a famine "inspired the working-out of agrarian issues that have been mute for a while," Arsen'ev noted.[17] Unlike *Notes of the Fatherland*, the *Herald* did not consider the landed nobility responsible for insufficient land allotments and famines, nor did it treat land ownership as a zero-sum game. Arsen'ev supported Populist writer Aleksandr Engelgardt's demand that the state cooperate with local social forces to facilitate land purchases for the impoverished peasants.[18] However, eliminating land shortage would not eliminate the chief problem, but "only facilitate our battle against it," Arsen'ev reminded his readers.[19] He proposed selling state allotments, organizing resettlements, and facilitating land purchases through micro-credit institutions.[20]

Resettlement had become a major issue in the late 1870s. By July 1881, the *Herald* maintained that the landless and unemployed proletariat in the Russian Empire had increased to 3 to 5 million persons.[21] Nikolai Iadrintsev argued that the "economic crisis" made resettlement and colonization "attract special attention."[22] The controversy had started over Prince Aleksandr Vasilchikov's book *Land Ownership and Agriculture in Russia and Other European States*, which came out of Mikhail Stasiulevich's print shop in 1876 and was reprinted in 1881. Vasilchikov's service in self-government institutions ingratiated him with the progressive intelligentsia.[23] He answered his critics on the *Herald*'s pages by arguing that the state could successfully regulate agricultural affairs only if it first reorganized two underdeveloped programs: micro-credits for land purchases and colonization.[24]

The *Herald* agreed with the importance of the commune in Russian agriculture and defended Vasilchikov against Boris Chicherin and historian Vladimir Ger'e, who descried socialist tendencies in Vasilchikov's proposals that would destabilize the political balance in the empire by undermining the nobility's economic position.[25] Stasiulevich, however, went a step beyond Vasilchikov in proposing that the peasants transform the communes into rural artels or semi-official cooperative associations—the commune could turn from economic equalizer into the root of cooperative labor. In November 1881, Arsen'ev argued that the second edition of Vasilchikov's book was "not only a priceless literary work, but a courageous act" because the author admitted the problem of land shortage.[26] In other words, colonization could become a solution without infringing on the nobility's property rights. Fyodor Voroponov argued that organizing colonization of the steppe regions should become the state's priority.[27]

The *Herald* consistently proposed making resettlement a legal, controlled, and rational process instead of something resembling "a national retreat before an invasion," as Iadrintsev eloquently put it.[28] He also proposed the closest thing to a program with a simple formula: state and local aid to migrants, zemstvo aid for purchasing neighboring plots, and short-term credit in addition to land-purchasing credits.[29] Iadrintsev pointed to the United States, where state-controlled settlement offices distributed land to newcomers. He also argued for a resettlement and colonization fund that would help migrants to relocate. These two measures, he believed, would be more beneficial than land credit and bank loans.[30] The zemstvos would ensure the fair implementation of these policies on the ground. Furthermore, Iadrintsev saw in colonization the guarantee of Russia's territorial integrity, especially in the Far East, where the presence of "European civilization" would stem the tide of Chinese encroachments.[31]

Herald articles never called for the redistribution of the gentry's lands. Instead, as Iadrintsev argued, colonization would ease capitalism's "intensive" development by "extensive" means. It would allow the state to avoid the "disasters and catastrophes" of economic progress "by opening in a timely fashion the valve of life."[32] The *Herald* thus proposed a minimalist agricultural improvement program. Both state and society had to help the village harmonize its functions with those of Russia's changing economy, but the

peasants and landowners were not necessarily on opposite sides of the economic fence. By synthesizing their interests, state policy could benefit both
groups. Micro- and short-term credit could form the basis of the state's agricultural policy and indirectly benefit the landowners, many of whom were
also facing bankruptcy.[33] The *Herald* liberals saw the well-being of the upper
classes as a corollary of the peasantry's well-being, which proved the journal's non-estate approach to agricultural issues. Unlike its Western varieties,
liberalism in Russia aimed to champion the interests of all estates and classes.

SOCIAL JUSTICE THROUGH TAX REFORM

While the *Herald*'s micro-credit and colonization proposals laid the groundwork for state-society cooperation, the journal's position on taxes subordinated middle class interests to those of the peasantry. Taxes became a concern
for the *Herald* after the Russo-Turkish War of 1877–1878 increased their disproportionate burden on the peasantry. As Voroponov explained, the main
problem with land taxes was that they were geographically "unjust": highest
in the non-black-earth regions; higher on the Poles than the Russians; lowest on the black-earth Russian landowners; and higher on the peasants of
western and northern Russia.[34] Since restrictions on movement from villages
into factories decreased employment opportunities, Arsen'ev opposed passport fees, which the state required to validate documents allowing the annual
post-harvest migration.[35] Without bribes, the process was slow, which constrained the movement of labor. Lawyer Anatolii Koni even called the passport system a "brake on the country's economic development," not least
because off-season income supplemented the family budget.[36]

The *Herald* targeted the soul tax as an "old patch of a different color" on
Russia's modern garb.[37] Arsen'ev, Pypin, and economist Iulii Zhukovskii
all favored decreasing the peasantry's tax burden by increasing taxes on
industry.[38] Zhukovskii proposed distributing the tax burden in the following way: 1/3 on the peasants and peasant property and 2/3 on movable property, industry, manufactures, trade, and the professions.[39] Leonid Polonskii
proposed a more radical solution: to implement income taxes and taxes on
ranks.[40] This sort of redistribution of the tax burden would become one of
the liberal program's pillars.

The *Herald*'s position on taxes was a version of "placing the responsibility on the strong," that is, on industry and the new professions that it was
breeding. The state finally organized a commission in March 1879, which

eliminated the soul tax in four consecutive stages in 1883, 1884, 1886, and 1887.[41] Having called for this since the early 1870s, the *Herald* was ahead of its time. However, in May 1882 Arsen'ev wrote pessimistically about the Emancipation's achievements: "The mass of the people, emancipated in all other senses, remains enslaved financially and economically, enslaved to such a degree that it is as if in the past twenty years no reform has taken place in the sense of eliminating all the sources of tensions between the estates."[42] Calling for cooperation between the zemstvos and the state and a fairer tax distribution, by the 1880s the *Herald* was parting ways even with moderate Populists.

LIBERALISM AS MATURE POPULISM

That the issue of the *tiers état* never acquired prominence on the *Herald*'s pages supports Arsen'ev's claim that Russian liberalism had little to do with its Western relatives because its genealogy was rooted not in the bourgeoisie, the urban classes, and capitalist production, but in what was more prevalent in Russia—agricultural issues, the peasantry's social status, and local self-government. Articulating the *Herald*'s position towards "legal Populism"— the non-radical, armchair variety—fell to Aleksandr Pypin, who maintained throughout the 1880s that Russian liberalism and legal Populism had common origins. Populism, however, was still a vague phenomenon in terms of theory, which inspired divergent judgments and attracted different adherents to it. The conceptual muddle of Populism also inspired Pypin to reexamine it as a cultural phenomenon.

Pypin's examination of Populism as a cultural phenomenon exposed a plethora of opinions and disagreements on the most important socio-economic group in the Russian Empire—the peasantry. However, despite the criticism that Pypin directed at the Populists, he did not mean to discredit them. On the contrary, he tried to eliminate what he believed were artificial ideological boundaries separating Populist from liberal values and to re-establish a common ground. He therefore hardly deserves the "anti-Populist liberal" label that some modern scholars have applied to him.[43] His central concern was that prominent Populist thinkers, such as Vasilii Vorontsov, had created an artificial distinction between two social theories that had emerged from the same humanistic literary tradition of the Great Reform era. However, in the process of defining Populism, Pypin uncovered a real ideological difference that the liberals could not overlook—the Populists were in essence paternalistic in their view of the peasantry even though they idealized it. This view was incompatible with the *Herald*'s crusade to empower the peasantry through greater representation in the zemstvos. According to Pypin, *Herald* liberalism was Populism stripped of its idealistic and elitist components, which is why literary historian Aleksandr Veselovskii was justified in calling Pypin a "unique and sincere Populist."[44]

Pypin applied the term "Populist," in its broadest sense, to people who were "especially devoted to the study of rural life and who actively aided the in-habitants of the countryside." In a narrower sense, Pypin applied the term to journalists, literary figures, and researchers of the 1850s and 1860s who took pride in their exclusive understanding of popular interests.[45] In the absence of conceptual clarity, however, these men ranged all over the political spectrum—agrarian socialism, Slavophilism, and conservatism.[46] Pypin traced Populism's origins to a dual legacy—a liberal-emancipatory tradition (Gogol, Belinskii, and Herzen) and a mystical-sentimental strain (the Slavophiles) from which the Populists inherited the idea of self-sufficiency (*samobytnost'*) and the intellectual's moral duty to the people.[47] Drawing on a plethora of preexisting and contradictory currents of thought that it never fully digested, Populism developed only one general characteristic—it was not statist.

Pypin identified three periods in the evolution of Populist thought. The first coincided with the preparation and execution of Emancipation, when social concern for the peasantry took on judicial and economic forms as it addressed the size of peasant allotments, the fate of the commune, and the importance of national education.[48] Although their passion for justice set them apart during the 1860s, the Populists could not support their historical arguments with solid scientific data.[49] Nikolai Uspenskii, Aleksandr Levitov, Fyodor Reshetnikov, Vasilii Sleptsov, and Gleb Uspenskii became the most influential non-revolutionary Populist writers of this era.[50] They distinguished themselves by fully supporting the reforms and helping the rural population by spreading education and encouraging local self-government, something the *Herald* group considered the pillars of social progress. However, Pypin also noted that their views did not entirely coincide with the general Populist spirit and, as an example, he used Levitov's refusal to idealize the rural lifestyle or to identify in the peasant world view a form of "ready wisdom." A strict sense of realism distinguished Levitov and the other writers of his time from the heady days of people-worship in the 1830s, 1840s, and 1850s.[51] Life exposed many of these writers to the realities of the peasant world, and destroyed the bookish illusions that they entertained as young men. Gleb

Uspenskii headed a local bank in Samara province; Levitov studied medicine and became a doctor in a village in Arkhangelsk province; while Reshetnikov worked as a local court clerk and a scribe in the provincial revenue chancery. Overall, Pypin evaluated the Populists of the 1860s positively for their practical dedication and the lack of an "unbridled idealization" of the peasantry that would characterize their successors.[52]

Mass participation combined with unrealistic expectations defined the second period in Populism's evolution during the 1870s. The "to the people" movement demonstrated a deep-seated instinct for social justice through collective effort, in Pypin's opinion, which finally brought the intelligentsia into direct contact with the people. In the process of studying rural life, the *intelligenty* came to understand the importance of national education. Pypin was aware that youthful naïveté and many political and socio-economic misconceptions lay behind the movement, yet his optimism pointed beyond the chaos of mistakes towards the slow process of reinterpretation and reconciliation between educated society and the village. In the context of the 1870s, Pypin especially praised the realistic work of writers and ethnographers Fillip Nefedov, Nikolai Naumov, Aleksandr Ertel, and Pavel Zasodimskii.[53] He also welcomed the honest and gritty descriptions of rural hardship and the belief that the intelligentsia could improve the peasants' lot. Pypin believed, as did his colleagues, in a mutual process of enlightenment. While education would bring the peasantry closer to the intelligentsia, the tortuous process of debunking preconceptions and illusions would bring the intelligentsia around to the peasant world view, which revolutionary agitation obscured.

The third and final period in Pypin's scheme included the 1880s and 1890s, when Populism became variegated and uneven in its ideological shades that ran the gamut from the folksy *Notes of the Fatherland* (until 1884) to the conservative *Rus*. While Pypin considered the in-depth studies of rural economic life, employment in rural schools, and service in other institutions as the most constructive Populist activities, he considered completely unproductive all attempts to ground Populist theory in the worship of "enlightened rural simplicity."[54] Not only did Pypin consider the Populist ideology of the 1880s and 1890s mediocre, vague, and incomplete, he criticized the Populists for denying the applicability of all Western political forms to Russia. Populism was embracing a peculiar mix of rural posing and elitist rhetoric that aspired to intellectual uniqueness and undeserved exclusivity. While some statisticians were busy studying rural conditions, Populist thinkers such as such as historian Mikhail Koialovich, writer Nikolai Zlatovratskii, and Pyotr

Chervinskii (himself a statistician), preached agrarian self-sufficiency and opposed popular education.[55]

Populist accusations of the intelligentsia having lost touch with the people baffled Pypin, who argued that the brightest representatives of the intelligentsia studied popular culture, examined rural conditions, and tried to improve them. This is why he repeatedly refused to grant the Populists the privilege of exclusive knowledge of popular thought patterns and sensibilities. Besides, he believed that knowledge of Russian folk ways was at the time insufficiently developed for anyone to lay claim to it.[56]

When in his *Foundations of Populism* (1882) Populist Iosif Kablits (pen name Iuzov) accused the Russian intelligentsia of forcing foreign customs upon a peasantry that traditionally based its world view on emotion and feeling, Pypin accused the author of "mysticism."[57] Responding to Pypin's criticism, the second part of *The Foundations of Populism* (1893) was even more relentlessly critical of the intelligentsia, which inspired Slonimskii to describe Kablits in a Brockhaus and Efron article as an aging romantic living "the illusion of a struggle for past ideals."[58] Moreover, Pypin challenged the idea that the intelligentsia "owed it" to the people to become involved in its education because he considered the intelligentsia's interests inseparable from those of the population.[59] However, only broad social support for state efforts could solve the problem of popular enlightenment.[60] On this point, Pypin anticipated a belief prevalent among development economists in the twentieth century that an educational system is not a luxury but a necessity for successful modernization.[61]

Pypin expected to find a competent theoretical explanation of Populism in the work of Vasilii Vorontsov, whose writings on rural economic development Pypin held in high regard. After graduating from medical school, Vorontsov had served as a zemstvo doctor for eight years before turning to economics.[62] However, Vorontsov's series of articles entitled "Attempts to Create a Foundation for Populism" in *Russian Wealth* (*Russkoe bogatstvo*, 1876–1918) disappointed Pypin.[63] He disagreed, for example, that the "communal form" was "an exclusive characteristic" of the Russian people and argued instead that commune-based agriculture was a historical stage of development in almost all communities.[64] Unlike Vorontsov, Pypin seriously doubted the capability of the peasant commune to withstand the evolution of capitalism in Russia. He admitted that it was still difficult to predict exactly how "economic conditions and the role of capitalism" would develop in Russia, but he was convinced that the village could not preserve its self-sufficiency or adapt without undergoing significant, and sometimes painful, socio-economic changes.[65]

The debate between Pypin and Vorontsov demonstrated how conceptually distant the liberals and Populists had become by the 1890s. In the field, a liberal and Populist would have worked side by side, but on paper, they rarely agreed. Pypin considered Vorontsov's identification of economic interests as exclusive determinants of social problems ("privileges on the one hand and oppression on the other") to be a complete misunderstanding of social evolution.[66] Pypin also disagreed with Vorontsov's belief that the intelligentsia served the interests of a privileged social minority and followed narrow bourgeois teachings.[67] In his reply, Vorontsov maintained that like most critics of Populism, Pypin had turned him into an intentionally grotesque opponent, which prevented Pypin from logically examining Populist views.[68]

According to Pypin, Populism's overall development followed a declining trajectory from the Emancipation-era scientific and social research and brilliant literary descriptions of life in the village to the "dark ages" of the 1880s and 1890s, during which Populism fell into "self-contented mysticism" and unjustified exclusivity.[69] Pypin was not alone in his pessimism about Populism's future. By the 1890s, even Populist thinker Nikolai Mikhailovskii became nostalgic for the active Populism of the 1860s, when its morals were consistent with its goals and the dichotomy between moral and effective activity did not exist.[70] In defining itself against the intelligentsia, Populism abandoned the struggle for what Mikhailovskii (and Pypin) valued most—individuality.

Pypin identified two major errors in Populist thinking. First, the Populists paid insufficient attention to the history of the Russian people, which caused them to make serious mistakes in their evaluations of its course and potential. Second, they believed that European civilization was "unnecessary and inapplicable" to Russia. According to Pypin, Populism shared this attitude with "the worst representatives of obscurantism."[71] However, unlike conservatives, Pypin argued, the Populists were interested neither in paternal monarchism, nor in Orthodoxy, nor in religion.[72] The total absence of any religious justifications for protecting the peasantry's interests was common to the *Herald* liberals and the Populists, which underlines the non-religious character of progressive thought in the 1890s and the Orthodox Church's conspicuous absence from the modernization project.

In general, Pypin characterized Populist ideology as a "mass of theoretical confusions" without a thorough conceptual grounding. Only theoretical clarity and social maturity would enable Populism to achieve the organizational and logistical force required to establish a constant and close interaction between the educated classes and the peasantry.[73] The Herald group believed that such clarity and organization existed in the guise of Russian liberalism, of which they considered themselves the leaders. The central idea behind Pypin's arguments was that liberalism was a mature form of Populism, which having gown out out of its adolescent solipsism, took account of the immense complexity of Russia's socio-economic conditions and tried to engage them through the zemstvos.

CULTURE AND PRAXIS BEYOND POPULISM

Pypin's debate with the Populists was more than just an intellectual exercise. In addition to his writing, his other responsibilities also demonstrated avenues of action that Russian intellectuals could take to make a difference in the lives of ordinary people. Pypin had dedicated his life to exploring the genealogy of Russian liberalism under the guise of academic research. If the topics he researched were to be arranged in historical order, they would appear in the following sequence: the Freemasons, Decembrism, Slavophilism, Westernism, and Populism. In all these, Pypin saw individuals as agents of change who brought "society into consciousness of its role in national development and led it through self-activity toward self-government."[74] Reformers accomplished results when the state treated them as allies in the cause of popular enlightenment, which gradually increased the population's right to govern itself. Each one of the socio-intellectual movements that Pypin explored shared in common the absence of state support at their inception and varying degrees of state censorship and even repression throughout their existence. The potential for self-development was necessary for liberalism's evolution in Russia. Pypin understood liberalism as "the direction of social thought that tends toward maximum social self-realization, toward the maximum freedom for personal individuality and personal thought."[75] In Pypin's eyes, Alexander I's advisor Mikhail Speranskii, members of the literary circles of the 1820s, the Petrashevsty, and the Slavophiles and Westernizers of the 1840s–1860s had all been liberals. Russian history was therefore full of examples worth emulating—from a passive receptacle of reforms, Russian society slowly evolved into an active agent of socio-economic evolution. Pypin's optimism reflected that of the *Herald* group in general, while his spectacular public service record justified his arguments.

In an 1886 article on Russian folk literature, Pypin wrote that the Russian scholar's role should not be exclusively scientific, but that "he must facilitate the growth of [enlightenment's] elementary shoots among the social masses."[76] A pioneering ethnographer, Pypin championed the study of local history and folklore by supporting the opening of the Saratov Radishchev Museum in 1885, and working closely with the Imperial Geographic Society to support local studies and conferences.[77] In 1886, a group of young Populists in Siberian exile thanked Pypin for "characterizing the most important epochs in the social and literary development" of Russian society, and asked him to publish another volume of collected articles since the first editions of his books had already become rarities.[78] Pypin's series of articles on the history of Russian ethnography, which appeared on the pages of the *Herald* between 1881 and 1889, appeared through Stasiulevich's printing house as *The History of Russian Ethnography* (1891), becoming the first systematic overview of the subject. In 1898 and 1899, he reworked a series of *Herald* articles into *The History of Russian Literature* (1898–1899), which examined literary genres "in the sequence of their historical development, their relations to each other and to dominant political and social events."

Pypin's energy did not diminish in the 1890s. He was in his sixties, his academic achievements had accumulated, and his intellectual energy reached its peak and showed no signs of deterioration until his sudden death on December 9, 1904. He was by then a member of one foreign and eight Russian academic societies, and an honorary member of two Russian universities, one museum, two local archival commissions, and the Russian Academy of Sciences, as well as two foreign scientific academies.[79] His public service also extended to education and publishing. In 1901, he joined the Education Ministry's commission "on the transformation of middle schools," where he opposed excessive emphasis on the learning of classical languages.[80] In 1895, he cooperated with the Imperial Free Economic Society as it published the collected works of Ivan Krylov, Aleksandr Pushkin, and Mikhail Lermontov, and in 1899 participated in the Petersburg Pedagogical Society of Mutual Aid, which oversaw the publication of affordable educational literature.[81]

Pypin believed that revolution was antithetical to the Russian national character and historically counterproductive. Referring to socialist tendencies as "purely Platonic," he argued that it was "ridiculous to dream of a socialist order within the Russian Empire."[82] Marxism, like Nietzsche's philosophy, was in his opinion a symptom of decadence and "a mistake, simplification, and monstrosity" that represented but an "episode" in European development, which it was an error to treat as "the ultimate limit of human thought and artistic creativity, and as guidance."[83] Throughout his career, Pypin defended the reformist spirit of the 1860s, advocated for further reforms, greater local autonomy, and more freedom for the arts and sciences. In Pypin's view, co-operation between the state, representative institutions, and the press could achieve all of these goals without bloodshed, while cultural enlightenment would ensure social stability.[84] Neither the Populist, nor the Marxist ideology offered a convincing solution to Russia's challenging socio-economic growing pains.

Toward a Liberal World View

Pypin's examination of Populism exposed deeper shades of late imperial socio-economic thinking than the Populist-Marxist wrangling over the primacy of classes and abstract socio-economic loyalties. Pypin's visceral distrust of essentialist arguments about agrarian self-sufficiency demonstrated that *Herald* "Westernism" had less to do with importing foreign ideals than with preventing Russia's socio-economic and cultural isolation from the developing world—a distinction worth pondering for contemporary Russian liberals and their opponents. Although the Populists claimed to protect the peasantry's traditions from the blind forces of modernization—which anticipated the Third Way movements of the twentieth century—Pypin's articles in combination with the *Herald*'s crusade to extend peasant participation in local self-government demonstrate that the liberals actually pointed to the institutions that could make this happen.

Having separated on the issue of radical terrorism, liberalism and Populism strayed even further apart theoretically. Although there are first-hand accounts of Populists such as Sergei Iuzhakov and Vasilii Vorontsov mixing easily in salons with liberals and zemstvo members such as Arsen'ev, such civil behavior did not indicate a rapprochement.[85] Unlike the Populists, the *Herald* liberals explored ways for the peasantry to coexist with capitalism and pointed to the zemstvo as the only viable medium by which Russian educated society could influence the rural population and create constructive feedback for the state.

Populists claimed to be the first to formulate difficult questions about Russia's socio-economic development strategy. Vorontsov opened his most famous work, *Fates of Capitalism in Russia* (1882), with a deceptively simple thesis—"Russia's organization of production is much more complex than the

Western European"—and dedicated his work to proving Russian capitalism's creative impotence and exploitative qualities.[86] Because the impoverished Russian population that constituted the domestic market could not absorb the products of industry, Vorontsov argued, subsidizing heavy industry was an economic dead end and imitating the German economy was a dangerous project.[87] Although this "Jeremiah of Populists" warned of the corrupting effects of foreign ideas, the *Herald* materials demonstrate that the Populists were by no means the only ones suspicious of transplanting foreign development models.[88]

Some scholars have argued that in opposition to the Marxists, the Populists "passionately defended free will and the right, power, and duty of the individual" to stand firmly against the objective forces of nature and history.[89] The *Herald* materials demonstrate that by the 1890s the Populists appeared to the liberals to be as obscurantist as the Marxists appeared indifferent. By the 1890s, Pypin was arguing that the liberals fully shared the humane sensibilities that the Populists claimed as exclusively their own, but that the liberals were the only ones carrying the torch of conscious and progressive efforts to humanize the painful but necessary modernization process. Mikhailovskii described Pypin's idée fixe as "the unity of [bourgeois] civilization" and argued that Pypin belonged to the ranks of "the few bona fide Westernizers we still have who believe in the unity of European civilization and who have sharpened their analytical knife primarily by criticizing nationalistic teachings, especially those of the Slavophiles."[90] In a way, Mikhailovskii was right—as a cultural historian, Pypin saw through and looked beyond Slavophilic and Populists tropes—but he was also concerned for the human being behind the statistic.

Some scholars have argued that Populism's suspicion of constitutionalism contributed to its inability to win converts, which set the unfortunate precedent of counterposing economic to political democracy.[91] Economic democracy, however, was exactly what the *Herald* group championed when it called for the delegation of state power to the zemstvos to compensate for the absence of political rights. In his analysis of Populist theory, Pypin pointed to its messianic overtones, which created an insurmountable obstacle to constructive activity. The *Herald*, by contrast, articulated its own socio-economic development program that justified the pains of modernization while simultaneously offering the chance to mitigate its worst side effects through the zemstvos.

When it came to social justice on the pages of the *Herald of Europe*, the zemstvo was at the center of the debate. It also happened to be at the center of economic and political battles between the ministries, state agencies, and the estates in the 1890s. The zemstvo was simultaneously the battleground and the prize. The *Herald* writers saw no promise for socialism in Russia and treated the commune as a temporary economic necessity during the transition to capitalism. They distrusted and argued against enforced modernization and envisioned the zemstvo as a negotiating link between rural interests, the intelligentsia, and the state. Russia's civil society evolved on the local level where the zemstvos became hubs of social activity that sent threads throughout the empire and into the capitals. But these connections only appear if the observer looks for them, which the *Herald* makes possible.

The readers of the *Herald of Europe* opened a window onto a rich world of local politics that functioned in extra-parliamentary ways. The journal was therefore a window not so much on the West, although it was also that, but on the kaleidoscope of local politics and nodes of local civil society in Russia. It was an information carrier that ran to and from the provinces along a network of subscribers. The journal soaked up news from the provinces, which its editors interpreted and then sent back in the form of programmatic articles. In the process of examining local issues, the *Herald* group began to articulate a development program that sought to empower the peasantry instead of saving it. In reaction to the famine of 1891–1892, the *Herald* group also began to deal with macro-economic issues just as Marxism emerged as a powerful intellectual force. And in the process of engaging with Marxism, the *Herald* articulated its own understanding of Russia's place in the world economy without losing sight of modernization's local effects or Russia's uniqueness.

PART III

The Emergence of a Liberal Program

What has happened in the past in the industrially advanced
countries has little bearing on us today. . . . Western economics,
therefore, though helpful, have little bearing on our present-day
problems. . . . We thus have to do our own thinking, profiting by
the example of others but essentially trying to find a path for
ourselves suited to our own conditions.

—JAWAHARLAL NEHRU, "Democracy, Communism, Socialism, and
Capitalism," *The New Leader*, September 8, 1958

7

Challenging the Ideology of Progress

Russia and the Global Economy

ECONOMIC DEVELOPMENT AFTER 1861

In the second half of the nineteenth century, when "state capitalism" was the norm and not a contradiction, Europe was enjoying the blessings of a global market. As John Maynard Keynes wrote of the decades preceding the Great War:

> The inhabitant of London could order by telephone, sipping his morning tea in bed, the various products of the whole earth—he could at the same time and by the same means adventure his wealth in the natural resources and new enterprise of any quarter of the world—he could secure forthwith, if he wished, cheap and comfortable means of transit to any country or climate without passport or other formality.[1]

The infrastructure to which Europe owed the second industrial revolution and the first global market was in large part the result of state-directed economic development, and Russia was no exception to this pattern. The Finance Ministry channeled funds into strategic sectors of the economy, and the volume and direction of these investments formed modernization vectors that functioned within broader fields of state interests determined by domestic conditions and international factors. The development vectors in the Russian Empire after the Great Reforms emphasized industry and railways. Since Emancipation, the Finance Ministry had paid little attention to the consequences of its policies in the countryside, which the *Herald* saw as the main problem in Russia's economic development. No highly placed bureaucrat could have doubted that agriculture was the linchpin of the Russian economy, yet the state largely ignored its needs.

Many scholars have observed that statistics-gathering by provincial zemstvos marked the last third of the nineteenth century and contributed to social awareness of rural conditions.[2] By the 1880s, publishers spared neither ink, nor paper in printing compendiums of figures about everything from soil types to macroeconomic trends. Like a victim of thirst, Russian society gulped down numbers that quantified changes in the Romanov Empire. When this passion for statistical exploration and rational discovery emerged during the reign of Nicholas I, it was an effort to gain real control over the immense space of the Russian Empire by systematizing information.[3] By the last quarter of the nineteenth century, this first step in creating an economic Cartesian grid turned into a feverish catching-up process. It was a time-consuming affair and by 1882, Vorontsov still complained that nobody was able to "paint a full economic picture of Russia."[4] Coming from the man who published the most comprehensive summary of the zemstvo findings together with agronomist and statistician Aleksei Fortunatov, this evaluation demonstrated how much work still lay ahead.[5] The enlightenment emanating from the Imperial Free Economic Society, of which Arsen'ev and *Herald* contributor Vladimir Stasov were members, was a drop in the ocean.[6] Nevertheless, each book that emerged from the printing presses was like another word in a rapidly growing vocabulary. Benjamin Disraeli once distinguished between "lies, damned lies, and statistics," and if his healthy skepticism held true for Great Britain in the 1870s, it certainly applied to Russia's immense territory too.

Russia's economic development figures for the period 1861–1890 reflected the uneven nature of economic development.[7] The railroad system became increasingly important and grew eighteen-fold between 1865 and 1890. Russia's banking system underwent rapid changes after 1861 as newly established joint-stock companies concentrated and mobilized private capital. The financial growth statistics demonstrated a great industrial thirst for capital and energy resources.[8] Even the *Herald*'s choice of novels to publish reflected the growing importance of the bourgeoisie and banking when in 1882 Boborykin's *Kitai-gorod*, which described the rise of a new, dynamic, and enlightened merchant class, appeared in the journal.

Working with late nineteenth-century Russian economic statistics, however, is a useful exercise in healthy skepticism. Although the absolute figures demonstrated economic growth, they told only part of a complicated story.[9]

Finance Ministry agendas before the 1890s demonstrated three things. First, having crossed the 1861 threshold, the Russian state had no coherent, long-term development program and became a hostage of socio-economic circumstances. Second, when industrialization emerged as the state's principal aim by the 1890s, the agrarian question fell from prominence, which jeopardized the gains of the Great Reforms. And third, social issues fell largely into the background of the development goals. These were all problems that the *Herald* consistently emphasized in its articles and surveys.

The Finance Ministry played the central role in planning and implementation, but the vertical administrative structure of the Russian Empire made it difficult for the center to appreciate or even stay abreast of local economic needs. The *Herald* addressed this problem by supporting zemstvo participation in economic reforms on the local level. For the first time since Russian rulers began to implement crash modernization programs, the empire had a well-established network of local institutions that could provide feedback to the center and help to implement its directives on the ground. The zemstvos could act as feelers and nodes of an economic democracy that evaluated modernization based on local benefits, not exchequer balances. However, none of the post-Reform finance ministers took advantage of this. On the contrary, financial policy became increasingly vertical.[10] Between the tenures of finance ministers Mikhail Reitern (1862–1878) and Ivan Vyshnegradskii (1887–1892), financial stability and industrialization superseded social issues. Although Emancipation had aimed at liberating the peasant, it produced unfavorable short-term effects. Collective financial responsibility, the preservation of the peasant commune, and limitations on migration all aimed to filter out some of the worst excesses of capitalization, but they often produced the opposite effects and, according to most contemporaries and scholars, these artificial filters allowed the most pernicious forms of financial exploitation to penetrate the villages.[11]

The great regional differences in how successfully rural communities adapted to the new economic conditions, however, did not negate the overall picture of relative rural decline compared to industrial growth. Toward the end of the nineteenth century, the Romanov Empire was a tapestry of pre-Emancipation, proto-capitalist, and agrarian-capitalist regional economies. These changes also negatively affected the landed nobility, which began to lose property to merchants, businessmen, and sometimes even to wealthy peasants. Its collective share of land fell from 78 percent in 1877 to 69 percent by 1887.[12] Such was the economic road to the 1890s, by which time the *Herald of Europe* had already articulated its basic views on the primacy of local self-government and peasant interests during the transition to an industrial economy and it would now have to examine this process in depth in depth in order to engage the Russian Marxists in an informed debate.

THE LABOR QUESTION

The labor question in Russia did not become a subject of state legislation until the 1880s. However, the *Herald* group's attention to the conditions and interests of labor in the 1870s demonstrated its foresight and awareness of international socio-economic trends.[13] In the 1870s, a wave of strikes rolled through Russian towns with high concentrations of factories, including Saint Petersburg.[14] Beyond Russia's borders, Europe was already struggling with the labor issue, the memory of the 1871 Paris Commune was fresh, and sections of the First International were operating across the continent. No Russian intellectual could overlook these facts and their implications, but unlike the more intransigent First International, the *Herald* liberals saw the labor question as yet another area of potential cooperation between state and society.

Arsen'ev argued by 1878 that Western Europe's failure to adequately deal with the agrarian question was the real cause of labor problems, which he called Western civilization's "Achilles heel."[15] The Russian liberals, Arsen'ev believed, had the advantage of preventing the problems that they were witnessing in the West before they appeared in Russia. The Populists made the same argument after one of their own—Nikolai Danielson—became the first translator into Russian of Marx's *Capital*, which in his view illustrated how *not* to modernize. While European socialists were in the process of challenging the classical liberal laissez-faire, laissez-passer school of thought during the 1870s, the *Herald* group supported a form of state socialism as long as it respected the interests of local self-government.

By the late 1870s, the *Herald* position on the labor question resembled in many ways the moderate intelligentsia's consensus that human beings deserved better. After an account of Siberian gold mine workers described the owners' "inhuman attitude" towards them in 1878, Polonskii warned that "the inadequacy of the workers' conditions" and the absence of labor legislation facilitated the spread of socialist ideas and turned working women and children into "martyrs calling to the state for protection."[16] Not only did Polonskii argue that there was nothing to fear from state initiatives to better workers' living conditions, but ignoring this problem would lead to social "strife" and "full economic decline."[17] The censors cut out this section of Polonskii's "Domestic Survey," demonstrating that the Russian state was aware of the labor problem and sensitive to criticism of its inaction, but as yet unprepared to tread on the interests of the factory owners.

However, the state was not the only responsible party. Journalist Pavel Abramov shifted the responsibility for the labor question onto society. "Education and the amelioration of workers' lives," he wrote, "have so far attracted insufficient attention from the Russian public."[18] Faithful to the liberal view, Abramov refused to interpret ignorance, indolence, poor hygiene, and alcoholism as inherent characteristics of the workers, seeing them instead as results of illiteracy, low wages, and poor living conditions.[19] He thus defined three problems for the Russian liberals to tackle—education, labor contracts, and hygiene. Meanwhile, Arsen'ev proposed building cheap, multistoried apartment houses for workers.[20] Articulating the vocabulary of the labor issue in the 1870s and 1880s, the *Herald* championed shorter working hours, especially for women and children; wage increases; better working and living conditions; universal primary education; evening and vocational schools for workers; a basic insurance system; and factory inspections.[21]

True to its title, the *Herald of Europe* looked to Western European solutions. It urged the Russian government to follow Bismarck's policy of placing the labor question "on the broad foundation of 'state socialism' according to Lassalle's principle."[22] The journal's foreign review sections, which Leonid Slonimskii took over in 1882, monitored the fate of German socialism. Arsen'ev welcomed Bunge's June 1882 laws regulating child labor and establishing factory inspectors as "a first step towards solving the problem."[23] Much like the local self-government issue, the labor question also became a battleground between the Finance and Interior Ministries.[24] The *Herald*, however, argued for a combined state-society effort to tackle labor problems, which inevitably raised the question of the individual's role in the process of modernization. In order to negotiate this relationship, the journal explored Western economic theory, and Marxism in particular, which was already polarizing the debate on the labor question in Europe.

MARXISM COMES TO RUSSIA

When Slonimskii began contributing to the *Herald* in 1878, he brought to the economic debate a thorough legal foundation and a broad contextual view of Russia's place in the world economy. Well acquainted with Western economic theory, Slonimskii examined Russian development alternatives with reference to prominent European theoreticians. His contributions marked the moment that the journal fully lifted its head above Russian conditions and took notice of debates beyond the empire's borders. Slonimskii became a regular contributor and editor at the same time as Marxism made its way into Russia, bringing the spirit of scientific inquiry into sociological questions that until then had been the bailiwick of literary figures, bureaucrats, and religious philosophers. Nevertheless, when he could he steered the debate on socio-economic development away from abstract theory and towards practical policies that addressed Russia's specific conditions.

The Westernizers had known of Marx as early as the 1840s. Writer Pavel Annenkov, a regular contributor to the *Herald*, was personally acquainted and corresponded with him. In their turn, Marx and Engels took notice of events in Russia in the early 1850s and by 1852 Engels was feverishly studying Russian and the basics of other Slavic languages. Early on, he predicted that the Pan-Slavists would "turn the ancient Slavic communal ownership into communism and portray the Russian peasants as Communists."[25] In 1858, Marx examined the economic situation in Russia on the eve of Emancipation—he predicted the disappearance of the landed gentry as a class and prophesied a "Russian year 1793."[26] From then on, Marx carefully monitored internal Russian developments, for which purpose economist Nikolai Danielson regularly sent him books and journals in Russian.

Ironically, it was not Marx the historian (the mind behind *The German Ideology*) and not even the revolutionary (the voice of the *Manifesto*), but Marx the economist that Russians came to know first with the translation of *Capital* in 1872. In a letter, Marx wrote, "My good friends the Russians" against whom "I had waged a battle for twenty-five years" are "my first benefactors."[27] Little did he know that the book was intended to be a how-*not*-to manual. Marx even sent the publisher, Nikolai Poliakov, a photograph of himself as requested. Poliakov presented the translation to the Petersburg censors and they passed it with the following justification:

> As was to be expected, many passages in the book demonstrate the socialist and antireligious attitudes of the notorious president of the International society. However, regardless of how strong and cutting Marx's remarks are about the treatment of workers by capitalists, the censor does not think that they will cause great harm because they drown in a mass of abstract, partly

obscure political-economic argumentation that constitutes the book's sub-
stance. It can be said with certainty that few people in Russia will read it, and
fewer will understand it.[28]

How right he was! The censors added that Marx did not accuse any specific persons or class of capitalism's excesses, but treated it as a lawful stage
of historical development. The censor further noted that since Marx analyzed English capitalism almost exclusively, the book was inapplicable to
Russia, "whose development unfolds differently, and where state interference limits free competition."[29] The censors correctly interpreted *Capital* as
economic analysis that neither called for the overthrow of governments, nor
left any room for personal influence on socio-economic development. However, the censorship committee was unaware that the book was the tip of
an iceberg—a crowning "scientific" justification for a socio-political program
that had preceded it. The censors also underestimated the Russian intelligentsia's gift for selective interpretation and its tendency to treat every text
as an Aesopian riddle. Simultaneously, the general dearth of native economic
theory made Marxism increasingly popular as it seeped into Russia from
Europe. By 1871, economist Nikolai Ziber, a regular *Herald* contributor,
had published his dissertation as a separate book entitled *D. Ricardo and
K. Marx in Their Socio-Economic Researches.* The volume sold well, although
Ziber focused exclusively on the theory of value, not on its revolutionary implications. He saw Marx as a talented economist and follower of the analytic
tradition of Adam Smith and David Ricardo. Revolutionary Marxism had
not yet appeared in Russia when in March 1872, the first Russian edition of
Capital sold out all three thousand copies.

The book's popularity was a result of two factors. On the one hand, it fell
onto parched intellectual ground. Conservative liberals such as Boris Chicherin blamed the stifling atmosphere of Tsar Nicholas I's regime for pushing
Russian youth toward "senseless propaganda" aimed at destroying a state
that was finally emancipating "twenty million subjects from two hundred
years of slavery." "Priceless gifts rained onto Russia from above," he wrote,
"the dawn of a new life was upon us, while on the bottom, serpents born in
the darkness of the previous reign prepared to exterminate this great historical event, to poison the roots of the still small forces growing out of the
ground."[30] The second factor involved the groups that used Marx as anti-
capitalist propaganda, especially on the pages of the Populist *Notes of the
Fatherland.* In his review of *Capital*, Mikhailovskii recommended the book

as "truly educational for the Russian reader," because it illustrated the pit-
falls of Western capitalist development from which it was not too late to save
Russia.[31] Both its enemies and proponents read the book.

In 1872, economist Illarion Kaufman published a review article of the
new translation in the *Herald of Europe*. His verdict was positive, although he
found fault with how Marx used statistics to support his arguments. Marx
was so happy with the appearance of the first translation that he removed
from the second German edition references to the "Muscovite Herzen," the
"Russian Kalmyks," and "the *knout*." In the epilogue, he praised Ziber's dissertation "D. Ricardo's Theory of Value and Capital," called Chernyshevskii
a "great Russian scholar and critic," and quoted parts of Kaufman's *Herald*
review article.[32]

For the book's tenth anniversary in 1877, economist Iulii Zhukovskii published another review of *Capital*. He wrote highly of Marx's lively style and
welcomed the departure from Hegel's assumption that the German state—
with its pseudo-constitutional structure in the 1870s—was the result of "the
Good becoming self-conscious of itself." Zhukovskii also argued, however,
that Marx had gone too far in applying Hegel's assumption of inherent and
constant antagonism to the process of production in an attempt to find in
this dialectic the "mystical source of a new Nile." The metaphysics upon
which Marx had based his economic theory confused readers who were un-
used to "dialectical games," and the text's clarity suffered from the endless
repetition of Hegelian steps. Marx could have made his point much clearer
had he stuck to the facts and jettisoned the philosophy.[33] Zhukovskii was not
alone in criticizing Marx for disfiguring facts and trends to fit into his a priori
construction—Boris Chicherin and finance minister Nikolai Bunge agreed in
their evaluations.[34]

The analysis of Marx's thought in Russia began with criticisms of his
methodology, to which Leonid Slonimskii dedicated the first article that
he published in the *Herald* in 1878. Slonimskii bemoaned the decomposi-
tion of Ricardian political economy with its "logical order and harmonious
unity" into a methodological free-for-all involving induction, deduction,
direct observation, abstraction, economic history, and philosophizing—Marx
was one of the worst "selectionist" offenders and essentially a "literary economist."[35] Slonimskii's article was illustrative of Russian economic theory in
its information-gathering stage and still wary of grand theorizing. The *Herald* argued that Russians would do well to cultivate education and a legal consciousness among the population before engaging in high-stakes economic

debates. And here again, Slonimskii restated the journal's central idea that state and civil society could find plenty of opportunities to cooperate.

EDUCATION AND LAND OWNERSHIP

Aware that Russia was only beginning to enter the age of capitalism, the *Herald* liberals redirected their readers' attention from Marxism to the national education system and the clear articulation of land ownership rights as preconditions for economic progress. Indeed, Marxist dialectics and the abstruse intricacies of "mean value" were still far from Russia's real economic concerns in the 1870s. Instead, Slonimskii examined Johann von Thünen's argument that mass education was a way to reduce socio-economic animosities by raising the workers' intellectual and moral levels.[36] Slonimskii believed that this argument could also apply to Russia's own proletariat as it slowly emerged out of the peasant masses, which meant educating the peasants first—a tall order that only cooperation between the state and the zemstvos could tackle.

It is a compliment to Slonimskii that he began to think along these lines in the late 1870s, long before concern for national education reached critical mass in the 1890s and produced its first milestone in *The Economic Evaluation of National Education* (1896). Born of a collective effort, the book argued, based on statistics, that state investments in education were not "acts of philanthropy," but a necessity. Economist Aleksandr Chuprov argued in his chapter that economic development progressed in direct proportion to professional education.[37] Ahead of its time, Slonimskii's emphasis on the importance of the human factor in economics formed the nucleus of his idea of humane modernization, which he would articulate over the next thirty years.

Throughout the 1880s, while Konstantin Arsen'ev monitored the evolution of self-government and factory legislation, Slonimskii explored sociological questions with an eye toward the unspoken assumptions behind European intellectual trends. Socialism fascinated Slonimskii not as an ideal, but as a political tool that wise European statesmen used to offset the bourgeoisie by bringing broader social groups into the process of government. Germany, Austria-Hungary, and Italy, "the most monarchical governments of Western Europe," were also the most tolerant of socialist ideas because their leaders "directed changes along purely economic lines around the ancient pillars of political organization," Slonimskii argued. The landed aristocracy and the

clergy used socialist rhetoric to wrest from the wealthy bourgeoisie its political achievements—hence "Christian" and "conservative" socialism. That the
European monarchies sought support from the poorest classes was not sur-
prising: "The monarchy emerged from the feudal period with a bourgeois
hue; it may emerge from the bourgeois era with a national-socialist shade."[38]
Written in 1884, these lines were ominously prophetic.

Some Russian statesmen in the 1880s were already thinking along European lines. Finance minister Nikolai Bunge encouraged the state to ensure a
wide distribution of profits by directing them into production—socialism
"could not be eliminated, only directed."[39] According to Bunge, socialism's
strength lay in its potential to coordinate and direct all social forces toward
achieving social well-being. Socio-economic stability was a practical affair,
not a scientific endeavor, Bunge argued, and in this, he foreshadowed Eduard
Bernstein's evolutionary socialism. It is no surprise then that Bunge's ministry spearheaded factory legislation in the 1880s.

In 1883, Slonimskii also began to explore private ownership of land in Russia, which he approached neither as de facto necessary, nor philosophically
illegitimate, but instead as a historical evolution of the institution of private
property.[40] Slonimskii got the inspiration for this approach from German
historical economists Karl Knies, Johann Karl Rodbertus, and Adolph Wagner, whom Sergei Witte also respected for emphasizing the historical relativ-
ity of economic systems.[41] Slonimskii gave the historical economists credit
for "relativizing" the property question, but criticized them for leaving its
development to "historical factors, as if that would naturally resolve the land
ownership debate."[42]

Slonimskii proposed splitting the concept of land into its spatial component (space on which people and things exist) and its financial component
(as a source of revenue). In the first case, land had a political and social character, whereas the second instance concerned private and economic rights.
The debate about land ownership often took on the form of two monologues,
Slonimskii argued, because proponents of private property saw in their position the principle of individual liberty, while those who saw land as a common
human habitat failed to perceive its inherent economic utility.[43] By equating
capital and land, European law facilitated the use of land for strictly financial
operations, although agricultural productivity could never compete with re-
turns on capital. Slonimskii proposed "special land-tenure and inheritance
laws [to] regulate ownership by giving significant space to the element of public interest."[44] Land speculation in France, Germany, and Austria-Hungary,

for example, decreased the amount of individually owned land and created latifundia with which individual farmers could not compete. As a result, they organized themselves into agricultural associations for pooling together resources—"where the commune's last traces have disappeared, its pale shadow was artificially recreated."[45] The European peasantry already had the chance to establish its private rights to land before resuscitating agricultural societies, whereas in Russia, Emancipation preserved the commune for tax purposes without restructuring the legal principles underlying land ownership.[46] Slonimskii suggested two reforms. First, he pointed to the example of the American Homestead and Exemption Laws that prevented creditors from seizing farmers' lands and property essential to labor and survival. Second, he suggested that taxation become a function of peasant income, not property value.[47]

Slonimskii maintained that by 1890, most Western European economists agreed that three central problems undermined agriculture. First, the legacy of Roman law did not distinguish between land ownership and other private property. Second, "one-sided individualism" triumphed over common interests. And third, credit and tax law—especially concerning arrears—had become outdated.[48] Capitalism took advantage of agriculture because the law did not protect the rural laborer from claims on his property—the creditor wielded disproportionate power over the debtor. Slonimskii suggested that in Russia, as in Europe, agricultural law should become an entity unto itself, like commercial and railway law. The first step in this direction was to peg agricultural micro-credit to productivity and profits (as commercial and industrial credit was), not to property. The second step was to prevent the justice system from becoming a tool in the hands of creditors "armed with formal documents" who used the courts to strip peasants of their last possessions. The law had to place human survival above "capital yield," and the courts had to consider the circumstances of every case. The "narrowly formalistic" interpretation of credit documents was inappropriate in an empire in which the majority of the population was illiterate.[49] It was up to the state to introduce these changes, Slonimskii believed, for the zemstvos to implement them, and for local courts to enforce compliance.

At no point did Slonimskii's proposals threaten the gentry's land rights. Nevertheless, he argued that by the mid-1880s the gentry's attitude toward Emancipation had switched from acquiescence to opposition. It had become abundantly clear to many landowners by this time that the economic foundation had forever disappeared from under their feet and the disgruntled din from the countryside grew louder in defense of "one-sided estate interests."[50]

Slonimskii accused the gentry of abandoning its natural ally, the peasantry, although the money economy threatened both. Unlike the German Junkers, Slonimskii argued, the Russian landed nobility lacked the practical under-standing of agriculture and was disorganized and impulsive in the pursuit of its interests. As a result, it pursued contradictory policies defending private property rights and opposing peasant ownership of land, protecting its pos-sessions and acting as an ally of commercial interests, demanding gentry privileges and supporting protective tariffs. Therefore, the artificial antago-nism of landowner and peasant existed only for those who treated their land as a guarantee for bank loans or sold commodities (such as timber) for im-mediate gain. With his articles, Slonimskii reinforced *Herald* liberalism's inclusive loyalties.

PROGRESS AND PLURALISM

An economic relativist, Slonimskii erred on the side of practice instead of ide-ology. In 1888, he published a programmatic article about the staunchly pro-laissez-faire Paris group that centered around the *Journal des économistes* and the Collège de France—Paul Leroy-Beaulieu, Gustave de Molinari, Yves Guyot, and Léon Say—which made it abundantly clear that Russian liberal-ism would not follow the classical liberal path.[51] Slonimskii pointed to bour-geois, or "trade-industrial," economists as the party guiltiest of ideological excesses in treating free competition as a natural law that had permeated human society since its origins.[52] Slonimskii agreed with Molinari's criticism of protectionism because it forced men to view "foreigners as competitors and enemies," treated economics as a zero-sum process, and fanned "narrow nationalism."[53] However, Slonimskii disagreed with Molinari's demand that the state withdraw from economics completely. Free trade, according to Slonimskii, was insufficient to guarantee "solidarity between nations and the unity of enlightened humanity."[54] Moreover, Slonimskii questioned the valid-ity of any universal standard of socio-economic evolution along with the stigma that deviance from it implied.

Slonimskii's article became a milestone that reemphasized the social ori-entation of *Herald* liberalism—some scholars have labeled it "social liberal-ism"—which envisioned the state as much more than an impartial economic judge and leveler.[55] The review also demonstrated that Slonimskii drew no cultural line and recognized no gradient between Russia and the West—the West was itself full of lines and gradients. Unlike Russian conservatives,

Slonimskii did not perceive change as destabilization or irreparable corruption and eschewed alarmist evaluations of Russia's economic development. Most importantly, Slonimskii refused to see economics as the ultimate standard of human activity on the international as well as the personal level—there was much more to civilization than its earnings reports and the density of its railroads.

Between the lines, Slonimskii was searching for new standards with which to define, evaluate, and justify progress. Furthermore, he began to question the assumption of convergent economic development with Europe as the universal model. Could Russia achieve Western production levels without compromising its cultural values? Marx himself had not been clear on the issue. In the introduction to the first edition of *Capital*, he argued that every developed country showed "the image of its own future" to the less developed one. Reacting to Iulii Zhukovskii's review of his work in the *Herald*, however, Marx wrote to *Notes of the Fatherland* in 1877 warning the Russians not to apply Western European schema to their society.[56] When Slonimskii criticized the ideology of progress, he not only used Marx's ideas to criticize economic ideology in general, but he also targeted the Finance Ministry, which aimed to replicate foreign economic achievements without the domestic conditions to do so.

Attempting to define the individual's place in Russia's modernization project, Slonimskii turned his attention from economics to theories of progress. He disagreed with the tendency of Victorian anthropologists to theorize about man's prehistoric ancestors by examining primitive societies as missing links in the development of the ape into the European.[57] The assumption of convergent evolutionism—that societies evolve upwards towards the European ideal—alarmed Slonimskii because of its implications in relation to "backward" social groups or countries. The Anglo-Saxon socio-economic model was a standard to which even Marx subscribed. Indeed, in his eulogy, Engels gave Marx credit for extending Darwin's theory to the study of the inner dynamics and change in human society.[58] Slonimskii did not have to look far for examples of how social Darwinism, which permeated Victorian ethnography, turned into practice during the scramble for Africa during the last quarter of the nineteenth century. Indeed, the British economic historian J. A. Hobson wrote of the British Empire: "So easily we glide from natural history to ethics, and find in utility a moral sanction for the race struggle. Now, Imperialism is nothing but this natural history doctrine regarded from the standpoint of one's own nation."[59]

Popular evolutionism was a dangerous underestimation of cultural variety, Slonimskii believed. And as long as sociology and economics used subjective methods of inquiry, Slonimskii argued, they would produce wildly inconsistent and impracticable results, whereas David Ricardo's "objective analysis of value, labor, and capital" had "helped the workers' cause immeasurably more than all the subjective defenders of labor taken together."[60] Slonimskii's reviews of Russian and foreign ethnographers and sociologists became the starting point of a major intellectual project to reconceptualize progress, but denying the assumption of socio-economic convergence demanded one of two things: either a new non-Western reference point or a pluralistic development model. In the late 1880s, Slonimskii began to explore conceptualizations that would allow backwardness and otherness to balance—and even cancel—each other out. This new way of looking at things would show that Russia could progress by tapping into its native potential and thereby avoid the cultural stigma of falling short of a foreign standard.

Serious social theorizing, Slonimskii believed, demanded a multilayered analysis of social phenomena and a synthesis of global historical trends.[61] Slonimskii agreed with the positivist belief that the intellectual supremacy of the scientific attitude was the most direct path to social progress, but he did not share Nikolai Mikhailovskii's vision of a utopia dominated by rural egalitarianism and primitive cooperation. None of the *Herald* editors believed that the peasant commune was a higher type of social organization at a lower stage of evolution, as Mikhailovskii argued, and none wanted to elevate this particular type of social organization to a higher stage of development. In this, Slonimskii was completely in harmony with Arsen'ev's preference for breaking down the artificial barrier between the peasant *volost'* (a unit of peasant local self-rule) and the zemstvo by creating an all-estate *volost'* and integrating the peasantry into all administrative structures by further economic decentralization of the countryside.

Slonimskii found in American economist Henry George a solid sociological theoretician, and wrote a lengthy review of his *Progress and Poverty* (1879), a study of industrial cycles and potential remedies. Slonimskii welcomed George's exploration of the paradox contained in the book's title and agreed with the author's conclusion that the "struggle for existence" theory so prevalent in the late nineteenth century was in essence "optimistic fatalism."[62] George postulated that "equality and social justice" comprised the second condition for progress after association. The root of social inequality for George was the private ownership of land, which absorbed all surplus capital from its laborers and produced unjustified profits for its owners.[63] Slonimskii agreed with George's diagnosis, but considered his solution—to confiscate land rents and redirect them into state coffers—simplistic because it assumed that state and society were synonymous.[64] Progress must start instead from an internal social principle, Slonimskii argued, in other words from the ability to understand one's capabilities and to develop them accordingly.[65] To do so, an active social debate had to explore alternative paths of socio-economic development, which is what the *Herald* offered to its readers.

THE ZEMSTVO AS CIVIL SOCIETY'S SANCTUARY

Having defended the pluralistic approach to socio-economic development strategies, Slonimskii began to examine the factors that made Russia's experience unique and even hinted at the possibility that some of them might make political progress more promising than in Western Europe. His conclusions were remarkably similar to those of Alexis de Tocqueville, who gave enormous credit for the success of the American political system to the functionality of local self-government. Following Tocqueville's logic, Russia's zemstvos gave cause for an optimistic prognosis for the growth and maturity of civil society.

As usual, Slonimskii began his examination of Russia from outside by identifying the two principles of late-nineteenth-century Western political culture: the blending into one another of state and society on the one hand and the triumph of individualism on the other. By depriving the individual of a social network, the second principle reinforced the first. In the economic sphere, Slonimskii argued, individualism led to the triumph of "rapacious instincts over the moral and social" ones. His diagnosis of this phenomenon's political consequences was creative—the decline of local autonomy, the extreme empowerment of the state mechanism, and state centralization.[66] He wrote:

> Without the cultivating influence of self-government, citizens with full rights represent a very unstable mass, which self-serving and popular leaders direct from one side to another, sometimes against the real interests of society. Without the habit of discussing the local needs of their communities and provinces, people are that much less likely to practice the delicate calculation and consistency of more abstract questions and goals of national policy. They follow accidental moods that take hold of society and which certain journalists support;

they fall prey to apparitions of external dangers and conflicts, which the press
inflates in its pursuit of novelty and effect.[67]

Published in September 1889, these lines had a double meaning. On the
one hand, they were a barely veiled criticism of the land captains whom the
July statutes had introduced to oversee the zemstvos. On a deeper level, however, Slonimskii was articulating a form of civic participation outside politics
in the Western sense. His views challenged the Russian statists, represented
by the late Konstantin Kavelin, who had argued that Russia's historical progress consisted in the gradual dissolution of patriarchal bonds and their re-
placement by the juridical order of the centralized state, which gave more
room for individual freedom, but undermined civil society.[68] Like Tocqueville
before him, Slonimskii distrusted the combination of mass politics and executive centralization. Local self-government was liberty's real guarantee in his
opinion.

The worst symptom of state centralization and individualism was nationalism, which had undergone a great metamorphosis in the late nineteenth
century from popular to state-sponsored, or as Slonimskii put it, "from revolutionary to conservative and even reactionary."[69] Anticipating J. A. Hobson,
Slonimskii argued that the militancy of modern nationalism fostered a siege
mentality and the conviction that all national interests, especially economic
ones, functioned in a zero-sum field wherein one state's success became
another's loss.[70] Slonimskii called "mystical" the assumption that the "unity
and organicism" of the state was the highest form of "personality"—an idea
that G. W. F. Hegel had championed and German economist Lorenz Stein
resurrected in the guise of his theory of "organic government," which equated
the tax-collecting interests of the state with that of the population. Slonimskii was suspicious of the extent to which some German economists had
identified state goals with social interests.[71]

By 1890, Slonimskii had articulated a balance between state involvement in economic affairs and local self-government's role in balancing its
excesses. He could not have chosen a better time to address these issues, as
the famine of 1891–1892 brought to light all the deficiencies of Russia's post-
Emancipation economic development and exposed the risks of heavy dependence on a precarious agricultural base while competing in a global market
with other grain producers, such as Canada, Australia, and the United States.
In the debate about the "agrarian crisis," which became increasingly important during the last quarter of the nineteenth century, the *Herald* firmly

maintained that the crisis was real and serious.[72] As a result, the journal raised the inevitable question of why poor harvests led to worse famines in Russia than in other European states. As a landowner from Penza province, Prince Dmitrii Drutskoi-Sokolninskii, argued in his "Articles from the Countryside," which the *Herald* published in the 1880s and early 1890s, that the problem was not only international prices, but also the peasantry's indigence brought on by an unreasonable taxes, which the state ploughed into industrial development.[73] Since Russia could not be isolated from the global market, the state had to find some mechanism to integrate local interests with global trade patterns. By the late nineteenth century, Russia faced the classic development problem—trade had integrated it into the global market, but the overwhelming majority of the population remained peripheral to the profits from this trade. What could facilitate its incorporation? The *Herald*'s examination of the famine would demonstrate in practice that the zemstvo could become the first and basic link of a complex mechanism of integration into the world economy.

8

〜◇〜

Solving the Agrarian Crisis
The Famine of 1891–1892 and the Zemstvo

It is textbook knowledge that the famine of 1891–1892 marked a milestone in the evolution of the public sphere in Russia.[1] After a series of localized crop failures in 1889 and 1890, a broader one struck sixteen of Russia's European provinces in the autumn of 1891.[2] Reports about rural conditions reinforced the moral imperative to question development policies. As the extent of the crop failure became apparent towards the end of 1891 and it became clear that its scale would cause starvation, the din of criticism grew. In its twenty-fifth year by this time, the *Herald of Europe* was ready to do battle, for which it had prepared by cutting its teeth on its critique of Tsar Alexander III's counter-reforms.

As long as the state's economic reforms coincided with political reaction under Alexander III, the intelligentsia's dissatisfaction aimed at the whole without distinguishing its parts. This combination sustained disillusioned but unvanquished Populist sensibilities and simultaneously provided fertile soil from which Russian Marxism drew its strength. The volatile mixture of political conservatism, accelerating economic development, and liberal opposition boiled under reaction's lid until the famine provided an excuse to vocalize the discontent and to debate economic policies openly. As the events of 1891–1892 demonstrated, the state had ignored the enormous potential that the zemstvos provided to soften the side effects of modernization, which most people believed was responsible for the conditions that led to the famine. For the *Herald*, the famine provided a chance once again to urge the public and the state to cooperate. Instead of allocating blame, the journal focused on famine prevention, but emphasized economic empowerment over political liberalization. The tragic famine sparked the debate that sharpened liberalism's language and clarified its aims by questioning the ultimate aim of modernization and the role of the zemstvo in this process.

Some modern scholars have reevaluated the state's intentions behind the zemstvo reform of 1864 by exploring the limited extent to which the government allowed or wished to encourage a genuine decentralization or devolution of power to the local level.[3] Economists and statisticians were aware of the government's distrust of the zemstvos at the time and the debate slowly gathered momentum as the nineteenth century drew to a close. At its root was the fundamental issue of the relationship between local self-government and modernization. On the one hand, the zemstvos and town councils could stimulate corporate identity, urban self-confidence, and economic and cultural progress across all sectors of society, including the peasantry. On the other hand, the state's strained relationship with local self-government was often symbolic of the failure, or unwillingness, of the tsarist regime to adapt to change and to establish an effective rapport with society. The state took the issue very seriously—the two statutes on local self-government of 1864 and 1890 comprised 120 and 138 articles respectively.

Arsen'ev treated the zemstvo as a barometer of social reactions to state policies. The weakening of the pulse of zemstvo life in the 1880s was symptomatic of alienation from the state, he argued, which allowed revolutionary groups to siphon off the energy and talent that should have served local self-government instead. Russian society and the press became almost indifferent to the role of local self-government until 1886, when conservative encroachments on it galvanized a counter-reaction.[4] The state crowned its infringement on local autonomy in 1889 with the introduction of the land captains—centrally appointed officials who monitored and approved zemstvo decisions. By the Statute of 1890, the government changed the election rules to favor the gentry, made all administrative posts appointed, and allowed governors to block zemstvo decisions. Although few instances of actual encroachments on local self-government took place, the law made administrative arbitrariness possible.

Instead of laying the foundation for a form of economic democracy through the zemstvos, the state turned them into administrative extensions. In order to save money, the state had outsourced administrative functions to provincial and urban self-government in 1864 and thereby encouraged the development of provincial society, but it also wanted to control local institutions and ensure above all that they perceived state obligations as greater priorities than local needs. The center feared the independence of local officials and subordinated them to appointed representatives and to ministries in the capital. Since the reign of Peter the Great, in fact, the Petersburg bureaucracy had developed a rich tradition of centralism when it came to local government, which only time or tragic circumstances could alter.

During the 1880s, conservative bureaucrats wanted to turn the zemstvo into an extension of the imperial administration and turn local administrators into state agents. Conservative publicists such as Prince Vladimir Meshcherskii used the inevitable mistakes and abuses of power by the zemstvos to justify tighter state control over them.[5] Arsen'ev fought tirelessly to draw his readers' attention to the legal changes underway and even tended to idealize the original institutions created in 1864 as loci of opposition to the autocracy. In January 1891, he warned that Russia stood to lose not the "terminally sick and dying" institution that the conservative press portrayed, but the original 1864 version that was strong and impervious to "modern influences," by which Arsen'ev meant radicalism.[6] The kind of "opposition to the autocracy" centered on the zemstvo that Arsen'ev was describing went to the heart of the unique liberal world view that the *Herald* group articulated, with economic activity as its essential component and the zemstvo as the mechanism for reinvesting wealth into the communities that generated it in the first place.

This, however, was not the intention of the Finance Ministry. Although finance minister Vyshnegradskii's economic policies led to an unprecedented industrial boom in the 1890s, they had serious defects. By the last quarter of the nineteenth century, peasants constituted just over three-quarters of the empire's population, while massive agricultural exports maintained a favorable trade balance that stabilized and strengthened the ruble. The Finance Ministry believed that this stability would attract European investments into Russia's heavy industry, which survived behind protective tariffs up to that point. The Ministry expected the peasants to weather the hard times, while it bought abundant grain cheaply immediately after the harvest and made a profit by selling it abroad at higher prices. Simultaneously, prohibitive import tariffs raised the cost of foreign agricultural tools and other agricultural necessities. Rural taxes subsidized industry, although the peasantry cared nothing about industrial strength, macroeconomic stability, and competition on foreign markets, let alone Russia's place among the elite club of European powers. By the late 1880s, state policy had split the national economy in two and made parasitism, not symbiosis, the modus operandi—Russian industry flourished at the expense of the village.[7]

What opposition there was to this state of affairs during the 1880s came from landowners who were also on the losing end of industrial favoritism. The nobility-dominated State Council became the first defender of zemstvo autonomy between 1880 and 1890.[8] As Russia entered the 1890s, the gentry's interests determined zemstvo agendas: financial credit for landowners, wholesale grain trade regulations, grain storehouses, stricter punishments for un-fulfilled labor contracts, and more favorable railroad tariffs. Peasant interests remained in the background.[9] The central issue in the 1880s therefore was not so much the survival of local self-government, but whose interests it served and how it did so. The *Herald of Europe* had opposed all encroachments on zemstvo independence consistently since the 1870s, and by 1890 began to bring peasant interests to the forefront and justified its case with economic arguments. Arsen'ev was ready for the debate that the famine of 1891–1892 inspired.

THE CONTEXT: ARSEN'EV'S 1882 LIBERAL PROGRAM

The journal's stand on several important issues in the 1880s deserves a closer examination in order to explain the attitudes and expectations with which the *Herald* approached the events of 1891–1892. An article in an 1882 issue of *Rus* argued that Russian liberalism had no definition or program and that there was no such thing as a "liberal party."[10] In response, Arsen'ev published a "liberal program" in the "Domestic Survey" of the *Herald*'s April 1882 issue, wherein he listed freedom of the press and freedom of conscience as liberalism's primary demands. Anticipating right-wing accusations of disloyalty to the state, he distinguished treachery from opposition and disagreement from calumny. Personal freedom and the inviolability of the individual were next in Arsen'ev's hierarchy—criticism of administrative arbitrariness had been the *Herald*'s dominant theme from its inception in 1866.

Progress in popular education formed another aspect of Arsen'ev's program. Referring to the educational counter-reforms of Katkov and education minister Tolstoi, Arsen'ev favored specialized, professional education.[11] He wrote, "A national school, developing freely and open to all is the first, but by far not the only, condition of national well-being."[12] He also called for a reorganization of local self-government through the establishment of the all-estate canton (*volost'*), a self-government unit below the zemstvo, and the lowering of property requirements for zemstvo elections.[13] Anticipating accusations of liberal bias, Arsen'ev added that the liberal press was not blind to the zemstvos' mistakes.

The all-estate canton first came up in the early 1880s when Loris-Melikov established the Kakhanov Commission (1881–1885), which proposed the creation of new and inclusive administrative units at the village and canton levels. The *Herald* wholeheartedly defended the commission's proposals and the all-estate canton acquired a central place in Arsen'ev's "Domestic Surveys," in which he argued that the council should become the "center of gravity" of local self-government. It would answer to the district zemstvo, but also enjoy a degree of independence.[14] Arsen'ev pictured the all-estate canton as an organic link between rural society and the state, which would act as the foundation for a harmonious administrative structure resting on a wide popular base.[15] Indeed, some scholars have argued convincingly that the local canton courts enabled Russian peasants to learn the skills and habits of citizenship.[16] The Kakhanov Commission's conclusions about the councils, however, proved unacceptable to Alexander III's government, which dissolved the body without implementing any of its proposals.[17]

Arsen'ev argued further that liberalism aimed to (1) uphold common property as a guarantee against rural pauperization through landlessness; (2) transfer more land to peasants with state and local help; (3) abolish restrictions on the colonization of land; (4) establish small peasant credit institutions; (5) abolish passport control and collective responsibility for taxes; (6) lower redemption payments where they exceeded the profit from the land; (7) abolish the soul tax; and (8) lower taxes on the peasantry by simultaneously raising them on the wealthier groups and cutting unproductive government spending. The liberals also supported a government of laws, to which end Arsen'ev favored the establishment of an Imperial Council of Representatives, although he did not clarify whether it was to be legislative or advisory. He warned, however, that it would take years of trial and error to make the new administrative bodies function smoothly and efficiently.[18]

Several assumptions underlay Arsen'ev's program. His analysis suggested that the incomplete conceptualization and inconsistent implementation of the Great Reforms had led to the regicide of 1881. Russian liberalism's immediate aim was therefore to complete the socio-economic changes that the Great Reforms had initiated. Although Arsen'ev was quite vague about the path along which economic development was to proceed, he was convinced that the victory of gentry, industrial, and urban interests over those of the peasantry boded ill for the future—something that the Populists also argued. The state's principal aim, Arsen'ev believed, should be to prevent social polarization and to minimize the rural costs of economic progress. Arsen'ev believed that the Great Reforms had introduced more humane and democratic principles into imperial administration, but civil and criminal legislation failed to keep pace with them. Writing immediately after the assassination of Alexander II, Arsen'ev urged the state to encourage more, not less, civil participation in administration, which would eradicate the last vestiges of serfdom in the form of the civic sloth from which political extremists drew their energy. Only with a complete overhaul of civil and administrative legislation and further reforms of self-government and local authority could the autocracy reestablish social stability. Arsen'ev denied that the majority of the population had any revolutionary tendencies.[19]

The 1882 program was a list of well-intentioned but vague ideals by which the *Herald of Europe* stood firmly during Alexander III's reign. Beginning in March of 1880, Arsen'ev wrote monthly commentaries on contemporary events in the journal's "Domestic Survey," which examined the problems and paradoxes of the new legislation pouring out of Saint Petersburg. He covered changes in zemstvo organization, urban statutes, labor rights, and rural taxes, which he examined meticulously as he weighed the pros and cons, the shades and overtones, and the practical results of both imperial and local legislation. Traces of his program were always behind Arsen'ev's thorough commentary, although it is sometimes overwhelmed by exhaustive detail and legalistic language. It was not until the famine of 1891–1892, however, that Arsen'ev crystallized his program's ideals and made them concrete and practical.

From the moment that Arsen'ev joined the journal in 1880 until 1901, he contributed 235 "Domestic Surveys" and 203 "Social Surveys." By 1891, he had dedicated most of the "360 [sixteen-page] printer's sheets" that he had composed to registering administrative encroachments upon zemstvo rights, repelling attacks by the conservative press, and systematically propagandizing the economic and cultural needs of local self-government.[20] He saw his monthly work as "dull and boring" and complained about introducing "little that is constructive, new, and original."[21] Indeed, the "Domestic Surveys" are not page-turners, but they contain the rudiments of the *Herald*'s liberal sensibility. Arsen'ev had first-hand knowledge of local self-government. As a member of the Luga district and Petersburg provincial zemstvos, he pushed for a four-year elementary school program, the abolition of corporal punishment for peasants, and the right for the zemstvo to petition the state directly for agricultural aid. Arsen'ev's dedication to peasant interests justified the argument he made to Populist Vasilii Vorontsov that Russian liberals were different from their western European colleagues who were primarily interested in defending their class interests.

Arsen'ev was also the link between the provincial and urban intelligentsia through informal meetings of the "zemstvo circle," which began in 1883 in Saint Petersburg and introduced zemstvo members from many provinces to literary figures, statisticians, and even students. According to contemporaries, the gatherings brought together the progressive youth of Saint Petersburg. Among the regular visitors were ethnologist Sergei Ol'denburg, liberal economist and *Herald* contributor Nikolai Vodovozov, Marxist Pyotr Struve, scientist Vladimir Vernadskii, and Pypin. The debates concerned local affairs but avoided politics.[22] The liberals, one member remembered, "tried to organize the youth for work in the zemstvo."[23]

When in 1890 the meetings moved to Moscow to avoid surveillance, most of the Petersburg intelligentsia stopped attending, but Arsen'ev often traveled to the old capital. Far from Petersburg, the members began to address more immediate concerns such as educational reform, the legal status of the peasantry, and the possibility for greater inter-zemstvo cooperation. A comparison of Arsen'ev's notes for the "Domestic Surveys" demonstrates that the debates at the zemstvo gatherings affected his choice of topics.[24] He attended regularly because he believed that only participation in local self-government could overcome endemic political apathy in Russia.[25] The famine of 1891–1892, however, finally gave Arsen'ev the excuse to combine his 1882 "program" with his personal experiences in local self-government and to articulate a blueprint of a socio-economic democracy that included all estates and classes.

The Zemstvos during the Famine

As the harvest failure unfolded in the summer of 1891, the conservative and liberal press clashed over the legacy of the Great Reforms. During the scramble to assess the damage in their locales, the zemstvos discovered that emergency grain reserves were insufficient to feed the population through the end of the year, which also meant that there would be no seed for the winter and spring sowing. Predictably, the responsibility of local self-government became the central and most divisive issue in the debate between conservatives and liberals, the latter reiterating once again that the tragedy of the famine could become the basis for cooperation between the state and the enormous mobilization of local forces through the zemstvos.

An August 1891 issue of Meshcherskii's ultra-conservative *Citizen* (*Grazhdanin*, 1872–1879, 1882–1914) blamed the zemstvo (and its entire twenty-five-year history) for frivolously spending money on public schools instead of preparing emergency grain supplies.[26] Arsen'ev responded that only zemstvo statistical works could ensure a successful campaign against the crisis. Modern historians have identified two basic methods to combat famine: traditional food storage networks and economic incentives to direct grain to the appropriate locales. The last reform of the relief system statutes in Russia had taken place in 1866, but by the late 1880s, taxes and redemption payments on the peasantry prevented the accumulation of grain reserves.[27] Arsen'ev clearly favored the economic approach to famine relief, but he had to remind conservative critics that it was not within the zemstvo's responsibilities to prohibit or encourage the production and sale of food. It was the Finance Ministry's responsibility to lower grain transportation tariffs, although only communication between the zemstvos could create a network sufficiently informed and efficient to inform the center which locales needed the grain most.[28]

The term "famine" first appeared in the *Herald*'s August 1891 "Domestic Survey" because Arsen'ev did not think it too early to sound the alarm bells about mass starvation in the hardest-hit areas.[29] Following the *Herald*'s lead, the Russian press began to explore the role of the land captains in assessing local needs and directing the relief effort. In answer to another article in the *Citizen*, Arsen'ev argued that the most serious problem was local distribution of aid to villages and micro-distribution to households and individuals—too broad a task for the land captains alone. Arsen'ev argued in favor of local, popularly elected officials who were closer to the peasantry. He believed that the need for all-estate cantons became especially acute in times of crisis that necessitated rapid communication.[30]

Arsen'ev pointed out that the land captains were Interior Ministry appointees and since the Russian people were distrustful of new faces in general—and officially sanctioned ones especially—new appointees needed time to acquaint themselves with the area and win the peasantry's confidence. Canton-level officials had an advantage because they already knew their locale and cared about their policies' effects on their reputations. Of the appointed land captains in the provinces in 1891, 50 percent were former military men and their military ethos created tensions with the peasantry. Among landowner land captains, many were also uneducated. Locally elected administrators could easily fill what Arsen'ev believed was a dearth of qualified personnel.[31]

Arsen'ev also argued that the state should encourage local social initiative and only punish the misuse of funds and abuses of authority. He welcomed the increasing number of private relief organizations that had already appeared before the Ministry of Interior officially permitted them in September 1891. However, state attempts to direct local initiative would be counterproductive, Arsen'ev warned.[32] The experience of the 1880–1881 crop failure had demonstrated the effectiveness of local initiative functioning with sufficient freedom to encourage individual enthusiasm and energy.[33] Reiterating his support, Arsen'ev wrote in November 1891: "The more varied the sources of relief, the deeper and wider the aid movement, the more chances of its success."[34] Regardless of how large the scale of private relief, however, Arsen'ev admitted that it could never match what the state could offer through the zemstvos by increasing their revenues with the implementation of a progressive income tax. In the mid-1880s, the government's proposal to withhold a percentage of all civil servant, non-governmental, estate, and stock-based organization salaries above two thousand rubles had already met with a storm of protest in the conservative press and was shelved. Many zemstvos had supported an all-estate tax since 1870.[35] Arsen'ev believed it timely to resurrect the idea.[36]

In Count Leo Tolstoy's plea for private assessments of grain reserves in every canton, Moscow's conservative press perceived a conspiracy against the state's directing role in the relief effort. Tolstoy did not question the state's abilities, Arsen'ev argued, he merely proposed a faster and more efficient way to estimate local needs. The *Moscow News* (*Moskovskie vedomosti*, 1756–1917) insisted that peasants would mislead private citizens by giving incorrect information. Arsen'ev answered that the speed and efficiency of relief were crucial and that good works would only reinforce the state's efforts, not impede them. If nothing else, therefore, Tolstoy's call for "social initiative" was a welcome antidote to a culture saturated with a tendency to act only when commanded.[37] It is remarkable how similar Arsen'ev's arguments sound to the Populist—and even anarchist—call for "spontaneous self-initiative."[38] The crucial difference was of course that Arsen'ev addressed educated members of society, not the peasants themselves.

When Tolstoy began opening private soup kitchens and called for their proliferation, Arsen'ev supported the idea, comparing the kitchens to practical schools. Most provincial governments had no time to learn how to establish them, but individuals could visit privately run soup kitchens, learn through observing them or working in them, and then transplant the institutions. Soup kitchens could become hands-on learning centers releasing threads in all directions. With time, private aid could develop into areas such as child care, care for the sick and elderly, aid to domestic and cottage industry, and the purchase of cattle and implements. Arsen'ev cautiously added, however, that having "come out in full support of total freedom for private aid, we in no way mean to overlook state efforts, which dwarf private initiative (72 versus 4 million rubles)."[39] Ever circumspect, Arsen'ev did not want to give the censors any excuses to descry belittlement of the state's contribution to the relief effort.

Arsen'ev supported thorough investigations instead of extraordinary measures against crimes committed during the famine. More transparency and fewer obstacles to uncovering "unpleasant facts" would make the legal system function properly, he argued. Dmitrii Samarin had proposed that local authorities implement obligatory statistics-gathering accompanied by severe penalties for false information. Arsen'ev proposed employing elected zemstvo officials for this task because they would be more effective executing it out of moral duty rather than obligation. Legal reform had not developed sufficiently for the state to punish misinformation, which would alienate the population further and encourage audacious evasions of the law.[40]

Arsen'ev came out in favor of public works projects, but only as long as they were voluntary, transparent, and locally based, encouraging peasants to stay close to their families. Mending local dirt roads would constitute the priority, since potholes were the most serious impediments to transporting grain. The tasks had to be of the simplest and non-specialized kind, such as working with spades and transporting materials. Arsen'ev considered grand projects, such as building railways, repairing riverbeds, excavating river ports, and ameliorating soil as too complex and less urgent than repairing local roads and bridges.[41] He admitted, however, that such unreasonable projects frequently originated in zemstvos themselves as they scrambled to use the Interior Ministry's offers to fund public works. The basic idea of public works was a sound one and had been used to advantage in the past, but the existing administrative structure provided no apparatus for managing such projects. As a result, the state had to work out everything from the top down in a very short time and implement it through regular administrative channels, which were in the hands of a small group of officials who could not adequately coordinate everything.[42] The center's dependence on ad hoc administrative appointments was proof of its inability to institutionalize functional administrative links, which it could have done easily through the zemstvos.

Arsen'ev made an example of the Nizhnii Novgorod Relief Commission's exhaustive publications of findings and reports. He wrote, "In a time like this, the role of the saving hand should not constitute a monopoly, no obstacles or snares should be placed between the needy and those ready to help."[43] The Nizhnii relief effort was remarkable for its transparency and demonstrated the advantages of the provincial authorities, the zemstvos, and private forces coming together voluntarily at a time of need. Arsen'ev praised Governor Nikolai Baranov of Nizhnii Novgorod for admitting that he shared his burdens "with comrades, not subordinates." The Samara provincial government followed the opposite path, however, by taking into its hands the entire relief effort and turning the zemstvos into executive outgrowths. As a result, its achievements lagged far behind Nizhnii's.[44] Cooperation between the state, the zemstvos, and social initiative was clearly an advantage, Arsen'ev believed.

THE JOURNAL AS RELIEF COORDINATOR

When it came to private involvement in the relief effort, Arsen'ev practiced what he preached. A large portion of his 1891–1892 personal correspondence deals with the allocation of relief funds that his friends and colleagues sent to the *Herald* office in Saint Petersburg. Beginning in December 1891, Arsen'ev corresponded regularly with famous Russian mineralogist Vladimir Vernadskii, who oversaw relief efforts in Tambov province from Moscow, where he organized regular zemstvo "discussions" and "lunches" and supplied Arsen'ev with minutes that made their way into the "Domestic Surveys."[45] Their man in Tambov was a certain retired V. V. Keller, who traveled all over Morshansk district and reported to Vernadskii exactly where to send the funds. In December 1891, Vernadskii and Arsen'ev channeled money into the district through the Literacy Committee, which organized a commission to help local preschoolers.[46] By January 1892, Keller reported that Boiarovka village no longer required relief and asked Arsen'ev's permission to redirect funds to Lipovka.[47] On January 12, 1892, Vernadskii informed Arsen'ev that unfortunately, most of the activity at the Literacy Committee revolved around publishing requests for aid in local papers and constant meetings about how to phrase the appeals: "It is horrible when you feel how your work is constrained and tied down."[48] Better news came from Morshansk district in February when Keller informed Vernadskii that local landowners had begun to hire peasants to do extra work on their estates. The better the operation was organized, the more people donated, Keller believed: "It seems to me that there are a lot of good people in Russia and the problem is that they cannot find each other due to enforced silence and fear."[49] Arsen'ev accepted all donations: eight rubles from a veterinarian in Kharkov province and ten rubles from General A. N. Ostrogorskii (which Pypin forwarded), one of Dmitrii Miliutin's closest advisors.[50] In April 1892, Arsen'ev sent 250 rubles to Voronezh province for soup kitchens and the local executor promised to forward to the *Russian News* (*Russkie vedomosti*, 1863–1918) a detailed account of the allocation of funds both for transparency and as an advertisement for potential donors.[51]

Arsen'ev's direct involvement in the famine relief effort became a testament to the hands-on attitude characteristic of the *Herald* group. In this, he followed in Stasiulevich's and Pypin's footsteps. That he was so closely involved in the day-to-day affairs of famine relief lent his articles not only emotional depth but also moral integrity. Arsen'ev's personal correspondence makes clear that he was abreast of what went on in the provinces. When he composed the "Domestic Survey" for the journal, he drew on his correspondence as well as his bureaucratic experience to present his readers with a full picture of the relief effort. Few analysts were as qualified as Arsen'ev to examine its social, economic and political implications.

FROM FAMINE TO REFORM

In the first months of 1892, the debate between the *Herald of Europe* and other publications shifted from zemstvo issues to the peasantry's relations with the state. Defending the peasants from accusations of excessive dependence on state aid in the *News* (*Novosti*, 1872–1918), Arsen'ev argued that the peasantry repaid annually not only its redemption debts but also the empire's foreign debt, which "the profits of state enterprises" did not cover.[52] As a result, the entire peasant population was indigent, although Russia's abundant land acted like a sponge that absorbed local poverty by distributing it equally among its many inhabitants.[53]

In Arsen'ev's opinion, the famine had uncovered a systemic problem in the Russian economy, which only the resurrection of the spirit of the 1860s—together with long-term and complex legal reforms—could remedy. He described the Russian economy as an organism with a chronic illness that had become acute by 1891–1892. In such a case, one treated first the aggravated

condition, that is, the famine, and afterward attacked the source of the initial
weakness—the national economy.[54]

In its own way, public participation in famine relief constituted a new
"going to the people" movement. This time, however, moral duty manifested
itself in material aid, not calls to revolution. The essential private contributions
were not the small donations, charity balls, or the "annoying solicitation
lists," but the quiet, small deeds that demanded personal sacrifices
and took place hourly all over the stricken areas. With a hint of Populism,
Arsen'ev encouraged Russians to abandon the city lifestyle, move into the
rural wilderness, examine the rural population's needs, and share its suffering,
which would constitute a personal investment in the struggle against
the famine. Thousands of people were doing it quietly, Arsen'ev argued, and
finding their reward and support in no more than the persistent execution of
their moral duty.[55]

Arsen'ev believed that the crop failure would not have struck with such
force had rural productivity been higher and the population better equipped
to deal with food shortages. This meant that zemstvo influence on economic
life had to increase. At the source of the rural crisis lay not the peasant's conservative
nature, Arsen'ev argued, but insufficient knowledge and poverty.
Arsen'ev held up the Moscow provincial zemstvo as an example of how to
spread enlightenment through its Provincial Economic Council and the Provincial
Economic Bureau—both organized in 1890. The agronomic section
introduced peasants to technical novelties in the areas of implements, seed
quality, crops, and grass sowing. The peasants reacted favorably, but had
insufficient funds to follow through.[56]

By early 1892, specialized studies of the famine's causes began to appear in
print, some of which proposed reforms. Arsen'ev examined some of these in
detail. He wrote specifically of two major works, *The State of Provisions* and
the *Harvest of 1891 in Nizhnii Novgorod Province*, published by the Moscow
and the Nizhnii provincial zemstvos, respectively. According to Arsen'ev,
both works agreed that the peasantry's general impoverishment began long
before the recent crop failure—unemployment and decreasing wages, the
shrinking of pastures, epizootics, and fires brought on the chronic malady in
Russia's agricultural sector. How could the state break the vicious cycle?[57]
In his memoirs, Arsen'ev recorded a zemstvo "lunch" he had attended in the
summer of 1892 in Saint Petersburg that explored agricultural problems and
solutions—"land shortage, the peasants' legal status, their ignorance and
alienation, and all forms of help within the zemstvo's powers."[58]

Reorganizing statistics on paper would achieve nothing, Arsen'ev argued in the summer of 1892, and only active exchanges of opinions among experts and witnesses would bring results. He maintained that Senate audits would be useful, but insufficient by themselves. In the immediate wake of the famine, Arsen'ev sought closure—an event that would allow zemstvo representatives to exchange opinions about crisis management. To this end, he proposed a conference in Saint Petersburg for administration and zemstvo officials from all regions of the empire. The free exchange of ideas would determine the famine's causes and work out measures against a similar calamity in the future.[59] In this, he anticipated the demands of Russia's "liberation movement" of the late 1890s. Nine addresses from zemstvos asked Nicholas II for institutionalized consultative zemstvo representation in the capital, which he curtly refused. This precipitated unsanctioned inter-zemstvo colloquia as a substitute for the suppressed annual zemstvo conferences—the first and only one of which took place in Nizhnii Novgorod in the summer of 1896.[60]

In January 1892, the Interior Ministry ordered a revision of the national foodstuffs statute by requesting that governors and relief committees articulate the most important problems concerning emergency grain supplies. Which local institutions should oversee the reserves? Who should compute and maintain grain elevator levels? What was the most effective organization of local distribution? How to identify the neediest households? How to maintain exact household statistics? The ministry even organized provincial conferences composed of local officials, zemstvo members, and other knowledgeable individuals to discuss these problems. Few government officials claimed that the state alone could manage local relief and few zemstvo members suggested that local self-government could handle the job by itself.[61]

The conclusions appeared in June 1892 as the "Official Report of the Special Committee on Famine Relief," which admitted that there was a shortage of local institutions to make and implement decisions—exactly what Arsen'ev had argued. He further maintained that the typhus epidemic's rapid and unpredictable spread in the wake of the famine also demanded functional local organizations to assess the infection's initial signs and to organize channels for outside medical help. However, the report did not go beyond proposing extraordinary commissions to deal with future crop failures. Arsen'ev argued instead that crises demanded not extraordinary measures, but elastic bodies that could immediately increase their cadres in response to pressing needs, a capability that only local institutions possessed, with their tradition of glasnost and proximity to the land guaranteeing efficient distribution. Nobody was born a zemstvo member, Arsen'ev wrote, but peasants and nobles acquired this experience through devotion to their locales. The famine had demonstrated that the key to effective relief lay in attracting fresh, new forces to local self-governing bodies.[62]

Arsen'ev further argued that an income tax would ease the burden on the peasantry. The *News* led the opposition by arguing that the state already taxed all property, inheritance, and businesses, so the new excise would fall on bureaucrats and professionals and would become a tax on intellectual productivity. The *Moscow News* doubted that the state could even accurately calculate private income. Arsen'ev proposed instead to exempt low incomes from taxes and to take into consideration family size, constancy of employment, and stable income and to implement progressive tax rates. As for intellectual labor, a tax would apply for its remuneration above a certain sum. High incomes, Arsen'ev argued, often paid for "needless luxuries, fantasies, and schemes," so fixed income from capital and property would be taxed higher than wages. In other words, the tax system would reward productive labor. Most western European governments, except for France, already had this arrangement by the 1890s.[63] Supporting a more just distribution of taxes, Arsen'ev reinforced *Herald* liberalism's universal appeal—it did not favor the "third estate" at the expense of the peasantry.[64]

DECENTRALIZATION OVER CONSTITUTIONALISM

With the tax proposals, Arsen'ev had restated his 1882 program in richer economic detail. He looked to the West for examples of how to organize and implement taxation. He looked to Russia's own experience with local self-government to justify a continuing policy of economic decentralization. Arsen'ev saw clearly the fundamental paradox in center-local relations. Local self-government could not flourish under state direction, but depended on the government's good graces financially. The low economic and cultural level in rural areas inhibited the growth of civil society, but was the only genuine source of civic consciousness. The *Herald* had to negotiate further delimitations of responsibilities between state and locale. This would not be easy, but Arsen'ev believed in learning by doing.

As Arsen'ev's articles demonstrate, the *Herald* group distinguished itself by evaluating Russia's economic development since the 1860s through the lens of achievements in local self-government, which, Arsen'ev firmly believed, were crucial components of successful economic development. The economic decentralization that he envisioned could even replace the peasant commune. In his detailed examination of famine relief, Arsen'ev not only specified the socio-economic responsibilities of local self-government, but also argued for greater cooperation between the state and local self-government institutions. Furthermore, he supported an imperial zemstvo organization to exchange ideas and debate broad domestic policies.

Some scholars have pointed to the 1890s as the turning point in the constitutional-reform movement as it tried to gather support from local self-government, but Arsen'ev's proposals demonstrate that not all liberals treated the zemstvos as "seedbeds of democracy" in its parliamentary form.[65] Constitutionalism was conspicuously absent from the pages of the *Herald* because Russian censorship forbid it, but this does not make the alternative directions for the growth of civil society that the *Herald* articulated any less valuable. Since the zemstvos remained underfunded and the peasantry poor, financial concerns remained more important than political aspirations. Arsen'ev's articles examining the handling of famine relief, which laid down the rudiments of a zemstvo-centered economic decentralization, demonstrate the profound economic turn in liberal thinking by the 1890s. The commune, which the Populists and agrarian socialists saw as the foundation of egalitarianism, and the state as the guarantee of stability, were conspicuously absent from Arsen'ev's articles because he conceived of rural autonomy outside of both. Nevertheless, Arsen'ev's thinking about the all-estate canton, soup kitchens, public works projects, and the redistribution of the tax burden carried Populist overtones, while his participation in unofficial zemstvo gatherings in both capitals demonstrated that the liberals and Populists could cooperate on practical matters.

Some scholars have argued that the weakness of the famine relief operations during 1891–1892 stemmed from the general inadequacy of local administration, especially the absence of firm institutional links with the peasant world, although the state had performed adequately to fill in the gaps.[66] The *Herald* came to the less sanguine conclusion that the government's ad hoc committees and empowered representatives were temporary ploys to surmount fatal flaws of its own making with no intention of repairing them. Arsen'ev called for the creation of an all-estate canton to further decentralize the economic administrative system and to make local self-government more representative and cohesive.

To the readers of the *Herald*, the dominant debate in the 1890s was therefore not about the zemstvo's political promise, but about economic efficiency on the local level. According to Arsen'ev, only local self-government units could govern effectively, but in order to do so, two things needed to happen. First, the state had to loosen central control over local self-government and increase zemstvo responsibilities. And second, the state had to create the all-estate canton, which would act as a natural guarantee that greater local responsibility would not become a breeding ground for radicalism and, more importantly, for irresponsible financial policies. The peasantry's inherent traditionalism and common sense would not allow that to happen, Arsen'ev believed, while socio-economic responsibility would become more optimized the closer it came to the peasant household. Rural poverty, however, remained the most serious drag on the promise of self-government, as it made it hostage to incentives from imperial authorities. Rural poverty and the belief in the general decline of Russian agriculture since Emancipation not only figured prominently on the journal's pages, but also played a crucial role in articulating the *Herald*'s attitude to the Russian Marxist movement.

9

∽∿∾

From Marxist Apologetics to a
Moral Economy

Having achieved its greatest popularity and influence by the 1890s, the *Herald of Europe* also had to adjust itself to the rapidly changing trends of the dawning Silver Age of Russian literature and philosophy. After the closing of *Notes of the Fatherland* in 1884, the *Herald of Europe* became Russia's most popular thick journal with around seven thousand monthly subscribers throughout the decade. By the 1890s, it became the standard-bearer for many intellectuals.[1] According to Koni, even Nicholas II read the journal.[2] Chernyshevskii described the *Herald* as a "good journal that commands respect from the majority of the public."[3] Anton Chekhov considered it the "best of the thick journals."[4] In 1897, even the Populist *Russian Wealth*, with which Pypin had argued, praised the *Herald*'s program of encouraging a "healthy civic life," the rule of law, the independence of the courts, and firm guarantees of individual rights.[5] Indeed, the *Herald* emphasized broad social activism outside of parliamentary politics and below the political radar of the censors, the police, and the Russian radicals.

In 1891, famous physician and writer Nikolai Belogolovyi noted that the journal's twenty-fifth anniversary marked "a truly momentous milestone" in a distinguished commitment to spread general enlightenment in Russia, especially during the era of the counter-reforms when "beasts roamed freely, but men sat in fear." Throughout the 1880s, Belogolovyi argued, the *Herald* managed to keep its ideals intact and never compromised, while the reactionary press attacked the journal with greater frequency and increasing support from the state.[6] Indeed, a censor summarized the journal's political attitude throughout the decade as "systematically and irreconcilably opposed to all state measures to reinforce national principles, the rule of law, and to clear minds of false and pernicious teachings."[7] The judgment read as a badge of honor. Describing the journal culture of the late imperial era, Marietta Shaginian noted in her memoirs how the "complex social life" of the time pulsated on the journals' pages and "galvanized and fed the imagination."[8] Vladimir Solovyov's nephew Sergei remembered how in the 1890s his uncle brought into their home "the mixed smell of incense, the Vatican, and the *Herald of Europe*," whose articles mitigated all the nationalistic tendencies of Sergei's siblings.[9] Symbolist poet Konstantin Balmont's wife Ekaterina remembered in her memoirs that when her parents locked the book cabinet, she would immerse herself in the thick journals, the *Herald of Europe* among them.[10]

The 1880s and 1890s witnessed the apex of the *Herald*'s intellectual influence before the journal's subscriptions began to decline at the turn of the century. These two decades also marked personal success for the journal's editors. In 1883, Slonimskii took over the journal's "Foreign Survey" and gave a series of presentations to the Saint Petersburg Juridical Society on issues of private property and the peasant commune in 1885 and 1891–1892.[11] Referring to Slonimskii as the journal's foreign minister, Stasiulevich nevertheless had to restrain the enthusiastic young writer: "Engage your opponents as a traveler engages a barking dog: never argue directly with the barking dog, but continue to walk quietly and without looking back."[12]

Throughout the 1880s, Pypin and Stasiulevich tried to determine the right balance between mass appeal and enlightenment value. Pypin complained to literary historian Vsevolod Miller that Stasiulevich was turning down specialized and lengthy articles in an attempt to make the *Herald* a popular journal. However, Pypin admitted in the same letter that "academics would do a great service if they came closer to their readers."[13] Both men worked hard on the Russian Library—affordable volumes that aimed to introduce ordinary Russian readers to famous writers.

The 1880s and 1890s witnessed the unraveling of the ties between social and literary criticism, whose close relationship had persisted since Belinskii's time. More and more intellectual currents separated themselves out of this tradition as the Silver Age offered new forms of creativity, artistic expression, and social criticism. The 1880s saw major shifts in Russia's journal culture. Katkov's *Russian Herald* ceased to be a literary influence by 1880. In 1884, *Notes of the Fatherland* was shut down. Vukol Lavrov established the Moscow monthly *Russian Thought* (*Russkaia Mysl'*, 1880–1918), which moved from a conservative toward a moderately liberal position by 1885 under Victor Goltsev's editorship. *Russian Wealth* went from a weak beginning to an important vehicle of Populist thought, especially after former *Notes of the Fatherland* critic Nikolai Mikhailovskii joined its staff in the mid-1880s and his anti-modernist views added spice to the journal. In 1885, *The Northern Herald* (*Severnyi vestnik*, 1885–1898) appeared, but was not yet fulfilling its role as the first major publication to welcome modernist writers.

In the late 1880s and early 1890s, the *Herald of Europe* published the first works of Silver Age poets Zinaida Gippius, Dmitrii Merezhkovskii, and Konstantin Balmont (whose first collection—*Under the Northern Sky*—also came out of Stasiulevich's printing shop). Other names followed—Aleksandr Ertel, Dmitrii Mamin-Sibiriak, Nikolai Minskii, Konstantin Staniukovich, Aleksei Apukhtin, and Afanasii Fet. Nonetheless, the *Herald* continued to publish journalistic literature, which is mostly forgotten today. One of the more outstanding writers of this school was Pyotr Boborykin, who produced naturalistic novels copiously. The journal referred to them as "human documents" and they reflected Stasiulevich's interest in photographic depictions of contemporary life. Boborykin had no equals in recording the dominant social and intellectual trends of late imperial Russia. Both Leo Tolstoy and Maksim Gorky respected his sensitivity for intellectual sensibilities and his attention to detail. After Turgenev's death in 1883, Boborykin became the magnet that attracted readers—every January, the journal would publish the first installment of one of his novels. In the 1890s, Stasiulevich also began to publish women writers with increasing frequency: Valentina Dmitrieva, Aleksandra Vinitskaia, Nataliia Stakhevich, and Nadezhda Khvoshchinskaia-Zaionchkovskaia. In 1893, Ivan Bunin made his literary debut on the *Herald*'s pages with his poem "Songs of the Spring."[14]

Unlike Bunin, Vladimir Solovyov came to the journal as an accomplished poet and thinker. Like the other members of the *Herald* group, he had also lost his academic job and the right to speak publicly as a result of an infamous lecture given in March 1881 that urged the state to amnesty Tsar Alexander's assassins. Having published in Slavophile journals until the mid-1880s, Solovyov joined the liberal camp after reconsidering his world view and began to submit his poems to Pypin and Stasiulevich in 1886. Many articles followed and Solovyov became a regular contributor, although he published in other periodicals as well. His turn to the *Herald* coincided with Solovyov's break with Slavophilism and especially with one the chief proponents of *pochvennichestvo* (the back-to-the-soil movement), Nikolai Strakhov. They clashed over Nikolai Danilevskii's *Russia and Europe*, which Solovyov re-viewed negatively on the pages of the *Herald* in 1888.[15] Strakhov published his replies in the *Russian Herald* and Suvorin's *New Time*. The argument revolved around the validity of the Europe-Russia standoff. In a letter to Stasiulevich, Solovyov complained that "contemporary quasi-Slavophilism" had split into the Byzantine, liberal, and "viscerally patriotic" varieties, each of which was developing in a separate direction.[16] Concerned more at this time with unity, Solovyov no longer shared the Slavophiles' desire to isolate Russia from the West, and he found welcome company amid the *Herald* group. He respected Pypin and loved to play chess with him. In the process of working on the Brockhaus and Efron encyclopedia, he also befriended Arsen'ev and then Slonimskii, becoming godfather to one of his sons in 1888.[17]

Not all the members of the editorial staff understood Solovyov's theories, however. Arsen'ev wrote to Stasiulevich in 1890 regarding one of Solovyov's articles: "I have to admit that it is total abracadabra to me. There are only a few comprehensible phrases at the very end."[18] Solovyov, in his turn, opposed the "art for art's sake" movement that was emerging with the first shoots of Russian symbolism in the 1890s. In 1894, he condemned the "aesthetic separatism" of Gippius, Merezhkovskii, Balmont, and especially Valerii Briusov. He even came out in defense of Chernyshevskii's utilitarian program for literature, albeit in a less radical form. In articles dedicated to traditional Russian poets, Solovyov praised Pushkin, Lermontov, and Tiutchev, among others, for their combination of beauty and the pursuit of truth, which he believed the new poets separated from each other to their art's peril. Solovyov's attitude anticipated and paralleled Leo Tolstoy's, whose *What Is Art?* (1897) argued similar points, albeit with the greater religious fervor characteristic of his late works. Nevertheless, the symbolists considered Solovyov their precursor, although only Slonimskii's sister-in-law Zinaida openly referred to Solovyov's poems themselves as "symbolist." Pypin argued that Russian literature as a whole had experienced a period of "decline" in the 1890s and referred to decadent poetry as "half-witted." On the *Herald*'s pages, writer and literary critic Evgenii Liatskii praised Chekhov's depictions of simple folk, but criticized severely his depressing portrayals of the Russian intelligentsia. He also found Gorky's "Nietzschean" experiments inferior to his depictions of the life of simple people and the beauty of nature.[19]

Solovyov's work did not find favor with conservatives such as Pobedonostsev who asked writer Evgenii Feoktistov: "What is Vl. Solovyov whoring on about [*bliadoslovit*] in the new issue of the 'Herald of Europe'? When you can, send me a copy."[20] Solovyov, in his turn, became friends with Stasiulevich and defended him against conservative attacks: "I do not know of another man in Russia who deserves more respect than this 'liberal'."[21] Solovyov even penned this humorous quatrain to Stasiulevich:

> Не болен я и не печален,
> Хоть вреден мне климат Москвы;
> Он чересчур континентален,—
> Здесь нет Галерной и Невы.

> [I am not sick and I am not saddened,
> Though Moscow's climate is bad for me;
> It is too continental,—
> There is no Galernaia or Neva here.][22]

Solovyov also published some of his major books through Stasiulevich's company: *The National Question in Russia* (1st ed. 1888, 2nd ed. 1891), *The Spiritual Foundations of Life* (1897), and *Poems* (1900). Stasiulevich wrote Pypin upon Solovyov's premature death in 1900: "He is more than a contributor to the journal—and we are not mourning so much the loss of a colleague as the irreplaceable loss of a person whom everybody loved."[23]

By 1897, Stasiulevich's publishing house was one of the ten largest printing companies in Saint Petersburg. Having turned 70 in 1896, he remained in control of the journal de jure, but relied increasingly on his loyal editors Arsen'ev, Pypin, and Slonimskii, whose ranks enlarged with the arrival of writer Mikhail Lemke and literary and social historian Mikhail Gershenzon. The infusion of new blood could not have been more timely because in the late 1890s Stasiulevich began to lose his eyesight.

By the 1890s, preoccupations with literary questions morphed into an interest in pedagogical issues that emphasized the formation of human consciousness, so a new generation of journals sprang up to satiate the public's interest in psychology and aesthetics. *Education* (*Obrazovanie*, 1892–1909) regularly printed psychological studies and reviews of psychological and psychiatric literature, including Schopenhauer, Ibsen, Durkheim, Max Nordau, and Wilhelm Wundt, among others. Authors explored the influence of dreams, hypnotism, poetry, and the psychology of women, predictions of racial degeneration manifested in neurosis, pessimism, and suicide. *God's World* (*Mir bozhii*, 1891–1906) also had a pedagogic mission that took a more social turn when former radical Angel Bogdanovich became its editor in 1894. The most serious and erudite of these newcomers was the journal of the Moscow Psychological Society, *Problems of Philosophy and Psychology* (*Problemy filosofii i psikhologii*, 1889–1918). Under Iakov Grot's editorship, the journal offered whatever help the broadest forms of learning might give in solving contemporary spiritual problems. It introduced Russia to Nietzsche and published Tolstoy's controversial *What is Art?* In 1899, *The World of Art* (*Mir iskusstva*, 1899–1904) began its short but remarkable career with a mission to revolutionize Russian taste and simultaneously to save Russia's artistic tradition from the dead hand of positivist interpretation. Editor Sergei Diaghilev and contributors Zinaida Gippius and Dmitrii Merezhkovskii determined the journal's direction.[24]

The *Herald* maintained its weight while these brilliant but short-lived aberrations in the history of Russian journalism lit up and fizzled out around it. Sustainable only in the special cultural conditions of the time, the artistic journals were reacting to the empire's political tradition and the social problems in its wake. The *Herald* also tackled this issue but in its own way by providing a rich tapestry of local news and practical administrative activity as the answer to Russia's growing pains. However, the journal's message also evolved further during the 1890s as it added to its "preserve the Great Reform legacy" refrain an ethical justification for the state to encourage local self-government initiative and for Russians to become involved in it.

THE PROBLEM WITH PROTECTIONISM

Although technological, scientific, and economic developments in the nineteenth century often eclipsed ethical concerns, the *Herald* liberals resisted the positivist tendency to evaluate progress based on scientific and technological advancements alone. The journal approached Marxism as a critical tool at best, but never as an ideology that justified sacrifices. In the cauldron of finance minister Sergei Witte's industrialization and in reaction to both Marxism and Populism, the journal produced a socially oriented market model that welcomed state involvement in directing modernization only as long as local self-government could mediate its effects by economically empowering the population on the local level. Unfortunately, historians of Russian liberalism have overlooked this crucial economic component of Russian liberalism and have overemphasized its social loyalties and political ideals (especially constitutionalism).

Under state protection and with minimal local involvement, Russian capitalism evolved with a rapacity witnessed only in European colonies. Although the *Herald* liberals criticized the Finance Ministry's misguided development policies, especially protectionism, the journal did not target capitalism as a whole. Instead, Leonid Slonimskii argued that the Finance Ministry's aping of the outdated trade balance theory was the main culprit behind rural poverty. In his view, by the 1890s the Russian state had acquired the role of a colonial office that profited at the expense of the Russian population. Obsessed with trade balance sheets, it failed to negotiate the complex balance between agricultural producers and the global market. Protectionism thus became Slonimskii's primary target.

In February 1892, Slonimskii examined the soundness of pursuing a positive trade balance, which according to the Finance Ministry had grown at an encouraging rate in 1891 as Russia exported 682 million rubles worth of goods and imported only 342 million.[25] Slonimskii concluded from this that if one were to judge economic welfare by international trade balances then the famine had enriched Russia. By the same logic, Russia should have made enormous cumulative profits ever since the 1877 import tariff tipped the balance in favor of exports. Why then, asked Slonimskii, were the results not evident in the villages? Or were they simply the mirages of financial minds? The very fact that famine years were very profitable by international trade standards should have caused suspicion, he noted. If a negative trade balance implied impoverishment, as protectionists argued, then England and France had been on the path to insolvency since the 1860s, when their annual imports consistently began to exceed their exports. Russia, on the other hand, had a positive annual balance throughout the 1880s, yet it suffered the most when foreigners "owed" it money. By the end of the nineteenth century, almost all advanced Western nations ran a negative trade balance. Indeed, despite her positive trade balances, creditors did not pour their investments into Russia. Was it possible, he asked, that the trade balance theory had outlived its utility?[26]

Slonimskii used the sugar industry as an example of how the state achieved a positive trade balance. Sugar cost 5 rubles per pood (16.38 kg) in Russia but only 2.6 rubles in London. The state returned the excise duties to producers in order to encourage exports. This eliminated competition on the international market and increased the state's profit from sales, but eventually rural taxes covered the difference in the loss from the return of the excise tax to producers. The protectionist doctrine aimed at preventing a flood of foreign goods onto the domestic market, while the state's financial interests

demanded increased exports *and* higher revenues. Slonimskii identified this
as the essential dilemma of finance minister Ivan Vyshnegradskii's economic
policy.[27] Slonimskii took the protectionist argument to its logical conclusion—that a predatory sell-off of Russia's natural resources with no purchases
from abroad would create the greatest trade balance in the world. At the same
time, protectionists would complain of "very poor" trade balances if the rural
population consumed the products of its own labor, bought cheaper domestic and advanced foreign goods, and raised its general standard of living.[28]

In order to prove that the Finance Ministry's mercantile ideology had
become obsolete, Slonimskii turned to European critics of protectionism, beginning in the eighteenth century. Slonimskii quoted David Hume: "Nations
suffer material losses not from the outflow of capital to foreigners, but from
the decline of their productivity, their energy, and entrepreneurship." He
also invoked Jeremy Bentham: "[If a] merchant chooses to send money to
Paris, it is because he thinks it profitable for himself; but the acute politician
finds that one man's profit is a whole nation's loss. To interfere with individual gain is therefore to prevent collective detriment." Inflated fears and illusory alarms were thus the fabric of protectionism, which treated economics
as a zero-sum game. Slonimskii quoted his contemporary (French politician
and economist) Yves Guyot:

> The proponents of protectionism periodically predict the complete ruin of
> France caused by imports of American pork, Russian wheat, or English cotton
> or metal goods. In the past forty years, the entire industry was expected to dis-
> appear, wages to decrease to zero, and the population to emigrate. Fields would
> grow fallow and all shops would close. However, none of this has happened.[29]

Slonimskii concluded that it was time to abandon the "dangerous siren"
that had caused grief under the harmless and deceptive name of "international trade balance." If logic and common sense were helpless in this case,
he concluded, perhaps a more convincing argument would be that Russia
maintained a superb trade balance during the less than excellent year of
1891.[30] The protectionism issue introduced Slonimskii to the latest trends
in European economic thinking, which could not have been more timely,
as Sergei Witte's rise to the post of finance minister ushered in a massive
industrialization program based on protectionism that was dismissive of the
zemstvos and oblivious to the fate of individuals caught in the grand scheme
of economic modernization. The *Herald* emerged as their champion.

A CAPITAL ECONOMY IN THE COUNTRYSIDE

As one scholar has argued about the evolution of Russian liberalism during the 1890s, its "defense of individual liberties and cultured creativity [. . .] seemed at best an untimely statement of noble principles and at worst an expression of the self-interest and uneasy conscience of the privileged."[31] It is impossible however to apply this characterization to the *Herald* group because it emphasized economic activity as the key to social participation. Moreover, there was always something of John Locke's distrust of enthusiasm in the group's political sensibilities. The *Herald* liberals were active zemstvo members who experienced firsthand the pressures under which this institution evolved in the 1890s. As the gentry and the Finance Ministry faced off on issues of control over local self-government, the rift created a window for the *Herald* cause of increasing the peasantry's participation in the zemstvos and enacting a major legal reform to accommodate the capitalization of agricultural productivity.

Witte's insufficient attention to agricultural problems reflected a broader shift of public interest from agricultural problems to the promises of industrialization. As Russia's major dailies analyzed the year 1892, they concentrated on industrial and protectionist concerns instead of rural issues. Only the *Russian News* placed agricultural concerns on its front page, but wrote of the danger "of allowing the rural economy to develop naturally."[32] On the pages of the *Herald*, Slonimskii focused instead on the peasantry's legal and economic conditions. Maintaining that the peasant commune was a remarkably protean institution that easily adapted to climatic and socio-economic circumstances, he argued that the object of agricultural reform was give the commune the legal and economic incentives to adapt itself to local conditions, to dissolve in some places and evolve in others.[33] The *Herald* argued that agriculture had to take precedence over industry on the Finance Ministry's agenda.

Witte saw things differently. His first major policies in 1893 concerned State Bank reform, negotiations with Germany over tariffs, and the preparation of the monopoly on alcohol. Indeed, during the 1890s the Ministry of Agriculture was reduced to gathering information on rural conditions while the Finance Ministry determined the direction of economic policy.[34] Witte's first agricultural move was a formalistic one: a review of rural statutes. He supported the law of December 14, 1893, requiring the approval of a two-thirds majority for individuals to leave the commune. He also remained a staunch supporter of the commune as a traditional pillar of socio-political stability in Russia. The only issues upon which the dailies agreed were the need to eliminate restrictions on colonization and the peasantry's inability to accept the Peasant Bank's terms of mortgage.[35]

In August 1893, Slonimskii suggested a realistic approach to the agrarian question that the state could take without compromising its ideology. His article took the form of a book review of *Sketches of Our Post-Reform Economy*, in which Populist Nikolai Danielson blamed Russia's agricultural problems on the capitalization of her agricultural market and the outflow of large portions of that capital into industry. Slonimskii saw it differently: "Economists do not notice the constant destructive influence of traditional jurisprudence and assign this influence to some conscious, malicious plan that the industrial class or 'capitalism' pursues in modern times."[36]

Slonimskii agreed with Danielson that a new production-for-market economy had established itself in Russia, but he did not see its commercial effects as the main problem. Instead, he pointed to the judicial confusion it had created. Laws that used to apply to consumer classes, roughly one-fifth of the population, now applied to the peasantry also. The commune now undertook monetary exchanges and suffered financial penalties. It had to take into account supply and demand trends, negotiate contracts and orders, and deal with mortgages and foreclosures. The French and Italian civil codes anticipated the legal aspects of agricultural capitalization, including microeconomic exchanges, loans, and mortgages. In Russia, however, Emancipation left the old legal apparatus intact.[37] Therefore, the problem was not the appearance of "western European capitalism" in Russia, which Slonimskii considered a positive development, but the state's tardiness in updating the legal structure to accommodate it in the countryside.[38]

Meanwhile, the first major legal revision that the Finance Ministry undertook under Witte concerned the passport system, which exerted an enormous drag on the free movement of labor. In February 1894, Witte and interior minister Pyotr Durnovo submitted to the State Council a joint project that aimed to eliminate the anachronistic socio-economic division between the taxed and un-taxed estates and groups. All classes, with the exception of the clergy and military, would henceforth pay taxes and receive passports good for five years (ten years for privileged classes). The State Council partially fulfilled the *Herald* expectations for tax reform when it approved the law and scheduled its implementation for the first day of 1895.[39]

Witte also passed laws to facilitate colonization. When he justified the construction of the Trans-Siberian Railroad to Alexander III in 1893, he used as one of his arguments for this project that the railway would bring to life Siberia's vast lands and decrease land shortage in parts of European Russia.[40] Crown Prince Nicholas, who was Chairman of the Siberian Railroad Committee at the time, took Witte's position. In addition to solving the land shortage in central Russia, colonization would also remove troublesome peasants to the empire's borders, strengthen Russia's strategic position in the Far East, and contribute to the Russification of the borderlands. In 1894, Witte increased migrant allowances by taking money from the Siberian Railroad Fund. He also set up medical and feeding points along the Cheliabinsk-Tiumen section and sent groups of surveyors beyond the Urals to prepare land plots for the colonizers.[41] Still, all of these changes failed to give Russian agriculture the full freedom to accommodate itself to the new economic circumstances, which is something that the Marxist-Populist debate ended up addressing.

MARXISM AS INDUSTRIALIZATION'S APOLOGIA

The debate about modernization erupted with unprecedented urgency after the rural catastrophe of 1891–1892. Writing the intellectual history of the 1890s, Western historians have focused primarily on the standoff between the Marxists and the Populists.[42] And indeed, the rift between these camps deepened in the 1890s leading to increased polarization and intellectual aggression characteristic of ideological battlefields. However, the Marxist-Populist fireworks obscured the liberal point of view on modernization, which was no less detailed than the Marxist position and in many ways more pragmatic than Populist alternatives.

As the debate about Russia's development alternatives began in the 1890s, Slonimskii initially accused it of distracting attention from the more important issue of the Finance Ministry's taxation policies, which retarded local economic development and prevented popular participation in modernization. The *Herald* argued for coordinating central modernization projects with local needs and evaluating success from the bottom up. In the process of criticizing Marxist ideology, Slonimskii exposed it as an apologia for forced industrialization. Indeed, non-agrarian Marxism entered Russia on the coattails of the Witte System. Arguing against the Marxists, Slonimskii offered a new and practical definition of a moral economy for the twentieth century, but instead of defining morality in religious terms, he did so in terms of economic decentralization rooted in local self-government. In other

words, a moral economy was one that took care of the socio-economic interests that its participants themselves defined.

Slonimskii first approached Russian Marxism by criticizing Populist Nikolai Danielson's 1893 book *Sketches of Our Post-Reform Communal Economy*,
which argued that capitalist production was making inroads into Russia and
had to be stopped. Slonimskii disagreed with Danielson's argument that capitalism alienated peasants from their labor. In his desire to demonstrate the
evils of capitalism as described by Marx, Danielson attributed to Russia's new
money-based economy all the characteristics of developed capitalism, on
which he blamed every imaginable entrepreneurial and moral abuse. Danielson, Slonimskii concluded, had accurately identified Russia's economic problems since Emancipation, but Marxist theory completely failed to explain
them.[43] Slonimskii reminded his readers that serfdom, not capitalism, had
caused Russia's economic woes. Correcting the historical record became one
of Slonimskii's projects.[44]

Indeed, Slonimskii argued, Russia had never had a coherent economic
policy. Instead, personnel changes determined economic tactics and strategies, while protectionism favored specific people, but not social groups, let
alone classes. Slonimskii referred to a brochure by Russian engineer Karl
Weber entitled *The Needs of Our National Economy* (1892) that pointed to the
resilience of the cottage industry flourishing all over Western Europe, including England. In England and Germany, small privately owned mills, weav-
ing, carpentry, and many other cottage forms of production "blossomed next
to large-scale production."[45] In Russia, however, the Populists were wrongly
convinced that the evolution of capitalism was undermining cottage industry. In Saxony, Weber wrote, peasant crafts flourished because the state encouraged them, invested in trade schools, and supported basic education. It
was the state's inattention to cottage industry, not capitalism per se, Slonimskii argued, that was undermining the Russian peasantry's non-agricultural
sources of income. Much as the Finance Ministry lacked a complex program
of reforms, inchoate Russian Marxism lacked a complex vision of Russia's
socio-economic problems.

In the 1890s, Slonimskii argued, the Romanov Empire resembled a socio-
economic museum whose exhibits ran the gamut from advanced technological urban achievements to villages based on subsistence agriculture.
No single theory could explain how this multiplicity functioned. Marxism,
which was about to flood Russia's intellectual life in 1894, was for him one
of many schools of economic thought.[46] Indeed, most Russian intellectuals

in the last quarter of the nineteenth century were tolerant of Marxism. For example, writer and economic historian Vladimir Sviatlovskii wrote, "For the young mind, Marx is undoubtedly important as a stage. Marx is a school—a token of the mind, the development and sharpening of one's social world view. And, above all, Marx is the emancipation from the constraints of teleology and pettiness; it is the implementation of a fine understanding of the materialistic structure of history, law, and sociology."[47] Some of the brightest stars in Russia's Silver Age firmament, such as Sergei Bulgakov, Pyotr Struve, and Mikhail Tugan-Baranovskii, went through a Marxist stage in their intellectual development. Tugan-Baranovskii wrote: "We need to go further than Marx, but through Marx, having used all that Marx has given to us."[48]

In 1894, Pyotr Struve published *Critical Notes on the Question of Russia's Economic Development,* in which he welcomed the transition from the natural to the exchange economy and examined the immense cultural changes that this entailed. Capitalism facilitated the development of agriculture as well as industry, he argued, and created an increasingly interconnected market across the empire. These arguments echoed Witte's and Dmitrii Mendeleev's ideas. In late nineteenth-century Russia, Struve's "legal" Marxism became synonymous with capitalism in that it championed industrialization. Unlike the Populists, against whom he argued in his work, Struve identified the natural rural economy, not nascent capitalism, as the principal cause of poverty in Russia. The state's responsibility in this process was to "clear the soil for economic progress and soften its social effects."[49]

Slonimskii descried in Struve's work the same economic gullibility he had criticized throughout the 1880s. He objected to Marxist dialectics that left little room for individual action and state policy and he argued that Russian "capitalism" manifested itself in "crude *kulachestvo*" (a greedy and self-serving modus operandi) both in the rural and industrial worlds. Despite Struve's attempt to debunk Populist economic theories, Slonimskii noticed that the Russian Marxists themselves had insufficiently articulated their world view. "Does this not demonstrate," he asked, "that we are dealing here not with a scientific debate, but with petty literary sectarianism, which revolves around a teacher's words?" Struve's greatest mistake, according to Slonimskii, was that he first decided that capitalism would triumph in Russia and then promised to prove this factually in his "next brochure."[50] The irony of this reversal was not lost on Slonimskii—Marx and Engels also developed historical materialism in the 1840s, but published the economic support for it in the 1860s. By the 1890s, the Russian Marxists emerged as great supporters of the Witte System and Slonimskii observed that their economic theories obscured their ethical aims. He would have agreed with Mikhailovskii's criticism that their actions were not consistent with their moral goals.[51]

Slonimskii viewed the 1890s, like the 1860s, as a thaw marked by great intellectual interest in cultural, philosophical, social, and economic questions. In the beginning of the 1890s, publisher Florentii Pavlenkov successfully sold twenty thousand copies of a translation of Henry Thomas Buckle's *History of Civilization in England*, the poster child of Victorian materialism, progressivism, and rationalism. Slonimskii also noticed that in the 1890s, as in the 1860s, the antagonism between materialistic and moral issues, economic and social interests, and moral and utilitarian ideas came to the fore. Works on ethics became popular once again: two editions of philologist Vasilii Modestov's translation of Spinoza's *Ethics*, the late Konstantin Kavelin's *The Goals of Ethics*, and Tolstoy's moral writings. Parallel to this interest in ethics, materialism also attracted followers and a new ban on Marx's *Capital* increased its popularity. However, Slonimskii argued, economic materialism in Russia took a wrong turn under German influence.[52] The application of Marxist concepts to Russia obscured the main lines of Russian development.[53]

Having challenged the ideology of progress and protectionism in the 1880s, Slonimskii now began to deconstruct Marxism. His principal criticism of *Capital* was that it focused narrowly on industry at the expense of "the primary importance of land ownership and agriculture"—crucial issues even in highly industrialized countries. Furthermore, Slonimskii argued, capital per se was an essential element of exchange economies and had "nothing in common with capitalism." Alienation from the means of production was also hardly a novel phenomenon, he maintained.[54] Russian followers of Marx blindly focused on the primacy of industrial issues and treated his "hypotheses as truths and examples as proofs," which bred scholastic debates about vocabulary while the useful economic research that rational materialism should have encouraged on all levels was proceeding only on the zemstvo level through its statistical committees.[55]

In 1896, Slonimskii argued that Marx's "commodity fetishism"—"consumerism" in modern terms—obscured the true economic forces behind social inequalities.[56] The "capitalist system" was no system at all, Slonimskii argued, and joined the growing ranks of Marx's critics such as Albert Shäffle, Karl Knies, Adolph Wagner, and Eugen von Böhm-Bawerk.[57] Slonimskii echoed what Mikhailovskii had written about Marxism in 1894:

The very foundations of economic materialism, repeated as axioms innumer-
able times, still remain unconnected among themselves and untested by facts,
which deserve attention, particularly in a theory that relies upon material and
tangible facts and arrogates to itself the title of being particularly "scientific."[58]

This was very different from Georgii Plekhanov's argument that Marx's
scientific generalizations were rigorously logical and open to empirical veri-
fication. Plekhanov, sometimes called the father of Russian Marxism, had
argued that Darwin and Marx made complementary contributions to ren-
dering the philosophy of history inseparable from science.[59] The connection between Darwinism and Marxism was not lost on Slonimskii either,
but he viewed Marxism as a variation of Victorian anthropology, which
assumed convergent, not pluralistic, development. Like the Populists, Slonimskii directed his most severe criticism at Marx's philosophy of history.
Unlike the Populists, however, he did not believe that Marx's analysis of
western European economic processes was basically sound and valuable.[60]

Behind the debate about Russia's economic development lay the fundamental question about the state's relationship to its subjects. Writing about
the political side of this rapport was taboo, but the economic repercussions
of a state-enforced modernization that affected the lives of millions begged
questions regarding the state's responsibilities and the population's loyalties.
The *Herald*'s most original contribution to Russian liberalism came in the
form of its evaluation of the Witte System that the Marxist-Populist debate
encouraged. Just like Witte, Slonimskii argued, the Marxists also underestimated modernization's social price. The "social question does not fit into the
economic value question," he wrote.[61]

RUSSIA'S FIRST MARXIST MINISTRY

Slonimskii interrupted his examination of Russian Marxism in May 1896 to
explore Witte's monetary reforms and the transition to the gold standard,
which allowed him to apply his economic acumen to concrete problems. In
the process, he confirmed his suspicion that Russian Marxism had become
an apologia for forced economic modernization as the Finance Ministry
implemented what Slonimskii defined as a Marxist program.

The Finance Ministry's policies had been paving the way since the 1880s
for pegging the paper ruble to the value of gold. When Witte began to promote the gold standard in the spring of 1895, he faced a storm of criticism

from the press. Brochures predicted that the gold standard would "encourage betting on the stock market and pernicious speculative tendencies among the public" and "benefit the stock markets and our enemies."[62] Slavophile and Populist voices warned of an "invasion of foreigner entrepreneurs who will buy up all of Russia."[63] Saint Petersburg University financial law professor L. V. Kholodkovskii gave a speech before the Imperial Free Economic Society in which he warned that gold would leak out of Russia to the last ounce.[64]

Witte spent the winter of 1895 and the spring of 1896 proving to the State Council, its various subcommittees, and the public that the financial reform would not only benefit industry, but also have no negative impact on everyday consumers and the peasantry. In the State Council, he came up against members of the gentry who believed that the depreciated paper ruble worked to their advantage.[65] The liberal dailies supported the reform. Only Suvorin's *New Time* published articles both for and against the gold standard.

Slonimskii turned to western European examples and found that France, Germany, and the United Kingdom kept silver reserves along with gold ones even though as highly industrialized nations they could afford a monometallic gold-based currency. In Russia, gold coins were too valuable for everyday rural exchange and the precious metal had a tendency to increase in price. Slonimskii maintained that only "large-scale industry, bankers, and Russian Marxists" supported Witte's reform.[66] The crux of Slonimskii's suggestion was that any financial reform had to benefit the lowest and the most populous social groups and to this end he called for a silver-pegged currency to be disseminated widely among the peasantry. Indeed, as foreign experience had demonstrated, monetary reform was too important to be left to the Finance Ministry since the Russian peasantry would eventually have to pay higher taxes to compensate for the flight of gold reserves.

Slonimskii recognized the shared urgency with which the Finance Ministry and the Marxists wanted to overcome socio-economic backwardness. However, when he examined the enterprises that Witte's protective tariffs encouraged he noticed something peculiar—the most lucrative ones belonged to foreigners who also ran them. The Russian "bourgeoisie" had "no faith in tomorrow," no trust in "legally defined rights," and "lacked access to knowledge and enlightenment."[67]

Slonimskii's central argument was that that modernization from above could only produce surface gloss. Like a parasite, the Russian bourgeoisie was feeding off economic development, but was not contributing to it. The

Russian Marxists were underestimating the cultural components that were necessary for socially stable capitalist development. The *Herald* group, on the other hand, believed that the rural population had to participate in modernization in order for it to produce long-term economic and cultural benefits. Blind economic forces could not produce all this and there had to be a conscious agency balancing development, Slonimskii argued. His suspicion of the bourgeoisie's guiding role was confirmed when in 1906 a Finance Ministry statistical study defined the "middle estate" as persons making no less than five thousand rubles a year and found that only 60,228 men fit this category.[68] In an empire of 160 million people, the financially defined "bourgeoisie" thus constituted approximately .01 percent of the population. This was clearly not the force behind a socially responsible transition to enlightened capitalism.

Industrial apologists, such as Tugan-Baranovskii, pretended to stand above ideological constraints, but in doing so reminded Slonimskii of Monsieur Jourdain from Molière's *Le Bourgeois Gentilhomme*, "who spoke prose without knowing it." Slonimskii constructed his review of *The Russian Factory in the Past and Present* around debunking Tugan-Baranovskii's central Marxist thesis that existence determined consciousness. The author's thesis that class-based antagonism determined reform priorities was simply inapplicable to contemporary Russia—the bourgeoisie was hardly absorbing the cultural lessons of Western capitalism. Slonimskii concluded that Tugan-Baranovskii's book contained many interesting facts about Russia's factories but succumbed to industrialist ideology masked as Marxism.[69]

Meanwhile, the poor harvest in the central provinces in 1896 and the consequent malnutrition and cholera outbreaks reinvigorated calls for agricultural reforms in the second half of 1897. The *News* proposed an income tax, which the *Herald* had consistently supported since the 1870s.[70] The *News* also turned against defenders of the commune, preferring to see it as a "healthily flexible" institution capable of adapting to circumstances, which echoed Slonimskii's view.[71] The *Russian News* also called for the elimination of indirect taxes, the brunt of which fell upon the peasantry, and supported the income tax.[72] *New Time* was the most outspoken on the peasantry's plight, which the paper considered the most important economic issue: "The gentry has received new privileges, but nothing has been done for the peasants."[73] Although industry was progressing, "almost everything was created by hands involved in agriculture."[74] The *Stock Exchange News* (*Birzhevye vedomosti*, 1861–1879, 1880–1917) called for a complete "reorganization of rural life into a capitalist mode, against the commune, and for introducing Russian agriculture to western European know-how."[75]

By 1898, the variety of proposals for agricultural reforms in the press made the Marxist-Populist debate appear ideological and reductionist and demonstrated that the real intellectual fault lines in the 1890s concerned the politics behind the state's agricultural policies. The papers agreed on one thing, however. With remarkable unanimity, they wrote off the landed gentry not only as an economic force, but also as an estate. Preserving the gentry was no longer an issue because a new money-based elite was emerging in Russia.

The failed harvest of 1897 also made Witte realize that he could no longer ignore the interests of the countryside. He came to believe, however, that the main culprit of Russia's agricultural woes was neither land hunger, nor the tax burden, but the peasant's legal status—an argument that Slonimskii had been developing for a decade and a half. Witte also came to believe that this legal muddle retarded the development of capitalism. For example, peasant rights to their allotments were different from their rights of possession over their private property, which led to a form of legal schizophrenia. Ironically, Witte borrowed the idea of turning "a peasant from a half-man into a man" from Pobedonostsev.[76] In a letter to Nicholas II in October 1898, Witte argued that the peasantry in its current state could not act as a support for the autocracy and that the peasants' legal disorder was the "joy of all outspoken and hidden" enemies of the state.[77] As a result, Witte's peasant reform emphasized the estate's legal status and education—exactly what the *Herald* had championed. Although he demonstrated a learning curve throughout the 1890s, industrial development and financial reform nevertheless remained central in the finance minister's development agenda.

When Slonimskii turned his attention to the state of Russia's economy in the wake of peasant uprisings during 1897, he described it with unusual pessimism. Wherever Slonimskii turned, he saw "rapacity and speculation, barbarity, intellectual darkness" while a national education system still "remained a question." The achievements of which Witte's ministry boasted in its annual reports did not grow naturally out of the rural population's development, Slonimskii argued. Meanwhile, "optimists of a new type," meaning Marxists such as Mikhail Tugan-Baranovskii and Sergei Bulgakov, consoled "themselves with the thought that out of a national disaster new and more perfected forms of life will arise." Russia was becoming an exporter of natural resources and her "role on the world market could not be considered respectable."[78] The tone of Slonimskii's articles reflected the bitter realization that Russian Populism had become distracted from the peasantry's real problems as it debated abstract problems with the Marxists and even began to mirror their views.

Slonimskii's articles dealing with Marxism in the mid-1890s may confuse the modern reader because instead of dealing with Marxists per se, they actually targeted Nikolai Mikhailovskii, Nikolai Danielson, and Vasilii Vorontsov, whose Populist theories Pypin was examining concurrently. Slonimskii approached Russian Marxism through the prism of Populism, but unlike Pypin, who tried to trace Populism's intellectual pedigree, Slonimskii saw it as a pure reaction to Marxism, which treated capitalism and the peasant economy as mutually exclusive economic processes.[79] So powerful had been *Capital*'s influence on the Populists that Slonimskii actually referred to them as Marxists. In fact, by the mid-1890s, publishing Marxist articles became so profitable that even contributors to the Populist periodical *Russian Wealth* began declaring their support for Marxism.[80] "The defenders of Russia's self-sufficiency stand firmly on the foundation of Marx's teachings, but deny only the applicability of his philosophic and historical formula to our conditions," Slonimskii wrote, adding humorously that "capitalist enterprises such as printing houses" were already producing Populist literature ruminating "about when capitalism would finally establish itself in Russia."[81]

Slonimskii disagreed with Danielson's claim that the Emancipation Manifesto became a socio-economic divide that brought capitalism to Russia and allowed it to take over the instrument of the state, ushering in "the beginning of the end."[82] Slonimskii's counterargument resembled Tugan-Baranovskii's ideas about the relationship between cottage crafts and factory production:[83]

Industrial production per se is not antagonistic to peasant agriculture; on the contrary, directly and indirectly it produces an increase in agricultural activity, facilitates the transition to more intensive systems of production and offers various side-earnings to peasants and rural communities. The antagonism arises only when one-sided policies favor large industrial enterprises, which acquire a predatory, speculative nature as a result; therefore, the key issue is the state's economic policy and the level of its accommodation of popular interests. Legislative acts cannot eliminate the capitalist principle, but the conditions and methods of its manifestation depend on legislation and state power.[84]

Vasilii Vorontsov, for whose statistical research Slonimskii had great respect, had also assumed the validity of Marx's arguments in *Fates of Capitalism in Russia* (1882). This "Populist-Marxist" text, according to Slonimskii, "pushed all of our economic writing into a doctrinal struggle with phantoms" as well as "improvable and unfounded assumptions."[85] Vorontsov's call to reorganize industry along communal principles was utopian. Instead, Slonimskii argued, the working class in any nation would achieve real results only by having its enlightened members negotiate better labor conditions. Instead, by the 1890s, Slonimskii argued, Populism had lost touch with Russian reality by trapping itself in the "vicious circle" of an ideological struggle against Marxism.

Slonimskii concluded his battle against the last glimmers of Populism by addressing the publication in 1901 of a collection of essays in honor of Nikolai Mikhailovskii and a separate brochure critical of his social theories by Nikolai Berdiaev.[86] Slonimskii drew a parallel between the Russian intelligentsia's obsession with Hegel in the beginning of the nineteenth century, Darwin and Spencer during its middle, and Marx towards its end. "The Populists were solving the world's social problems by referring to Marx and Engels, correcting Spencer's sociology, and arguing about subjective ideals and the struggle for an integrated individuality," Slonimskii complained.[87] Meanwhile, Russian liberalism addressed the practical concerns of the time.

Slonimskii thus reiterated his argument that the source of rural problems was not capitalism per se but the Finance Ministry's failure to anticipate the impact of its policies on the village. Once again, the *Herald* demonstrated its non-bourgeois loyalties and showed itself as the champion of the peasantry ready to engage the state on the issue of real economic reforms. Slonimskii's articles also supported Aleksandr Pypin's claim that *Herald* liberalism was mature Populism, while contemporary Populists overlooked the peasantry's interests because they were too busy sparring with Marxist abstractions.

THE REAL DEBATE OF THE 1890S:
MODERNIZATION AND THE ZEMSTVO

The central debate during the 1890s centered on the zemstvo's role as an administrative tool. As a result, it became a battleground of very powerful and uncompromising interests. The central issue was no longer whether local self-government was viable, but whose purpose it served. For the liberals, the zemstvo was an alternative source of civic and economic education. This was not how the Finance Ministry saw things, however. Witte's attempts to simultaneously strong-arm and appease local self-government became an integral subplot in the debate about Russian modernization. For Witte, local self-government was inconvenient because of its opposition to the Finance Ministry's plans. He viewed the zemstvos as executive tools and expected the Finance Ministry to delegate and revoke whatever powers local officials exercised.[88]

Witte's views were on a collision course with Arsen'ev's argument that smaller, all-estate cantons could make the local administrative structure more organic by absorbing the peasants into it en masse. Slonimskii made a parallel argument that endowing them with clear property rights would guarantee the social stability of this lowest administrative rung by "democratizing" it economically.[89] The problem was that by the 1890s, the zemstvo had become the nobility's last stronghold, which explains why Witte was initially distrustful of local self-government.[90] Witte wrote that his attempts to curb the nobility's privileges and the strength of communal land ownership "aroused against me all those nobles who hold to the principle that the Russian Empire exists in order to feed them."[91]

The beginning of Witte's service as finance minister coincided with an increase in public works projects, many of which were holdovers from the famine. Throughout his tenure, he tried his best to channel as many funds as possible into state coffers and to limit expenditure on items not contributing directly to industry. The zemstvos were already in debt to the state after the famine and Witte placed a tight rein on further treasury subsidies for public projects. In 1893, the Finance Ministry sent provincial officials to supervise zemstvo tax assessments. A law passed in 1895 ordered the zemstvos to deposit most of the funds not used for operating expenses into the imperial treasury. In 1898, the Finance Ministry drafted Russia's earliest progressive tax reform, which proposed to free all rural dwellers from industrial taxes, thereby depriving the zemstvo of its claims on the handicraft taxes of peasants hiring no outside labor.[92]

Witte articulated his views on the agrarian problem in his 1899 "Report on State Revenues and Expenditures." That poor harvests did not produce such disastrous results in any other European country, Witte argued, demonstrated that the Russian peasantry had not developed an economy that could overcome low yields. Witte said nothing about the tax burden, but pointed once again to the peasantry's vague legal status.[93] He specifically targeted such institutions as corporal punishment, incarceration as a component of tax-collection, and outdated self-government and court institutions.[94] Exactly what he meant by the latter he did not specify. By the turn of the century,

Witte had developed a broad agricultural reform program based on six points: (1) a gradual reform of communal landholding; (2) the elimination of collective financial responsibility; (3) the abolition of corporal punishment; (4) limitations of land captains' powers; (5) the elimination of the peasantry's legal isolation; and (6) a reorganization of peasant self-government, courts, and the codification of local laws. Except for the conspicuous absence of an educational component, which was beyond the Finance Ministry's competence anyway, the finance minister's program was, point for point, the one that the *Herald* group had pursued all along. The views of Russia's progressive bureaucrats and liberals were converging under the pressure of economic necessity, but the methods of implementation differed radically. Witte envisioned his ministry as the engine of reform, while the *Herald* group believed that the initiative should belong to the zemstvos.

In 1899, Witte published *Autocracy and the Zemstvo*, in which he argued that the principle of local self-government contradicted the monarchical principle. He vigorously denounced the zemstvo for its costliness and fiscal irresponsibility. He also prevailed on Nicholas II to replace interior minister Ivan Goremykin with deputy finance minister Dmitrii Sipiagin, which allowed the two ministries to "settle in an alliance that seemed to zemstvo leaders to mark the beginning of a conspiracy against them." In June 1900, Witte and Sipiagin produced laws placing a 3 percent per annum limit on the increase of zemstvo budgets and removing the zemstvo from the organization of food relief for which Arsen'ev had argued since 1891.[95]

Witte clearly understood the authority with which the right to tax and spend empowered the zemstvo. In the 1890s, the most heated conflicts between central and local administrations concerned taxation and, in particular, the right to raise income to provide for education and health care.[96] In Arsen'ev's scheme, the state and the zemstvos would cooperate in developing projects. In reality, the Finance Ministry's financial interests ran against those of the zemstvos as Witte rushed to industrialize the country.

Meanwhile, Russia's conservative press identified the zemstvo as the cause of modernization's ills in the late 1890s. The *Moscow News* and the *Citizen* mounted a relentless crusade against local self-government and blamed all social ills on the "nomadic intelligentsia of petty administrators." They argued that no ministry could supersede "independent social life in the country," by which Slonimskii took them to mean not the zemstvos, of course, but the combination of the gentry, the governors with their bureaucracies, and the land captains. In response, Slonimskii upheld the liberal formula of "self-government, glasnost, and public control." Since the last two remained unfulfilled in Russia, he praised the zemstvos for absorbing the country's brightest minds from the universities and hiring talented scientists, statisticians, and writers.[97] Slonimskii thus articulated an ideal socio-administrative amalgam for successful modernization—while self-government encouraged all socio-economic classes to formulate local needs, a responsive and enlightened central administration, aware of foreign economic developments and intellectual trends, would direct modernization with constant reference to its effects on the ground. It was a respectable dream.

By 1900, the effects of the general European economic recession finally reached Russia and the conservative *Moscow News* and the *Citizen* turned against both the liberals and Witte. In a rare show of support for the enlightened bureaucracy, Slonimskii addressed a series of articles by writer Dmitrii Tsertelev in the *Moscow News* that blamed the "nomadic petty bureaucratic intelligentsia" for severing the ties between the people and the tsar.[98] In an editorial article, the *Citizen* also blamed "the ministries" for stamping out the last vestiges of independent activity within the empire and concluded that the zemstvos and juries should be abolished, while governors aided exclusively by the land captains should take over all local affairs. The conservatives even accused the landed gentry of collaborating with the bureaucrats by participating in local self-government.[99]

Slonimskii defended Russia's "newest" bureaucracy by arguing that each year the ministries "absorbed the best intelligent minds," while the majority of university graduates joined state chanceries. Every ministry, especially Finance and Agriculture, boasted many honest, bright, experienced, and talented writers and thinkers who made priceless contributions to their subjects and disseminated crucial practical knowledge among the public.[100] It was best to leave agricultural development policy in their care (as opposed to the gentry), the countryside to the zemstvos, and justice to the juries, Slonimskii concluded.

The trickle of economic coverage from the dailies indicated that despite its economic achievements, Russia remained a traditional autocracy whose policies were factors of court preferences. As Witte went on the defensive during the recession, support for him in the media declined. The *Stock Exchange News* all but stopped covering economic issues in 1900 and redirected its attention to education and foreign affairs.[101] The *Russian News* concentrated its attention on the industrial crisis and identified two explanations for it: the influx of foreign capital and the peasantry's weak purchasing power.[102] The paper maintained that Russia's agriculture should depend on private, small-scale rural production units in the form of the commune, which the paper now argued was worth preserving.[103]

In 1900, *New Time* declared that "free labor" was now the central economic issue "because the Russian people feels itself constrained by rusted fetters on the international market and even at home." "Give it this freedom," the paper demanded, while admitting that agriculture was in a poor state although the economy was essentially healthy.[104] By 1902, Suvorin's daily gave up on attempts to influence the Finance Ministry's industrialization and financial policies and proposed "raising [the interests of] agriculture above industry."[105] A debate about the role of the commune took place on the pages of the *News* between those who considered it a drag on the peasant economy and those who saw its positive socio-economic functions.[106] Former *Herald* staff member Leonid Polonskii, now with the *Saint Petersburg News*, attempted to moderate by arguing that the peasants would choose their own socio-economic institutions.[107]

By 1902, the poor harvests of 1899 and 1901 and the peasant disturbances that followed them once again forced the state to consider agricultural reforms. However, it went about it in the typical way by setting up two independent bodies—the Special Committee on the Needs of Agriculture under Witte and the Editing Commission on the Question of Peasant Jurisdiction under interior minister Dmitrii Sipiagin. The commissions worked independently of each other and could not escape the ideological predilections of their parent ministries. In 1893, interior minister Ivan Durnovo had organized it so that peasant reform was de facto within the Interior Ministry's purview, which complicated Witte's ability to direct the successful agricultural reform that he needed to salvage his career.

In January 1902, Witte submitted a proposal to set up a joint committee to discuss reforms. All state ministries connected to agriculture, including Finance, Interior, State Property, Agriculture, and others, would be represented. Witte admitted in this report that the peasantry's conditions of life "improved disproportionately" with the "the development of state needs" and that "the Russian people's material and spiritual well being depended on the state of agriculture."[108] Nicholas approved the creation of the Special Committee on the Needs of Agriculture under Witte and promised to endorse its decisions personally.[109] Although Witte tried to convince Nicholas to take personal charge of discussing legal reform, as Alexander II had, the tsar refused.[110]

The press welcomed the formation of Witte's Special Committee on the Needs of Agriculture. Suvorin's *New Time* called the committee's formation "a decisive step towards helping agriculture."[111] When *New Time* closely monitored its proceedings and suggested that the committee consider the landed gentry's problems only within the broader context of agricultural reform. "Everything that was done for the landowner should also be done for the peasant," it demanded.[112] State Bank director and long-time contributor to the *Herald* A. P. Nikol'skii argued for the abolition of the commune, the extension of universal civil and criminal rights to the peasantry, and peasant self-government.[113] The *Russian News* also welcomed the Special Committee, but wrote that only glasnost and cooperation with "local forces" would guarantee its success.[114] In a timely volume, Arsen'ev argued in his introduction to *The Small Zemstvo Unit* (1902)—a collection of essays that argued for the extension of local self-government rights—that the government should "extend and deepen its connection" with the rural population before undertaking any reforms. "This is such a simple truth that one feels it before one understands it," Arsen'ev pleaded.[115]

It seemed that state-zemstvo cooperation had become possible when eighty-two provincial and 536 district and local committees were established to report on regional agricultural needs. However, the ministers excluded the zemstvos from the committees' inquiries into agrarian problems. The assassination of Dmitrii Sipiagin on April 2, 1902, resulted in Viacheslav Pleve becoming interior minister, which boded ill for Witte's agricultural reform plans. Had Witte co-opted the zemstvos into his reform plans earlier, their support could have ensured continuity despite the change of ministers. Senator and State Council member Fyodor Terner, who contributed articles on state agrarian policies to the *Herald*, wrote in his memoirs that "the Witte committee collected a mass of priceless material regarding the situation of the peasantry and worked out some problems, but only a few of these were seen through to their conclusion."[116]

As a result, in 1902 the Russian liberals' attention began to shift from the zemstvos to forming alternative organizations with broader programs beyond local self-government.[117] The proportion of constitutionalists in the Beseda circle, the unofficial meetings of liberals and constitutionalists, grew rapidly at this time. The pressure of the mounting social crisis, government disinterest in public opinion, and bureaucratic incompetence mobilized the men of the 1880s into political opposition, abandoning the gospel of small deeds and the path of strict legality. Beseda facilitated political communication within zemstvo ranks and between zemstvo men and the intelligentsia, which led to the creation of the Union of Liberation, the Union of Zemstvo Constitutionalists, and eventually the Constitutional Democratic Party. Beseda was the group in which a number of prominent zemstvo men took their first steps outside the zemstvo institutions in seeking the realization of their political goals.[118] Witte was in a bind. By excluding zemstvo representatives from direct participation in the committees and appealing directly to the peasantry's interests, he eliminated the local self-government obstacle, but the payoff was the creation of a liberal backlash that pointed toward 1905.

WITTE AND THE LIBERALS

While submitting the 1903 budget to the State Council, Witte admitted that in 1902 rural taxation "had reached its extreme limit" and that increasing it further would have deleterious effects on the economy.[119] This realization came too late, however, when in August 1903 Tsar Nicholas dismissed Witte by appointing him chairman of the Council of Ministers. In his new post, Witte had very little influence over state policy, which was precisely Nicholas's intention.

Witte's dismissal elicited a mixed response in the press. The *Stock Exchange News* bemoaned his departure, not least because Witte had left Russia's rural problems unresolved.[120] Suvorin's *New Time* echoed this concern and criticized Witte for "over-developing the state sector."[121] The *News* wrote, "It is hard to imagine something greater, brighter, more vibrant, than the eleven years during which Sergei Iul'evich Witte directed our Finance Ministry."[122] Nevertheless, the paper considered protectionism the leading cause of the economic crisis that began in 1900.[123] The *Russian News* supported Witte's policies and argued that his failures were not entirely his fault and that "changes were necessary."[124] A month later, the *Russian News* published a series of articles condemning the "Witte System" as a whole.[125]

Arsen'ev argued that Witte's tenure crowned the twenty-year process of "the return of government," which the Great Reforms had temporarily interrupted. The Finance Ministry, he argued, had spearheaded an administrative crusade with Witte at its helm. Government superseded self-government and Witte never camouflaged his distrust of the zemstvo. In 1899, his interference prevented the expansion of self-government institutions to the empire's western provinces. The top-down approach that produced greater profits for railroads, argued Arsen'ev, was unacceptable when it came to governing a country. The zemstvos made possible the network of peasant schools and recruited an "army of doctors" that had brought modern medicine to the rural areas. They produced valuable statistical analysis "based on personal observation" that penetrated into "the depths of local life." Unfortunately, Witte's tenure dismissed and sometimes even undermined these achievements. Nevertheless, Arsen'ev praised Witte's Committee on the Needs of Agriculture and its attention to the peasants' legal status and spoke highly of Witte's educational legacy, although he almost completely ignored rural schools in favor of middle and higher education.[126]

In the same issue of the journal, Arsen'ev praised Witte's specialized education in contrast to the "numbing ultra-classicism" that had become a political weapon in the 1870s. After Witte's dismissal a rumor swept through Saint Petersburg that the Education Ministry would take over all the higher education institutions. By preventing competition between schools, Arsen'ev argued, this would stifle innovation, discourage educational experiments, and stunt the culture of knowledge in Russia. Only decentralized education wherein ministries ran their own network of institutions allowed specialization and competition for students, and Witte had contributed to this phenomenon.[127]

Slonimskii evaluated Witte's legacy in early 1904 by reviewing statistics.[128] It is rare that a man can paint a picture with numbers, but Slonimskii's gift for language enabled him to produce a very bleak canvas of rural conditions. Between 1893 and 1903, the exchequer annually exceeded its collections by 1.3 million rubles above its 1893 estimates. Instead of coming from the rising productivity of Russia's economy, however, the profit came at the peasantry's expense. Indirect taxes increased from three rubles per capita in the 1870s to five rubles in 1901, so the price of goods such as kerosene, sugar, tea, coffee, rice, herring, and vodka rose while the price of agricultural commodities fell. Protectionism was behind this artificial imbalance.[129] Slonimskii agreed with the prevailing view among zemstvo representatives that the center was taking too much from the provinces and leaving little to invest in basic and professional education. A survey of local demands narrowed them down to three principle issues: (1) ending industrial protectionism, (2) easing the tax burden, and (3) implementing the income tax. "Agriculture," Slonimskii concluded, "demanded not privileges, but equal treatment."[130] Overall, Slonimskii was skeptical of bureaucratic reform plans that identified isolated factors as kernels of the agricultural crisis and he reiterated his belief that the first step in the variegated process of reform was the elimination of the peasantry's "special status."[131] His view coincided with Witte's.

Witte summarized his conclusions on the agrarian question in his famous *Memorandum on Peasant Affairs*, which the *Herald of Finances* published in 1904. Witte agreed with the conclusion of the local committees that the rural economy would improve once legal reforms "encouraged the development of economic entrepreneurship and initiative," while "technical and economic" measures would have an "insignificant" impact on the rural economy.[132] Witte suggested reorganizing rural self-government along an all-estate structure. While village communities would decide on questions of communally held land, all-estate cantons would oversee everything else and cooperate with the zemstvo by acting as its local extensions (albeit under the supervision of the land captains). The peasant canton court would become the basic all-estate link in the legal structure.

Although there is no direct proof that Witte read the *Herald*, his memoirs prove that he knew Arsen'ev personally.[133] Directed by necessity, Witte's solution to Russia's agricultural problems was tactical and only satisfied Slonimskii's side of the *Herald* program. The zemstvo issue, Arsen'ev's side, remained an unbridgeable gulf and Stolypin would continue in the Witte tradition and implement his reforms from the top down. The *Herald* program remained unfulfilled as a whole. The state's conduct continued to demonstrate a deep suspicion of the rural masses, and this distrust echoed the Populist conviction that the peasants were unable to help themselves. The *Herald* group, however, believed that the peasantry was capable of articulating its interests if only given the chance through all-estate cantons and greater state-zemstvo cooperation.

MODERNIZATION AND THE INDIVIDUAL

Parallel to his examination of Finance Ministry policies and local participation in modernization, in the late 1890s, Slonimskii also began to question the validity of associating capitalism exclusively with the "West." He worked out a development program at the center of which stood neither *Homo economicus*, nor the peasant commune, but the individual—a crucial modern concept that the Witte System neglected. Exploring how the individual negotiated with a modernizing state in the absence of political institutions became the unique contribution that the *Herald* group made to the Russian liberal tradition. The *Herald* approached the individual externally, through local self-government rights that protected the individual's socio-economic interests from the encroachments of Russia's modernization project, of which the Witte System marked the apex. In the process, the *Herald* defined a personal sphere of local socio-economic activity that gave the individual room for self-definition.

Even though by the early twentieth century, Russian Marxists began to rethink their tenets by contextualizing them historically and geographically, but Slonimskii argued that even such works as Tugan-Baranovskii's *Sketches of the Newest History of Political Economy* (1903) did not produce a sufficiently practical result. In his pioneering revisionist work, Tugan-Baranovskii began by explaining that the economic situation of the 1840s had led Marx to assume that the impoverishment of the working class would increase until a breaking point, but the nineteenth century had proven him wrong. The trade-unionist movements proved as valuable for the cause of the working classes as socialist participation in legislatures and cabinets. Marx's greatest contribution to economic theory, Tugan-Baranovskii maintained, was to explain the concentration of production under capitalism and the social and political effects this would have. However, Marxist theory did not explain agricultural production trends and even in relation to industry, it explained only specific periods in specific places.[134]

Slonimskii, however, criticized Tugan-Baranovskii for reevaluating too little in his revisionism—political economy had to go further, abandon its industrial focus, and look beyond "theories of exchange." "The foundations of national economies have little to do with commodity trade," Slonimskii argued, "but lie much deeper; they depend first of all on agricultural relations, which determine a country's economic life and give the national economy a general tone regardless of the industrial system."[135] Were Russian economists to explore rural problems, they would be justified in creating "a special path" of economic research. It was no longer a question of "reworking, cleaning, and transforming" Marxism, as Tugan-Baranovskii had argued in his preface.[136] Slonimskii argued instead that economic theorists would do better to start with "the groundwork of economic life—the foundations of the agricultural economy and landownership relations."[137]

A month after Witte's dismissal from the Finance Ministry, Leonid Slonimskii used the publication of *Problems of Idealism* as an occasion to evaluate his country's economic achievements and Russian Marxism as a whole. He wrote the book off as pointless idealistic musings that completely ignored the economic injustices, judicial abuses, and administrative arbitrariness that took place in the real world. "The lyrical excesses of idealism are as groundless as the sorry theoretical attempts of Marxism," he wrote. He saw the flight to metaphysics as a natural consequence of Marxist idealism, which had little to do with positivist sensibilities, let alone materialism. Finance ministers Reitern and Bunge had already made capitalist development the official state doctrine and Vyshnegradskii had already crowned the process before the Russian Marxists even appeared on the scene in the 1890s to "prove that capitalism was a reality." Slonimskii maintained that Russian Marxism was a form of idealistic apologetics and a Panglossian illusion—a form of metaphysical idealistic indifference.[138] He failed to recognize that, like the *Herald* liberals themselves, the contributors to *Problems of Idealism* were also attempting to re-articulate the individual freedom and intellectual independence of a flourishing civil society with no political outlets.

Capitalism per se was not the central concern for the *Herald* liberals. They focused instead on the Finance Ministry's development policies. Slonimskii evaluated the Witte System not from the central point of view, but from the local level. The increasing "centralization of revenue," he argued, has left "the province less civilized and poorer." The local agricultural committees that Witte had created to collect information under the auspices of the Committee on the Needs of Agriculture asked for no special privileges, Slonimskii argued. They demanded from the center no more than equal treatment in economic terms—less preference for industry, lower taxes on the peasantry, and a gradual implementation of an income tax. They demanded the creation of smaller local self-government units and "the abolition or limitation of the functions" of the land captains. They demanded that the state grant full civil rights to the peasants who could still be incarcerated for non-fulfillment of labor agreements, criminally prosecuted for profligacy and drunkenness, held in jail on a bread-and-water diet, and corporally punished. Last, but not least, the committees demanded a broader and more inclusive basic education system. In order to galvanize the local initiative and participation necessary for these changes, the state should "open the valves that are repressing local social forces" and the Russian "provinces will become transformed within one generation."[139] These words articulately summed up the crux of the journal's economic program.

Leonid Slonimskii's examination of Marxism restated and supplemented what Konstantin Arsen'ev and Aleksandr Pypin had also argued on the pages of the *Herald*. Legal reform was absolutely necessary, but insufficient by itself. Socially stable and economically successful modernization would produce long-term results only if the state extended the rights and responsibilities of local self-government and made the Russian population a participant

in modernization, not a subject of economic experiments. Ideological justifications for reform—be they Populist, Marxist, or other—had little to do with
reality regardless of the objectivity to which their proponents laid claim. The
social stability that would come with popular participation would compensate for the slower pace of economic development, but would make it less
likely that social backlashes would reverse it or that revolutions would erupt
in its wake.

Theory and Practice: Mikhail Stasiulevich's Public Service

The Marxist-Populist debate unfolded at the dawn of the Silver Age of Russian culture, which witnessed a proliferation of intellectual and religious quests
for social justice. Among the kaleidoscopic variety of alternatives, Mikhail
Stasiulevich chose public service through local self-government and engagement in civil society to improve public well-being and the lot of the average
citizen. Stasiulevich remained level-headed, rational, and cool during this
turbulent period when many Russian intellectuals passionately espoused
Marxism one day, neo-Kantianism the next, and Christian mysticism the
week after. Perhaps the predictable frequency of his trips to the censorship
bureau in Theater Square contributed to his self-discipline and consistency.
Perhaps the responsibility of running a successful publishing business in
an unpredictable environment and a precarious market demanded Job-like
patience and superb diplomatic skills. Whatever it was, Stasiulevich never
saw profits and commerce as ends in themselves. Even Plekhanov wrote of
him: "Stasiulevich deserves great respect as an honest, unselfish, staunch,
and productive person. But the convictions of this honest, unselfish, and productive person bear upon them the imprint characteristic of abstract Russian
liberalism, which, according to its very nature, is condemned to complete
debility."[140] Plekhanov severely misjudged Stasiulevich and *Herald* liberalism
as a whole.

Much like Pypin's, Stasiulevich's life also became a testament to what a
Russian liberal could do for his country. From 1881, Stasiulevich was a member of the Petersburg City Duma, which elected him deputy chairman in
1883, although the interior minister prevented the appointment. In the same
year, Stasiulevich became the executive head of the city's water supply commission and spearheaded the campaign to install water filters. After the water
supply authorities took the case to court, the city won. Although childless,

Stasiulevich dedicated himself to the cause of education in Saint Petersburg. From 1884, he was a member of the city educational commission and became its chairman in 1890. At the time, Petersburg had 262 gymnasia, 118 of them for women, but by 1900 there were 344. Sunday schools increased from 8 to 22 on Stasiulevich's watch. He explained his dedication in rather interesting terms in a speech given before the city gymnasia commission on November 17, 1897:

> Our educated society is on a par with those of European countries, but beneath the great writers, scientists, and artists, there is an immense chasm. In the West, enlightenment rests on a broad foundation of national education, while in our country it represents an oasis in an enormous desert of national ignorance—a bright spot upon a dark background. It is customary to measure material and physical conditions based on the mortality rate. If it rises above thirty per thousand, even the healthy become endangered. If, on the contrary, it decreases below twenty per thousand, then even the sick can find support. The same can be said about education: where the percentage of illiteracy rises above a certain level, intellectual death strikes at a young age. [. . .] We are only a hair above countries that we consider uncultured when it comes to national education. In Russia, the question of national education is gaining ground and may have already become preeminent.[141]

Even after he resigned in 1900 as chairman of the city education commission due to disagreements with the City Duma chairman, he remained an active member of that body. He was also a member of the Duma's executive commission and a representative of the City Duma in the zemstvo of Petersburg province. Between 1887 and 1899, Stasiulevich served as an honorary justice of the peace. He passionately championed civic participation and believed that every elected member of a local organization must face "the judgment of his peers if he has been called by them to fulfill a social function for the city." He was a member of a commission that allocated stipends to students and supported orphans (1884–1895); chairman and then member of the Financial Commission (1884–1894); chairman of the City Duma election reform commission (1884); city representative to the council on prison and poverty issues (1886); member of the commission on buying flour (1891); member of the commission on the number of city justice of the peace districts (1892); city representative to the commission on the poor laws (1892); member of the special Duma group on the building of the Troitskii Bridge

(1894); and member of the board of the Alexander III Shelter (1895). This list does not exhaust all the posts he held. On the fiftieth anniversary of Stasiule-vich's public service in 1897, Arsen'ev sent him a congratulatory letter, which demonstrated both Stasiulevich's achievements and a fellow intellectual's gratitude:

> You were lucky: you spent the best years of your youth in a university. Unfor-tunately, you had to leave it too early. But regardless of the reasons, you man-aged to create a new academic department for yourself—and such a solid one that despite the storms and problems, it has survived for thirty years. The *Her-ald of Europe*'s audience is not as close to you as that of students to their pro-fessor, but it is undoubtedly wider and has listeners who have been faithful to you from the very beginning. How much kindness and feeling it has towards you! You witnessed this during the journal's twenty-fifth anniversary. In addi-tion to your professorship, I have always respected your public service with its struggles and victories. This included immense organizational duties that befall few other city and zemstvo activists.[142]

Arsen'ev's lines show genuine sympathy and respect for half a century of service to society. The truncated list of Stasiulevich's responsibilities proves that Arsen'ev's awe was well founded. Stasiulevich practiced what his jour-nal preached—social change through civic involvement instead of abstract theorizing.[143]

Conclusion

ALTHOUGH ITS POPULARITY AND IMPACT noticeably decreased on the eve of the 1905 revolution, the *Herald of Europe* left an important legacy. The journal never questioned Russia's belonging to European culture and never took the "us versus them" approach to it, although the editors believed that Russia followed a unique socio-economic evolution. Focusing its readers' attention on Russia's domestic conditions, the *Herald* never allowed them to lose sight of the extended family of Western nations to which Russia belonged and made comparisons to its Western neighbors without encouraging inferiority complexes. In other words, *Herald* liberalism held the promise of non-convergent socio-economic evolution without the stigma of backwardness.

By analyzing Russia's socio-economic trends, the role of the state in directing modernization, and the part of local self-government in this process, the *Herald of Europe* helped its readers to articulate questions about modernization in terms of civic participation that challenged the autocratic model of state-society relations without undermining social stability. Immersion in local self-government eliminated the conflict between private and political life and integrated the individual by allowing him or her to acquire extra-parliamentary social significance. It is no accident that many Russian liberals who became prominent in the Duma era emerged out of the pre-1905 zemstvo movement. Modernization according to the *Herald* model encouraged Russians to understand themselves through participating in local self-government—a constructive act that nurtured individuality within a pluralistic environment.

Contextualizing Russian liberalism in the experiences of its Central European cousins during the age of mass politics sheds valuable light on *Herald* liberalism's advantages. Having challenged the rights of the crown in favor of the up-and-coming educated and economically empowered minorities, European liberalism led to the appearance of mass politics by the end of the nineteenth century, which in turn began to threaten liberalism's core values. While in England, "piecemeal widening of the franchise . . . slowed and modulated the arrival of mass politics, making life easier for the liberal-minded," liberalism's experience in Central Europe proved a lot more complicated.[1] For example, fin de siècle Austrian liberals experienced a rude awakening when their *Vereine*-based vision of civil society proved unrealizable. Mass politics, it turned out, no longer resembled a club with voluntary membership that enforced universal rules of conduct and ran under an invisible hierarchy of active and peripheral members. In order to safeguard the purity of their message, Austrian liberals embraced nationalist rhetoric.[2] In Germany, liberals embraced individualism and elitism that reflected their ambivalence towards democracy, while the metropolitan ideals that enabled political differentiation for German liberals eventually morphed into national chauvinism.[3] *Herald* liberalism's emphasis on local self-government prevented it from following the Central European path. Nonetheless, it faced opposition from a government unable to distinguish between social spontaneity and subversion, loyal opposition and radicalism.

The censors' attitude to the journal after 1881 demonstrates the arbitrariness of judgment that hung over the journal. In 1889, a censor wrote that the *Herald of Europe* "was in open opposition to the state" and suspiciously sympathetic "to the widest possible autonomy for our borderlands."[4] Four years later, another censor described the journal's "extraordinary uprightness and prudent moderation" in "melancholically dragging one foot" in its efforts to remind society "of the benefits of social self-government."[5] The attitude towards the *Herald* during the 1890s was indicative of the tsarist government's increasing inability to perceive real threats.

In 1895, Pobedonostsev's protégé Mikhail Solovyov was placed in charge of the Main Department of the Press and every journal issue's fate became more precarious. Pages were repeatedly cut and printing arbitrarily stopped and then allowed again. Stasiulevich wrote in 1895: "Our journalism now has to think less about what it says than about what it must not say."[6] The conservatives who engineered the fading of Witte's star around 1900 also created problems for the *Herald*. For example, Anatolii Koni wrote that interior minister Pleve criticized him face-to-face for cooperating with Stasiulevich.[7] Was there no greater threat to social stability than a liberal journal?

In 1889, the *Herald* still had only one warning, but this changed after the governor of Finland, Nikolai Bobrikov, complained to censorship chief Solov-yov that the *Herald* supported national aspirations and incited opposition to the governor's initiatives in Finland.[8] As a result, the Interior Ministry issued its second official warning to the journal in February 1899, bringing it per-ilously close to being shut down. Not only did the journal remain afloat, however, but its two senior editors reached the pinnacle of their academic and public careers after this second warning, demonstrating that there was more to *Herald* liberalism than words. Stasiulevich and Pypin practiced what they preached not only by participating in local self-government, but also by achieving professional recognition. However, Stasiulevich's deteriorating eye-sight, and Pypin's death in 1904, placed increasing responsibility on Arsen'ev's shoulders as the Romanov Empire approached the threshold of 1905 that would mark the bursting forth of mass politics in Russia.

Stasiulevich's personal reaction to the revolution demonstrated the diffi-cult position in which the older liberals found themselves. After learning that all 121 workers of his printing shop had joined the general strike in Decem-ber 1905, he wrote: "Where are we headed?! You would think that Russia wants to end its history by suicide!!"[9] In reaction to the violence of 1905, the *Herald* also moved to the right, which both Leo Tolstoy and Maksim Gorky noted.[10] However, this did not prevent Gorky from contributing materials to the journal in 1912 and 1913.

A decade earlier, in 1895, a group of publishers and writers submitted a petition to Tsar Nicholas II asking for a revision of the censorship statutes. Although Nikolai Mikhailovskii was the petition's principal author, Arsen'ev and Spasovich contributed a "Note on the Changes of the Laws on the Press" as an appendix, while Stasiulevich became one of the signatories. It took another ten years and the 1905 revolution before the state finally began to re-vise the statutes regulating the press. Stasiulevich, Arsen'ev, and Koni joined Dmitrii Kobeko's Special Council charged with this revision in 1905. Their colleagues were ultraconservative Vladimir Meshcherskii, Aleksei Suvorin, and economist and member of the Black Hundreds Dmitrii Pikhno. The lib-erals' minimum program aimed at no more than the substitution of judicial for administrative control over the press. By this time, however, the more radical members of the Council already considered Stasiulevich and Arsen'ev "rightist liberals."[11]

The *Herald*'s popularity declined in the wake of the 1905 revolution to four thousand monthly subscribers by 1908, when Stasiulevich left the running of the journal to Arsen'ev, Slonimskii, and Mikhail Gershenzon.[12] The proliferation of new journals diluted the literary pool from which the editors chose materials to publish. The very age that the *Herald* helped to create caused its popularity to decline as its unique stature slowly evaporated. The liberal movement, which gathered strength throughout the 1890s as a result of Witte's policies, led to inchoate political organizations and groups, most of which established their own papers, journals, and printing houses, as the *Herald* dissolved in the maelstrom of prerevolutionary political activity. The *Herald* editors tried to enter the political fray by creating the *Poriadok* (*Order*) Party, but the process never progressed beyond announcements and declarations. The party's platform of a hereditary constitutional monarchy failed to reflect increasingly radical popular demands that even the Constitutional (Kadet) Party satisfied only partially.[13]

On the eve of the revolution, Stasiulevich tried to make up for the lag in journal subscriptions with books. The publishing house turned to scientific and educational literature, the most successful of which was a series of unorthodox and provocative textbooks on the history of the Russian Empire and Western Europe by Nikolai Kareev and Aleksandr Trachevskii. Stasiulevich also remained loyal to his old friends. Kavelin's works came out in four volumes in 1897, although Stasiulevich understood that the current "age was not interested in idealism and the highest ethics."[14] When in 1902 he offered a subscription to Pypin's *History of Russian Literature*, only 793 people ordered the books.[15] There were other non-commercial publications of works by Kostomarov, Belinskii, Spasovich, Ziber, and Ianzhul, as well as famous anatomist and surgeon Nikolai Pirogov and poet Aleksei Zhemchuzhnikov. In 1907, Stasiulevich turned to works by younger writers Vladimir Kuzmin-Karavaev and Nikolai Rusanov and literary historian and sociologist Razumnik Vasil'evich Ivanov, as well as translations of Pierre-Joseph Proudhon. However, it was too late for intellectual somersaults. Stasiulevich and his journal were falling behind the revolutionary times.

The journal's cautious but practical liberalism, which it adapted to Russian conditions, sounded increasingly out of tune with the aesthetic solipsism, philosophical idealism, Christian mysticism, and Marxist radicalism that characterized the eve of the 1905 revolution. More disappointing, however, was the eclipse of the journal's moderate self-government message by the increasingly vicious rhetoric, radical demands, and the inevitable counter reaction that characterized Russia's parliamentary experiment between 1905 and 1914. Unlike many schools of thought during and after 1905, the *Herald* liberals never positioned themselves as prophets with moral and national authority, nor did they see their readers as devout and ardent acolytes. Victor Frank once described in a metaphor the gentry manors as "cradles of civilization" in Russia:

> [Their] pseudo-classical contours with moulding [sic] on the façade, surrounded by neglected parks and overgrown ponds, became for Russia what the cities had been for ancient Greece, the monasteries for medieval Europe, the 'manses' of Presbyterian ministers of Scotland, the *Pfarrhäuser* for protestant Germany.[16]

When the Russian gentry (and their manors) lost this influence after the Great Reforms, the thick journals carried on the civilizing mission. Through the wide-ranging topics on their pages, they made accessible an immense repository of intellectual and spiritual treasures. Indeed, the *Herald of Europe* consistently drew its readers' attention to the zemstvos. After 1905, however, the focus of attention switched to Duma politics, which was ironically a loss for the cause of local self-government. This caused the abstract liberal ideals of constitutionalism and civil rights to become increasingly incomprehensible to the larger population because they no longer dealt with the local issues that had dominated socio-economic discourse before 1905. In time, perhaps this comprehension gap could have been closed, but the persistent rift proved disastrous by 1917.

The *Herald* editors' participation in local self-government demonstrated that this was a necessary component of the Russian liberal's life-style. In the absence of political institutions, the Russian liberals could grow not only internally and intellectually, but also locally. The journal's set of extra-parliamentary liberal values provided the individual sufficient room for self-expression and self-fulfillment on the local level, which is something that post-Soviet Russian liberals have still not grasped fully. Was this a form of escapism? It would have been had the *Herald of Europe* gone no further than encouraging immersion in local affairs, but the issues it covered also went well beyond zemstvo politics.

It is misleading to identify Russian liberalism as a doomed reconciliation project that tried in vain to bring together the late Romanov Empire's political extremes—it never aimed to do so. Vital and resilient, the *Herald* spread public enlightenment by exposing its readers to alternative world views and nurtured civic values by encouraging participation in local self-government. Ironically, the achievements of 1905—the legalization of political parties and the creation of the Duma—redirected public attention from grass-roots politics to the imperial stage, and the rift once again began to deepen between political passions in the two capitals and social participation in consolidating the revolution's gains on the local level.

Herald liberalism produced an important echo in 1910, which demonstrated the damage that the revolution did to its legacy, but also the hope for a resurrection of *Herald* ideals. In the wake of the revolution of 1905, which they saw as an utter failure, seven intellectuals published the result of their reflections on this event as *Vekhi (Milestones)* in March 1909. The authors were Nikolai Berdiaev, Sergei Bulgakov, Mikhail Gershenzon, Bogdan Kistiakovskii, Pyotr Struve, Semyon Frank, and Aleksandr Izgoev. Mikhail Gershenzon—an editor of the *Herald* at this point—articulated the book's central argument, which urged the Russian intelligentsia to "admit the theoretical and practical primacy of spiritual existence above outward forms of social existence." Since the individual's inner life was "the only creative force of human existence," Gershenzon argued, failure to understand this had undermined the intelligentsia's attempt to "liberate the people" in 1905.[17] The authors articulated four central propositions: that the revolution of 1905 was primarily destructive and therefore a failure; that the Russian intelligentsia (from whose ranks the *vekhovtsy* extricated themselves by distinguishing between the intelligentsia and the educated class) was to blame; that the Russian intelligentsia had lost its national character; and that Russian socialism did not go beyond the redistribution of material and spiritual goods. The conclusion was that in order to prevent further revolutionary cataclysms, the intelligentsia had to undergo psychological and spiritual catharsis.

Vekhi inspired a broad and powerful reaction in over 220 articles and reviews, one of the most prominent of which was *Intelligentsiia v Rossii (The Intelligentsia in Russia)*, which appeared in 1910.[18] The eight contributors to this collective response were Ivan Petrunkevich, Konstantin Arsen'ev, Nikolai Gredeskul, Maksim Kovalevskii, Pavel Miliukov, Dmitrii Ovsianiko-Kulikovskii, Maksim Slavinskii, and Mikhail Tugan-Baranovskii. Three of the authors were associated with the *Herald of Europe*—Arsen'ev, Slavinskii (who joined the journal's editorial board in 1911), and cultural historian and linguist Ovsianiko-Kulikovskii (who joined in 1914). While *Vekhi* saw 1905 as a total failure and a tragedy leading to catharsis—a "Crimean War" of the Russian intelligentsia, so to speak—*Intelligentsiia v Rossii* saw it as the culmination of two century's worth of struggle and a quantum leap into the next stage of the liberation movement in Russia.

The *Intelligentsiia* authors did not mince words. Arsen'ev argued that although *Vekhi*'s sermon aroused curiosity, it failed to stir the passions that it targeted, neither emerging from a religious trend, nor containing the necessary ingredients to inspire one. Although the *Vekhi* volume was a welcome wake-up call to the Russian intelligentsia, Miliukov suggested, *intelligenty* should do the exact opposite of what the *vekhovtsy* recommended. The Russian educated classes should use all their strength to finish Russia's political structure by "complet[ing] the roof of this 'spacious' but incomplete house."[19]

The *Vekhi* volume was Russia's elitist and proto-nationalist answer to the explosion of mass politics in the guise of the revolution of 1905. The *vekhovtsy* followed the Austrian and German liberal traditions in breaking away from mainstream politics in order to safeguard the intellectual and cultural values that Central European liberals also believed mass politics to threaten. However, instead of treating the Russian intelligentsia as a post-Reform monstrosity, as the *vekhovtsy* did, *Intelligentsiia v Rossii* represented another stream of liberal thinking when it offered a more historicist view of the Russian intelligentsia's evolution, one that that may have strayed, but also corrected its own trajectory. Instead of abandoning the political world of "outward forms" for the sake of mystical withdrawal, *Intelligentsiia v Rossii* urged political and social engagement even if it came at the expense of overemphasizing the achievements of 1905 rather than dwelling on its problems. Politics, after all, is often (as much as nationalism) a function of inventing constructive traditions.

The term "Duma" appears once in *Vekhi* and twice in *Intelligentsiia v Rossii*, but the absence of any meaningful discussion of the zemstvos in either work indicates that post-1905 Russian liberalism took an unfortunate turn towards imperial politics at the expense of focusing on the day-to-day business of local self-government. In this sense, *Intelligentsiia v Rossii* also missed the mark by overestimating popular support for liberal interpretations of civil rights and dismissing the grass-roots institutions that could bring these ideals closer to the Russian people. Post-Soviet liberals repeated this mistake. In the 1990s, Aleksandr Solzhenitsyn was the only prominent intellectual to propose the resurrection of local self-government to provide a link between the individual and the nation. While the Yeltsin government was implementing shock therapy reforms and privatizing the spoils of the Soviet economy under the guidance of the IMF, Solzhenitsyn argued, it squandered the chance to enable "the democracy of small spaces." Solzhenitsyn called upon the Russian intelligentsia to "become the driving and working force of local self-government," just as it had in the late imperial period. He thereby articulated a grass-roots democratic movement to challenge the top-down reforms of the Yeltsin era. "If we are not ready to organize ourselves," he argued, "we have no one else to blame."[20]

Notes

INTRODUCTION

1. The zemstvos existed in thirty-four European provinces of Russia in 1864, in thirty-five by 1875, and in forty-three by 1917.

2. Terence Emmons and Wayne Vucinich, eds., *The Zemstvo in Russia: An Experiment in Local Self-Government* (Cambridge: Cambridge University Press, 1982); Thomas S. Pearson, *Russian Officialdom in Crisis: Autocracy and Local Self-Government, 1861–1900* (Cambridge: Cambridge University Press, 1989); Thomas Earl Porter, *The Zemstvo and the Emergence of Civil Society in Late Imperial Russia, 1864–1917* (San Francisco: Mellen Research University Press, 1991); and Alfred B. Evans and Vladimir Gelman, eds., *The Politics of Local Government in Russia* (Lanham, MD: Rowman & Littlefield Publishers, 2004). Of the Russian works, the most readable are O. A. Salov, *Zemstvo: Pervyi real'nyi institut mestnogo samoupravleniia v Rossii* (Moscow: Ekonomika, 2004); and A. P. Korelin, N. G. Koroleva, and L. F. Pisar'kova, eds., *Zemskoe samoupravlenie v Rossii, 1864–1918*, 2 vols. (Moscow: Nauka, 2005).

3. Edith W. Clowes, Samuel D. Kassow, and James L. West, eds., *Between Tsar and People: Educated Society and the Quest for Public Identity in Late Imperial Russia* (Princeton: Princeton University Press, 1991); Harley D. Balzer, ed., *Russia's Missing Middle Class: The Professions in Russian History* (Armonk, NY: M. E. Sharpe, 1996); Joseph Bradley, *Voluntary Associations in Tsarist Russia: Science, Patriotism, and Civil Society* (Cambridge: Harvard University Press, 2009).

4. Jacob Walkin, *The Rise of Democracy in Pre-Revolutionary Russia* (New York: Praeger, 1962); A. D. Stepanskii, *Obshchestvennye organizatsii v Rossii na rubezhe XIX–XX vv.* (Moscow: Moskovskii gosudarstvennyi istoriko-arkhivnyk institute, 1982); B. Pietrov-Ennker and G. N. Ul'ianova, eds., *Grazhdanskaia identichnost' i sfera grazhdanskoi deiatel'nosti v Rossiiskoi imperii: Vtoraia polovina XIX–nachalo XX veka* (Moscow: Rosspen, 2007); L. V. Koshman, *Gorod i gorodskaia zhizn' v*

Rossii XIX stoletiia: Sotsial'nye i kul'turnye aspekty (Moscow: Rosspen, 2008); A. S. Tumanova, *Obshchestvennye organizatsii i russkaia publika v nachale XX veka* (Moscow: Novyi khronograf, 2008); and A. A. Iartsev, *Senat i zemstvo: Administrativnaia iustitsiia i mestnoe samoupravlenie v dorevoliutsionnoi Rossii, 1864–1890* (Kaliningrad: Iskra, 2008), E. Iu. Kazakova-Aprakimova, *Formirovanie grazhdanskogo obshchestva: Gorodskie soslovnye korporatsii i obshchestvennye organizatsii na Srednem Urale (vtoraia polovina XIX-nachalo XX v.)* (Ekaterinburg: RAN-Ural'skoe otdelenie, Institut istorii i arkheologii, 2008).

5. For the evolution of public opinion and the Russian state's attempts to come to terms with it, see V. G. Chernukha, *Pravitel'stvennaia politika v otnoshenii pechati 60–70-e gody XIX veka* (Leningrad: Nauka, 1989).

6. V. E. Kel'ner, *Chelovek svoego vremeni: M. M. Stasiulevich, izdatel'skoe delo i liberal'naia oppositsiia* (St. Petersburg: Izd-vo Rossiiskoi natsional'noi biblioteki, 1993), 241, 297.

7. Robert L. Belknap, "Survey of Russian Journals, 1840–1880," *Literary Journals in Imperial Russia*, ed. Deborah A. Martinsen (Cambridge: Cambridge University Press, 1997), 92.

8. Quoted from Priscilla Reynolds Roosevelt, *Apostle of Russian Liberalism: Timofei Granovsky* (Newtonville, MA: Oriental Research Partners, 1986), 101.

9. Quoted from V. B. Smirnov, *"Otechestvennye zapiski" i russkaia literatura 70–80-kh godov XIX veka* (Volgograd: Izd-vo Vologogradskogo gos. universiteta, 1998), 9.

10. For a discussion of the latest themes in historiography, please see Adele Lindenmeyr, "'Primordial and Gelatinous'? Civil Society in Imperial Russia," *Kritika: Explorations in Eurasian History* 12, no. 3 (Summer 2011): 705–720.

11. Donald Treadgold, "The Constitutional Democrats and the Russian Liberal Tradition," *American Slavic and East European Review* 10, no. 2 (1951): 85–94; Evgenii Lampert, *Sons against Fathers: Studies in Russian Radicalism and Revolution* (Oxford: Clarendon Press, 1965); Charles E. Timberlake, ed., "Introduction," in *Essays on Russian Liberalism* (Columbia: University of Missouri Press, 1972), 5–7; William Rosenberg, *Liberals in the Russian Revolution: The Constitutional Democratic Party, 1917–1921* (Princeton: Princeton University Press, 1974); G. M. Hamburg, *Boris Chicherin & Early Russian Liberalism, 1828–1866* (Stanford: Stanford University Press, 1992), 221; Melissa Stockdale, *Paul Miliukov and the Quest for a Liberal Russia, 1880–1918* (Ithaca: Cornell University Press, 1996), xii, 124.

12. First quote in Thornton Anderson, *Russian Political Thought: An Introduction* (Ithaca: Cornell University Press, 1967), 272–273; and second in Daniel Field, "Kavelin and Russian Liberalism," *The Slavic Review* 32, no.1 (1973): 59.

13. The most articulate critique of the *Sonderweg* approach remains David Blackbourn and Geoff Eley's *The Peculiarities of German History: Bourgeois Society and Politics in Nineteenth-Century Germany* (New York: Oxford University Press, 1984); as well as James Sheehan, *German Liberalism in the Nineteenth Century*

(Chicago: University of Chicago Press, 1978). For the Austrian case, see Pieter Judson, *Exclusive Revolutionaries: Liberal Politics, Social Experience, and National Identity in the Austrian Empire, 1848–1914* (Ann Arbor: University of Michigan Press, 1996).

14. Scholars such as Boris Mironov have emphasized Russia's normality among the European nations during the imperial age. See B. N. Mironov, *Sotsial'naia istoriia Rossii perioda imperii: XVIII-nachalo XX v.* (St. Petersburg: Dmitrii Bulanin, 1999), 1:13–17.

15. George Fischer, *Russian Liberalism: From Gentry to Intelligentsia* (Cambridge: Harvard University Press, 1958), viii.

16. Richard Pipes, *Struve: Liberal on the Left, 1870–1905* (Cambridge: Harvard University Press, 1970), 82–83.

17. Theodore Von Laue, "*Struve: Liberal on the Left, 1870–1905*, Richard Pipes," *The American Historical Review* 77, no. 4 (1972): 1163.

18. V. V. Leontovitsch, *Istoriia liberalizma v Rossii: 1762–1914* (Moscow: Russkii put', 1995).

19. Andrzej Walicki, *Legal Philosophies of Russian Liberalism* (Notre Dame: University of Notre Dame Press, 1992); Hamburg, *Boris Chicherin.*

20. Randall Poole, "Introduction," in *Problems of Idealism: Essays in Russian Social Philosophy*, ed. and trans. Randall Poole (New Haven: Yale University Press, 2003), 6–78.

21. George F. Putnam, *Russian Alternatives to Marxism: Christian Socialism and Idealistic Liberalism in Twentieth-Century Russia* (Knoxville: University of Tennessee Press, 1977).

22. Terence Emmons, *The Formation of Political Parties and the First National Elections in Russia* (Cambridge: Harvard University Press, 1983), 45–46.

23. Stockdale, *Paul Miliukov*, xii, 124.

24. V. A. Kitaev, *Liberal'naia mysl' v Rossii, 1860–1880 gg.* (Saratov: Izdatel'stvo Saratovskogo universiteta, 2004).

25. Daniel Balmuth, "Liberals and Radicals in the Era of Reforms," *Canadian Slavic Studies* 3 (1969): 466–467; P. N. Zyrianov and V. V. Shelokhaev, *Pervaia russkaia revoliutsiia v amerikanskoi i angliiskoi burzhuaznoi istoriografii* (Moscow: Nauka, 1976), 126.

26. G. M. Hamburg, *Politics of the Russian Nobility, 1881–1905* (New Brunswick, NJ: Rutgers University Press, 1984), 32.

27. Leopold Haimson, "The Problem of Social Identities in Early Twentieth-Century Russia," *Slavic Review* 47, no. 1 (1988): 1–20. For liberal attempts to bridge the gulfs, see Rosenberg, *Liberals in the Russian Revolution.*

28. I. F. Gindin, "Russkaia burzhuaziia v period kapitalizma, ee razvitie i osobennosti," *Istoriia SSSR* 2 (1963): 1–42.

29. V. S. Diakin, *Samoderzhavie, burzhuaziia i dvorianstvo v 1907–1911 gg.* (Leningrad: Nauka, 1978); A. Ia. Avrekh, *Tsarizm i IV Duma, 1912–1914 gg.*

(Moscow: Izdatel'stvo Nauka, 1981); V. V. Shelokhaev, *Kadety—Glavnaia partiia liberal'noi burzhuazii v bor'be s revoliutsiei, 1905–1907 gg.* (Moscow: Nauka, 1983); V. S. Diakin and B. V. Ananich, eds., *Krizis samoderzhaviia v Rossii, 1895–1917* (Leningrad: Nauka, 1984); K. F. Shatsillo, *Russkii liberalizm nakanune revoliutsii, 1905–1907 gg.: Organizatsiia, programmy, taktika* (Moscow: Nauka, 1985); N. M. Pirumova and V. Ia. Laverychev, eds., *Zemskaia intelligentsiia i ee rol' v obshchestvennoi bor'be do nachala XX v.* (Moscow: Nauka, 1986); N. M. Pirumova, V. A. Tvardovskaia, and V. Ia. Laverychev, eds., *Obshchestvennoe dvizhenie v Rossii XIX veka: Sbornik statei* (Moscow: Institut istorii SSSR AN SSSR, 1986); R. Sh. Ganelin, *Rossiiskoe samoderzhavie v 1905 godu: Reformy i revoliutsiia* (St. Petersburg : Nauka, 1991).

30. N. M. Pirumova, *Zemskoe liberal'noe dvizhenie: Sotsial'nye korni i evoliutsiia do nachala XX veka* (Moscow: Nauka, 1977).

31. Shatsillo, *Russkii liberalizm.*

32. V. R. Leikina-Svirskaia, *Intelligentsiia v Rossii vo vtoroi polovina XIX v.* (Moscow: Mysl', 1971), and *Russkaia intelligentsia v 1900–1917 gg.* (Moscow: Mysl', 1981).

33. Pirumova and Laverychev, *Zemskaia intelligentsiia.*

34. V. V. Shelokhaev, "Russkii liberalizm kak istoriograficheskaia i istoriosofskaia problema," *Voprosy istorii* 4 (1998): 36.

35. V. I. Prilenskii, *Opyt issledovaniia mirovozzreniia rannikh russkikh liberalov* (Moscow: Rossiiskaia akademiia nauk, 1995); A. V. Gogolevskii, *Ocherki istorii russkogo liberalizma XIX–nachala XX veka* (St. Petersburg: Izd-vo Sankt-Peterburgskogo universiteta, 1996).

36. B. S. Itenberg and V. V. Shelokhaev, eds., *Rossiiskie liberaly: Sbornik statei* (Moscow: Rosspen, 2001), 9.

37. The journal *Russian Studies in History* deserves great credit for translating Russian scholarly articles on liberalism that are difficult to access in the West. See the edition from winter 1998–1999, which covered "Russian Liberalism"; the summer 2003 issue explored "The Russian Nobility and Local Society"; liberals and reforms were analyzed in the summer 2007 issue, entitled "Historians Honor Their Teacher: The P. A. Zaionchkovskii Centenary Conference."

38. V. F. Pustarnakov and I. F. Khudushina, eds., *Liberalizm v Rossii* (Moscow: Rossiiskaia akademiia nauk, 1996).

39. B. S. Itenberg, "Nekotorye voprosy izucheniia russkogo liberalizma XIX veka," in *Russkii liberalizm: Istoricheskie sud'by i perspektivy; Materialy mezhdunarodnoi nauchnoi konferentsii, Moskva, 27–29 maia 1998 g.*, ed. V. V. Shelokhaev et al. (Moscow: Rossiiskaia politicheskaia entsiklopediia, 1999), 494.

40. B. I. Esin, *Russkaia zhurnalistika 70-80-kh godov XIX veka* (Moscow: MGU, 1963), esp. 116–125; A. A. Savenkov, "Vestnik Evropy," in *Ocherki po istorii russkoi zhurnalistiki i kritiki* (Leningrad: LGU, 1965), 367–376; B. I. Esin, "Burzhuazno-liberalnaia pressa," *Istoriia russkoi zhurnalistiki XIX veka*, vol 2, *Vtoraia polovina*

XIX veka, ed. V. E. Evgen'ev-Maksimov (Moscow: MGU, 1969); B. P. Baluev, *Politicheskaia reaktsiia 80-kh godov XIX veka i russkaia zhurnalistika* (Moscow: MGU, 1971), esp. 178–192; B. I. Esin, "Russkaia legal'naia pressa kontsa XIX–nachala XX v.," in *Iz istorii russkoi zhurnalistiki kontsa XIX–nachala XX v.* (Moscow: MGU, 1973), 3–67; M. A. Nikitina, "Vestnik Evropy," in *Literaturnyi protsess i russkaia zhurnalistika kontsa XIX–nachala XX veka: 1890–1904. Burzhuazno-liberal'nye i modernistskie izdaniia*, ed. B. A. Bialik, V. A. Keldysh, and V. R. Shcherbina (Moscow: Nauka, 1982), 4–44.

41. Lousie McReynolds, *The News Under Russia's Old Regime: The Development of a Mass-Circulation Press* (Princeton: Princeton University Press, 1991), 14.

42. Daniel Balmuth, *The Russian Bulletin, 1863–1917: A Liberal Voice in Tsarist Russia* (New York: Peter Lang, 2000).

43. Kel'ner, *Chelovek svoego vremeni*; D. A. Balykin, *A. N. Pypin kak issledovatel' techenii russkoi obshchestvennoi mysli* (Briansk: Grani, 1996); A. A. Alafaev, *Russkii liberalizm na rubezhe 70–80-kh gg. XIX v.: Iz istorii zhurnala "Vestnik Evropy"* (Moscow: Institut Istorii SSSR, 1991).

44. James Billington, *Mikhailovsky and Russian Populism* (Oxford: Clarendon Press, 1958); Arthur Mendel, *Dilemmas of Progress in Tsarist Russia: Legal Marxism and Legal Populism* (Cambridge: Harvard University Press, 1961); Richard Kindersley, *The First Russian Revisionists: A Study of "Legal Marxism" in Russia* (Oxford: Clarendon Press, 1962); Richard Wortman, *The Crisis of Russian Populism* (London: Cambridge University Press, 1967); Andrzej Walicki, *The Controversy Over Capitalism: Studies in the Social Philosophy of the Russian Populists* (Notre Dame, IN: University of Notre Dame Press, 1969); Margaret Canovan, *Populism* (New York: Harcourt Brace Jovanovich, 1981); and Edward H. Judge and James Y. Simms Jr., eds., *Modernization and Revolution: Dilemmas of Progress in Late Imperial Russia: Essays in Honor of Arthur P. Mendel* ([Boulder, CO]: East European Monographs; New York: Distributed by Columbia University Press, 1992).

45. Pieter Judson and James Sheehan have argued the same point about Austrian and German liberalism, respectively. Judson, *Exclusive Revolutionaries*; and Sheehan, *German Liberalism*.

46. Lately think-tank research has conflated liberalism with libertarianism. In *Pragmatizm i liberal'noe mirovozzrenie* (Moscow: Institut ekonomiki perekhodnogo perioda, 2002), Pyotr Kaznacheev argued that the way out of Russia's economic woes was through total non-interference in the economy by the state. In April 2004, the CATO Institute sponsored a conference in Moscow entitled "A Liberal Agenda for the New Century: A Global Perspective" (see http://www.cato.org/events/russianconf2004/index.html). Andrei Illarionov, economic advisor to President Vladimir Putin at the time, gave the keynote address. The conference investigated the following set of questions: How much of an obstacle to growth and a free society is the continuing large size of government in many reforming countries? What are the most important elements of economic freedom? What is the

probable evolution of the rule of law in developing and transition countries? What is the relationship between property rights and authoritarian government?

CHAPTER 1. BORN UNDER THE IRON TSAR

1. R.Sh. Ganelin, et al., eds. *Sankt-Peterburg: 300 let istorii* (St. Petersburg: Nauka, 2003), 169.

2. Richard Stites, *Serfdom, Society, and the Arts in Imperial Russia: The Pleasure and the Power* (New Haven: Yale University Press, 2005), 18.

3. E. A. Ignatova, *Zapiski o Peterburge: Zhizneopisanie goroda so vremeni ego osnovaniia do 40-kh godov XX veka* (St. Petersburg: Amfora, 2003), 172.

4. M. S. Kagan, *Grad Petrov v istorii russkoi kul'tury* (St. Petersburg: Paritet, 2006), 135.

5. Ganelin, *Sankt-Peterburg*, 181.

6. Kagan, *Grad Petrov*, 118.

7. T. J. Binyon, *Pushkin: A Biography* (New York: Knopf, 2003), 215–250.

8. Walter Arndt, *Pushkin Threefold: Narrative, Lyric, Polemic, and Ribald Verse* (New York: Dutton, 1972), 27.

9. Iu. M. Lotman, *Karamzin* (St. Petersburg: Iskusstvo-SPB, 1997), 17.

10. Arndt, *Pushkin Threefold*, 34.

11. Joseph Frank, *Dostoevsky: The Seeds of Revolt, 1821–1849* (Princeton: Princeton University Press, 1976), 9.

12. M. K. Lemke, ed., *M. M. Stasiulevich i ego sovremenniki v ikh perepiskie* (St. Petersburg: Tipografiia M. M. Stasiulevicha, 1911–1913), 1:301.

13. Ibid., 1:27.

14. Konstantin Blumberg, *Piatidesiatiletie S.-Peterburgskoi Larinskoi Gimnazii, 1839–1886* (St. Petersburg: Tip. M. M. Stasiulevicha, 1886), 1–12.

15. Cynthia H. Whittaker, *The Origins of Modern Education: An Intellectual Biography of Sergei Uvarov, 1786–1855* (DeKalb: Northern Illinois University Press, 1984), 147. For an overall discussion of the gymnasia, see 143–151.

16. James G. Hart, "From Frontier Outpost to Provincial Capital: Saratov, 1590–1860," in *Politics and Society in Provincial Russia: Saratov, 1590–1917*, eds. Rex Wade and Scott Seregny (Columbus: Ohio State University Press, 1989), 35.

17. Quoted from A. P. Lanshchikov, *N. G. Chernyshevskii* (Moscow: Sovremennik, 1982), 11. For an excellent analysis of life in provincial towns at this time, see A. I. Kupriianov, *Gorodskaia kul'tura russkoi provintsii: Konets XVIII–pervaia polovina XIX veka* (Moscow: Novyi khronograf, 2007).

18. Lanshchikov, *Chernyshevskii*, 10–11; A. A. Demchenko, *Molodye gody Nikolaia Chernyshevskogo* (Saratov: Privolzhskoe knizhnoe izdatel'stvo, 1989), 16.

19. Quoted Lanshchikov, *Chernyshevskii*, 11.

20. A. N. Pypin, *Moi zametki* (Saratov: Sootechestvennik, 1996), 50, 57; William F. Woehrlin, *Chernyshevskii: The Man and the Journalist* (Cambridge: Harvard University Press, 1971), 19.

21. Woehrlin, *Chernyshevskii*, 17.

22. For an excellent analysis of peasant utopias see K. V. Chistov, *Russkaia narodnaia utopiia: Genezis i funktsii sotsial'no-utopicheskikh legend* (St. Petersburg: Dmitrii Bulanin, 2003).

23. Pypin, *Moi zametki* (1996), 56–57.

24. Woehrlin, *Chernyshevskii*, 14.

25. N. Chernyshevskii to A. N. Pypin, 30 May 1846, in N. G. Chernyshevskii, *Polnoe sobranie sochinenii* (Moscow: Goslitizdat, 1939–1953), 14:13.

26. N. Chernyshevskii to family, 28 June 1846, ibid., 14:23–25.

27. Chernyshevskii, *Polnoe sobranie*, 14:61–62, 71, 75, 106, 114.

28. Francis B. Randall, *N. G. Chernyshevskii* (New York: Twayne Publishers, 1967), 24.

29. Chernyshevskii, *Polnoe sobranie*, 14:47–48.

30. D. A. Balykin, *A. N. Pypin kak issledovatel' techenii russkoi obshchestvennoi mysli* (Briansk: Grani, 1996), 19.

31. P. P. Pekarskii, ed. *Istoricheskie bumagi, sobrannye Konstantinom Ivanovichem Arsen'evym* (St. Petersburg: Tip. Imperatorskoi Akademii Nauk, 1872), 15–19.

32. Susan Smith-Peter, "Defining the Russian People: Konstantin Arsen'ev and Russian Statistics before 1861," *History of Science* 45, no. 1 (March 2007), 50–51.

33. L. M. Liashenko, *Aleksandr II, ili, Istoriia trekh odinochestv* (Moscow: Molodaia gvardiia, 2002), 46; Pekarskii, *Istoricheskie bumagi*, 33.

34. Pekarskii, *Istoricheskie bumagi*, 39.

35. S. N. Semanov, *Aleksandr II: Istoriia tsaria-osvoboditelia, ego ottsa i ego syna* (Moscow: Algoritm, Eksmo, 2003), 75; V. A. Nikolaev, *Aleksandr Vtoroi: Biografiia* (Moscow: Zakharov, 2005), 27, 52, 77.

36. On the embrace of statistics at this time, see Ian Hacking, *The Taming of Chance* (Cambridge: Cambridge University Press, 1990).

37. W. Bruce Lincoln, *In the Vanguard of Reform: Russia's Enlightened Bureaucrats 1825–1861* (DeKalb: Northern Illinois University Press, 1982), 106.

38. Daniel T. Orlovsky, *The Limits of Reform: The Ministry of Internal Affairs in Imperial Russia, 1802–1881* (Cambridge: Harvard University Press, 1981), 30–31.

39. Smith-Peter, "Defining the Russian People," 53.

40. K. I. Arsen'ev, *Tsarstvovanie Petra II* (St. Petersburg: Tipografiia Imperatorskoi Rossiiskoi Akademii, 1839); Arsen'ev, *Tsarstvovanie Ekateriny I* (St. Petersburg: Tipografiia Imperatorskoi Rossiiskoi Akademii, 1856).

41. A. G. Iashchenko, ed., *Russkoe geograficheskoe obshchestvo: 150 let* (Moscow: Progress/Pangeia, 1995), 12.

42. Lincoln, *In the Vanguard of Reform*, 93.

43. Pekarskii, *Istoricheskie bumagi*, 58–59.

44. Ibid., 45–49.

45. K. K. Arsen'ev, "Vospominaniia K. K. Arsen'eva ob uchilishche pravove-deniia, 1849–1855 gg.," *Russkaia starina* 50, no. 4 (1886): 204.

46. See family tree and short biographies in Tatiana Zaitseva and Raisa Slonim-skaia, *Volnye mysli: K iubileiu Sergeia Slonimskogo* (St. Petersburg: Kompozitor, 2003), 256–262.

47. Benjamin Nathans, *Beyond the Pale, The Jewish Encounter with Late Imperial Russia* (Berkeley: University of California Press, 2002), 5.

48. Jonathan Frankel, *Prophecy and Politics: Socialism, Nationalism, and the Russian Jews, 1862–1917* (Cambridge: Cambridge University Press, 1981); David Vital, *The Origins of Zionism* (Oxford: Clarendon Press, 1975).

49. V. E. Kel'ner, *Ocherki po istorii russko-evreiskogo knizhnogo dela vo vtoroi polovine XIX–nachale XX v.* (St. Petersburg: Rossiiskaia natsional'naia biblioteka, 2003), 12.

50. The article "Glorious Pages in the History of National Science and Technology" appeared in *The Red Star* on August 19, 1952. The authors concluded: "Thus the examination of historical evidence leads to the conclusion that our fatherland holds the priority on the duplex system of electric telegraphy made public by the Russian scientist Z. Ia. Slonimskii 12 years before Stirnes and 15 years before Edison." Quoted from Nicolas Slonimsky, *Perfect Pitch: A Life Story* (Oxford: Oxford University Press, 1988), 23.

51. M. L. Slonimskii, *Kniga vospominanii* (Moscow: Sovetskii pisatel', 1966), 9–10.

52. Leonid Slonimskii to Mikhail Stasiulevich, July 24, 1899, Institut Russkoi Literatury (IRLI), Arkhiv M. M. Stasiulevicha, f. 293, op. 1, ed. khr. 1317; Leonid Slonimskii to M. Stasiulevich, August 2, 1901, ibid.

53. Eli Lederhendler, *The Road to Modern Jewish Politics: Political Tradition and Political Reconstruction in the Jewish Community of Tsarist Russia* (Oxford: Oxford University Press, 1989), 110.

54. G. G. Branover, ed., *Rossiiskaia evreiskaia entsiklopediia* (Moscow: Rossiiskaia akademiia estestvennykh nauk, 1994–), 71.

55. Joseph Jacobs and Judah David Eisenstein, "Meridian, Date-," in JewishEncyclopedia.com, http://www.jewishencyclopedia.com/view.jsp?artid=478&letter=M&search=meridian%20date, accessed on May 3, 2008. See also Slonimsky, *Perfect Pitch*, 25.

56. John Doyle Klier, *Imperial Russia's Jewish Question, 1855–1881* (Cambridge: Cambridge University Press, 1995), 241.

57. A. I. Paperna, "Iz nikolaevskoi epokhi," in *Evrei v Rossii: XIX vek*, ed. V. E. Kel'ner (Moscow: Novoe literaturnoe obozrenie, 2000), 176.

58. Lederhendler, *The Road to Modern Jewish Politics*, 113.

59. Slonimskii, *Kniga vospominanii*, 9.

60. Polina Vengerova, *Vospominaniia babushka: Ocherki kul'turnoi istorii evreev Rossii v XIX veke* (Moscow: Mosty kul'tury, 2003), 245.

61. Patrick L. Alston, *Education and the State in Tsarist Russia* (Stanford: Stanford University Press, 1969), 31.

Chapter 2. Formative Years

1. Other historians have made this argument with regard to Russian urban politics at a later age, but the *Herald* story extends it backward in time. See Blair Ruble, *Second Metropolis: Pragmatic Pluralism in Gilded Age Chicago, Silver Age Moscow, and Meiji Osaka* (Cambridge: Cambridge University Press, 2001); and Robert W. Thurston, *Liberal City, Conservative State: Moscow and Russia's Urban Crisis, 1906–1914* (New York: Oxford University Press, 1987).

2. Cynthia H. Whittaker, *The Origins of Modern Russian Education: An Intellectual Biography of Count Sergei Uvarov, 1786–1855* (DeKalb: Northern Illinois University Press, 1984), 153.

3. P. A. Pletnev, "Istoricheskaia zapiska o pervom dvadtsatipiatiletii universiteta, chitannaia 8 fevralia, 1844 goda," in *Otchety o sostoianii Imperatorskogo Sanktpeterburgskogo Universiteta, sostavlennye rektorom ego Petrom Pletnevym* (St. Petersburg: Tipografiia voenno-uchebnykh zavedenii, 1845), 109–221.

4. V. V. Grigor'ev, *Imperatorskii s..peterburgskii universitet v techenie pervykh piatidesiati let ego sushchestvovaniia* (St. Petersburg: V. Bezobrazov i Komi, 1870), 127.

5. Priscilla Reynolds Roosevelt, *Apostle of Russian Liberalism: Timofei Granovsky* (Newtonville, MA: Oriental Research Partners, 1986), 84.

6. Whittaker, *The Origins of Modern Russian Education*, 116.

7. Pletnev, "Istoricheskaia zapiska," 225–226.

8. Grigor'ev, *Imperatorskii s. peterburgskii universitet*, 116–117.

9. Ibid., 213–216.

10. M. K. Lemke, ed. *M. M. Stasiulevich i ego sovremenniki v ikh perepiskie* (St. Petersburg: Tipografiia M. M. Stasiulevicha, 1911–1913), 1:38–39; Chernyshevskii to parents, 15 February 1847, in N. G. Chernyshevskii, *Polnoe sobranie sochinenii* (Moscow: Goslitizdat, 1939–1953), 14:113.

11. M. M. Stasiulevich, *Afinskaia igemoniia* (St. Petersburg: Tipografiia Imperatorskoi Akademii Nauk, 1849).

12. Lemke, *M. M. Stasiulevich i ego sovremenniki*, 1:237.

13. Roosevelt, *Apostle of Russian Liberalism*, 144–146; Lemke, *M. M. Stasiulevich i ego sovremenniki*, 1:237.

14. Derek Offord, *Portraits of Early Russian Liberals: A Study of the Thought of T. N. Granovsky, V. P. Botkin, P. V. Annenkov, A. V. Druzhinin, and K. D. Kavelin* (Cambridge: Cambridge University Press, 1985), 51.

15. M. M. Stasiulevich, *Likurg Afinskii* (St. Petersburg: Tipografiia Imperatorskoi Akademii Nauk, 1851), 13–14.

Notes to pages 38–44

16. Stasiulevich to I. F. Knorring, 29 December 1850/January 9 1851, in Lemke, *M. M. Stasiulevich i ego sovremenniki*, 1:51.

17. Stasiulevich to M. S. Kutorga, 10/21 July 1850, 1:239.

18. A. N. Pypin, *Moi zametki* (Saratov: Sootechestvennik, 1996), 76.

19. Whittaker, *The Origins of Modern Russian Education*, 116.

20. A. N. Pypin, "Nekrolog, V. I. Grigorovich," *Vestnik Evropy* 2 (1877): 892–893.

21. N. Chernyshevskii to parents, 22 November 1849, in Chernyshevskii, *Polnoe sobranie sochinenii*, 14:167.

22. D. A. Balykin, *A. N. Pypin kak issledovatel' techenii russkoi obshchestvennoi mysli* (Briansk: Grani, 1996), 21.

23. Pypin, *Moi zametki* (1996), 93.

24. Ibid., 105.

25. Ibid., 106.

26. Ibid., 122.

27. Ibid., 126.

28. For an overview of late imperial literary scholarship, see Andy Byford, *Literary Scholarship in Late Imperial Russia: Rituals of Academic Institutionalization* (London: Legenda, 2007).

29. A. P. Lanshchikov, *N. G. Chernyshevskii* (Moscow: Sovremennik, 1982), 73–74; A. A. Demchenko, *Molodye gody Nikolaia Chernyshevskogo* (Saratov: Privol'zhskoe knizhnoe izdatel'stvo, 1989), 155–165.

30. Pypin, *Moi zametki* (1996), 131.

31. Ibid., 114.

32. Ibid., 137–138.

33. Ibid., 292.

34. For a list of Pypin's works, see Ia. L. Barskov, *Spisok trudov akademika A. N. Pypina, 1853–1903* (St. Petersburg: Izdanie Otdeleniia russkogo iazyka i slovesnosti Imperatorskoi Akademii Nauk, 1903).

35. Chernyshevskii to parents, 14 September 1853, in Chernyshevskii, *Polnoe sobranie sochinenii*, 14:241; Chernyshevskii to parents, 21 September 1853, 14:243.

36. Chernyshevskii to parents, 6 December 1854, 14:279.

37. Pypin, *Moi zametki* (1996), 156.

38. For a discussion of Orthodoxy's influence on secular thinking, see Laurie Manchester, *Holy Fathers, Secular Sons: Clergy, Intelligentsia, and the Modern Self in Revolutionary Russia* (DeKalb: Northern Illinois University Press, 2008).

39. Pypin, *Moi zametki* (1996), 144.

40. Ibid., 160.

41. Chernyshevskii to parents, 10 May 1855, in Chernyshevskii, *Polnoe sobranie sochinenii*, 14:299.

42. Balykin, *A. N. Pypin*, 28.

43. Chernyshevskii to parents, 7 January 1858, in Chernyshevskii, *Polnoe sobranie sochinenii*, 14:352–353.

Notes to pages 44–49 215

44. Chernyshevskii to parents, 2 November 1854, in N. G. Chernyshevskii, 14:273.

45. E. P. Aksenova, *A. N. Pypin o slavianstve* (Moscow: Indrik, 2006), 31.

46. The other elite school was the Tsarskoe Selo Lyceum, where Aleksandr Pushkin had studied, and the two institutions were rivals. I. A. Tiutchev, "V uchilishche pravovedeniia v 1847–1852 gg.," *Russkaia starina* 48, no. 12 (1885): 677.

47. Iu. R. Shreier, ed., *Piatidesiatiletnii iubilei Ego Imperatorskogo Vysochestva printsa Petra Georgievicha Ol'denburgskogo* (St. Petersburg: Zibert i Foss, 1881), 1:72.

48. Allen A. Sinel, "The Socialization of the Russian Bureaucratic Elite, 1811–1917: Life at the Tsarskoe Selo Lyceum and the School of Jurisprudence," *Russian History* 3, no. 1 (1976): 1–2; Whittaker, *The Origins of Modern Education*, 166–167.

49. W. Bruce Lincoln, *In the Vanguard of Reform, Russia's Enlightened Bureaucrats, 1825–1861* (DeKalb: Northern Illinois University Press, 1982), 74.

50. Tiutchev, "V uchilishche pravovedeniia," *Russkaia starina* 48, no. 11 (1885): 438.

51. Tiutchev, "V uchilishche pravovedeniia," *Russkaia starina* 49, no. 2 (1885): 370.

52. K. K. Arsen'ev, "Vospominaniia K. K. Arsen'eva ob uchilishche pravovedeniia, 1849–1855 gg.," *Russkaia starina* 50, no. 4 (1886): 199–204.

53. Arsen'ev, "Vospominaniia," 211.

54. P. U., *Obshchestvennoe vospitanie i obrazovanie v Rossii: Zapiski ob uchilishche pravovedeniia* (St. Petersburg: V. Demakov, 1869), xiii.

55. Arsen'ev, "Vospominaniia," 220.

56. Nicolas Slonimsky, *Perfect Pitch: A Life Story* (Oxford: Oxford University Press, 1988), 9.

57. M. F. Vladimirovskii-Budanov, *Istoriia Imperatorskogo Universiteta Sv. Vladimira* (Kiev: Tipografiia universiteta Sv. Vladimira, 1884), 1:85–160; Whittaker, *The Origins of Modern Russian Education*, 191, 193–197.

58. V. S. Chevazhevskii, "Iz proshlogo Kievskogo universiteta i studencheskoi zhizni," *Russkaia starina* 150, no. 6 (1912): 581–582.

59. Michael F. Hamm, *Kiev: A Portrait, 1800–1917* (Princeton: Princeton University Press, 1993), 18–54, 117–134.

60. Benjamin Nathans, *Beyond the Pale: The Jewish Encounter with Late Imperial Russia* (Berkeley: University of California Press, 2002), 234.

61. Patrick L. Alston, *Education and the State in Tsarist Russia* (Stanford: Stanford University Press, 1969), 55.

62. V. G. Sarbei et al., eds., *Istoriia Kieva* (Kiev: Naukova Dumka, 1982), 2:214–228; Chevazhevskii, "Iz proshlogo," 567–572.

63. Vladimirovskii-Budanov, *Piatidesiatiletie Imperatorskogo Universiteta*, 38–40.

64. Chevazhevskii, "Iz proshlogo," 564–566.

65. I. I. Ianzhul, *Otchet o prakticheskikh zaniatiiakh na iuridicheskikh fakul'te-takh vos'mi russkikh universitetov* (St. Petersburg: V. Bezobrazov i Ko., 1903), 1–3.

66. Vladimirovskii-Budanov, *Piatidesiatiletie Imperatorskogo Universiteta*, 17–24.

67. Chevazhevskii, "Iz proshlogo," 578–580.

68. N. P. Iasnopol'skii, *Spetsializatsiia uchebnykh planov prepodavaniia i zaniatii naukami iuridicheskimi, gosudarstvennymi i ekonomicheskimi v universitetakh Rossii* (Kiev: Tipografiia universiteta Sv. Vladimira, 1907), 165–174.

69. See Susan Heuman, *Kistiakovsky: The Struggle for National and Constitutional Rights in the Last Years of Tsarism* (Cambridge: Harvard University Press, 1998), 8–16.

70. Nathans, *Beyond the Pale*, 248.

71. V. L. Stepanov, *N. Kh. Bunge: Sud'ba reformatora* (Moscow: Rosspen, 1998), 52.

72. Chevazhevskii, "Iz proshlogo," 577–578.

73. Stepanov, *N. Kh. Bunge*, 23–31.

74. M. M. Stasiulevich, "Nekrolog, Nikolai Khristianovich Bunge," *Vestnik Evropy* 8 (1895): 422–426.

75. Stepanov, *N. Kh. Bunge*, 44–53.

CHAPTER 3. NO PLACE FOR TALENT

1. For an in-depth study of the *raznochintsy*, see Elise Kimerling Wirtschafter, *Structures of Society: Imperial Russia's "People of Various Ranks"* (DeKalb: Northern Illinois University Press, 1994); and Nathaniel Knight, "Was the Intelligentsia Part of the Nation? Visions of Society in Post-Emancipation Russia," *Kritika: Explorations in Eurasian History* 7, no. 4 (Fall 2006), 733–758.

2. Derek Offord, *Portraits of Early Russian Liberals: A Study of the Thought of T. N. Granovsky, V. P. Botkin, P. V. Annenkov, A. V. Druzhinin, and K. D. Kavelin* (Cambridge: Cambridge University Press, 1985), 197–199.

3. Quoted from Offord, *Portraits of Early Russian Liberals*, 224.

4. Quoted from Priscilla Reynolds Roosevelt, *Apostle of Russian Liberalism: Timofei Granovsky* (Newtonville, MA: Oriental Research Partners, 1986), 122.

5. M. K. Lemke, ed., *M. M. Stasiulevich i ego sovremenniki v ikh perepiskie* (St. Petersburg: Tipografiia M. M. Stasiulevicha, 1911–1913), 1:28.

6. I. V. Porokh, "Londonskie vstrechi A. N. Pypina s A. I. Gertsenom (k voprosu ob ikh vzaimootnosheniiakh)," *Osvoboditel'noe dvizhenie v Rossii* 14 (1992): 18.

7. A. N. Pypin, *Moi zametki* (Saratov: Sootechestvennik, 1996), 168.

8. Ibid., 180–181.

9. Ibid., 180.

10. Chernyshevskii to parents, 30 September 1858, in N. G. Chernyshevskii, *Polnoe sobranie sochinenii* (Moscow: Goslitizdat, 1939–1953), 14:364; Chernyshevskii to parents, 14 October 1858, 14:365.

11. Pypin, *Moi zametki* (1996), 185.

12. Ibid., 204.

13. Ibid., 207.

14. Ibid., 200.

15. *Piatidesiatiletie nauchno-literaturnoi deiatel'nosti akademika A. N. Pypina* (St. Petersburg: A. E. Vineke, 1903), 23.

16. Quoted from Offord, *Portraits of Early Russian Liberals*, 142.

17. The Petersburg press took note of it: "A millionaire's daughter marries not 'his highness' . . . but a poor, young academic," in Lemke, *M. M. Stasiulevich i ego sovremenniki*, 1:118.

18. V. E. Kel'ner, *Chelovek svoego vremeni: M. M. Stasiulevich, izdatel'skoe delo i liberal'naia oppositsiia* (St. Petersburg: Izd-vo Rossiiskoi natsional'noi biblioteki, 1993), 16.

19. These lines belong to Longin Panteleev, a member of the radical Land and Freedom organization and a successful publisher in his own right, who was one of Stasiulevich's students in the 1860s. L. F. Panteleev, *Vospominaniia* (Moscow: Gos. izd-vo khudozh. lit-ry, 1958), 195–196.

20. A. V. Nikitenko, *Dnevnik* (Leningrad: Gos. izd-vo khudozh. lit-ry, 1955), 2:56.

21. V. P. Ostrogorskii, *Iz istorii moego uchitel'stva* (St. Petersburg: Tip. Popova, 1895), 52–53.

22. A. M. Skabichevskii, *Literaturnye vospominaniia* (Moscow: Agraf, 2001), 73–80.

23. Offord, *Portraits of Early Russian Liberals*, 52.

24. Chernyshevskii to parents, 20 June 1860, in Chernyshevskii, *Polnoe sobranie sochinenii*, 14:395.

25. Chernyshevskii to parents, 10 October 1860, 14:411. See also N. I. Kostomarov, *Istoricheskie proizvedeniia: Avtobiografiia* (Kiev: Tip. Kievskogo gos. universiteta, 1989), 571.

26. Kel'ner, *Chelovek svoego vremeni*, 263.

27. V. Obruchev, "Iz perezhitogo," *Vestnik Evropy* 5 (1907): 132; V. D. Spasovich, "Vospominaniia o K. D. Kaveline," in *Polnoe sobranie sochinenii*, ed. K. D. Kavelin (St. Petersburg: Tip. M. M. Stasiulevicha, 1897–1900), 1:xvii; A. Ia. Panaeva, *Vospominaniia* (Moscow: Zakharov, 2002), 282.

28. Abbott Gleason, *Young Russia: The Genesis of Russian Radicalism in the 1860s* (New York: Viking, 1980), 115.

29. V. D. Spasovich, "Piatidesiatiletie Peterburgskogo universiteta," *Vestnik Evropy* 4 (1870) and 5 (1870); and Nikitenko, *Dnevnik*, 2:373.

30. Erich Haberer, *Jews and Revolution in Nineteenth-Century Russia* (Cambridge: Cambridge University Press, 1995), 21–26.

31. V. D. Spasovich, "Piatidesiatiletie Peterburgskogo universiteta," *Vestnik Evropy* 4 (1870): 318–340.

32. Institut Russkoi Literatury (IRLI), f. 250, op. 1, ed. khr. 48, 1. 50.

33. Stasiulevich to wife, 3 June 1862, in Lemke, *M. M. Stasiulevich i ego sovremenniki*, 1:404.

34. V. V. Mavrodin, ed., *Leningradskii universitet v vospominaniiakh sovremennikov* (Leningrad: Izd. Leningradskogo universiteta, 1963), 1:278. The quotes come from the memoirs of N. V. Shelgunov.

35. Stasiulevich to wife, 20 May 1862, in Lemke, *M. M. Stasiulevich i ego sovremenniki,,*1:398.

36. D. A. Balykin, *A.N. Pypin kak issledovatel' techenii russkoi obshchestvennoi mysli* (Briansk: Grani, 1996), 34, 150.

37. N. M. Chernyshevskaia, ed., *Delo Chernyshevskogo: Sbornik dokumentov* (Saratov: Privol'zhskoe knizhnoe izd-vo, 1968), 92, 94, 104, 111, 113, 134, 592; and Chernyshevskii to A. N. and E. N. Pypin, 30 June [1863], in Chernyshevskii, *Polnoe sobranie sochinenii*, 484.

38. Chernyshevskaia, *Delo Chernyshevskogo*, 104.

39. M. K. Lemke, *Politicheskie protsessy v Rossii 1860-kh gg. (po arkhivnym dokumentam)*, 2nd ed. (Moscow: Petrograd gos. izdat., 1923), 235, 240.

40. S. A. Vengerov, ed., *Iubileinyi sbornik literaturnogo fonda, 1859–1909* (St. Petersburg: Tip. t-va Obshchestvennaia pol'za, 1909), 72–73.

41. The debate about the causes of the split among the journal's editors is ongoing. N. P. Emelianov, *"Otechestvennye zapiski" N. A. Nekrasova i M. E. Saltykova-Shchedrina, 1868–1884* (Leningrad: Khudozhestvennaia literatura, 1986), 17, 19–21.

42. IRLI, f. 250, op. 2, ed. khr. 1, 1. 25.

43. IRLI, f. 163, op. 4, ed. khr. 41, 1l. 35–37.

44. William F. Woehrlin, *Chernyshevskii: The Man and the Journalist* (Cambridge: Harvard University Press, 1971), 330–331.

45. Kostomarov, *Istoricheskie proizvedeniia*, 572.

46. The reform also required not only that the censor state his reasons for warning a publication but also that the periodical publish that statement. This practice, designed to chasten editors and writers and to make clear the limits on public discourse, served to place in full view of the public what often seemed to be vague and petty rulings by censors. Charles A. Ruud, *Fighting Words: Imperial Censorship and the Russian Press, 1804–1906* (Toronto: University of Toronto Press, 1982), 228.

47. N. A. Nekrasov, *Polnoe sobranie sochinenii i pisem* (Leningrad: Nauka, 1981–2000), 12:53.

48. IRLI, f. 250, op. 2, ed. khr. 73, 1l. 115–120.

49. Ruud, *Fighting Words*, 161.

50. N. A. Nekrasov, *Perepiska N. A. Nekrasova* (Moscow: Khudozh. lit-ra, 1987), 1:500.

51. K. K. Arsen'ev, "Iz dalekikh vospominanii," *Golos minuvshego* 2 (1915): 124.

52. For a thorough discussion of this topic, see Richard S. Wortman, *The Development of a Russian Legal Consciousness* (Chicago: University of Chicago Press, 1976).

53. E. P. Karnovich, *Ocherki nashikh poriadkov administrativnykh, sudebnykh i obshchestvennykh* (St. Petersburg: Skariatin, 1873), 1–17.

54. "K kakoi prinadlezhim my partii?," *Russkii vestnik* 37 (1862): 843.

55. Arsen'ev, "Iz dalekikh vospominanii," 161.

56. The "October Affair," as he referred to the officially sanctioned purges that followed the student disturbances, was a foretaste of the authorities' conduct that "cast a dark shadow upon the following decades." Ibid., 161.

57. Ibid., 164–167.

58. See M. G. Korotkikh, *Samoderzhavie i sudebnaia reforma 1864 goda v Rossii* (Voronezh: Izd. Voronezhskogo universiteta, 1989); Peter H. Solomon Jr., ed., *Reforming Justice in Russia, 1864–1996: Power, Culture, and the Limits of Legal Order* (Armonk, NY: M. E. Sharpe, 1997), 3–82.

59. Pavel Kalinnikov, ed., "Arsen'ev Konstantin Konstantinovich," *Russkii Biograficheskii Slovar'*, 20 June 2006, http://rulex.ru/01010686.htm.

60. Ruud, *Fighting Words*, 160.

61. Ibid., 184.

62. K. K. Arsen'ev, "Russkie zakony o pechati," *Vestnik Evropy* 4 (1869): 810.

63. Ruud, *Fighting Words*, 232–233.

64. Nicolas Slonimsky, *Perfect Pitch: A Life Story* (Oxford: Oxford University Press, 1988), 8.

65. Slonimsky, *Perfect Pitch*, text under pictures between 120 and 121.

66. Pauline Wengeroff, *Rememberings: The World of a Russian-Jewish Woman in the Nineteenth Century* (Potomac: University Press of Maryland, 2000), 217.

67. Benjamin Nathans, *Beyond the Pale: The Jewish Encounter with Late Imperial Russia* (Berkeley: University of California Press, 2002), 222–224.

68. Slonimsky, *Perfect Pitch*, 9.

69. Ibid., 14–15.

70. G. B. Sliozberg, *Dela minuvshikh dnei: Zapiski russkogo evreia* (Paris: Imprimerie Pascal, 1933), 1:261.

Chapter 4. Birth Pangs Full of Promise

1. Linda K. Hughes and Michael Lund, eds., *The Victorian Serial* (Charlottesville: University Press of Virginia, 1991), chap. 1, especially 1–11.

2. Ibid., 73.

3. Patricia Okker, *Social Stories: The Magazine Novel in Nineteenth-Century America* (Charlottesville: University of Virginia Press, 2003), 5–8.

4. Louise McReynolds, *The News Under Russia's Old Regime: The Development of a Mass-Circulation Press* (Princeton: Princeton University Press, 1991), 18–24.

5. Kitaev, *Liberal'naia mysl'*, 287–290.

6. Stasiulevich to wife, 6 June 1862, in *M. M. Stasiulevich i ego sovremenniki v ikh perepiskie*, ed. M. K. Lemke (St. Petersburg: Tipografiia M. M. Stasiulevicha, 1911–1913), 1:405.

7. Institut Russkoi Literatury (IRLI), f. 293, op. 1, ed. khr. 105, 1. 101.

8. Stasiulevich to P. A. Pletnev, 10/22 November 1865, in Lemke, *M. M. Stasiulevich i ego sovremenniki*, 98–99.

9. Pavel Kalinnikov, ed., "Karamzin Nikolai Mikhailovich," *Russkii Biograficheskii Slovar'*, Studiia Kolibri, 20 November 2006, http://www.rulex.ru/01110594.htm.

10. N. I. Kostomarov, *Avtobiografiia N. I. Kostomarova* (Moscow: Zadruga, 1922), 376–377.

11. Pavel Kalinnikov, ed., "Valuev Petr Aleksandrovich," *Russkii Biograficheskii Slovar'*, Studiia Kolibri, 11 May 2006, http://www.rulex.ru/01030018.htm.

12. Lemke, *M. M. Stasiulevich i ego sovremenniki*, 226.

13. E. J. Dillon, *Russian Traits and Terrors: A Faithful Picture of the Russia of To-day* (Boston: B. R. Tucker, 1891), 267.

14. V. E. Kel'ner, *Chelovek svoego vremeni: M. M. Stasiulevich, izdatel'skoe delo i liberal'naia oppositsiia* (St. Petersburg: Izd-vo Rossiiskoi natsional'noi biblioteki, 1993), 23.

15. *Sovremennoe obozrenie* 2 (1868): 106. Another expression of the journal's goal was "to gather new riches, instead of reditributing the old ones." N. P. Emelianov, "*Otechestvennye zapiski*" *N. A. Nekrasova i M. E. Saltykova-Shchedrina, 1868–1884* (Leningrad: Khudozhestvennaia literatura, 1986), 24.

16. IRLI, f. 293, op. 1, ed. khr. 105, 1l. 89, 93.

17. IRLI, f. 293, op. 1, ed. khr. 102, 1. 1.

18. A. N. Pypin to M. E. Saltykov, 2 April 1871, in M. E. Saltykov-Shchedrin, *Polnoe sobranie sochinenii* (Moscow: Izd. Khudozhestvennaia literatura, 1933–1941), 18:2:346.

19. Alexis Pogorelskin, "'The Messenger of Europe'," in *Literary Journals in Imperial Russia*, ed. Deborah A. Martinsen (Cambridge: Cambridge University Press, 1997), 131.

20. Kel'ner, *Chelovek svoego vremeni*, 30–31.

21. *Vestnik Evropy* 12 (1867), vii–viii.

22. IRLI, f. 293, op. 1, ed. khr. 101, 1. 82.

23. G. G. Branover, ed., *Rossiiskaia evreiskaia entsiklopediia* (Moscow: Rossiiskaia akademiia estestvennykh nauk, 1994), 1:315–316. See also G. B. Sliozberg, *Dela minuvshikh dnei: Zapiski russkogo evreia* (Paris: Imprimerie Pascal, 1933), 263–295.

24. Quoted from Martin Katz, *Mikhail N. Katkov: A Political Biography, 1818–1887* (The Hague: Mouton, 1966), 83–84.

25. M. N. Katkov, "Usilenie pol'skoi intrigi v nekotorykh peterburgskikh sferakh i gazetakh," *Moskovskie vedomosti*, no. 46, March 2, 1868.

26. Kitaev, *Liberal'naia mysl' v Rossii*, 230.

27. A. N. Pypin, "Pol'skii vopros v russkoi literature," *Vestnik Evropy* 2 (1880): 704.

28. Alexis E. Pogorelskin, "*Vestnik Evropy* and the Polish Question in the Reign of Alexander II," *Slavic Review* 46, no. 1 (Spring, 1987), 91.

29. For further reading on Russian policies in the western provinces, see Theodore R. Weeks, *Nation and State in Late Imperial Russia: Nationalism and Russification on the Western Frontier, 1863–1914* (DeKalb: Northern Illinois University Press, 1996); and M. D. Dolbilov and A. I. Miller, eds., *Zapadnye okrainy Rossiiskoi imperii* (Moscow: Novoe literaturnoe obozrenie, 2006).

30. M. P. Dragomanov, "Vostochnaia politika Germanii i obrusenie," *Vestnik Evropy* 2 (1872): 640.

31. V. D. Spasovich, "Pol'skie fantazii na slavianofilskuiu temu," *Vestnik Evropy* 8 (1872): 741.

32. Kitaev, *Liberal'naia mysl' v Rossii*, 230–233.

33. L. G. Lopatinskii, "Pis'mo," *Vestnik Evropy* 3 (1873): 934.

34. Kitaev, *Liberal'naia mysl'*, 235–236.

35. Pogorelskin, "*Vestnik Evropy* and the Polish Question," 98.

36. Kitaev, *Liberal'naia mysl'*, 244.

37. Pavel Kalinnikov, ed., "Bezobrazov Vladimir Pavlovich," *Russkii Biograficheski' Slovar'*, Studiia Kolibri, 11 May 2006, http://www.rulex.ru/01021112.htm.

38. IRLI, f. 293, op. 1, ed. khr. 101, 1. 75.

39. IRLI, f. 293, op. 1, ed. khr. 102, 1. 101.

40. IRLI, f. 293, op. 1, ed. khr. 101, 1. 64.

41. A. K. Tolstoi to Stasiulevich, 22 November 1868, in Lemke, *M. M. Stasiulevich i ego sovremenniki*, 2:317.

42. A. K. Tolstoi to Stasiulevich, 13 January 1869, 2:323.

43. Turgenev to A. A. Fet, 26 March/6 April 1866, in I. S. Turgenev, *Polnoe sobranie sochinenii i pisem* (Moscow-Leningrad: Nauka, 1965), 6:66.

44. G. E. Vinnikova, *Turgenev i Rossiia* (Moscow: Sovetskaia Rossiia, 1986), 262.

45. Stasiulevich to wife, 25 September 1883, in Lemke, *M. M. Stasiulevich i ego sovremenniki*, 3:238.

46. Lemke, *M. M. Stasiulevich i ego sovremenniki*, 4:307.

47. N. K. Piksanov, *Roman Gonacharova "Obryv" v svete sotsial'noi istorii* (Leningrad: Nauka, 1968), 148–149.

48. D. L. Mordovtsev to Stasiulevich, 26 April 1868, in Lemke, *M. M. Stasiulevich i ego sovremenniki*, 2:17–18.

49. Stasiulevich to wife, 28 March 1868, 4:1.

50. Charles A. Moser, *Antinihilism in the Russian Novel of the 1860's* (The Hague: Mouton, 1964), 184–185.

51. L. S. Utevskii, *Zhizn' Goncharova: Vospominaniia, pis'ma, dnevniki* (Moscow: Agraf, 2000), 209.

52. Iu. M. Loshchits, *Goncharov* (Moscow: Molodaia gvardiia, 1986), 281.

53. Utevskii, *Zhizn' Goncharova*, 225.

54. Evgenii Utin, "Literaturnye spory nashego vremeni," *Vestnik Evropy* 11 (1869).

55. Stasiulevich to A. K. Tolstoi, 10 May 1869, in Lemke, *M. M. Stasiulevich i ego sovremenniki*, 2:331.

56. Piksanov, *Roman Gonacharova*, 116.

57. Ibid., 145.

58. Utevskii, *Zhizn' Goncharova*, 229–243.

59. P. D. Boborykin, *Vospominaniia* (Moscow: Izd-vo khudozhestvennoi literatury, 1965), 2:439.

60. Stasiulevich to A. K. Tolstoi, 10 May 1869, in Lemke, *M. M. Stasiulevich i ego sovremenniki*, 2:331.

61. Utevskii, *Zhizn' Goncharova*, 243.

62. N. I. Barsov, "Vospominanie ob I. A. Goncharove," in *I. A. Goncharov v vospominaniiakh sovremennikov*, ed. V. V. Grigorenko et al. (Leningrad: Khudozhestvennaia literatura, 1969), 152.

63. A. F. Koni, "Ivan Aleksandrovich Goncharov," in Grigorenko, *I. A. Goncharov*, 257–258.

64. Pavel Kalinnikov, ed., "Kruze Nikolai Fedorovich (fon)," *Russkii Biograficheskii Slovar'*, Studiia Kolibri, 11 May 2006, http://www.rulex.ru/01110346.htm.

65. Lemke, *M. M. Stasiulevich i ego sovremenniki*, 5:159.

66. M. P. Pogodin to Stasiulevich, 3 January 1872, 2:115.

67. Kitaev, *Liberal'naia mysl'*, 272–277.

68. *Vestnik Evropy* 2 (1870): 935. Some scholars such as B. S. Itenberg and V. A. Kitaev have posited that Pypin was the actual author of the obituary. See Kitaev, *Liberal'naia mysl' v Rossii*, 293.

69. Pogorelskin, "'The Messenger of Europe'," 137.

70. M. M. Stasiulevich, "Zametka o russkoi pochte," *Vestnik Evropy* 7 (1871): 405.

71. It was founded in 1862. B. S. Itenberg, *P. L. Lavrov v russkom revoliutsionnom dvizhenii* (Moscow: Nauka, 1988) 75.

72. Kel'ner, *Chelovek svoego vremeni*, 69.

73. M. E. Saltykov-Shchedrin, "Samodovol'naia sovremennost'." *Otechestvennye zapiski* 10 (1871): 67.

74. *Russkie knigi v bibliotekakh K. Marksa i F. Engel'sa* (Moscow: Politizdat, 1979), 159.

75. K. K. Arsen'ev, "Vzgliad na proshloe 'Vestnika Evropy' (1866–1908)," *Vestnik Evropy* 1 (1908): 230.

76. IRLI, f. 293, op. 1, ed. khr. 102, 1. 99.

77. Pavel Kalinnikov, ed., "Sol'skii Dmitrii Martynovich," *Russkii Biograficheskii Slovar'*, Studiia Kolibri, 11 May 2006, http://www.rulex.ru/01180858.htm.

78. A. V. Golovnin to Stasiulevich, 16 October 1871, in Lemke, *M. M. Stasiulevich i ego sovremenniki*, 1:501, 502, 507.

79. A. V. Golovnin to Stasiulevich, 13 November 1868, 1:503.

80. A. V. Golovnin to Stasiulevich, 2 February 1871, 1:504.

81. "Otzyv chlena soveta Glavnogo upravleniia po delam pechati F. F. Veselago o napravlenii zhurnala," Rossiskii Gosudarstvennyi Istoricheskii Arkhiv (RGIA), f. 776, op. 5, ed. khr. 15, 11. 2–9.

82. Pogorelskin, "'The Messenger of Europe'," 133.

Chapter 5. Publishing as Philanthropy

1. V. A. Kitaev, *Liberal'naia mysl' v Rossii, 1860–1880 gg.* (Saratov: Izdatel'stvo Saratovskogo Universiteta, 2004), 281.

2. Rossiiskaia Natsional'naia Biblioteka (RNB), f. 621, op. 1, ed. khr. 823, 1. 16.

3. Institut Russkoi Literatury (IRLI), f. 293, op. 1, ed. khr. 165/1, 1. 3.

4. E. P. Aksenova, *A. N. Pypin o slavianstve* (Moscow: Indrik, 2006), 38–50.

5. K. K. Arsen'ev, "Piatidesiatiletie '*Vestnika Evropy*'," *Vestnik Evropy* 2 (1915): 111.

6. IRLI, f. 250, op. 3, ed. khr. 45, 1. 1.

7. K. K. Arsen'ev, "Politicheskii protsess 1869–1871 gg.," *Vestnik Evropy* 11 (1871): 302.

8. K. D. Kavelin to Stasiulevich, 29 November 1871, in *M. M. Stasiulevich i ego sovremenniki v ikh perepiske*, ed. M. K. Lemke (St. Petersburg: Tipografiia M. M. Staiulevicha, 1911–1913), 2:121.

9. *Vestnik Evropy* 12 (1870): 970; 12 (1871): 932; 12 (1872): 822.

10. N. O. Pruzhanskii, "Moe znakomstvo s M. M. Stasiulevichem," *Istoricheskii Vestnik* 4 (1911): 200.

11. E. J. Dillon, *Russian Traits and Terrors: A Faithful Picture of the Russia of To-day* (Boston: B. R. Tucker, 1891), 265–266.

12. *Vestnik Evropy* 4 (1874): 900–904.

13. *Vestnik Evropy* 6 (1876)—see advertisement in the back.

14. Lemke, *M. M. Stasiulevich i ego sovremenniki*, 3:39.

15. I. S. Turgenev, "Otchet po izdaniiu pervykh piati tomov 'Russkoi biblioteki'," in *Aleksandr Sergeevich Griboedov* (St. Petersburg: Tip. M. M. Stasiulevicha, 1875), v–vi.

16. Turgenev to P. V. Annenkov, 18/30 September 1875, in I. S. Turgenev, *Polnoe sobranie sochinenii i pisem* (Moscow-Leningrad: Nauka, 1965), 11:132–133.

17. *Russkie knigi v bibliotekakh K. Marksa i F. Engel'sa* (Moscow: Politizdat, 1979), 33, 204.

18. Aleksandr Bakhrakh, "Bunin v khalate," in *Bunin v khalate i drugie portrety: Po pamiati, po zapisiam* (Moscow: Vagrius, 2005), 81.

19. Kitaev, *Liberal'naia mysl'*, 330–331.

20. G. E. Vinnikova, *Turgenev i Rossiia* (Moscow: Sovetskaia Rossiia, 1986), 273–278.

21. Ernest Alfred Vizetelly, *Émile Zola, Novelist and Reformer: An Account of His Life and Work* (London: John Lane, 1904), 150; and Colette Becker, *Les apprentissages de Zola: Du poète romantique au romancier naturaliste, 1840–1867* (Paris: Presses universitaires de France, 1993). See the chronological list of published works at the end of the volume.

22. Turgenev to M. M. Stasiulevich, 6/18 January 1875, in Turgenev, *Polnoe sobranie*, 11:7.

23. P. D. Boborykin, *Vospominaniia* (Moscow: Izd-vo khudozhestvennoi literatury, 1965), 2:502.

24. Turgenev to Émile Zola 19/31 October 1874, in Turgenev, *Polnoe sobranie*, 10:315.

25. Frederick Brown, *Zola: A Life* (New York: Farrar, Strauss, Giroux, 1995), 315.

26. Matthew Josephson, *Zola and His Time* (New York: Russell & Russell, 1969), 194.

27. Alexis Pogorelskin, "'The Messenger of Europe'," in *Literary Journals in Imperial Russia*, ed. Deborah A. Martinsen (Cambridge: Cambridge University Press, 1997), 142.

28. Brown, *Zola*, 317.

29. V. E. Kel'ner, *Chelovek svoego vremeni: M. M. Stasiulevich, izdatel'skoe delo i liberal'naia oppositsiia* (St. Petersburg: Izd-vo Rossiiskoi natsional'noi biblioteki, 1993), 136.

30. Emile Zola to Stasiulevich, 14 December 1877, in Lemke, *M. M. Stasiulevich i ego sovremenniki*, 3:622.

31. Pavel Kalinnikov, ed., "Engelgardt Anna Nikolaevna," *Russkii Biograficheskii Slovar'*, 17 May 2006, http://www.rulex.ru/01300035.htm.

32. N. K. Mikhailovskii, "Literaturnye zametki," *Otechestvennye zapiski* 9 (1879): 112.

33. Boborykin, *Vospominaniia*, 1:329, 2:162.

34. Kitaev, *Liberal'naia mysl' v Rossii*, 285.

35. Boborykin, *Vospominaniia*, 2:134.

36. Kel'ner, *Chelovek svoego vremeni*, 152.

37. IRLI, f. 293, op. 1, ed. khr. 102, 1. 77.

38. Turgenev to A. A. Fet, 21 August/2 September 1873, in Turgenev, *Polnoe sobranie*, 10:143.

39. IRLI, f. 293, op. 1, ed. khr. 102, 1. 77.

40. Dillon, *Russian Traits and Terrors*, 275.

41. Pogorelskin, "'The Messenger of Europe'," 144.

42. P. L. Lavrov, *Lavrov—gody emigratsii: Arkhivnye materialy v dvukh tomakh* (Dordrecht: Reidel, 1974), 1:193.

43. B. S. Itenberg, *P. L. Lavrov v russkom revoliutsionnom dvizhenii* (Nauka: Moscow, 1988), 169–171.

44. A. V. Golovnin, "Perepiska so Stasiulevichem," *Vestnik Evropy* 1 (1877): 130–141.

45. A. V. Golovnin to Stasiulevich, 8 December 1876, in Lemke, *M. M. Stasiulevich i ego sovremenniki*, 1:511–512.

46. O. V. Aptekman, *Obshchestvo 'Zemlia i volia' semidesiatykh godov* (Prague, 1924), 34.

47. Kitaev, *Liberal'naia mysl'*, 218–220.

48. Karl Marx to P. V. Annenkov, 28 December (no year), in Lemke, *M. M. Stasiulevich i ego sovremenniki*, 3:458–462.

49. Louise McReynolds, *The News Under Russia's Old Regime: The Development of a Mass-Circulation Press* (Princeton: Princeton University Press, 1991), 73–92.

50. Kitaev, *Liberal'naia mysl'*, 246–248.

51. Ibid., 248–250.

52. McReynolds, *The News*, 73–92.

53. Kitaev, *Liberal'naia mysl'*, 251–257.

54. IRLI, f. 250, op. 2, ed. khr. 1, 1. 40.

55. D. A. Balykin, *A. N. Pypin kak issledovatel' techenii russkoi obshchestvennoi mysli* (Briansk: Grani, 1996), 53.

56. *Vestnik Evropy* 12 (1881): 940.

57. Kel'ner, *Chelovek svoego vremeni*, 286–287.

58. Kitaev, *Liberal'naia mysl'*, 299–300.

59. Ibid., 221–225.

60. Charles Ruud, *Fighting Words: Imperial Censorship and the Russian Press, 1804–1906* (Toronto: University of Toronto Press, 1982), 306.

61. Koni to E. F. Raden, 8 November 1880, in A. F. Koni, *Sobranie sochinenii* (Moscow: Iurid. lit-ra, 1969), 8:45.

62. "Rech' Stasiulevicha Kommissii po revizii zakonov o pechati, 1880," in Lemke, *M. M. Stasiulevich i ego sovremenniki*, 1:544–549.

63. P. A. Valuev, *Dnevnik, 1877–1884* (Prague, 1919), 126.

64. RNB, f. 621, ed. khr. 831, 1l. 44–45.

65. RNB, f. 621, ed. khr. 835, 1. 47.

66. RNB, f. 621, ed. khr. 829, 1. 36.

67. RNB, f. 621, ed. khr. 362, 1. 24–24 ob.

68. L. Z. Slonimskii, "M. M. Stasiulevich kak redaktor," *Vestnik Evropy* 3 (1911): 410–411.

69. S. A. Muromtsev, *Sbornik statei* (Moscow: Izd. M. i S. Sabashikovykh, 1911), 412.

70. Turgenev to M. M. Stasiulevich, 25 February/9 March 1881, in Turgenev, *Polnoe sobranie*, 13:1:66–67.

71. K. P. Pobedonostsev to Stasiulevich, 6 January 1881 and 3 February 1881, in Lemke, *M. M. Stasiulevich i ego sovremenniki*, 1:484–485.

72. Kel'ner, *Chelovek svoego vremeni*, 173.

73. Pogorelskin, "'The Messenger of Europe'," 129.

74. Ibid., 140.

75. D. M. Sol'skii to Stasiulevich, 15 February 1879, in Lemke, *M. M. Stasiulevich i ego sovremenniki*, 1:340.

76. IRLI, f. 293, op. 1, ed. khr. 165, 1. 33.

77. Kitaev, *Liberal'naia mysl'*, 334.

78. *Zemlia i Volia*, no. 1, October 25, 1878, in *Revoliutsionnaia zhurnalistika semidesiatykh godov*, ed. B. Bazilevskii (Paris: Société nouvelle de librairie et d'edition, 1905), 118.

79. L. A. Polonskii, "Vnutrennee obozrenie," *Vestnik Evropy* 9 (1878): 394.

80. *Zemlia i Volia*, no. 1, October 25, 1878, in Bazilevskii, *Revoliutsionnaia zhurnalistika*, 161.

81. Polonskii, "Vnutrennee obozrenie," 842.

82. *Zemlia i Volia*, no. 3, January 15, 1879, in Bazilevskii, *Revoliutsionnaia zhurnalistika*, 274.

83. *Zemlia i Volia*, no. 5, February 8, 1879, 239.

84. *Zemlia i Volia*, no. 1, October 1, 1879, 7.

85. K. K. Arsen'ev, "Vnutrennee obozrenie," *Vestnik Evropy* 3 (1880): 398–399.

86. Polonskii, "Vnutrennee obozrenie," 835. He would change his opinion on the feasibility of "state socialism" in the early 1880s after leaving the *Herald*. Polonskii published an extensive article in *Birzhevye vedomosti* on June 8, 1883, taking the classical liberal approach to state involvement in economics.

87. Ibid., 841.

88. *Zemlia i Volia*, no. 3, January 15, 1879, in Bazilevskii, *Revoliutsionnaia zhurnalistika*, 837.

89. Pavel Kalinnikov, ed., "Klements Dmitrii Aleksandrovich," *Russkii Biograficheskii Slovar'*, 11 September 2006, http://rulex.ru/01111304.htm.

90. *Zemlia i Volia*, no. 3, January 15, 1879, in Bazilevskii, *Revoliutsionnaia zhurnalistika*, 246–285.

91. L. Lukianov, "Nado zhit: Rasskaz," *Vestnik Evropy* 12 (1878): 767.

92. Ibid., 790.

93. L. A. Polonskii, "Vnutrennee obozrenie: Vyrezannoe tsenzuroi iz I knigi V. E. 1879," in Lemke, *M. M. Stasiulevich i ego sovremenniki*, 1:475.

94. Polonskii, "Vnutrennee obozrenie," 787.

95. Ibid.

96. K. K. Arsen'ev, "Literaturnoe obozrenie," *Vestnik Evropy* 2 (1879): 780.

97. K. K. Arsen'ev, *Vospominaniia (1910–1913)*, IRLI, f. 359, op. 1, d. 3, 1. 159.

98. Kitaev, *Liberal'naia mysl'*, 192.

99. *Narodnaia volia*, no. 2, November 1, 1879, in *Literatura partii "Narodnoi voli"* (Moscow: K-vo Bor'ba i pravo, 1907), 46.

100. *Narodnaia volia*, no. 3, January 1, 1880, in *Literatura partii "Narodnoi voli"*, 88.

101. N. A. Morozov, *Povesti moei zhizni: Memuary* (Moscow: Nauka, 1965), 2:375.

102. V. K. Debogorii-Mokrievich, *Vospominaniia* (Stuttgart: J. H. W. Dietz, 1903), 373–374.

103. *Narodnaia volia*, nos. 8–9, February 5, 1882, in *Literatura partii "Narodnoi voli"*, 244.

104. *Vestnik Evropy* 12 (1881): 940.

105. K. K. Arsen'ev, "Vnutrennee obozrenie," *Vestnik Evropy* 4 (1881): 772.

106. *Narodnaia Volia*, nos. 8–9, February 5, 1882, in *Literatura partii "Narodnoi voli"*, 245.

107. M. M. Stasiulevich, *Chernyi peredel reform imperatora Aleksandra II: Pis'ma iz Moskvy za granitsu par bonté* (Berlin: B. Behr, 1882), 67–74.

108. K. K. Arsen'ev, "Vnutrennee obozrenie," *Vestnik Evropy* 1 (1882): 336.

109. Quoted from B. S. Itenberg and V. V. Shelokhaev, "Predislovie," in *Rossiiskie liberaly: Sbornik statei* (Moscow: Rosspen, 2001), 7.

110. A. F. Koni, *Graf Loris-Melikov: Na zhiznennom puti* (Berlin, n.d.), 3:1:6.

111. Kel'ner, *Chelovek svoego vremeni*, 173.

112. E. M. Feoktistov, *Vospominaniia: Za kulisami politiki i literatury, 1848–1896* (Leningrad: Priboi, 1929), 182.

113. A. A. Alafaev, "Agrarnyi vopros v zhurnale 'Vestnik Evropy,' 1878–1882 gg.," in *Vtoraia revoliutsionnaia situatsiia v Rossii: Otkliki na stranitsakh pressy; Sbornik statei*, ed. N. M. Pirumova and V. A. Tvardovskaia (Moscow: Akademiia nauk SSSR, 1981), 38.

114. RNB, f. 621, ed. khr. 832, 1. 13.

115. *K. P. Pobedonostsev i ego korrespondenty: Pis'ma i zapiski* (Prague, 1923), 1:1:85.

116. V. I. Lenin, "Goniteli zemstva i annibaly liberalizma," in *Polnoe sobranie sochinenii*, 5th ed. (Moscow: Gos. izd-vo polit. lit-ry, 1964), 5:44–45.

117. K. K. Arsen'ev, "Vnutrennee obozrenie," *Vestnik Evropy* 9 (1882): 337.

118. The letter is dated January 15, 1882. "Iz pisem K. D. Kavelina k gr. D. A. Miliutinu, 1882–1884 gg." *Vestnik Evropy* 1 (1909): 15.

CHAPTER 6. A PARTING OF WAYS

1. For a distinction between the two, see Franco Venturi's superb *Roots of Revolution: A History of the Populist and Socialist Movements in Nineteenth-Century Russia*, trans. Francis Haskell (New York: Grosset & Dunlap, 1966); and

Richard Wortman's *The Crisis of Russian Populism* (London: Cambridge University Press, 1967).

2. N. E. Nikoladze, "Osvobozhdenie N.G. Chernyshevskogo," in *N. G. Chernyshevskii v vospominaniiakh sovremennikov*, ed. Iu. G. Oksman (Saratov: Saratovskoe knizhnoe izd-vo, 1959), 2:264.

3. *Poriadok*, April 27 and April 28, 1881.

4. *Golos*, October 1, 1880.

5. D. F. Samarin, "Teoriia o nedostatochnosti krest'ianskikh nadelov, po ucheniiu professora Iu. E. Iansona," *Rus*, no. 3, October 15, 1880, 2.

6. Ibid.

7. S. F. Sharapov, "Eshche neskol'ko slov ob 'opyte' g. Iansona," *Rus*, no. 7, December 27, 1880, 4.

8. F. F. Voroponov, "Teoriia dostatochnosti krest'ianskikh nadelov," *Vestnik Evropy* 2 (1881): 786–788.

9. N. M. Iadrintsev, "Nashi vyseleniia i kolonizatsiia," *Vestnik Evropy* 6 (1880): 448.

10. F. F. Voroponov, "Po povodu vliianiia zemel'nogo nadela na blagosostoianie," *Vestnik Evropy* 11 (1880): 394.

11. K. K. Arsen'ev, "Literaturnoe obozrenie," *Vestnik Evropy* 9 (1881): 434.

12. A. I. Vvedenskii, "Literaturnye mechtaniia i deistvitel'nost'," *Vestnik Evropy* 9 (1882): 178.

13. *Literatura partii "Narodnoi voli"* (Moscow: K-vo Bor'ba i pravo, 1907), 7 for the "colossus" quote.

14. K. K. Arsen'ev, "Vnutrennee obozrenie," *Vestnik Evropy* 3 (1881): 356.

15. "Materialy revizii Arsen'evym K. K. Samarskoi i Saratovskoi gub. (1880–1881)," Institut Russkoi Literatury (IRLI), f. 359, op. 1, d. 63, 1l. 7 and 11.

16. K. D. Kavelin, "Putevye pis'ma," *Vestnik Evropy* 10 (1882): 698.

17. K. K. Arsen'ev, "Vnutrennee obozrenie," *Vestnik Evropy* 3 (1881): 353.

18. K. K. Arsen'ev, "Vnutrennee obozrenie," *Vestnik Evropy* 9 (1882): 334.

19. K. K. Arsen'ev, "Vnutrennee obozrenie," *Vestnik Evropy* 3 (1881): 356–357.

20. K. K. Arsen'ev, "Vnutrennee obozrenie," *Vestnik Evropy* 3 (1881): 357.

21. M. P. Petrovskii, "Retrogradnaia pechat' i golos provintsii," *Vestnik Evropy* 7 (1881): 329.

22. Iadrintsev, "Nashi vyseleniia," 483.

23. Pavel Kalinnikov, ed., "Vasilchikov Aleksandr Illarionovich," *Russkii Biograficheskii Slovar'*, 30 August 2006, http://rulex.ru/01030446.htm.

24. A. I. Vasilchikov, "Po povodu kritik i retsenzii na knigu 'Zemlevladenie i zemledelie'," *Vestnik Evropy* 2 (1878): 813.

25. F. Migrin, "Sel'skii byt i sel'skoe khoziaistvo v Rossii," *Vestnik Evropy* 6 (1881): 883.

26. K. K. Arsen'ev, "Vnutrennee obozrenie," *Vestnik Evropy* 11 (1881): 371.

27. F. F. Voroponov, "Melkii zemel'nyi kredit i krest'ianskie pereseleniia," *Vestnik Evropy* 10 (1880): 732.

28. N. M. Iadrintsev, "Polozhenie pereselentsev v Sibiri," *Vestnik Evropy* 8 (1881): 602.

29. Voroponov, "Melkii zemel'nyi kredit," 733.

30. Iadrintsev, "Polozhenie pereselentsev," 619.

31. Iadrintsev, "Nashi vyseleniia," 486.

32. Ibid., 465.

33. Vasilchikov, "Po povodu kritik," 809.

34. F. F. Voroponov, "Nashi pozemel'nye nalogi," *Vestnik Evropy* 5 (1878): 334.

35. K. K. Arsen'ev, "Vnutrennee obozrenie," *Vestnik Evropy* 2 (1881): 810.

36. A. F. Koni, "Spornyi vopros nashego trudoustroistva," *Vestnik Evropy* 1 (1881): 224.

37. K. K. Arsen'ev, "Vnutrennee obozrenie," *Vestnik Evropy* 5 (1882): 354.

38. K. K. Arsen'ev, "Vnutrennee obozrenie," *Vestnik Evropy* 2 (1881): 806; Iu. G. Zhukovskii, "Priamye nalogi v Rossii," *Vestnik Evropy* 2 (1881): 517; A. N. Pypin, "Izuchenie russkoi narodnosti," *Vestnik Evropy* 9 (1881): 317.

39. Zhukovskii, "Priamye nalogi v Rossii," 524.

40. L. A. Polonskii, "Vnutrennee obozrenie," *Vestnik Evropy* 8 (1878): 723.

41. V. G. Chernukha, *Krest'ianskii vopros v pravitel'stvennoi politike Rossii (60–70-e gody XIX v.)* (Leningrad: Nauka, 1972), 121.

42. K. K. Arsen'ev, "Vnutrennee obozrenie," *Vestnik Evropy* 5 (1882): 354.

43. B. P. Baluev, *Liberal'noe narodnichestvo na rubezhe XIX–XX vekov* (Moscow: Nauka, 1995), 110.

44. *Piatidesiatiletie nauchno-literaturnoi deiatel'nosti akademika A. N. Pypina* (St. Petersburg: A. E. Vineke, 1903), 25.

45. A. N. Pypin, "Teorii narodnichestva," *Vestnik Evropy* 10 (1892): 706, 710–712.

46. A. N. Pypin, *Istoriia russkoi etnografii* (St. Petersburg: Tip. M. M. Stasiulevicha, 1890–1892), 2:375.

47. A. N. Pypin, "Narodniki i narod. Sobranie sochinenii N. Zlatovratskogo," *Vestnik Evropy* 2 (1891): 660–661. See also *Istoriia russkoi etnografii*, 2:354, 383.

48. Pypin, "Teorii narodnichestva," 725.

49. A. N. Pypin, "Belletrist-narodnik shestidesiatykh godov," *Vestnik Evropy* 8 (1884): 354.

50. For excellent treatments of these writers see also Cathy A. Frierson, *Peasant Icons: Representations of Rural People in Late Nineteenth-Century Russia* (New York: Oxford University Press, 1993); and Wortman, *The Crisis of Russian Populism*.

51. A. N. Pypin, "Narodnost' i narodnichestvo," *Vestnik Evropy* 2 (1888): 388; Pypin, "Belletrist-narodnik shestidesiatykh godov," 672–673, 683; Pypin, *Istoriia russkoi etnografii*, 2:407.

52. Pypin, "Teorii narodnichestva," 708–710.

53. Pypin, *Istoriia russkoi etnografii*, 2:408.

54. Pypin, "Teorii narodnichestva," 745–746.

55. A. N. Pypin, "Po povodu 'Otkrytogo pis'ma' g. Zlatovratskogo," *Vestnik Evropy* 4 (1884): 840.

56. Pypin, *Istoriia russkoi etnografii,* 395–399.

57. A. N. Pypin, "Narodnichestvo (Statia vtoraia)," *Vestnik Evropy* 2 (1882): 722.

58. Pavel Kalinnikov, ed., "Kablits Iosif Ivanovich (Iuzov)," *Russkii Biografich-eskii Slovar',* 12 March 2007, http://rulex.ru/011110371.htm.

59. A. N. Pypin, "Prugavin A. S. Zaprosy naroda i obiazannosti intelligentsii v oblasti prosveshcheniia i vospitaniia. 2-e izd. SPb., 1895," *Vestnik Evropy* 3 (1895): 386, 393.

60. A. N. Pypin, "Narodnaia gramotnost'," *Vestnik Evropy* 1 (1891): 255–256, 278–279.

61. Rondo Cameron, "Some Lessons of History for Developing Nations," *The American Economic Review* 57, no. 2 (1967): 318–319.

62. Pavel Kalinnikov, ed., "Vorontsov Vasilii Pavlovich," *Russkii Biograficheskii Slovar',* 6 March 2007, http://rulex.ru/01030853.htm.

63. The articles appeared in *Russkoe bogatstvo* beginning in February 1892.

64. Pypin, "Teorii narodnichestva," 720; Pypin, "Eshche o teoriiakh narodnich-estva," *Vestnik Evropy* 2 (1893): 765.

65. Pypin, "Teorii narodnichestva," 721–722.

66. Ibid., 730, 740.

67. Ibid., 731.

68. V. P. Vorontsov, "Popytki obosnovaniia narodnichestva," *Russkoe bogatstvo* 10 (1892): 7; and Vorontsov, "Kritik narodnichestva," *Russkoe bogatstvo* 4 (1893): 5, 27.

69. Pypin, *Istoriia russkoi etnografii,* 2:383; Pypin, "Po povodu 'Otkrytogo pis'ma'," 870.

70. Arthur P. Mendel, "N. K. Mikhailovskij and His Criticism of Russian Marx-ism," *American Slavic and East European Review* 14, no. 3 (1955): 341–343.

71. Pypin, *Istoriia russkoi etnografii,* 2:418.

72. Janko Lavrin, "Populists and Slavophiles," *Russian Review* 21, no. 4 (1962): 307.

73. Pypin, "Eshche o teoriiakh narodnichestva," 760; Pypin, *Istoriia russkoi etnografii,* 383–384.

74. A. N. Pypin, "Idealisty i realisty," *Vestnik Evropy* 10 (1871): 942.

75. A. N. Pypin, "Perezhivaemye dni," *Poriadok,* April 28, 1881.

76. A. N. Pypin, "Novye razyskaniia v narodno-poeticheskoi starine," *Vestnik Evropy* 12 (1886): 791–792.

77. A. N. Pypin, "Otkrytie Radishchevskogo muzeia, osnovannogo A. P. Bogoli-ubovym v Saratove," *Vestnik Evropy* 8 (1885): 836–844.

78. The signatories were Leonid Zhebunev, Evgenii Sidorenko, Maria Shi-blakova, Lidiia Panova, Aleksandr Panov, and Sofiia Subbotina. V. A. Kitaev,

Liberal'naia mysl' v Rossii (1860–1880 gg.) (Saratov: Izdatel'stvo Saratovskogo Universiteta, 2004), 285–286.

79. Societies in Russia included the Russian Society of History and Ancient Studies, the Society of Natural Science, Anthropology, and Ethnography, Moscow University's Society of Russian Philology, Petersburg University's Neo-Philological Society, the Society of Friends of Ancient Writing, the Pushkin Lyceum Society, the Russian Bibliographical Society, and the Petersburg Imperial Russian Historical Society. Foreign societies included the Bulgarian Scientific Society of Sophia. He became honorary member of Iur'ev University and Kazan University and Moscow's Public Rumiantsev Museum. He was also member of the Prague Academy of Knowledge, Sciences, and the Arts as well as the Serbian Academy of Sciences. He was also a member of the Saratov Province Scientific Archive Commission and the Scientific Archival Commission of Nizhnii Novgorod. IRLI, f. 250, op. 2, ed. khr. 1, 1l. 40–41; ed. khr. 41, 1. 59; ed. khr. 61, 1l. 5, 49, 70, 96; ed. khr. 66, 1. 1.

80. A. N. Pypin, *Istoriia russkoi literatury* (St. Petersburg: Tip. M. M. Stasiulevicha, 1907), 4:v–vi.

81. IRLI, f. 250, op. 2, ed. khr. 41, 1. 1.

82. A. N. Pypin, *Moi zametki* (Moscow: L. E. Bukhgeim, 1910), 77, 65–66.

83. A. N. Pypin, "Borozdin A. K. Sto let literaturnogo razvitiia. Kharakeristika russkoi literatury XIX stoletiia. Spb., 1900," *Vestnik Evropy* 10 (1900): 840–841.

84. "Perezhivaemye dni."

85. V. V. Bartenev, "Vospominaniia peterburzhtsa o vtoroi polovine 1880-x godov," in *Ot narodnichestva—k marksizmu: Vospominaniia uchastnikov revoliutsionnogo dvizheniia v Peterburge (1883–1894 gg.),* ed. S. S. Volk (Leningrad: Lenizdat, 1987), 197–198.

86. V. P. Vorontsov, *Sud'by kapitalizma v Rossii* (St. Petersburg: Tip. M. M. Stasiulevicha, 1882), 9.

87. Theodore Von Laue, "The High Cost and Gamble of the Witte System: A Chapter in the Industrialization of Russia," *Journal of Economic History* 13, no. 4 (Autumn 1953), 443.

88. Theodore Von Laue, "The Fate of Capitalism in Russia: The Narodnik Version," *American Slavic and East European Review* 13, no. 1 (1954): 18.

89. Ibid., 18.

90. N. K. Mikhailovskii, *Polnoe sobranie sochinenii,* 7th ed. (St. Petersburg, 1909), 7:666.

91. Arthur P. Mendel, *Dilemmas of Progress in Tsarist Russia: Legal Marxism and Legal Populism* (Cambridge: Harvard University Press, 1961), 241.

CHAPTER 7. CHALLENGING THE IDEOLOGY OF PROGRESS

1. John Maynard Keynes, *The Economic Consequences of the Peace* (London: Macmillan, 1919), 11.

2. Esther Kingston-Mann, "Marxism and Russian Rural Development: Problems of Evidence, Experience, and Culture," *The American Historical Review* 86, no. 4 (1981): 732.

3. W. Bruce Lincoln, *In the Vanguard of Reform: Russia's Enlightened Bureaucrats, 1825–1861* (DeKalb: Northern Illinois University Press, 1982).

4. V. P. Vorontsov, *Sud'by kapitalizma v Rossii* (St. Petersburg: Tip. M. M. Stasiulevicha, 1882), 12.

5. Kingston-Mann, "Marxism and Russian Rural Development," 733.

6. V. V. Oreshkin, *Vol'noe ekonomicheskoe obshchestvo v Rossii, 1765–1917: Istoriko-economicheskii ocherk* (Moscow: Izd-vo Akademii nauk SSSR, 1963), 22.

7. The bibliography on this subject is rich. Works of the time include A. N. Gur'ev, *Reforma denezhnogo obrashcheniia* (St. Petersburg: Tip. V. Kirshbauma, 1896), 54; D. A. Timiriazev, *Obzor razvitiia glavneishikh otraslei promyshlennosti i torgovli v Rossii za poslednee dvadtsatiletie* (St. Petersburg: A. Il'in, 1876), 4–6; I. P. Taburno, *Eskiznyi obzor finansovo-ekonomicheskogo sostoianiia Rossii za poslednie 20 let (1882–1901 gg.)* (St. Petersburg: Tip. E. Novitskogo, 1904), 18–21. For later works, see B. V. Ananich and R. Sh. Ganelin, eds., *Vlast' i reformy: Ot samoderzhavnoi k sovetskoi Rossii* (Moscow: DB, 1996), 403.

8. Ian M. Drummond, "The Russian Gold Standard, 1897–1914," *The Journal of Economic History* 36, no. 3 (September 1976), 663; A. N. Gur'ev, *Denezhnoe obrashchenie v Rossii v XIX stoletii: Istoricheskii ocherk* (St. Petersburg: Kirshbaum, 1903), 65.

9. Alexander Gerschenkron, *Economic Backwardness in Historical Perspective* (Cambridge: Belknap Press, 1962), 26–28.

10. B. B. Glinskii, "Period tverdoi vlasti," *Istoricheskii vestnik* 8 (1912): 682–683; A. N. Kulomzin, *M. Kh. Reitern: Biograficheskii ocherk* (St. Petersburg: Tip. Sel'skogo vestnika, 1919), 42; B. V. Ananich, *Rossiia i mezhdunarodnyi kapital, 1897–1914: Ocherki istorii finansovykh otnoshenii* (Leningrad: Nauka, 1970), 9; L. E. Shepelev, *Tsarizm i burzhuaziia vo vtoroi polovine XIX veka: Problemy torgovo-promyshlennoi politiki* (Leningrad: Nauka, 1981), 71–82; V. L. Stepanov, "Nikolai Khristoforovich Bunge," *Istoriia SSSR* 1 (1991): 20; V. L. Stepanov, "Rabochii vopros v sotsial'no-ekonomicheskikh vozzreniiakh N. Kh. Bunge," *Vestnik MGU, Istoriia* 3 (1987): 17–25.

11. K. N. Tarnovskii, *Sotsial'no-ekonomicheskaia istoriia Rossii: Nachalo XX v.* (Moscow: Nauka, 1990), 54.

12. Taburno, *Eskiznyi obzor*, 17.

13. In this it was not alone, as Reginald Zelnik has shown in his minutely researched *Labor and Society in Tsarist Russia: The Factory Workers of St. Petersburg, 1855–1870* (Stanford: Stanford University Press, 1971).

14. A. A. Alafaev, *Russkii liberalizm na rubezhe 70–80-kh XIX v.: Iz istorii zhurnala "Vestnik Evropy"* (Moscow: Institut istorii SSSR, 1991), 48.

15. K. K. Arsen'ev, "Literaturnoe obozrenie," *Vestnik Evropy* 3 (1882): 410.

16. P. M. Romanov, "Nasha zolotopromyshlennost' i ee usloviia," *Vestnik Evropy* 3 (1880): 368; L. A. Polonskii, "Vnutrennee obozrenie," *Vestnik Evropy* 12 (1878): 833; Polonskii, "Vnutrennee obozrenie," *Vestnik Evropy* 11 (1879): 330. For child labor legislation, see Boris Gorshkov, *Russia's Factory Children: State, Society, and Law, 1800–1917* (Pittsburgh, PA: University of Pittsburgh Press, 2009).

17. L. A. Polonskii, "Vnutrennee obozrenie," *Vestnik Evropy* 12 (1878): 834; L. A. Polonskii, "Vnutrennee obozrenie: Vyrezannoe tsenzuroi iz I knigi V. E. 1879," in *M. M. Stasiulevich i ego sovremenniki v ikh perepiskie* (St. Petersburg: Tipografiia M. M. Stasiulevicha, 1911–1913), 1:477.

18. P. Abramov, "Obrazovanie i obespechenie byta rabochikh v Rossii," *Vestnik Evropy* 1 (1879): 326.

19. Ibid., 325.

20. K. K. Arsen'ev, "Vnutrennee obozrenie," *Vestnik Evropy* 3 (1882): 353–354.

21. See Reginald Zelnik's chapter on the Sunday School Movement in *Labor and Society in Tsarist Russia*.

22. A. V. Kairova, "Pis'ma iz Germanii," *Vestnik Evropy* 10 (1881): 858.

23. K. K. Arsen'ev, "Vnutrennee obozrenie," *Vestnik Evropy* 8 (1882): 722.

24. Jacob Walkin, "The Attitude of the Tsarist Government toward the Labor Problem," *American Slavic and East European Review* 13, no. 2 (1954): 163–184; Gaston V. Rimlinger, "Autocracy and the Factory Order in Early Russian Industrialization," *Journal of Economic History* 20, no. 1 (1960): 67–92; Theodore Von Laue, "Factory Inspection under the 'Witte System': 1892–1903," *American Slavic and East European Review* 19, no. 3 (1960): 347–362; Von Laue, "Russian Peasants in the Factory, 1892–1904," *Journal of Economic History* 21, no. 1 (1961): 61–80; Von Laue, "Tsarist Labor Policy, 1895–1903," *Journal of Modern History* 34, no. 2 (1962): 135–145.

25. Engels to Marx, 23 March 1852, in Karl Marx and Friedrich Engels, *Sochineniia*, 2nd ed. (Moscow: Izd. Politicheskoi literatury, 1968–1979), 28:30–31.

26. Marx and Engels, *Sochineniia*, 12:605, 701.

27. Marx to L. Kugelman, 13 October 1868, 32:472.

28. "Sochineniia Karla Marksa v russkoi tsenzure (Arkhivnaia spravka)," *Dela i dni* 1 (1920): 323–324.

29. Ibid., 324.

30. B. N. Chicherin, *Vospominaniia Borisa Nikolaevicha Chicherina: Moskovskii universitet* (Moscow: Izd. M. i S. Sabashnikovykh, 1929), 22.

31. N. K. Mikhailovskii, "Po povodu russkogo izdaniia knigi Karla Marksa," in *Narodnicheskaia ekonomicheskaia literatura: Izbrannye proizvedeniia*, ed. N. K. Karataev (Moscow: Izd-vo sotsial'no-ekon. lit-ry, 1958), 167–168.

32. Marx and Engels, *Sochineniia*, 13;17–18, 19, 21.

33. Iu. G. Zhukovskii, "Karl Marks i ego kniga o kapitale," *Vestnik Evropy* 5 (1877): 72–74.

34. See B. N. Chicherin, "Nemetskie sotsialisty. II. Karl Marks," *Sbornik gosudarstvennykh znanii* 6 (1878): 3; and N. Kh. Bunge, *Ocherki politiko-ekonomicheskoi literatury* (St. Petersburg: Tip. V. Kishbauma, 1895), 139–140.

35. L. Z. Slonimskii, "Zabytye ekonomisty Tiunen i Kurno," *Vestnik Evropy* 9 (1878): 24–25; and "Zabytye ekonomisty Tiunen i Kurno," *Vestnik Evropy* 9 (1878): 5–7. Present-day scholars echo Slonimskii's criticism. According to Mark Blaug, for example, von Thünen was the "founder of marginal cost analysis of the nineteenth century." See Mark Blaug, *Economic Theory in Retrospect* (Cambridge: Cambridge University Press, 1997), 299.

36. Slonimskii, "Zabytye ekonomisty Tiunen i Kurno," 13.

37. I. I. Ianzhul, "Znachenie obrazovaniia dlia uspekhov promyshlennosti i torgovli," *Ekonomicheskaia otsenka narodnogo obrazovaniia: Ocherki* (St. Petersburg, 1899), 3; and A. I. Chuprov, "Znanie i narodnoe bogatstvo," in *Ekonomicheskaia otsenka*, 51.

38. L. Z. Slonimskii, "Gosudarstvennyi sotsializm v politike i literature," *Vestnik Evropy* 7 (1884): 287–289.

39. N. Kh. Bunge, "Zagrobnye zametki: Sotsializm ne ugas i prinimaet groznuiu formu. (Zapiska, naidennaia v bumagakh N. Kh. Bunge)," *Istochnik* 10 (1993): 38–39.

40. L. Z. Slonimskii, "Pozemel'naia sobstvennost v teoriiakh ekonomistov i sotsiologov," *Vestnik Evropy* 1 (1883): 239.

41. On Russian and German historical economics, see Esther Kingston-Mann, *In Search of the True West: Culture, Economics, and Problems of Russian Development* (Princeton: Princeton University Press, 1999).

42. Slonimskii, "Pozemel'naia sobstvennost'," 245.

43. For a discussion of the differences between early modern conceptions of communal property and modern "absolute property," see John Brewer and Susan Staves, eds., *Early Modern Conceptions of Property* (New York: Routledge, 1995).

44. L. Z. Slonimskii, "Pozemel'nyi vopros v Evrope i Rossii," *Vestnik Evropy* 3 (1885): 189.

45. L. Z. Slonimskii, "Pozemel'nyi vopros v Evrope i Rossii," *Vestnik Evropy* 4 (1885): 756 (France); 759 (Prussia, Austria).

46. This is a well-known argument carried on by contemporary Western scholars. See Janko Lavrin, "Populists and Slavophiles," *Russian Review* 21, no. 4 (1962): 307–317.

47. Slonimskii, "Pozemel'nyi vopros v Evrope i Rossii," 773.

48. L. Z. Slonimskii, "Voprosy pozemel'noi politiki," *Vestnik Evropy* 9 (1890): 323.

49. Ibid., 331–337.

50. L. Z. Slonimskii, "Ekonomicheskie zametki," *Vestnik Evropy* 7 (1897): 319.

51. Even Joseph Schumpeter, who entertained no socialist sympathies whatsoever, called these men "laissez-faire ultras" and "anti-*étatistes*" who "indulged in a

belief to the effect that the main business of economists is to refute socialist doctrines and to combat the atrocious fallacies implied in all plans of social reform and of state interference of any kind." The school stood "staunchly by the drooping flag of unconditional free trade and laissez-faire" and cared less for the "purely scientific aspects" of economic analysis, than for articulating an ideology. Joseph Schumpeter, *History of Economic Analysis* (New York: Oxford University Press, 1954), 809–841.

52. L. Z. Slonimskii, "Ekonomicheskie idealy," *Vestnik Evropy* 9 (1888): 323.

53. Ibid., 330.

54. Ibid., 333.

55. V. A. Kitaev, "The Unique Liberalism of Vestnik Evopy (1870–1880)," *Russian Studies in History* 46, no. 1 (2007): 59.

56. As Bertram Wolfe has noted, the "progressive" epochs that Marx had earlier outlined in the *Contribution to the Critique of Political Economy* could have been typological listings, not a developmental scheme. Marx also used the term "pregnancy" in reference to economic systems, but he never defined exactly what he meant by it. Bertram D. Wolfe, "Backwardness and Industrialization in Russian History and Thought," *Slavic Review* 26, no. 2 (1967): 180–181.

57. L. Z. Slonimskii, "O teoriiakh progressa," *Vestnik Evropy* 3 (1889): 265. Historian of Victorian anthropology George W. Stocking argued that from the 1860s "savages no longer stood on the fringes of human history, but their inferiority reduced them to the missing links in the evolutionary chain, they were subjects of study not in and for themselves, but as tools to cast light about how the ape developed into the British gentleman." George W. Stocking, *Victorian Anthropology* (New York: Free Press, 1987), 185.

58. Alexander Vucinich, *Darwin in Russian Thought* (Berkeley: University of California Press, 1988), 356.

59. J. A. Hobson, *Imperialism: A Study* (New York: Gordon Press, 2006), 156.

60. Slonimskii, "O teoriiakh progressa," 265.

61. L. Z. Slonimskii, "Mnimaia sotsiologiia," *Vestnik Evropy* 5 (1889): 147.

62. L. Z. Slonimskii, "Genri Dzhordzh i ego teoriia progressa," *Vestnik Evropy* 7 (1889): 334.

63. Evaluating George's economic theories, Schumpeter wrote: "The abolition of this *Bodensperre* ["land-fence"] is (substantially) what his Liberal socialism that made a hit with many minds amounts to." Schumpeter, *History of Economic Analysis*, 854.

64. Slonimskii, "Genri Dzhordzh," 343–344.

65. Ibid., 350–351.

66. L. Z. Slonimskii, "Progress v politike," *Vestnik Evropy* 9 (1889): 247–248.

67. Ibid., 250.

68. Andrzej Walicki, "Russian Social Thought: An Introduction to the Intellectual History of Nineteenth-Century Russia," *Russian Review* 36, no. 1 (1977): 13.

69. L. Z. Slonimskii, "Natsionalizm v politike," *Vestnik Evropy* 11 (1889): 286.

70. Hobson wrote in 1902: "The assumption that there is only a given quantity of trade, and that if one nation gets any portion of it another nation loses just so much, shows a blind ignorance of the elements of international trade. It arises from a curiously perverse form of separatism which insists upon a nation keeping a separate account with every other nation, and ignoring altogether the round-about trade which is by far the most important business of an advanced industrial nation." Hobson, *Imperialism*, 66.

71. L. Z. Slonimskii, "Poniatiia o gosudarstve," *Vestnik Evropy* 4 (1890): 727.

72. Among the prerevolutionary proponents of the crisis were M. I. Tugan-Baranovskii, *Zemel'naia reforma: Ocherk dvizheniia v pol'zu zemel'noi reformy i prakticheskie vyvody* (St. Petersburg: Tip. I. N. Skorokhodova, 1905); V. I. Lenin's 1893 essay "Novye khoziaistvennye dvizheniia v krest'ianskoi zhizni: Po povodu knigi V. E. Postnikova—'Iuzhno-russkoe krest'ianskoe khoziaistvo'" in *Polnoe sobranie sochinenii* (Moscow: Gos. izd-vo polit. lit-ry, 1958–1965), volume 1, and *The Development of Capitalism in Russia* (Moscow: Progress Publishers, 1967), chapter 2. Among the Soviet historians, supporters of the "agrarian crisis" theory were, among others, I. D. Koval'chenko and L. V. Milov, *Vserossiiskii agrarnyi rynok: XVIII–nachalo XX veka* (Moscow: Nauka, 1974); B. N. Mironov, *Khlebnye tseny v Rossii za dva stoletiia (XVIII–XIX vv.)* (Leningrad: Nauka, 1985); I. D. Koval'chenko, *Agrarnyi stroi Rossii vtoroi poloviny XIX–nachala XX vv.* (Moscow: Nauka, 2004). In the West after the Second World War, the crisis also became a contentious issue. The argument hinged on three Russia-specific assumptions: first, that the post-Emancipation land allotments were too small to support the peasants who worked them; second, that the village commune was a severe obstacle to productivity; and third, that the redemption payments made it impossible to accumulate the required financial reserves to raise productivity. See Richard G. Robbins Jr., *Famine in Russia, 1891–1892: The Imperial Government Responds to a Crisis* (New York: Columbia University Press, 1975), 4. As a result of these factors, agricultural output fell short of population growth, thereby producing general rural poverty, which the famine of 1891–1892 eventually demonstrated. See Paul Gregory, "Rents, Land Prices, and Economic Theory: The Russian Agrarian Crisis," in *Economy and Society in Russia and the Soviet Union, 1860–1930: Essays for Olga Crisp*, ed. Linda Edmondson and Peter Waldron (New York: St. Martin's Press, 1992), 7–12. The Western proponents of the agrarian crisis theory were Alexander Gerschenkron, "Agrarian Policies and Industrialization: Russia, 1861–1917," in *The Cambridge Economic History of Europe*, vol. 6, *The Industrial Revolution and After: Incomes, Population, and Technological Change*, ed. H. J. Habakkuk and M. Postan (Cambridge: Cambridge University Press, 1965), 2:706–800; Arcadius Kahan, *The Plow, the Hammer, and the Knout: An Economic History of Eighteenth-Century Russia* (Chicago: University of Chicago Press, 1985), chapter 2; and Lazar Volin, *A Century of Russian Agriculture: From Alexander II to*

Khrushchev (Cambridge: Harvard University Press, 1970), especially 57–60. However, a revisionist school soon appeared. See Paul Gregory, "The Agrarian Crisis Revisited," in *The Soviet Rural Economy*, ed. Robert Stuart (Totowa, NJ: Rowman & Allanheld, 1984), 21–32; S. G. Wheatcroft, "Grain Production and Utilization in Russia and the USSR before Collectivization" (PhD diss., University of Birmingham, 1980) and "Crises and the Condition of the Peasantry in Late Imperial Russia," in *Peasant Economy, Culture, and Politics of European Russia, 1800–1921*, ed. Esther Kingston-Mann and Timothy Mixter (Princeton: Princeton University Press, 1991), 129–175; Richard Rudolph, "Agricultural Structure and Proto-Industrialization in Russia: Economic Development with Unfree Labor," *The Journal of Economic History* 44, no. 1 (March 1985), 47–69; James Y. Simms Jr., "The Crisis in Russian Agriculture at the End of the Nineteenth Century: A Different View," *Slavic Review* 36, no. 3 (1977): 377–398; James Y. Simms Jr., "On Missing the Point: A Rejoinder," *Slavic Review* 37, no. 3 (September 1978), 487–490. See also G. M. Hamburg's critical response to Simms, "The Crisis in Russian Agriculture: A Comment," *Slavic Review* 37, no. 3 (September 1978), 481–486; and Simms's to Hamburg: "The Crop Failure of 1891: Soil Exhaustion, Technological Backwardness, and Russia's 'Agrarian Crisis'," *Slavic Review* 41, no. 2 (Summer 1982), 236–250; John Thomas Sanders, "'Once More Into the Breach, Dear Friends': A Closer Look at Indirect Tax Receipts and the Condition of the Russian Peasantry, 1881–1899," *Slavic Review* 43, no. 4 (Winter 1984), 657–666; James Y. Simms Jr., "'Once More Into the Breach, Dear Friends': A Closer Look at Indirect Tax Receipts and the Condition of the Russian Peasantry, 1881–1899: Reply," *Slavic Review* 43, no. 4 (Winter 1984), 236–250; Simms, "More Grist for the Mill: A Further Look at the Crisis of Russian Agriculture at the End of the Nineteenth Century," *Slavic Review* 50, no. 4 (Winter 1991), 999–1009.

73. Dmitrii Drutskoi-Sokolninskii, "Nashe sel'skoe khoziaistvo i ego budushchnost'," *Vestnik Evropy* 10 (1891): 699–724.

CHAPTER 8. SOLVING THE AGRARIAN CRISIS

1. For example, see Hugh Seton-Watson, *The Russian Empire, 1801–1917* (Oxford: Clarendon Press, 1967), 512–513; Nicholas V. Riasanovsky, *A History of Russia* (New York: Oxford University Press, 1993), 405; and Catherine Evtuhov, David Goldfrank, Lindsey Hughes, and Richard Stites, *A History of Russia: Peoples, Legends, Events, Forces* (Boston: Houghton Mifflin, 2004), 497.

2. Perm, Viatka, Ufa, Orenburg, Samara, Kazan, Nizhnii Novgorod, Simbirsk, Penza, Saratov, Riazan, Tula, Tambov, Orel, Voronezh, Kursk, and Kharkov.

3. Janet M. Hartley, "Provincial and Local Government," in *The Cambridge History of Russia*, vol. 2, *Imperial Russia*, ed. Dominic Lieven (Cambridge: Cambridge University Press, 2006), 449–468.

4. B. B. Veselovskii, *Istoriia zemstva za sorok let* (Cambridge, England: Oriental Research Partners, 1973), 3:365. Veselovskii was an eminent zemstvo historian, a member of the Social Democratic Party, and eventually a Menshevik. Originally published in 1909, this work is the first definitive study of the zemstvo.

5. I. E. Dronov, "Put' konservatora," in *Grazhdanin konservator*, by V. P. Meshcherskii (Moscow: Ikhtios, 2005), 17–29.

6. K. K. Arsen'ev, "Vnutrennee obozrenie," *Vestnik Evropy* 1 (1891): 369.

7. For a general discussion of the peasantry's state before the famine, see Richard Robbins Jr., *Famine in Russia, 1891–1892: The Imperial Government Responds to a Crisis* (New York: Columbia University Press, 1975), 1–13.

8. W. E. Mosse, "Aspects of Tsarist Bureaucracy: The State Council in the Late Nineteenth Century," *The English Historical Review* 95, no. 375 (April 1980), 282–284.

9. Veselovskii, *Istoria zemstva*, 3:369–371; Roberta Thompson Manning, "The Zemstvo and Politics," in *The Zemstvo in Russia: An Experiment in Local Self-Government*, ed. Terence Emmons and Wayne S. Vucinich (Cambridge: Cambridge University Press, 1982), 133–176.

10. I. A. Aksakov founded *Rus* in 1880. It was a conservative weekly paper, which reflected Aksakov's Slavophilic and Pan-Slavic views. See *Entsiklopedicheskii slovar', reprintnoe vosproizvedenie izdaniia F. A. Brokgauz-I. A. Efron 1890 g.* (Iaroslavl, 1992), 53:367. Effie Ambler refers to *Rus* as a neo-Slavophile semimonthly in her *Russian Journalism and Politics, 1861–1881: The Career of Aleksei S. Suvorin* (Detroit: Wayne State University Press, 1972), 166.

11. As Alexander Vucinich has argued, Tolstoi's 1871 curriculum was "one of the most potent mechanisms that government had employed in its effort to stem the tide of 'natural science materialism,' interpreted as a major enemy of autocratic institutions." Alexander Vucinich, *Darwin in Russian Thought* (Berkeley: University of California Press, 1988), 103–104.

12. K. K. Arsen'ev, "Vnutrennee obozrenie," *Vestnik Evropy* 4 (1882): 803.

13. For a basic introduction to the *volost'* and the debates around it, see D. Kuzmin-Karavaev's article "Vsesoslovnaia volost'," in *Novyi Entsiklopedicheskii Slovar'*, ed. K. K. Arsen'ev (St. Petersburg: Tip. Aktsionernogo ob-va Brokgauz-Efron, 1911–1916), 11:157–159.

14. K. K. Arsen'ev, "Vnutrennee obozrenie," *Vestnik Evropy* 8 (1881): 825.

15. K. K. Arsen'ev, "Vnutrennee obozrenie," *Vestnik Evropy* 7 (1881): 366.

16. On the role of the *volost'* courts, see Stephen P. Frank, *Crime, Cultural Conflict, and Justice in Rural Russia, 1856–1914* (Berkeley: University of California Press, 1999); and Jane Burbank, *Russian Peasants Go to Court: Legal Culture in the Countryside, 1905–1917* (Bloomington: Indiana University Press, 2004).

17. Robbins, *Famine in Russia*, 27–28.

18. K. K. Arsen'ev, "Vnutrennee obozrenie," *Vestnik Evropy* 4 (1882): 806.

19. For a discussion of *Vestnik Evropy* in the Russian liberal movement of the time, see A. A. Alafaev, *Russkii liberalizm na rubezhe 70-80-kh gg. XIX v.: Iz istorii zhurnala "Vestnik Evropy"* (Moscow: Institut istorii SSSR, 1991).

20. N. I. Pirumova, *Zemskoe liberal'noe dvizhenie: Sotsial'nye korni i evoliutsiia do nachala XX veka* (Moscow: Nauka, 1977), 93.

21. Ibid., 94.

22. N. A. Kotliarevskii, *Kholmy rodiny* (Berlin: Obelisk, 1923), 144.

23. V. V. Bartenev, "Vospominaniia peterburzhtsa o vtoroi polovine 1880-x godov," in *Ot narodnichestva—k marksizmu: Vospominaniia uchastnikov revoliutsionnogo dvizheniia v Peterburge (1883–1894 gg.)*, ed. S. S. Volk (Leningrad: Lenizdat, 1987), 203–205, 210.

24. Pirumova, *Zemskoe liberal'noe dvizhenie*, 192.

25. K. K. Arsen'ev, "Vnutrennee obozrenie," *Vestnik Evropy* 2 (1899): 800–802.

26. *Grazhdanin* was published by the "troubadour of reaction," Prince V. P. Meshcherskii, from funds supplied by the Winter Palace. The paper defended Alexander III's reign. Meshcherskii argued for putting an end to all reforms in Russia. Louise McReynolds, *The News Under Russia's Old Regime: The Development of a Mass-Circulation Press* (Princeton: Princeton University Press, 1991), 99–101.

27. Robbins, *Famine in Russia*, 14–16.

28. K. K. Arsen'ev, "Vnutrennee obozrenie," *Vestnik Evropy* 8 (1891): 866–869.

29. Ibid., 866.

30. K. K. Arsen'ev, "Vnutrennee obozrenie," *Vestnik Evropy* 9 (1891): 426–428.

31. K. K. Arsen'ev, "Vnutrennee obozrenie," *Vestnik Evropy* 1 (1891): 370–378.

32. K. K. Arsen'ev, "Vnutrennee obozrenie," *Vestnik Evropy* 10 (1891): 808.

33. K. K. Arsen'ev, "Vnutrennee obozrenie," *Vestnik Evropy* 11 (1891): 354–357.

34. K. K. Arsen'ev, "Vnutrennee obozrenie," *Vestnik Evropy* 9 (1891): 424.

35. Pirumova, *Zemskoe liberal'noe dvizhenie*, 139.

36. K. K. Arsen'ev, "Vnutrennee obozrenie," *Vestnik Evropy* 9 (1891): 425–426.

37. K. K. Arsen'ev, "Vnutrennee obozrenie," *Vestnik Evropy* 12 (1891): 872–873.

38. Theodore Von Laue, "The Fate of Capitalism in Russia: The Narodnik Version," *American Slavic and East European Review* 13, no. 1 (1954): 11–28.

39. K. K. Arsen'ev, "Vnutrennee obozrenie," *Vestnik Evropy* 2 (1892): 859.

40. K. K. Arsen'ev, "Vnutrennee obozrenie," *Vestnik Evropy* 12 (1891): 874–880.

41. K. K. Arsen'ev, "Vnutrennee obozrenie," *Vestnik Evropy* 1 (1892): 383–384.

42. Robbins, *Famine in Russia*, 111, 123.

43. Arsen'ev, "Vnutrennee obozrenie," *Vestnik Evropy* 1 (1892): 388.

44. Ibid., 388–390.

45. Pirumova, *Zemskoe liberal'noe dvizhenie*, 192.

46. Institut Russkoi Literatury (IRLI), f. 359, no. 184, 19 December 1891.

47. IRLI, f. 359, no. 184, 18 January 1892.

48. IRLI, f. 359, no. 184, 12 January 1892.

49. IRLI, f. 359, no. 184, 18 February 1892.

50. IRLI, f. 359, no. 37, 23 April 1892; IRLI, f. 359, no. 419, 26 February 1892.
51. IRLI, f. 359, no. 152, 1 May 1892.
52. *Novosti* was short for *Novosti dnia i birzhevaia gazeta*, which O. K. Notovich ran beginning in 1880. It had a liberal orientation and a westward slant, but it was inconsistent in its editorial policies, drawing on many contributors, as Notovich tried to fill each issue with material. McReynolds, *The News*, 132–133.
53. K. K. Arsen'ev, "Vnutrennee obozrenie," *Vestnik Evropy* 2 (1892): 853–858.
54. K. K. Arsen'ev, "Vnutrennee obozrenie," *Vestnik Evropy* 3 (1892): 400.
55. Ibid., 392–393.
56. Ibid., 392–399.
57. K. K. Arsen'ev, "Vnutrennee obozrenie," *Vestnik Evropy* 4 (1892): 372.
58. Pirumova, *Zemskoe liberal'noe dvizhenie*, 189.
59. K. K. Arsen'ev, "Vnutrennee obozrenie," *Vestnik Evropy* 6 (1892): 824–827.
60. Terence Emmons, "The Beseda Circle, 1899–1905," *Slavic Review* 32, no. 3 (1973): 464–465.
61. Robbins, *Famine in Russia*, 178.
62. K. K. Arsen'ev, "Vnutrennee obozrenie," *Vestnik Evropy* 7 (1892): 401–404. See also Robbins, *Famine in Russia*, 104.
63. Arsen'ev, "Vnutrennee obozrenie," *Vestnik Evropy* 7 (1892): 405–410.
64. K. K. Arsen'ev, "Vnutrennee obozrenie," *Vestnik Evropy* 5 (1893): 449–450.
65. Emmons, "The Beseda Circle," 462.
66. Robbins, *Famine in Russia*, 168–175.

CHAPTER 9. FROM MARXIST APOLOGETICS TO A MORAL ECONOMY

1. *Vestnik Evropy* 12 (1891): 886; 12 (1892): 890; and 12 (1893): 922.
2. M. A. Nikitina, "Vestnik Evropy," in *Literaturnyi protsess i russkaia zhurnalistika kontsa XIX–nachala XX veka: 1890–1904; Burzhuazno-liberal'nye i modernistskie izdaniia*, ed. B. A. Bailik, V. A. Keldysh, and V. R. Shcherbina (Moscow: Nauka, 1982), 6.
3. Chernyshevskii to K. T. Soldatenkov, 26 December 1888, in N. G. Chernyshevskii, *Polnoe sobranie sochinenii* (Moscow: Goslitizdat, 1950), 15:784–785.
4. A. P. Chekhov, *Polnoe sobranie sochinenii i pisem* (Moscow: Izd-vo khudozhestvennoi literatury, 1949), 17:12.
5. Nikitina, "Vestnik Evropy," 5.
6. N. A. Belogolovyi to K. K. Arsen'ev, 15 March 1892, Institut Russkoi Literatury (IRLI), f. 359, no. 151.
7. "Vypiska iz zhurnala zasedaniia Soveta ob otnoshenii zhurnala Vestnik Evropy k reforme zemskikh uchrezhdenii [December 1889]," Rossiiskii Gosudarstvennyi Istoricheskii Arkhiv (RGIA), f. 776, op. 2, ed. khr. 24, ll. 177–179.
8. M. S. Shaginian, *Chelovek i vremia: Istoriia chelovecheskogo stanovleniia* (Moscow: Khudozhestvennaia literatura, 1980), 61.

9. S. M. Solov'ev, *Vospominaniia* (Moscow: Novoe literaturnoe obozrenie, 2003), 171.

10. E. A. Andreeva-Balmont, *Vospominaniia* (Moscow: Shabashnikovy, 1997), 167.

11. Pavel Kalinnikov, ed., "Slonimskii Leonid-Liudvig Zinov'evich," in *Russkii Biograficheskii Slovar'*, 23 June 2006, http://rulex.ru/01181124.htm.

12. IRLI, f. 293, op. 1, ed. khr. 98, 1. 42.

13. D. I. Abramovich, ed., *Iz perepiski deiatelei Akademii nauk* (Leningrad: Gosudarstvennaia publichnaia biblioteka, 1925), 40.

14. I. A. Goncharov to Stasiulevich, 30 October 1882, in *M. M. Stasiulevich i ego sovremenniki v ikh perepiskie*, ed. M. K. Lemke (St. Petersburg: Tipografiia M. M. Stasiulevicha, 1911–1913), 4:370.

15. V. S. Solov'ev, "Rossiia i Evropa," *Vestnik Evropy* 2 (1888): 340–357; and 4 (1888): 568–588.

16. The letter was dated December 1888. Quoted from A. F. Losev's *Vladimir Solov'ev i ego vremia* (Moscow: Molodaia gvardiia, 2000), 67.

17. Nikitina, "Vestnik Evropy," 15.

18. IRLI, f. 293, op. 1, ed. khr. 165/4, 1. 100.

19. Nikitina, "Vestnik Evropy," 16–20, 38, 40–42. For a full list of Solovyov's works in the *Herald*, see *Vestnik Evropy* 11 (1900): 425–426.

20. *Literaturnoe nasledstvo* (Moscow: Zhurnal'no-gazetnoe ob"edinenie, 1935), 22:544.

21. V. S. Solov'ev, *Pis'ma* (Prague, 1923), 5.

22. V. S. Solov'ev, *Stikhotvoreniia i shutochnye p'esy* (Munich: W. Fink, 1968), 171. This is my translation.

23. Rossiiskaia Natsional'naia Biblioteka (RNB), f. 621, ed. khr. 850, 1. 13.

24. For an excellent overview of the era's publications, see Joan Delaney Grossman's "Rise and Decline of the 'Literary' Journal: 1880–1917," in *Literary Journals in Imperial Russia*, ed. Deborah A. Martinsen (Cambridge: Cambridge University Press, 1997), 92.

25. Leonid Slonimskii, "Nash torgovyi balans," *Vestnik Evropy* 2 (1892): 792–793.

26. Ibid., 794–797.

27. Ibid., 797–802.

28. Ibid., 802–805.

29. Ibid., 808.

30. Ibid., 805–809.

31. George F. Putnam, *Russian Alternatives to Marxism: Christian Socialism and Idealistic Liberalism in Twentieth-Century Russia* (Knoxville: University of Tennessee Press, 1977), 10.

32. "Poslednie dva neurozhainykh goda vydvinuli na pervyi plan interesy sel'skogo naseleniia i zemledelcheskoi promyshlennosti," *Russkie vedomosti*, January 30, 1893.

33. L. Z. Slonimskii, "Novye materialy dlia starogo spora," *Vestnik Evropy* 8 (1892): 770–777.

34. Richard G. Robbins Jr., *Famine in Russia, 1891–1892: The Imperial Government Responds to a Crisis* (New York: Columbia University Press, 1975), 180.

35. *Russkie vedomosti*, May 29, 1893, 2; June 22, 1893, 3; July 10, 1893; *Birzhevye vedomosti*, 4 and 7 December 1893.

36. L. Z. Slonimskii, "Ekonomicheskiia reformy i zakonodatel'stvo," *Vestnik Evropy* 8 (1893): 735.

37. Ibid., 736–737.

38. Ibid., 756.

39. B. V. Ananich and R. Sh. Ganelin, "Vstuplenie," in *Vlast' i reformy: Ot samoderzhavnoi k sovetskoi Rossii* (Moscow: DB, 1996), 50–51.

40. For an excellent discussion of the strategic purpose behind the railroad's construction, see Steven G. Marks' *Road to Power: The Trans-Siberian Railroad and the Colonization of Asian Russia, 1850–1917* (Ithaca: Cornell University Press, 1991).

41. I. V. Ostrovskii, *Agrarnaia politika tsarizma v Sibiri perioda imperializma* (Novosibirsk: Izd-vo Novosibirskogo universiteta, 1991), 119.

42. The main works on the subject are James Billington, *Mikhailovsky and Russian Populism* (Oxford: Clarendon Press, 1958); Arthur Mendel, *Dilemmas of Progress in Tsarist Russia: Legal Marxism and Legal Populism* (Cambridge: Harvard University Press, 1961); Richard Kindersley, *The First Russian Revisionists: A Study of "Legal Marxism" in Russia* (Oxford: Clarendon Press, 1962); Richard Wortman, *The Crisis of Russian Populism* (London: Cambridge University Press, 1967); Andrzej Walicki, *The Controversy Over Capitalism: Studies in the Social Philosophy of the Russian Populists* (Notre Dame, IN: University of Notre Dame Press, 1969); Margaret Canovan, *Populism* (New York: Harcourt Brace Jovanovich, 1981); and Edward H. Judge and James Y. Simms Jr., eds., *Modernization and Revolution: Dilemmas of Progress in Late Imperial Russia; Essays in Honor of Arthur P. Mendel* ([Boulder, CO?]: East European Monographs; New York: Distributed by Columbia University Press, 1992).

43. L. Z. Slonimskii, "Ekonomicheskiia nedorazumeniia," *Vestnik Evropy* 6 (1894): 774–777.

44. Slonimskii, "Ekonomicheskiia nedorazumeniia," 784.

45. Ibid., 774.

46. A. I. Chuprov, *O sovremennom znachenii i zadachakh politicheskoi ekonomii* (Moscow: Tip. Rus. ved., 1874), 14.

47. V. V. Sviatlovskii, *Ocherki po istorii ekonomicheskikh vozzrenii* (St. Petersburg, 1913), 275.

48. M. I. Tugan-Baranovskii, "Osnovnaia oshibka abstraktnoi teorii kapitalizma Marksa," *Nauchnoe obozrenie* 5 (1899): 974.

49. P. B. Struve, *Kriticheskie zametki k voprosu ob ekonomicheskom razvitii Rossii* (St. Petersburg: Tip. I. N. Skorokhodova, 1894), 282–285.

50. L. Z. Slonimskii, "Zametka: Nekul'turnost' i kapitalizm," *Vestnik Evropy* 12 (1894): 875–882.

51. Arthur Mendel, "N. K. Mikhailovskij and His Criticism of Russian Marxism," *American Slavic and East European Review* 14, no. 3 (1955): 338.

52. L. Z. Slonimskii, "Marks i ego shkola," *Vestnik Evropy* 3 (1896): 290–292.

53. Jacob Walkin, "The Attitude of the Tsarist Government toward the Labor Problem," *American Slavic and East European Review* 13, no. 2 (1954): 164.

54. Slonimskii, "Marks i ego shkola," 300.

55. Ibid., 304–306.

56. L. Z. Slonimskii, "Ekonomicheskaia teoriia Marksa," *Vestnik Evropy* 4 (1896): 825.

57. Slonimskii, "Marks i ego shkola," 371.

58. Quoted from Alexander Vucinich's *Darwin in Russian Thought* (Berkeley: University of California Press, 1988), 363.

59. Vucinich, *Darwin in Russian Thought*, 357–358.

60. Mendel, *Dilemmas of Progress*, 155.

61. L. Z. Slonimskii, "Kapitalizm v doktrine Marksa," *Vestnik Evropy* 7 (1896): 372.

62. I. Bortkevich, *O denezhnoi reforme, proektirovannoi Ministerstvom finansov* (St. Petersburg: Tip. E Arngol'da, 1896), 31.

63. S. D. Martynov, *Gosudarstvo i ekonomika: Sistema Vitte* (St. Petersburg: Nauka, 2002), 161.

64. P. P. Migulin, *Reforma denezhnogo obrashcheniia i promyshlennyi krizis v Rossii (1893–1902)* (Moscow: Obshchestvo kuptsov i promyshlennikov Rossii, 2006), 127.

65. Sidney Harcave, *Count Sergei Witte and the Twilight of Imperial Russia: A Biography* (Armonk, NY: M. E. Sharpe, 2004), 67.

66. L. Z. Slonimskii, "Denezhnaia reforma," *Vestnik Evropy* 5 (1896): 343.

67. L. Z. Slonimskii, "Ekonomicheskie zametki," *Vestnik Evropy* 4 (1898): 760.

68. *Materialy k proektu polozheniia o gosudarstvennom podokhodnom nalogie: Opyt priblizitel'nogo ischisleniia narodnogo dokhoda po razlichnym ego istochnikam i po razmeram v Rossii* (St. Petersburg: Tip. P. P. Soikina, 1906), 21.

69. L. Z. Slonimskii, "Promyshlennaia ideologiia," *Vestnik Evropy* 6 (1898): 768–783.

70. *Novosti*, November 5, 1897.

71. *Novosti*, December 2, 1897.

72. *Russkie vedomosti*, December 18, 1897.

73. *Novoe vremia*, January 1, 1898.

74. *Novoe vremia*, February 1, 1898.

75. *Birzhevye vedomosti*, September 2, 1898.

76. S. Iu. Witte, *Vospominaniia* (Moscow: Izd-vo sotsial'no-ekon. lit-ry, 1960), 2:524.

77. Ibid., 2:527.

78. Slonimskii, "Ekonomicheskie zametki," 751–759.

79. Theodore Von Laue, "The Fate of Capitalism in Russia: The Narodnik Version," *American Slavic and East European Review* 13, no. 1 (1954): 18.

80. Mendel, *Dilemmas of Progress*, 129.

81. L. Z. Slonimskii, "Karl Marks v russkoi literature," *Vestnik Evropy* 9 (1897): 301–303.

82. Nikolai-on, "Ocherki nashego po-reformennogo obshchestvennogo khoziaistva," *Slovo* 10 (1880): 77–142.

83. See chapter 7 of M. N. Tugan-Baranovskii's *Russkaia fabrika v proshlom i nastoiashchem: Istoriko-ekonomicheskie issledovanie* (St. Petersburg: Izd. L. F. Pantel'eva, 1898).

84. Slonimskii, "Karl Marks v russkoi literature," 293.

85. Ibid., 294.

86. *Na slavnom postu (1860–1900): Literaturnyi sbornik, posviashchennyi N. K. Mikhailovskomu* (St. Petersburg: Tip. N. N. Klobukova, 1901); and N. A. Berdiaev, *Sub"ektivizm i individualizm v obshchestvennoi filosofii: Kriticheskii etiud o N. K. Mikhailovskom; S predisloviem Petra Struve* (St. Petersburg: Izd-vo O. N. Popovoi, 1901).

87. L. Z. Slonimskii, "Nashi napravleniia," *Vestnik Evropy* 12 (1901): 808–824.

88. For a discussion of "under-government" in Russia, see S. Frederick Starr, *Decentralization and Self-Government in Russia, 1830–1870* (Princeton: Princeton University Press, 1972), 281–282.

89. For a discussion of peasant views of the zemstvos, see Dorothy Atkinson, "The Zemstvo and the Peasantry," in *The Zemstvo in Russia: An Experiment in Local Self-Government*, ed. Terence Emmons and Wayne S. Vucinich (Cambridge: Cambridge University Press, 1982), 79–133; William G. Rosenberg, "The Zemstvo in 1917 and Its Fate Under Bolshevik Rule," in Emmons and Vucinich, *The Zemstvo in Russia*, 383–423.

90. For a discussion of nobility participation in local self-government, see W. E. Mosse, "Aspects of Tsarist Bureaucracy: The State Council in the Late Nineteenth Century," *The English Historical Review* 95, no. 375 (April 1980), 278; Roberta Thompson Manning, "The Zemstvo and Politics," in Emmons and Vucinich, *The Zemstvo in Russia*, 133–176; Thomas S. Fallows, "The Russian Fronde and the Zemstvo Movement: Economic Agitation and Gentry Politics in the Mid-1890s," *Russian Review* 44, no. 2 (1985): 129, 137.

91. Witte, *Vospominaniia*, 2:515.

92. Thomas Fallows, "The Zemstvo and the Bureaucracy," in Emmons and Vucinich, *The Zemstvo in Russia*, 214–217.

93. "Vsepoddaneishii doklad ministra finansov o gosudarstvennoi rospisi dokhodov i raskhodov na 1898 g.," *Vestnik finansov promyshlennosti i torgovli* 1 (1899): 6.

94. Ibid., 8–9.

95. Fallows, "The Zemstvo and the Bureaucracy," 217–218.

96. Janet M. Hartley, "Provincial and Local Government," in *The Cambridge History of Russia*, vol. 2, *Imperial Russia*, ed. Dominic Lieven (Cambridge: Cambridge University Press, 2006), 453.

97. L. Z. Slonimskii, "Sovremennyia nedoumeniia," *Vestnik Evropy* 5 (1900): 238–249.

98. Ibid., 240.

99. Ibid., 242–243.

100. Ibid., 244.

101. *Birzhevye vedomosti*, January 27, 1901, 1, 16; May 25, 1901; July 25, 1901.

102. *Russkie vedomosti*, December 9 and 15, 1901; February 20, 1902.

103. *Russkie vedomosti*, November 26, 1900.

104. *Novoe vremia*, January 1, 1900.

105. *Novoe vremia*, January 28, 1902.

106. *Novosti*, May 27, 1900; June 20, 1900; July 3, 1900.

107. *Novosti*, September 2 and 5, 1900.

108. M. S. Simonova, *Krizis agrarnoi politiki tsarizma nakanune pervoi rossiiskoi revoliutsii* (Moscow: Nauka, 1987), 13.

109. *Pravitel'stvennyi vestnik*, January 24 (February 6), 1902.

110. Ibid., 117.

111. *Novoe vremia*, January 25, 1902.

112. *Novoe vremia*, January 4 and 27, 1902.

113. *Novoe vremia*, March 23, 1902.

114. *Russkie vedomosti*, January 29, 1902.

115. K. K. Arsen'ev, "Vvedenie," in *Melkaia zemskaia edinitsa* (St. Petersburg: Obshchestvennaia pol'za, 1902), i.

116. F. G. Terner, *Vospominaniia zhizni F. G. Ternera* (St. Petersburg: Izd. M. G. i E. G. Terner, 1911), 2:133–134.

117. Gregory L. Freeze, "A National Liberation Movement and the Shift in Russian Liberalism, 1901–1903," *Slavic Review* 28, no. 1 (1969): 87, 89.

118. Terence Emmons, "The Beseda Circle, 1899–1905," *Slavic Review* 32, no. 3 (1973): 487–488, 462.

119. *Ministr i gosudarstvennyi sovet o finansovom polozhenii Rossii: Zhurnal obshchego sobraniia gosudarstvennogo soveta 30 dekabria 1902 g.* (Stuttgart: J. W. Deitz, 1903), 6.

120. *Birzhevye vedomosti*, August 18, 1903; November 5, 1903.

121. *Novoe vremia*, August 22 and 24, 1903; September 7, 1903.

122. *Novosti*, August 18, 19, and 30, 1903.

123. *Novosti*, August 28 and 31, 1903.

124. *Russkie vedomosti*,August 2 and 18, 1903.

125. *Russkie vedomosti*, September 16, 1903.

126. K. K. Arsen'ev, "Vnutrennee obozrenie," *Vestnik Evropy* 10 (1903): 776–780.

127. K. K. Arsen'ev, "Obshchestvennaia khronika," *Vestnik Evropy* 10 (1903): 873–875.

128. This was a review article of four works: A. A. Radtsig, *Finansovaia politika Rossii s 1887 goda: Sbornik statei po finansovym i ekonomicheskim voprosam* (St. Petersburg: Narodnaia pol'za, 1903); M. S. Tolmachev, *Krest'ianskii vopros po vzgliadam zemstva i mestnykh liudei* (Moscow: Tipo-lit T-va I. N. Kushnerev, 1903); A. E. Voskresenskii, *Obshchinnoe zemlevladenie i krest'ianskoe malozemel'e* (St. Petersburg: Tip. i lit. V. A. Tikhonova, 1903); A. A. Rittikh, *Zavisimost' krest'ian ot obshchiny i mira* (St. Petersburg: Tip. V. F. Kirshbauma, 1903).

129. L. Z. Slonimskii, "Nashi ekonomicheskie zadachi i krest'ianskii vopros," *Vestnik Evropy* 1 (1904): 237–241.

130. Ibid., 245.

131. L. Z. Slonimskii, "Noveishie protivniki obshchiny," *Vestnik Evropy* 2 (1904): 772.

132. S. Iu. Witte, *Zapiska po krest'ianskomu delu* (St. Petersburg: Kirshbaum, 1904), 47.

133. Witte, *Vospominaniia*, 2:342, 357.

134. Alexander Gerschenkron, "An Economic History of Russia," *Journal of Economic History* 12, no. 2 (1952): 149.

135. L. Z. Slonimskii, "Nauchnye illiuzii," *Vestnik Evropy* 2 (1903): 757.

136. M. N. Tugan-Baranovskii, *Ocherki iz noveishei istorii politicheskoi ekonomii* (St. Petersburg: Izd. zhurnala Mir Bozhii, 1903), vi.

137. Slonimskii, "Nauchnye illiuzii," 769.

138. L. Z. Slonimskii, "Noveishie idealisty," *Vestnik Evropy* 9 (1903): 313–325.

139. Slonimskii, "Nashi ekonomicheskie zadachi," 237–253.

140. G. V. Plekhanov, *Sochineniia* (Leningrad, 1927), 26:66.

141. "Pis'mo Stasiulevicha Sankt Peterburgskoi gorodskoi uchilishchnaia komissii, 17-ogo noiabria 1897 goda," RGB, Fond D. A. Miliutina, op. 1, shifr 169, no. 75, no. 51.

142. IRLI, f. 293, op. 1, ed. khr. 165, 1.1.

143. Pavel Kalinnikov, ed. "Stasiulevich Mikhail Matveevich," in *Russkii Biograficheskii Slovar'*, Studiia Kolibri, 23 June 2006, http://rulex.ru/01181219.htm.

CONCLUSION

1. Philip Nord, "Introduction," in *Civil Society before Democracy: Lessons from Nineteenth-Century Europe*, ed. Nancy Bermeo and Philip Nord (Lanham, MD: Rowman & Littlefield Publishers, 2000), xix.

2. Pieter Judson, *Exclusive Revolutionaries: Liberal Politics, Social Experience, and National Identity in the Austrian Empire, 1848–1914* (Ann Arbor: University of Michigan Press, 1996).

3. James Sheehan, *German Liberalism in the Nineteenth Century* (Chicago: University of Chicago Press, 1978).

4. "Vypiska iz zhurnala zasedaniia Soveta ob otnoshenii zhurnala Vestnik Evropy k reforme zemskikh uchrezhdenii [December 1889]," Rossiiskii Gosudarstvennyi Istoricheskii Arkhiv (RGIA), f. 776, op. 2, ed. khr. 24, 1. 178.

5. "O kharaktere napravleniia gazety (otzyv tsenzora) [25 February 1893]," RGIA, f. 777, op. 4, ed. khr. 205, 11. 12–120b.

6. Institut Russkoi Literatury (IRLI), f. 293, op. 1, ed. khr. 99/2, 1. 43.

7. A. F. Koni, "Vestnik Evropy (Fevral 1911 g.)," in *Sobranie sochinenii* (Moscow: Iurid. lit-ra, 1969), 7:231.

8. V. E. Kel'ner, *Chelovek svoego vremeni: M. M. Stasiulevich, izdatel'skoe delo i liberal'naia oppositsiia)* (St. Petersburg: Izd-vo Rossiiskoi natsional'noi biblioteki, 1993), 254.

9. Stasiulevich to A. M. Zhemchuzhnikov, 9 December 1905, in *M. M. Stasiulevich i ego sovremenniki v ikh perepiskie*, ed. M. K. Lemke (St. Petersburg: Tipografiia M. M. Stasiulevicha, 1911–1913), 4:412.

10. For Tolstoy see *Literaturnoe nasledstvo* (Moscow: Zhurnal'no-gazetnoe ob"edinenie, 1979), 90:2:359 and 90:3:181. For Gorky see M. Gor'kii, *Sobranie sochinenii* (Moscow: Izd-vo Khudozhestvennoi literatury, 1955), 29: 45.

11. M. M. Stasiulevich and K. K. Arsen'ev, "Zapiska chetyrnadtsati redaktsii i otvet na nee dvukh chlenov osobogo soveshchaniia po pechati," *Vestnik Evropy* 3 (1905): 105.

12. IRLI, f. 293, op. 3, ed. khr. 17, 1. 6, 8, 17, 140, 151, 181.

13. *Vestnik Evropy* 2 (1906): 786–793.

14. D. A. Korsakov to Stasiulevich, 3 February 1896, in Lemke, *M. M. Stasiulevich i ego sovremenniki*, 2:235.

15. Rossiiskaia Natsional'naia Biblioteka (RNB), f. 621, ed. khr. 852, 1. 14.

16. Quoted from Derek Offord's *Portraits of Early Russian Liberals: A Study of the Thought of T. N. Granovsky, V. P. Botkin, P. V. Annenkov, A. V. Druzhinin, and K. D. Kavelin* (Cambridge: Cambridge University Press, 1985), 228.

17. M. Gershenzon, "Predislovie," in *Vekhi: Intelligentsiia v Rossii; Sborniki statei, 1909–1910*, ed. N. Kazakova (Moscow: Molodaia gvardiia, 1991), 23.

18. V. Shelokhaev, "Predislovie," in Kazakova, *Vekhi*, 5.

19. P. N. Miliukov, "Intelligentsiia i istoricheskaia traditsiia," in Kazakova, *Vekhi*, 378.

20. Alexander Solzhenitsyn, "Russia in Collapse," in *The Solzhenitsyn Reader: New and Essential Writings, 1947–2005*, ed. Edward E. Ericson and Daniel J. Mahoney (Wilmington, DE: ISI Books, 2006), 480–481.

Bibliography

Archival Materials

Moscow

Institut Nauchnykh Issledovanii Obshchestvennykh Nauk (INION)
Rossiiskaia Gosudarstvennaia Biblioteka (RGB)

St. Petersburg

Institut Russkoi Literatury (IRLI)
Rossiiskaia Natsional'naia Biblioteka (RNB)
Rossiiskii Gosudarstvennyi Istoricheskii Arkhiv (RGIA)

Published Works

Newspapers and Journals

Birzhevye vedomosti. St. Petersburg, 1880–1917.
Moskovskie vedomosti. Moscow, 1756–1917.
Narodnaia volia. St. Petersburg, 1879–1885.
Novoe vremia. St. Petersburg, 1868–1917.
Novosti. St. Petersburg, 1876–1917.
Osvobozhdenie. St. Petersburg, 1902–1905.
Poriadok. St. Petersburg, 1872–1873.
Pravitel'stvennyi vestnik. St. Petersburg, 1869–1917.
Rus. Moscow, 1880–1886.
Russkie vedomosti. St. Petersburg, 1863–1918.
Vestnik Evropy. St. Petersburg, 1866–1918.
Vestnik finansov, promyshlennosti i torgovli. St. Petersburg, 1885–1917.

Primary Published Sources

Abramov, P. "Obrazovanie i obespechenie byta rabochikh v Rossii." *Vestnik Evropy* 1 (1879): 321–340.

Abramovich, D. I., ed. *Iz perepiski deiatelei Akademii nauk*. Leningrad: Gosudar- stvennaia publichnaia biblioteka, 1925.

Andreeva-Balmont, E. A. *Vospominaniia*. Moscow: Shabashnikovy, 1997.

Aptekman, O. V. *Obshchestvo 'Zemli i volia' semidesiatykh godov*. Prague, 1924.

Arsen'ev, K. I. *Tsarstvovanie Petra II*. St. Petersburg: Tipografiia Imperatorskoi Rossii- skoi Akademii, 1839.

———. *Tsarstvovanie Ekateriny I*. St. Petersburg: Tipografiia Imperatorskoi Rossii- skoi Akademii, 1856.

Arsen'ev, K. K. "Iz dalekikh vospominanii." *Golos minuvshego* 2 (1915): 113–135.

———. "Literaturnoe obozrenie." *Vestnik Evropy* 2 (1879): 768–776.

———. "Literaturnoe obozrenie." *Vestnik Evropy* 9 (1881): 433–439.

———. "Literaturnoe obozrenie." *Vestnik Evropy* 3 (1882): 405–412.

———. "Obshchestvennaia khronika." *Vestnik Evropy* 10 (1903): 870–875.

———. "Piatidesiatiletie 'Vestnika Evropy'." *Vestnik Evropy* 2 (1915): 105–119.

———. "Politicheskii protsess 1869–1871 gg." *Vestnik Evropy* 11 (1871): 290–315.

———. "Russkie zakony o pechati." *Vestnik Evropy* 4 (1869): 805–817.

———. "Vnutrennee obozrenie." *Vestnik Evropy* 3 (1880): 392–403.

———. "Vnutrennee obozrenie." *Vestnik Evropy* 2 (1881): 794–816.

———. "Vnutrennee obozrenie." *Vestnik Evropy* 3 (1881): 348–360.

———. "Vnutrennee obozrenie." *Vestnik Evropy* 4 (1881): 772–781.

———. "Vnutrennee obozrenie." *Vestnik Evropy* 7 (1881): 360–370.

———. "Vnutrennee obozrenie." *Vestnik Evropy* 8 (1881): 819–827.

———. "Vnutrennee obozrenie." *Vestnik Evropy* 11 (1881): 364–373.

———. "Vnutrennee obozrenie." *Vestnik Evropy* 1 (1882): 336–345.

———. "Vnutrennee obozrenie." *Vestnik Evropy* 3 (1882): 349–359.

———. "Vnutrennee obozrenie." *Vestnik Evropy* 4 (1882): 800–811.

———. "Vnutrennee obozrenie." *Vestnik Evropy* 5 (1882): 345–356.

———. "Vnutrennee obozrenie," *Vestnik Evropy* 8 (1882): 715–726.

———. "Vnutrennee obozrenie." *Vestnik Evropy* 9 (1882): 326–337.

———. "Vnutrennee obozrenie." *Vestnik Evropy* 11 (1882): 355–365.

———. "Vnutrennee obozrenie." *Vestnik Evropy* 1 (1891): 369–380.

———. "Vnutrennee obozrenie." *Vestnik Evropy* 8 (1891): 860–871.

———. "Vnutrennee obozrenie." *Vestnik Evropy* 9 (1891): 419–430.

———. "Vnutrennee obozrenie." *Vestnik Evropy* 10 (1891): 800–811.

———. "Vnutrennee obozrenie." *Vestnik Evropy* 11 (1891): 351–362.

———. "Vnutrennee obozrenie." *Vestnik Evropy* 12 (1891): 870–880.

———. "Vnutrennee obozrenie." *Vestnik Evropy* 1 (1892): 380–391.

———. "Vnutrennee obozrenie." *Vestnik Evropy* 2 (1892): 850–860.

———. "Vnutrennee obozrenie." *Vestnik Evropy* 3 (1892): 390–401.

———. "Vnutrennee obozrenie." *Vestnik Evropy* 4 (1892): 370–380.

———. "Vnutrennee obozrenie." *Vestnik Evropy* 6 (1892): 820–829.

———. "Vnutrennee obozrenie." *Vestnik Evropy* 7 (1892): 400–410.

———. "Vnutrennee obozrenie." *Vestnik Evropy* 5 (1893): 440–451.

———. "Vnutrennee obozrenie," *Vestnik Evropy* 2 (1899): 800–810.

———. "Vnutrennee obozrenie." *Vestnik Evropy* 10 (1903): 770–780.

———. "Vospominaniia K. K. Arsen'eva ob uchilishche pravovedeniia, 1849–1855 gg." *Russkaia starina* 50, no. 4 (1886): 190–215.

———. *Vospominaniia (1910–1913).* IRLI, f. 359, op. 1, d. 3, l. 1–234.

———. "Vvedenie." In *Melkaia zemskaia edinitsa.* St. Petersburg: Obshchestvennaia pol'za, 1902.

———. "Vzgliad na proshloe '*Vestnika Evropy*' (1866–1908)." *Vestnik Evropy* 1 (1908): 223–238.

Barskov, Ia. L., ed. *Spisok trudov akademika A. N. Pypina, 1853–1903.* St. Petersburg: Izdanie Otdeleniia russkogo iazyka i slovesnosti Imperatorskoi Akademii Nauk, 1903.

Barsov, N. I. "Vospominanie ob I. A. Goncharove." In *I. A. Goncharov v vospominaniiakh sovremennikov,* edited by V. V. Grigorenko et al. Leningrad: Khudozhestvennaia literatura, 1969.

Bartenev, V. V. "Vospominaniia peterburzhtsa o vtoroi polovine 1880-x godov." In *Ot narodnichestva—k marksizmu: Vospominaniia uchastnikov revoliutsionnogo dvizheniia v Peterburge (1883–1894 gg.),* edited by S. S. Volk, 185–112. Leningrad: Lenizdat, 1987.

Berdiaev, N. A. *Sub"ektivizm i individualizm v obshchestvennoi filosofii: Kriticheskii etiud o N. K. Mikhailovskom; S predisloviem Petra Struve.* St. Petersburg: Izd-vo O. N. Popovoi, 1901.

Blumberg, Konstantin. *Piatidesiatiletie S.-Peterburgskoi Larinskoi Gimnazii, 1836–1886.* St. Petersburg: Tip. M. M. Stasiulevicha, 1886.

Boborykin, P. D. *Vospominaniia.* Moscow: Izd-vo khudozhestvennoi literatury, 1965.

Bortkevich, I. *O denezhnoi reforme, proektirovannoi Ministerstvom finansov.* St. Petersburg: Tip. E. Arngol'da, 1896.

Bunge, N. Kh. *Ocherki politiko-ekonomicheskoi literatury.* St. Petersburg: Tip. V. Kirshbauma, 1895.

———. "Zagrobnye zametki: Sotsializm ne ugas i prinimaet groznuiu formu. (Zapiska, naidennaia v bumagakh N. Kh. Bunge)." *Istochnik* 10 (1993): 36–43.

Chekhov, A. P. *Polnoe sobranie sochinenii i pisem.* 25 vols. Moscow: Izd-vo khudozhestvennoi literatury, 1949.

Chernyshevskii, N. G. *Polnoe sobranie sochinenii.* 15 vols. Moscow: Goslitizdat, 1939–1953.

Chernyshevskaia, N. M., ed. *Delo Chernyshevskogo: Sbornik dokumentov.* Saratov: Privol'zhskoe knizhnoe izd-vo, 1968.

Chevazhevskii, V. S. "Iz proshlogo Kievskogo universiteta i studencheskoi zhizni." *Russkaia starina* 150, no. 6 (1912): 574–590.

Chicherin, B. N. "Nemetskie sotsialisty. II. Karl Marks." *Sbornik gosudarstvennykh znanii* 6 (1878): 2–12.

———. *Vospominaniia Borisa Nikolaevicha Chicherina: Moskovskii universitet.* Moscow: Izd. M. i S. Sabashnikovykh, 1929.

Chuprov, A. I. *O sovremennom znachenii i zadachakh politicheskoi ekonomii.* Moscow: Tip. Rus. ved., 1874.

———. "Znanie i narodnoe bogatstvo." In *Ekonomicheskaia otsenka narodnogo obrazovaniia: Ocherki.* St. Petersburg, 1899.

Debogorii-Mokrievich, V. K. *Vospominaniia.* Stuttgart: J. H. W. Dietz, 1903.

Dillon, E. J. *Russian Traits and Terrors: A Faithful Picture of the Russia of To-day.* Boston: B. R. Tucker, 1891.

Dragomanov, M. P. "Vostochnaia politika Germanii i obrusenie." *Vestnik Evropy* 2 (1872): 640–653.

Drutskoi-Sokolninskii, D. "Nashe sel'skoe khoziaistvo i ego budushchnost'." *Vestnik Evropy* 10 (1891): 698–719.

Feoktistov, E. M. *Vospominaniia: Za kulisami politiki i literatury, 1848–1896.* Leningrad: Priboi, 1929.

Glinskii, B. B. "Period tverdoi vlasti." *Istoricheskii vestnik* 8 (1912): 681–695.

Golovnin, A. V. "Perepiska so Stasiulevichem." *Vestnik Evropy* 1 (1877): 130–141.

Gor'kii, M. *Sobranie sochinenii.* 30 vols. Moscow: Izd-vo Khudozhestvennoi literatury, 1949–1956.

Gur'ev, A. N. *Denezhnoe obrashchenie v Rossii v XIX stoletii: Istoricheskii ocherk.* St. Petersburg: Kirshbaum, 1903.

———. *Reforma denezhnogo obrashcheniia.* St. Petersburg: Tip. V. Kirshbauma, 1896.

Hobson, J. A. *Imperialism: A Study.* New York: Gordon Press, 2006.

Iadrintsev, N. M. "Nashi vyseleniia i kolonizatsiia." *Vestnik Evropy* 6 (1880): 464–490.

———. "Polozhenie pereselentsev v Sibiri." *Vestnik Evropy* 8 (1881): 601–630.

Ianzhul, I. I. *Otchet o prakticheskikh zaniatiiakh na iuridicheskikh fakul'tetakh vos'mi russkikh universitetov.* St. Petersburg: V. Bezobrazov i Ko., 1903.

———. "Znachenie obrazovaniia dlia uspekhov promyshlennosti i torgovli." In *Ekonomicheskaia otsenka narodnogo obrazovaniia: Ocherki,* 1–16. St. Petersburg, 1899.

"Iz pisem K. D. Kavelina k gr. D. A. Miliutinu, 1882–1884 gg." *Vestnik Evropy* 1 (1909): 5–27.

Kairova, A. V. "Pis'ma iz Germanii." *Vestnik Evropy* 10 (1881): 858–867.

Karnovich, E. P. *Ocherki nashikh poriadkov administrativnykh, sudebnykh i obshchestvennykh.* St. Petersburg: Skariatin, 1873.

Katkov, M. N. "Usilenie pol'skoi intrigi v nekotorykh peterburgskikh sferakh i gazetakh." *Moskovskie vedomosti,* no. 46, March 2, 1868.

Kavelin, K. D. "Putevye pis'ma." *Vestnik Evropy* 10 (1882): 685–703.

Kazakova, N. A., ed. *Vekhi: Intelligentsiia v Rossii; Sborniki statei, 1909–1910.* Moscow: Molodaia gvardiia, 1991.

Keynes, John Maynard. *The Economic Consequences of the Peace*. London: Macmillan, 1919.

"K kakoi prinadlezhim my partii?" *Russkii vestnik* 37 (1862): 820–851.

Koni, A. F. *Graf Loris-Melikov: Na zhiznennom puti*. 3 vols. Berlin, n.d.

———. "Ivan Aleksandrovich Goncharov." In *I. A. Goncharov v vospominaniiakh sovremennikov*, ed. V. V. Grigorenko et al. Leningrad: Khudozhestvennaia literatura, 1969.

———. *Sobranie sochinenii*. 7 vols. Moscow: Iurid. lit-ra, 1966–1969.

———. "Spornyi vopros nashego trudoustroistva." *Vestnik Evropy* 1 (1881): 217–225.

———. "Vestnik Evropy (Fevral 1911 g.)." In *Sobranie sochinenii*, 4:225–246.

Kostomarov, N. I. *Avtobiografiia N. I. Kostomarova*. Moscow: Zadruga, 1922.

———. *Istoricheskie proizvedeniia: Avtobiografiia*. Kiev: Tip. Kievskogo gos. universiteta, 1989.

Kotliarevskii, N. A. *Kholmy rodiny*. Berlin: Obelisk, 1923.

K. P. Pobedonostsev i ego korrespondenty: Pis'ma i zapiski. 2 vols. Prague, 1923.

Kuzmin-Karavaev, D. "Vsesoslovnaia volost'." In *Novyi Entsiklopedicheskii Slovar'*, edited by K. K. Arsen'ev, vol. 11, 157–159. St. Petersburg: Tip. Aktsionernogo ob-va Brokgauz-Efron, 1911–1916.

Lavrov, P. L. *Lavrov—gody emigratsii: Arkhivnye materialy v dvukh tomakh*. Dordrecht: Reidel, 1974.

Lemke, M. K. *Politicheskie protsessy v Rossii 1860-kh gg. (po arkhivnym dokumentam)*. 2nd ed. Moscow: Petrograd gos. izdat., 1923.

———, ed. *M. M. Stasiulevich i ego sovremenniki v ikh perepiskie*. St. Petersburg: Tipografiia M. M. Stasiulevicha, 1911–1913.

Lenin, V. I. *The Development of Capitalism in Russia*. Moscow: Progress Publishers, 1967.

———. *Polnoe sobranie sochinenii*. 5th edition. 55 vols. Moscow: Gos. izd-vo polit. lit-ry, 1958–1965.

Literatura partii "Narodnoi voli." Moscow: K-vo Bor'ba i pravo, 1907.

Literaturnoe nasledstvo. Moscow: Zhurnal'no-gazetnoe ob"edinenie, 1931–.

Lopatinskii, L. G. "Pis'mo." *Vestnik Evropy* 3 (1873): 933–938.

Lukianov, L. "Nado zhit: Rasskaz." *Vestnik Evropy* 12 (1878): 755–800.

Martynov, S. D. *Gosudarstvo i ekonomika: Sistema Vitte*. St. Petersburg: Nauka, 2002.

Marx, Karl, and Friedrich Engels. *Sochineniia*. 2nd ed. 59 vols. Moscow: Izd. Politicheskoi literatury, 1968–1979.

Materialy k proektu polozheniia o gosudarstvennom podokhodnom nalogie: Opyt priblizitel'nogo ischisleniia narodnogo dokhoda po razlichnym ego istochnikam i po razmeram v Rossii. St. Petersburg: Tip. P. P. Soikina, 1906.

Mavrodin, V. V., ed. *Leningradskii universitet v vospominaniiakh sovremennikov*. Vol. 1. Leningrad: Izd. Leningradskogo universiteta, 1963.

Migrin, F. "Sel'skii byt i sel'skoe khoziaistvo v Rossii." *Vestnik Evropy* 6 (1881): 877–899.

Migulin, P. P. *Reforma denezhnogo obrashcheniia i promyshlennyi krizis v Rossii (1893–1902)*. Moscow: Obshchestvo kuptsov i promyshlennikov Rossii, 2006.

Mikhailovskii, N. K. "Literaturnye zametki." *Otechestvennye zapiski* 9 (1879): 105–123.

———. *Polnoe sobranie sochinenii*. 12 vols. 7th ed. St. Petersburg, 1909.

———. "Po povodu russkogo izdaniia knigi Karla Marksa." In *Narodnicheskaia ekonomicheskaia literatura: Izbrannye proizvedeniia*, edited by N. K. Karataev, 165–169. Moscow: Izd-vo sotsial'no-ekon. lit-ry, 1958.

Ministr i gosudarstvennyi sovet o finansovom polozhenii Rossii: Zhurnal obshchego sobraniia gosudarstvennogo soveta 30 dekabria 1902 g. Stuttgart: J. W. Deitz, 1903.

Morozov, N. A. *Povesti moei zhizni: Memuary*. 2 vols. Moscow: Nauka, 1965.

Muromtsev, S. A. *Sbornik statei*. Moscow: Izd. M. i S. Sabashnikovykh, 1911.

Na slavnom postu (1860–1900): Literaturnyi sbornik, posviashchennyi N. K. Mikhailovskomu. St. Petersburg: Tip. N. N. Klobukova, 1901.

Nekrasov, N. A. *Perepiska N. A. Nekrasova*. 2 vols. Moscow: Khudozh. lit-ra, 1987.

———. *Polnoe sobranie sochinenii i pisem*. 15 vols. Leningrad: Nauka, 1981–2000.

Nikitenko, A. V. *Dnevnik*. Leningrad: Gos. izd-vo khudozh. lit-ry, 1955.

Nikoladze, N. G. "Osvobozhdenie N. G. Chernyshevskogo." In *N.G. Chernyshevskii v vospominaniiakh sovremennikov*, 67–98. Saratov: Saratovskoe knizhnoe izd-vo.

Nikolai-on (Danielson), "Ocherki nashego po-reformennogo obshchestvennogo khoziaistva." *Slovo* 10 (1880): 77–142.

"Ob izdanii v 1868 g. zhurnala 'Sovremennoe obozrenie'." *Sovremennoe obozrenie* 2 (1868): 16–23.

Obruchev, V. "Iz perezhitogo." *Vestnik Evropy* 5 (1907): 120–145.

Ostrogorskii, V. P. *Iz istorii moego uchitel'stva: Kak ia sdelalsia uchitelem*. St. Petersburg: Tip. Popova, 1895.

Panaeva, A. Ia. *Vospominaniia*. Moscow: Zakharov, 2002.

Panteleev, L. F. *Vospominaniia*. Moscow: Gos. izd-vo khudozh. lit-ry, 1958.

Pekarskii, P. P., ed. *Istoricheskie bumagi, sobrannye Konstantinom Ivanovichem Arsen'evym*. St. Petersburg: Tip. Imperatorskoi Akademii Nauk, 1872.

Perepiska N. A. Nekrasova. 2 vols. Moscow: Khudozh. lit-ra, 1987.

Petrovskii, M. P. "Retrogradnaia pechat' i golos provintsii." *Vestnik Evropy* 7 (1881): 324–351.

Piatidesiatiletie nauchno-literaturnoi deiatel'nosti akademika A. N. Pypina. St. Petersburg: A. E. Vineke, 1903.

Pisarev, D. I. *Sochineniia*. 4 vols. Moscow: Gos. izd-vo khudozh. lit-ry, 1955–1956.

Plekhanov, G. V. *Sochineniia*. 23 vols. Petrograd-Leningrad, 1920–1927.

Pletnev, P. A. "Istoricheskaia zapiska o pervom dvadtsatipiatiletii universiteta, chitannaia 8 fevralia, 1844 goda." In *Otchety o sostoianii Imperatorskogo Sanktpeterburgskogo Universiteta, sostavlennye rektorom ego Petrom Pletnevym*. St. Petersburg: Tipografiia voenno-uchebnykh zavedenii, 1845.

Polonskii, L. A. "Vnutrennee obozrenie." *Vestnik Evropy* 8 (1878): 740–751.

———. "Vnutrennee obozrenie." *Vestnik Evropy* 9 (1878): 359–372.

———. "Vnutrennee obozrenie." *Vestnik Evropy* 12 (1878): 782–794.

———. "Vnutrennee obozrenie." *Vestnik Evropy* 11 (1879): 316–331.

———. "Vnutrennee obozrenie: Vyrezannoe tsenzuroi iz I knigi V. E. 1879." In *M. M Stasiulevich i ego sovremenniki v ikh perepiskie*, 1:464–482. St. Petersburg: Tipografiia M. M. Stasiulevicha, 1911–1913.

Pruzhanskii, N. O. "Moe znakomstvo s M. M. Stasiulevichem." *Istoricheskii Vestnik* 4 (1911): 193–212.

Pypin, A. N. "Belletrist-narodnik shestidesiatykh godov." *Vestnik Evropy* 8 (1884): 648–670.

———. "Borozdin A. K. Sto let literaturnogo razvitiia. Kharakteristika russkoi literatury XIX stoletiia. Spb., 1900." *Vestnik Evropy* 10 (1900): 831–840.

———. "Eshche o teoriiakh narodnichestva." *Vestnik Evropy* 2 (1893): 760–774.

———. "Idealisty i realisty." *Vestnik Evropy* 10 (1871): 940–951.

———. *Istoriia russkoi literatury*. 4 vols. St. Petersburg: Tip. M. M. Stasiulevicha, 1907.

———. *Istoriia russkoi etnografii*. 4 vols. St. Petersburg: Tip. M. M. Stasiulevicha, 1890–1892.

———. "Izuchenie russkoi narodnosti." *Vestnik Evropy* 9 (1881): 283–300.

———. *Moi zametki*. Moscow: L. E. Bukhgeim, 1910.

———. *Moi zametki*. Saratov: Sootechestvennik, 1996.

———. "Narodnaia gramotnost'." *Vestnik Evropy* 1 (1891): 245–260.

———. "Narodnichestvo (Statia vtoraia)." *Vestnik Evropy* 2 (1882): 720–731.

———. "Narodniki i narod: Sobranie sochinenii N. Zlatovratskogo." *Vestnik Evropy* 2 (1891): 655–668.

———. "Narodnost' i narodnichestvo." *Vestnik Evropy* 2 (1888): 375–390.

———. "Nekrolog, V. I. Grigorovich." *Vestnik Evropy* 2 (1877): 892–893.

———. "Novye razyskaniia v narodno-poeticheskoi starine." *Vestnik Evropy* 12 (1886): 778–797.

———. "Otkrytie Radishchevskogo muzeia, osnovannogo A. P. Bogoliubovym v Saratove." *Vestnik Evropy* 8 (1885): 836–849.

———. "Pol'skii vopros v russkoi literature." *Vestnik Evropy* 2 (1880): 703–729.

———. "Po povodu 'Otkrytogo pis'ma' g. Zlatovratskogo." *Vestnik Evropy* 4 (1884): 866–875.

———. "Prugavin A. S. Zaprosy naroda i obiazannosti intelligentsii v oblasti prosveshcheniia i vospitaniia. 2-e izd. SPb., 1895." *Vestnik Evropy* 3 (1895): 385–393.

———. "Teorii narodnichestva." *Vestnik Evropy* 10 (1892): 704–720.

P. U. *Obshchestvennoe vospitanie i obrazovanie v Rossii: Zapiski ob uchilishche pravovedeniia*. St. Petersburg: V. Demakov, 1869.

Radtsig, A. A. *Finansovaia politika Rossii s 1887 goda: Sbornik statei po finansovym i ekonomicheskim voprosam*. St. Petersburg: Narodnaia pol'za, 1903.

Rittikh, A. A. *Zavisimost' krest'ian ot obshchiny i mira*. St. Petersburg: Tip. V. F. Kirshbauma, 1903.

Romanov, P. M. "Nasha zolotopromyshlennost' i ee usloviia." *Vestnik Evropy* 3 (1880): 354–371.

Russkie knigi v bibliotekakh K. Marksa i F. Engel'sa. Moscow: Politizdat, 1979.

Saltykov-Shchedrin, M. E. "Samodovol'naia sovremennost'." *Otechestvennye zapiski* 10 (1871): 58–73.

———. *Polnoe sobranie sochinenii.* 20 vols. Moscow: Izd. khudozhestvennaia literatura, 1933–1941.

Samarin, D. F. "Teoriia o nedostatochnosti krest'ianskikh nadelov, po ucheniiu professora Iu. E. Iansona." *Rus*, no. 3, October 15, 1880, 2.

Sharapov, S. F. "Eshche neskol'ko slov ob 'opyte' g. Iansona." *Rus*, no. 7, December 27, 1880, 4.

Shreier, Iu. R., ed. *Piatidesiatiletnii iubilei Ego Imperatorskogo Vysochestva printsa Petra Georgievicha Ol'denburgskogo.* St. Petersburg: Zibert i Foss, 1881.

Skabichevskii, A. M. *Literaturnye vospominaniia.* Moscow: Agraf, 2001.

Sliozberg, G. B. *Dela minuvshikh dnei: Zapiski russkogo evreia.* 3 vols. Paris: Imprimerie Pascal, 1933.

Slonimskii, L. Z. "Denezhnaia reforma." *Vestnik Evropy* 5 (1896): 338–350.

———. "Ekonomicheskiia nedorazumeniia." *Vestnik Evropy* 6 (1894): 772–789.

———. "Ekonomicheskiia reformy i zakonodatel'stvo." *Vestnik Evropy* 8 (1893): 735–756.

———. "Ekonomicheskaia teoriia Marksa." *Vestnik Evropy* 4 (1896): 809–836.

———. "Ekonomicheskie idealy." *Vestnik Evropy* 9 (1888): 318–333.

———. "Ekonomicheskie zametki." *Vestnik Evropy* 4 (1898): 750–765.

———. "Ekonomicheskie zametki." *Vestnik Evropy* 7 (1897): 318–333.

———. "Genri Dzhordzh i ego teoriia progressa." *Vestnik Evropy* 7 (1889): 333–351.

———. "Gosudarstvennyi sotsializm v politike i literature." *Vestnik Evropy* 7 (1884): 287–315.

———. "Kapitalizm v doktrine Marksa." *Vestnik Evropy* 7 (1896): 357–372.

———. "Karl Marks v russkoi literature." *Vestnik Evropy* 9 (1897): 288–307.

———. "Marks i ego shkola." *Vestnik Evropy* 3 (1896): 289–308.

———. "M. M. Stasiulevich kak redaktor." *Vestnik Evropy* 3 (1911): 405–415.

———. "Mnimaia sotsiologiia." *Vestnik Evropy* 5 (1889): 130–147.

———. "Nashi ekonomicheskie zadachi i krest'ianskii vopros." *Vestnik Evropy* 1 (1904): 237–253.

———. "Nashi napravleniia." *Vestnik Evropy* 12 (1901): 808–835.

———. "Nash torgovyi balans." *Vestnik Evropy* 2 (1892): 792–815.

———. "Nauchnye illiuzii." *Vestnik Evropy* 2 (1903): 750–770.

———. "Natsionalizm v politike." *Vestnik Evropy* 11 (1889): 281–300.

———. "Noveishie idealisty." *Vestnik Evropy* 9 (1903): 313–325.

———. "Noveishie protivniki obshchiny." *Vestnik Evropy* 2 (1904): 756–772.

———. "Novye materialy dlia starogo spora." *Vestnik Evropy* 8 (1892): 754–790.

———. "O teoriiakh progressa." *Vestnik Evropy* 3 (1889): 265–297.

———. "Poniatiia o gosudarstve." *Vestnik Evropy* 4 (1890): 725–750.

———. "Pozemel'naia sobstvennost' v teoriiakh ekonomistov i sotsiologov." *Vestnik Evropy* 1 (1883): 200–249.

———. "Pozemel'nyi vopros v Evrope i Rossii." *Vestnik Evropy* 3 (1885): 172–211.

———. "Pozemel'nyi vopros v Evrope i Rossii." *Vestnik Evropy* 4 (1885): 744–777.

———. "Progress v politike." *Vestnik Evropy* 9 (1889): 235–253.

———. "Promyshlennaia ideologiia." *Vestnik Evropy* 6 (1898): 768–783.

———. "Sovremennyia nedoumeniia." *Vestnik Evropy* 5 (1900): 238–249.

———. "Voprosy pozemel'noi politiki." *Vestnik Evropy* 9 (1890): 321–339.

———. "Zabytye ekonomisty Tiunen i Kurno." *Vestnik Evropy* 9 (1878): 5–27.

———. "Zametka: Nekul'turnost' i kapitalizm." *Vestnik Evropy* 12 (1894): 875–882.

Slonimskii, M. L. *Kniga vospominanii*. Moscow: Sovetskii pisatel', 1966.

Slonimsky, Nicolas. *Perfect Pitch: A Life Story*. Oxford: Oxford University Press, 1988.

Solov'ev, S. M. *Vospominaniia*. Moscow: Novoe literaturnoe obozrenie, 2003.

Solov'ev, V. S. *Pis'ma*. Prague, 1923.

———. "Rossiia i Evropa." *Vestnik Evropy* 2 (1888): 340–357 and 4 (1888): 568–588.

———. *Stikhotvoreniia i shutochnye p'esy*. Munich: W. Fink, 1968.

Solzhenitsyn, Alexander. *The Solzhenitsyn Reader: New and Essential Writings, 1947–2005*, edited by Edward E. Ericson and Daniel J. Mahoney. Wilmington, DE: ISI Books, 2006.

Spasovich, V. D. "Piatidesiatiletie Peterburgskogo universiteta." *Vestnik Evropy* 4 (1870): 765–779.

———. "Piatidesiatiletie Peterburgskogo universiteta." *Vestnik Evropy* 5 (1870): 312–331.

———. "Pol'skie fantazii na slavianofilskuiu temu." *Vestnik Evropy* 8 (1872): 738–757.

———. "Vospominaniia o K. D. Kaveline." In *Polnoe sobranie sochinenii*, edited by K. D. Kavelin, 1:i–xx. St. Petersburg: Tip. M. M. Stasiulevicha, 1897.

Stasiulevich, M. M. *Afinskaia igemoniia*. St. Petersburg: Tipografiia Imperatorskoi Akademii Nauk, 1849.

———. *Chernyi peredel reform imperatora Aleksandra II: Pis'ma iz Moskvy za granitsu par bonté*. Berlin: B. Behr, 1882.

———. *Likurg Afinskii*. St. Petersburg: Tipografiia Imperatorskoi Akademii Nauk, 1851.

———. "Nekrolog, Nikolai Khristianovich Bunge." *Vestnik Evropy* 8 (1895): 422–426.

———. "Zametka o russkoi pochte." *Vestnik Evropy* 7 (1871): 404–412.

Stasiulevich, M. M., and K. K. Arsen'ev. "Zapiska chetyrnadtsati redaktsii i otvet na nee dvukh chlenov osobogo soveshchaniia po pechati." *Vestnik Evropy* 3 (1905): 97–115.

Struve, P. B. *Kriticheskie zametki k voprosu ob ekonomicheskom razvitii Rossii*. St. Petersburg: Tip. I. N. Skorokhodova, 1894.

Sviatlovskii, V. V. *Ocherki po istorii ekonomicheskikh vozzrenii.* St. Petersburg, 1913.

Taburno, I. P. *Eskiznyi obzor finansovo-ekonomicheskogo sostoianiia Rossii za poslednie 20 let (1882–1901 gg.).* St. Petersburg: Tip. E. Novitskogo, 1904.

Terner, F. G. *Vospominaniia zhizni F. G. Ternera.* St. Petersburg: Izd. M. G. i E. G. Terner, 1911.

Timiriazev, D. A. *Obzor razvitiia glavneishikh otraslei promyshlennosti i torgovli v Rossii za poslednee dvadtsatiletie.* St. Petersburg: A. Il'in, 1876.

Tiutchev, I. A. "V uchilishche pravovedeniia v 1847–1852 gg." *Russkaia starina* 48, no. 11 (1885): 425–447; 48, no. 12 (1885): 668–682; 49, no. 2 (1885): 345–380.

Tolmachev, M. S. *Krest'ianskii vopros po vzgliadam zemstva i mestnykh liudei.* Moscow: Tipo-lit T-va I. N. Kushnerev, 1903.

Tugan-Baranovskii, M. I. *Ocherki iz noveishei istorii politicheskoi ekonomii.* St. Petersburg: Izd. zhurnala Mir Bozhii, 1903.

——. "Osnovnaia oshibka abstraktnoi teorii kapitalizma Marksa." *Nauchnoe obozrenie* 5 (1899): 965–981.

——. *Russkaia fabrika v proshlom i nastoiashchem: Istoriko-ekonomicheskoe issledovanie.* St. Petersburg: Izd. L. F. Pantel'eva, 1898.

——. *Zemel'naia reforma: Ocherk dvizheniia v pol'zu zemel'noi reformy i prakticheskie vyvody.* St. Petersburg: Tip. I. N. Skorokhodova, 1905.

Turgenev, I. S. "Otchet po izdaniiu pervykh piati tomov 'Russkoi biblioteki'." In *Aleksandr Sergeevich Griboedov,* i–vi. St. Petersburg: Tip. M. M. Stasiulevicha, 1875.

——. *Polnoe sobranie sochinenii i pisem.* 28 vols. Moscow-Leningrad: Nauka, 1965.

Utin, Evgenii. "Literaturnye spory nashego vremeni." *Vestnik Evropy* 11 (1869): 347–367.

Valuev, P. A. *Dnevnik, 1877–1884.* Prague, 1919.

Vasilchikov, A. I. "Po povodu kritik i retsenzii na knigu 'Zemlevladenie i Zemledelie'." *Vestnik Evropy* 2 (1878): 802–815.

Vengerova, Polina. *Vospominaniia babushki: Ocherki kul'turnoi istorii evreev Rossii v XIX veke.* Moscow: Mosty kul'tury, 2003.

Veselovskii, B. B. *Istoriia zemstva za sorok let.* Cambridge, England: Oriental Research Partners, 1973.

Vengerov, S. A., ed. *Iubileinyi sbornik literaturnogo fonda, 1859–1909.* St. Petersburg: Tip. t-va Obshchestvennaia pol'za, 1909.

Vladimirovskii-Budanov, M. F. *Istoriia Imperatorskogo Universiteta Sv. Vladimira.* Kiev: Tipografiia universiteta Sv. Vladimira, 1884.

——. *Piatidesiatiletie Imperatorskogo Universiteta Sv. Vladimira, 1834–1884, rech proiznesennaia na iubileinom akte universiteta.* Kiev: Tipografiia universiteta Sv. Vladimira, 1884.

Vorontsov, V. P. "Kritik narodnichestva." *Russkoe bogatstvo* 4 (1893): 1–30.

——. "Popytki obosnovaniia narodnichestva." *Russkoe bogatstvo* 10 (1892): 1–23.

——. *Sud'by kapitalizma v Rossii.* St. Petersburg: Tip. M. M. Stasiulevicha, 1882.

Voroponov, F. F. "Melkii zemel'nyi kredit i krest'ianskie pereseleniia." *Vestnik Evropy* 10 (1880): 725–739.

———. "Nashi pozemel'nye nalogi." *Vestnik Evropy* 5 (1878): 325–335.

———. "Po povodu vliianiia zemel'nogo nadela na blagosostoianie." *Vestnik Evropy* 11 (1880): 386–400.

———. "Teoriia dostatochnosti krest'ianskikh nadelov." *Vestnik Evropy* 2 (1881): 773–797.

Voskresenskii, A. E. *Obshchinnoe zemlevladenie i krest'ianskoe malozemel'e.* St. Petersburg: Tip. i lit. V. A. Tikhonova, 1903.

"Vsepoddaneishii doklad ministra finansov o gosudarstvennoi rospisi dokhodov i raskhodov na 1898 g." *Vestnik finansov promyshlennosti i torgovli* 1 (1899): 5–10.

Vvedenskii, A. V. "Literaturnye mechtaniia i deistvitel'nost'." *Vestnik Evropy* 9 (1882): 160–195.

Wengeroff, Pauline. *Rememberings: The World of a Russian-Jewish Woman in the Nineteenth Century.* Potomac: University Press of Maryland, 2000.

Witte, S. Iu. *Vospominaniia.* 3 vols. Moscow: Izd-vo sotsial'no-ekon. lit-ry, 1960.

———. *Zapiska po krest'ianskomu delu.* St. Petersburg: Kirshbaum, 1904.

Zemlia i Volia, no. 1, October 25, 1878. In *Revoliutsionnaia zhurnalistika semidesiatykh godov,* edited by B. Bazilevskii, 158–165. Paris: Société nouvelle de librairie et d'edition, 1905.

Zemlia i Volia, no. 1, October 1, 1879. In *Revoliutsionnaia zhurnalistika,* 5–13.

Zemlia i Volia, no. 3, January 15, 1879. In *Revoliutsionnaia zhurnalistika,* 270–276.

Zemlia i Volia, no. 5, February 8, 1879. In *Revoliutsionnaia zhurnalistika,* 237–242.

Zhukovskii, Iu. G. "Karl Marks i ego kniga o kapitale." *Vestnik Evropy* 5 (1877): 64–79.

———. "Priamye nalogi v Rossii." *Vestnik Evropy* 2 (1881): 503–525.

Secondary Works

Aksenova, E. P. *A. N. Pypin o slavianstve.* Moscow: Indrik, 2006.

Alafaev, A. A. "Agrarnyi vopros v zhurnale 'Vestnik Evropy,' 1878–1882 gg." In *Vtoraia revoliutsionnaia situatsiia v Rossii: Otkliki na stranitsakh pressy; Sbornik statei,* edited by N. M. Pirumova and V. A. Tvardovskaia, 35–58. Moscow: Akademiia nauk SSSR, 1981.

———. *Russkii liberalizm na rubezhe 70–80-kh gg. XIX v.: Iz istorii zhurnala "Vestnik Evropy."* Moscow: Institut istorii SSSR, 1991.

Alston, Patrick L. *Education and the State in Tsarist Russia.* Stanford: Stanford University Press, 1969.

Ambler, Effie. *Russian Journalism and Politics, 1861–1881: The Career of Aleksei S. Suvorin.* Detroit: Wayne State University Press, 1972.

Ananich, B. V. *Rossiia i mezhdunarodnyi kapital, 1897–1914: Ocherki istorii finansovykh otnoshenii.* Leningrad: Nauka, 1970.

Ananich, B. V., and R. Sh. Ganelin. *Vlast' i reformy: Ot samoderzhavnoi k sovetskoi Rossii*. Moscow: DB, 1996.

Anderson, Thornton. *Russian Political Thought: An Introduction*. Ithaca: Cornell University Press, 1967.

Arndt, Walter. *Pushkin Threefold: Narrative, Lyric, Polemic, and Ribald Verse*. New York: Dutton, 1972.

Atkinson, Dorothy. "The Zemstvo and the Peasantry." In *The Zemstvo in Russia: An Experiment in Local Self-Government*, edited by Terence Emmons and Wayne S. Vucinich, 79–133. Cambridge: Cambridge University Press, 1982.

Avrekh, A. Ia. *Tsarizm i IV Duma, 1912–1914 gg*. Moscow: Izdatel'stvo Nauka, 1981.

Bakhrakh, Aleksandr. "Bunin v khalate." In *Bunin v khalate i drugie portrety: Po pamiati, po zapisiam*, 17–73. Moscow: Vagrius, 2005.

Balmuth, Daniel. "Liberals and Radicals in the Era of Reforms." *Canadian Slavic Studies* 3 (1969): 460–479.

———. *The Russian Bulletin, 1863–1917: A Liberal Voice in Tsarist Russia*. New York: Peter Lang, 2000.

Baluev, B. P. *Politicheskaia reaktsiia 80-kh godov XIX veka i russkaia zhurnalistika*. Moscow: MGU, 1971.

———. *Liberal'noe narodnichestvo na rubezhe XIX–XX vekov*. Moscow: Nauka, 1995.

Balykin, D. A. *A. N. Pypin kak issledovatel' techenii russkoi obshchestvennoi mysli*. Briansk: Grani, 1996.

Balzer, Harley D., ed. *Russia's Missing Middle Class: The Professions in Russian History*. Armonk, NY: M. E. Sharpe, 1996.

Bartenev, V. V. "Vospominaniia peterburzhtsa o vtoroi polovine 1880-x godov." In *Ot narodnichestva—k marksizmu: Vospominaniia uchastnikov revoliutsionnogo dvizheniia v Peterburge (1883–1894 gg.)*, edited by S. S. Volk, 190–215. Leningrad: Lenizdat, 1987.

Becker, Colette. *Les apprentissages de Zola: Du poète romantique au romancier naturaliste, 1840–1867*. Paris: Presses universitaires de France, 1993.

Belknap, Robert L. "Survey of Russian Journals, 1840–1880." In *Literary Journals in Imperial Russia*, edited by Deborah A. Martinsen, 91–116. Cambridge: Cambridge University Press, 1997.

Billington, James. *Mikhailovsky and Russian Populism*. Oxford: Clarendon Press, 1958.

Binyon, T. J. *Pushkin: A Biography*. New York: Knopf, 2003.

Blackbourn, David, and Geoff Eley. *The Peculiarities of German History: Bourgeois Society and Politics in Nineteenth-Century Germany*. New York: Oxford University Press, 1984.

Blaug, Mark. *Economic Theory in Retrospect*. Cambridge: Cambridge University Press, 1997.

Bradley, Joseph. *Voluntary Associations in Tsarist Russia: Science, Patriotism, and Civil Society*. Cambridge: Harvard University Press, 2009.

Branover, G. G., ed. *Rossiiskaia evreiskaia entsiklopediia*. Moscow: Rossiiskaia akademiia estestvennykh nauk, 1994–.

Brewer, John, and Susan Staves, eds. *Early Modern Conceptions of Property*. New York: Routledge, 1995.

Brown, Frederick. *Zola: A Life*. New York: Farrar, Strauss, Giroux, 1995.

Burbank, Jane. *Russian Peasants Go to Court: Legal Culture in the Countryside, 1905–1917*. Bloomington: Indiana University Press, 2004.

Byford, Andy. *Literary Scholarship in Late Imperial Russia: Rituals of Academic Institutionalization*. London: Legenda, 2007.

Cameron, Rondo. "Some Lessons of History for Developing Nations." *The American Economic Review* 57, no. 2 (1967): 312–324.

Canovan, Margaret. *Populism*. New York: Harcourt Brace Jovanovich, 1981.

Chernukha, V. G. *Krest'ianskii vopros v pravitel'stvennoi politike Rossii (60–70-e gody XIX v.)*. Leningrad: Nauka, 1972.

———. *Pravitel'stvennaia politika v otnoshenii pechati: 60–70-e gody XIX veka*. Leningrad: Nauka, 1989.

Chistov, K. V. *Russkaia narodnaia utopiia: Genezis i funktsii sotsial'no-utopicheskikh legend*. St. Petersburg: Dmitrii Bulanin, 2003.

Clowes, Edith W., Samuel D. Kassow, and James L. West, eds. *Between Tsar and People: Educated Society and the Quest for Public Identity in Late Imperial Russia*. Princeton: Princeton University Press, 1991.

Demchenko, A. A. *Molodye gody Nikolaia Chernyshevskogo*. Saratov: Privol'zhskoe knizhnoe izdatel'stvo, 1989.

Diakin, V. S. and B. V. Ananich, eds. *Krizis samoderzhaviia v Rossii, 1895–1917*. Leningrad: Nauka, 1984.

———. *Samoderzhavie, burzhuaziia i dvorianstvo v 1907–1911 gg*. Leningrad: Nauka, 1978.

Dinershtein, E. A. *Rossiiskoe knigoizdanie: Konets XVIII–XX v.; Izbrannye stat'i*. Moscow: Nauka, 2004.

Dolbilov, M. D., and A. I. Miller, eds. *Zapadnye okrainy Rossiiskoi imperii*. Moscow: Novoe literaturnoe obozrenie, 2006.

Dronov, I. E. "Put' konservatora." In *Grazhdanin konservator*, by V. P. Meshcherskii, 17–29. Moscow: Ikhtios, 2005.

Drummond, Ian. "The Russian Gold Standard, 1897–1914." *Journal of Economic History* 36, no. 3 (September 1976): 663–688.

Edmondson, Linda, and Peter Waldron, eds. *Economy and Society in Russia and the Soviet Union, 1860–1930: Essays for Olga Crisp*. New York: St. Martin's Press, 1992.

Emelianov, N. P. *"Otechestvennye zapiski" N. A. Nekrasova i M. E. Saltykova-Shchedrina, 1868–1884*. Leningrad: Khudozhestvennaia literatura, 1986.

Emmons, Terence. "The Beseda Circle, 1899–1905." *Slavic Review* 32, no. 3 (1973): 461–490.

———. *The Formation of Political Parties and the First National Elections in Russia.* Cambridge: Harvard University Press, 1983.

Entsiklopedicheskii slovar' reprintnoe vosproizvedenie izdaniia F. A. Brokgauz-I .A. Efron 1890 g. 55 vols. Iaroslavl, 1992.

Esin, B. I. *Istoriia russkoi zhurnalistiki XIX veka.* Moscow: MGU, 1989.

———. "Russkaia legal'naia pressa kontsa XIX–nachala XX v." In *Iz istorii russkoi zhurnalistiki kontsa XIX–nachala XX v,* 3–67. Moscow: MGU, 1973.

Evans, Alfred B., and Vladimir Gelman, eds. *The Politics of Local Government in Russia.* Lanham, MD: Rowman & Littlefield Publishers, 2004.

Evtuhov, Catherine, David Goldfrank, Lindsey Hughes, and Richard Stites. *A History of Russia: Peoples, Legends, Events, Forces.* Boston: Houghton Mifflin, 2004.

Fallows, Thomas S. "The Russian Fronde and the Zemstvo Movement: Economic Agitation and Gentry Politics in the Mid-1890s." *Russian Review* 44, no. 2 (1985): 119–138.

———. "The Zemstvo and the Bureaucracy." In *The Zemstvo in Russia: An Experiment in Local Self-Government,* edited by Terence Emmons and Wayne S. Vucinich, 133–241. Cambridge: Cambridge University Press, 1982.

Field, Daniel. "Kavelin and Russian Liberalism." *Slavic Review* 32, no. 1 (1973): 59–78.

Fischer, George. *Russian Liberalism: From Gentry to Intelligentsia.* Cambridge: Harvard University Press, 1958.

Frank, Joseph. *Dostoevsky: The Seeds of Revolt, 1821–1849.* Princeton: Princeton University Press, 1976.

Frank, Stephen P. *Crime, Cultural Conflict, and Justice in Rural Russia, 1856–1914.* Berkeley: University of California Press, 1999.

Frankel, Jonathan. *Prophecy and Politics: Socialism, Nationalism, and the Russian Jews, 1862–1917.* Cambridge: Cambridge University Press, 1981.

Freeze, Gregory. "A National Liberation Movement and the Shift in Russian Liberalism, 1901–1903." *Slavic Review* 28, no. 1 (1969): 81–91.

Frierson, Cathy A. *Peasant Icons: Representations of Rural People in Late Nineteenth-Century Russia.* New York: Oxford University Press, 1993.

Ganelin, R. Sh. *Rossiiskoe samoderzhavie v 1905 godu: Reformy i revoliutsiia.* St. Petersburg: Nauka, 1991.

——— et al., eds. *Sankt-Peterburg: 300 let istorii.* St. Petersburg: Nauka, 2003.

Gerschenkron, Alexander. "Agrarian Policies and Industrialization: Russia, 1861–1917." In *The Cambridge Economic History of Europe.* Vol. 6, *The Industrial Revolution and After: Incomes, Population, and Technological Change,* edited by H. J. Habakkuk and M. Postan, 2:706–800. Cambridge: Cambridge University Press, 1965.

———. *Economic Backwardness in Historical Perspective.* Cambridge: Belknap Press, 1962.

———. "An Economic History of Russia." *Journal of Economic History* 12, no. 2 (1952): 146–159.

Gindin, I. F. "Russkaia burzhuaziia v period kapitalizma, ee razvitie i osobennosti." *Istoriia SSSR* 2 (1963): 1–42.

Gleason, Abbott. *Young Russia: The Genesis of Russian Radicalism in the 1860s.* New York: Viking, 1980.

Gogolevskii, A. V. *Ocherki istorii russkogo liberalizma XIX–nachala XX veka.* St. Petersburg: Izdatel'stvo Sankt-Peterburgskogo universiteta, 1996.

Gorshkov, Boris. *Russia's Factory Children: State, Society, and Law, 1800–1917.* Pittsburgh, PA: University of Pittsburgh Press, 2009.

Gregory, Paul. "The Agrarian Crisis Revisited." In *The Soviet Rural Economy,* edited by Robert Stuart, 21–32. Totowa, NJ: Rowman & Allanheld, 1984.

———. "Rents, Land Prices, and Economic Theory: The Russian Agrarian Crisis." In *Economy and Society in Russia and the Soviet Union, 1860–1930: Essays for Olga Crisp,* edited by Linda Edmondson and Peter Waldron, 7–12. New York: St. Martin's Press, 1992.

Grigor'ev, V. V. *Imperatorskii s. peterburgskii universitet v techenie pervykh piatidesiati let ego sushchestvovaniia.* St. Petersburg: V. Bezobrazov i Komi, 1870.

Grossman, Joan Delaney. "Rise and Decline of the 'Literary' Journal: 1880–1917." In *Literary Journals in Imperial Russia,* edited by Deborah A. Martinsen, 80–98. Cambridge: Cambridge University Press, 1997.

Haberer, Erich. *Jews and Revolution in Nineteenth-Century Russia.* Cambridge: Cambridge University Press, 1995.

Hacking, Ian. *The Taming of Chance.* Cambridge: Cambridge University Press, 1990.

Haimson, Leopold. "The Problem of Social Identities in Early Twentieth-Century Russia." *Slavic Review* 47, no. 1 (1988): 1–20.

Hamburg, G. M. *Boris Chicherin & Early Russian Liberalism, 1828–1866.* Stanford: Stanford University Press, 1992.

———. *Politics of the Russian Nobility, 1881–1905.* New Brunswick, NJ: Rutgers University Press, 1984.

———. "The Crisis in Russian Agriculture: A Comment." *Slavic Review* 37, no. 3 (September 1978): 481–486.

Hamm, Michael F. *Kiev: A Portrait, 1800–1917.* Princeton: Princeton University Press, 1993.

Harcave, Sidney. *Count Sergei Witte and the Twilight of Imperial Russia: A Biography.* Armonk, NY: M. E. Sharpe, 2004.

Hart, James G. "From Frontier Outpost to Provincial Capital: Saratov, 1590–1860." In *Politics and Society in Provincial Russia: Saratov, 1590–1917,* edited by Rex Wade and Scott Seregny, 10–28. Columbus: Ohio State University Press, 1989.

Hartley, Janet M. "Provincial and Local Government." In *The Cambridge History of Russia.* Vol. 2, *Imperial Russia,* edited by Dominic Lieven, 449–468. Cambridge: Cambridge University Press, 2006.

Heuman, Susan. *Kistiakovsky: The Struggle for National and Constitutional Rights in the Last Years of Tsarism.* Cambridge: Harvard University Press, 1998.

Hughes, Linda K., and Michael Lund, eds. *The Victorian Serial*. Charlottesville: University Press of Virginia, 1991.

Iartsev, A. A. *Senat i zemstvo: Administrativnaia iustitsiia i mestnoe samoupravlenie v dorevoliutsionnoi Rossii, 1864–1890*. Kaliningrad: Iskra, 2008.

Iasnopol'skii, N. P. *Spetsializatsiia uchebnykh planov prepodavaniia i zaniatii naukami iuridicheskimi, gosudarstvennymi i ekonomicheskimi v universitetakh Rossii*. Kiev: Tipografiia universiteta Sv. Vladimira, 1907.

Ignatova, E. A. *Zapiski o Peterburge: Zhizneopisanie goroda so vremeni ego osnovaniia do 40-kh godov XX veka*. St. Petersburg: Amfora, 2003.

Isachenko, A. G., ed. *Russkoe geograficheskoe obshchestvo: 150 let*. Moscow: Progress/ Pangeia, 1995.

Itenberg, B. S. *P. L. Lavrov v russkom revoliutsionnom dvizhenii*. Moscow: Nauka, 1988.

———. "Nekotorye voprosy izucheniia russkogo liberalizma XIX veka." In *Russkii liberalizm: Istoricheskie sud'by i perspektivy; Materialy mezhdunarodnoi nauchnoi konferentsii, Moskva, 27–29 maia 1998 g.*, edited by V. V. Shelokhaev et al., 491–503. Moscow: Rossiiskaia politicheskaia entsiklopediia, 1999.

Itenberg, B. S., and V. V. Shelokhaev, eds. *Rossiiskie liberaly: Sbornik statei*. Moscow: Rosspen, 2001.

Josephson, Matthew. *Zola and His Time*. New York: Russell & Russell, 1969.

Judge, Edward H., and James Y. Simms Jr., eds. *Modernization and Revolution: Dilemmas of Progress in Late Imperial Russia; Essays in Honor of Arthur P. Mendel*. [Boulder, CO?]: East European Monographs; New York: Distributed by Columbia University Press, 1992.

Judson, Pieter. *Exclusive Revolutionaries: Liberal Politics, Social Experience, and National Identity in the Austrian Empire, 1848–1914*. Ann Arbor: University of Michigan Press, 1996.

Kagan, M. S. *Grad Petrov v istorii russkoi kul'tury*. St. Petersburg: Paritet, 2006.

Kahan, Arcadius. *The Plow, the Hammer, and the Knout: An Economic History of Eighteenth-Century Russia*. Chicago: University of Chicago Press, 1985.

Katz, Martin. *Mikhail N. Katkov: A Political Biography, 1818–1887*. The Hague: Mouton, 1966.

Kazakova-Aprakimova, E. Iu. *Formirovanie grazhdanskogo obshchestva: Gorodskie soslovnye korporatsii i obshchestvennye organizatsii na Srednem Urale (vtoraia polovina XIX-nachalo XX v.)*. Ekaterinburg: RAN-Ural'skoe otdelenie, Institut istorii i arkheologii, 2008.

Kaznacheev, P. *Pragmatizm i liberal'noe mirovozzrenie*. Moscow: Institut ekonomiki perekhodnogo perioda, 2002.

Kel'ner, V. E. *Ocherki po istorii russko-evreiskogo knizhnogo dela vo vtoroi polovine XIX-nachale XX v.* St. Petersburg: Rossiiskaia natsional'naia biblioteka, 2003.

———. *Chelovek svoego vremeni: M. M. Stasiulevich, izdatel'skoe delo i liberal'naia oppositsiia*. St. Petersburg: Izd-vo Rossiiskoi natsional'noi biblioteki, 1993.

Kindersley, Richard. *The First Russian Revisionists: A Study of "Legal Marxism" in Russia*. Oxford: Clarendon Press, 1962.

Kingston-Mann, Esther. *In Search of the True West: Culture, Economics, and Problems of Russian Development*. Princeton: Princeton University Press, 1999.

———. "Marxism and Russian Rural Development: Problems of Evidence, Experience, and Culture." *The American Historical Review* 86, no. 4 (1981): 731–752.

Kitaev, V. A. *Liberal'naia mysl' v Rossii, 1860–1880 gg.* Saratov: Izdatel'stvo Saratovskogo Universiteta, 2004.

———. "The Unique Liberalism of Vestnik Evopy (1870–1880)." *Russian Studies in History* 46, no. 1 (2007): 50–67.

Klier, John Doyle. *Imperial Russia's Jewish Question, 1855–1881*. Cambridge: Cambridge University Press, 1995.

Knight, Nathaniel. "Was the Intelligentsia Part of the Nation? Visions of Society in Post-Emancipation Russia." *Kritika: Explorations in Eurasian History* 7, no. 4 (Fall 2006): 733–758.

Korelin, A. P., N. G. Koroleva, and L. F. Pisar'kova, eds. *Zemskoe samoupravlenie v Rossii 1864–1918*. 2 vols. Moscow: Nauka, 2005.

Korotkikh, M. G. *Samoderzhavie i sudebnaia reforma 1864 goda v Rossii*. Voronezh: Izd. Voronezhskogo universiteta, 1989.

Koshman, L. V. *Gorod i gorodskaia zhizn' v Rossii XIX stoletiia: Sotsial'nye i kul'turnye aspekty*. Moscow: Rosspen, 2008.

Koval'chenko, I. D. *Agrarnyi stroi Rossii vtoroi poloviny XIX–nachala XX vv.* Moscow: Rosspen, 2004.

Koval'chenko, I. D., and L. V. Milov. *Vserossiiskii agrarnyi rynok: XVIII–nachalo XX veka*. Moscow: Nauka, 1974.

Kulomzin, A. N. *M. Kh. Reitern: Biograficheskii ocherk*. St. Petersburg: Tip. Sel'skogo vestnika, 1919.

Kupriianov, A. I. *Gorodskaia kul'tura russkoi provintsii: Konets XVIII–pervaia polovina XIX veka*. Moscow: Novyi khronograf, 2007.

Lampert, Evgenii. *Sons against Fathers: Studies in Russian Radicalism and Revolution*. Oxford: Clarendon Press, 1965.

Lanshchikov, A. P. *N. G. Chernyshevskii*. Moscow: Sovremennik, 1982.

Lavrin, Janko. "Populists and Slavophiles." *Russian Review* 21, no. 4 (1962): 307–317.

Lederhendler, Eli. *The Road to Modern Jewish Politics: Political Tradition and Political Reconstruction in the Jewish Community of Tsarist Russia*. Oxford: Oxford University Press, 1989.

Leikina-Svirskaia, V. R. *Intelligentsiia v Rossii vo vtoroi polovina XIX v.* Moscow: Mysl', 1971.

———. *Russkaia intelligentsia v 1900–1917 gg.* Moscow: Mysl', 1981.

Leontovitsch, V. V. *Istoriia liberalizma v Rossii: 1762–1914*. Moscow: Russkii put', 1995.

Liashenko, L. M. *Aleksandr II, ili, Istoriia trekh odinochestv*. Moscow: Molodaia gvardiia, 2002.

Lincoln, W. Bruce. *In the Vanguard of Reform: Russia's Enlightened Bureaucrats, 1825–1861*. DeKalb: Northern Illinois University Press, 1982.

Lindenmeyr, Adele. "'Primordial and Gelatinous'? Civil Society in Imperial Russia." *Kritika: Explorations in Eurasian History* 12, no. 3 (Summer 2011): 705–720.

Losev, A. F. *Vladimir Solov'ev i ego vremia*. Moscow: Molodaia gvardiia, 2000.

Loshchits, Iu. M. *Goncharov*. Moscow: Molodaia gvardiia, 1986.

Lotman, Iu. M. *Karamzin*. St. Petersburg: Iskusstvo-SPB, 1997.

Manchester, Laurie. *Holy Fathers, Secular Sons: Clergy, Intelligentsia, and the Modern Self in Revolutionary Russia*. DeKalb: Northern Illinois University Press, 2008.

Manning, Roberta Thompson. "The Zemstvo and Politics." In *The Zemstvo in Russia: An Experiment in Local Self-Government*, edited by Terence Emmons and Wayne S. Vucinich, 133–176. Cambridge: Cambridge University Press, 1982.

Marks, Steven G. *Road to Power: The Trans-Siberian Railroad and the Colonization of Asian Russia, 1850–1917*. Ithaca: Cornell University Press, 1991.

McReynolds, Louise. *The News Under Russia's Old Regime: The Development of a Mass-Circulation Press*. Princeton: Princeton University Press, 1991.

Mendel, Arthur. *Dilemmas of Progress in Tsarist Russia: Legal Marxism and Legal Populism*. Cambridge: Harvard University Press, 1961.

———. "N. K. Mikhailovskij and His Criticism of Russian Marxism." *American Slavic and East European Review* 14, no. 3 (1955): 331–345.

Migulin, P. P. *Reforma denezhnogo obrashcheniia i promyshlennyi krizis v Rossii (1893–1902)* Moscow: Obshchestvo kuptsov i promyshlennikov Rossii, 2006.

Mironov, B. N. *Khlebnye tseny v Rossii za dva stoletiia (XVIII–XIX vv.)*. Leningrad: Nauka, 1985.

———. *Sotsial'naia istoriia Rossii perioda imperii: XVIII–nachalo XX v.* 2 vols. St. Petersburg: Dmitrii Bulanin, 1999.

Moser, Charles A. *Antinihilism in the Russian Novel of the 1860's*. The Hague: Mouton, 1964.

Mosse, W. E. "Aspects of Tsarist Bureaucracy: The State Council in the Late Nineteenth Century." *The English Historical Review* 95, no. 375 (April 1980): 268–292.

Nathans, Benjamin. *Beyond the Pale: The Jewish Encounter with Late Imperial Russia*. Berkeley: University of California Press, 2002.

Nehru, Jawaharlal. "Democracy, Communism, Socialism, and Capitalism." *The New Leader*, September 8, 1958, 1–13.

Nikitina, M. A. "Vestnik Evropy." In *Literaturnyi protsess i russkaia zhurnalistika kontsa XIX–nachala XX veka: 1890–1904; Burzhuazno-liberal'nye i modernistskie izdaniia*, edited by B. A. Bialik, V. A. Keldysh, and V. R. Shcherbina, 4–44. Moscow: Nauka, 1982.

Nikoladze, N. E. "Osvobozhdenie N. G. Chernyshevskogo." In *N. G. Chernyshevskii v vospominaniiakh sovremennikov*, edited by Iu. G. Oksman, 2:251–279. Saratov: Saratovskoe knizhnoe izd-vo, 1959.

Nikolaev, V. A. *Aleksandr Vtoroi: Biografiia*. Moscow: Zakharov, 2005.

Nord, Philip. "Introduction." In *Civil Society before Democracy: Lessons from Nineteenth-Century Europe*, edited by Nancy Bermeo and Philip Nord, i–xxix. Lanham, MD: Rowman & Littlefield Publishers, 2000.

Offord, Derek. *Portraits of Early Russian Liberals: A Study of the Thought of T. N. Granovsky, V. P. Botkin, P. V. Annenkov, A. V. Druzhinin, and K. D. Kavelin*. Cambridge: Cambridge University Press, 1985.

Okker, Patricia. *Social Stories: The Magazine Novel in Nineteenth-Century America*. Charlottesville: University of Virginia Press, 2003.

Oreshkin, V. V. *Vol'noe ekonomicheskoe obshchestvo v Rossii, 1765–1917: Istoriko-ekonomicheskii ocherk*. Moscow: Izd-vo Akademii nauk SSSR, 1963.

Orlovsky, Daniel T. *The Limits of Reform: The Ministry of Internal Affairs in Imperial Russia, 1802–1881*. Cambridge: Harvard University Press, 1981.

Ostrovskii, I. V. *Agrarnaia politika tsarizma v Sibiri perioda imperializma*. Novosibirsk: Izd-vo Novosibirskogo universiteta, 1991.

Paperna, A. I. "Iz nikolaevskoi epokhi." In *Evrei v Rossii: XIX vek*, edited by V. E. Kel'ner, 27–177. Moscow: Novoe literaturnoe obozrenie, 2000.

Pearson, Thomas S. *Russian Officialdom in Crisis: Autocracy and Local Self-Government, 1861–1900*. Cambridge: Cambridge University Press, 1989.

Pietrov-Ennker, B., and G. N. Ul'ianova, eds. *Grazhdanskaia identichnost' i sfera grazhdanskoi deiatel'nosti v Rossiiskoi imperii: Vtoraia polovina XIX–nachalo XX veka*. Moscow: Rosspen, 2007.

Piksanov, N. K. *Roman Gonacharova "Obryv" v svete sotsial'noi istorii*. Leningrad: Nauka, 1968.

Pipes, Richard. *Struve: Liberal on the Left, 1870–1905*. Cambridge: Harvard University Press, 1970.

Pirumova, N. I. *Zemskoe liberal'noe dvizhenie: Sotsial'nye korni i evoliutsiia do nachala XX veka*. Moscow: Nauka, 1977.

Pirumova, N. I., and V. Ia. Laverychev. *Zemskaia intelligentsiia i ee rol' v obshchestvennoi bor'be do nachala XX v.* Moscow: Nauka, 1986.

Pirumova, N. I., V. A. Tvardovskaia, and V. Ia. Laverychev, eds. *Obshchestvennoe dvizhenie v Rossii XIX veka: Sbornik statei*. Moscow: Institut istorii AN SSSR, 1986.

Pogorelskin, Alexis. "'The Messenger of Europe'." In *Literary Journals in Imperial Russia*, edited by Deborah A. Martinsen, 129–149. Cambridge: Cambridge University Press, 1997.

———. "*Vestnik Evropy* and the Polish Question in the Reign of Alexander II." *Slavic Review* 46, no. 1 (Spring 1987): 87–105.

Poole, Randall. "Introduction." In *Problems of Idealism: Essays in Russian Social Philosophy*, edited and translated by Randall Poole, 6–78. New Haven: Yale University Press, 2003.

Porokh, I. V. "Londonskie vstrechi A. N. Pypina s A. I. Gertsenom (k voprosu ob ikh vzaimootnosheniiakh)." *Osvoboditel'noe dvizhenie v Rossii* 14 (1992): 1–20.

Porter, Thomas Earl. *The Zemstvo and the Emergence of Civil Society in Late Imperial Russia, 1864–1917*. San Francisco: Mellen Research University Press, 1991.

Prilenskii, V. I. *Opyt issledovaniia mirovozzreniia rannikh russkikh liberalov*. Moscow: Rossiiskaia akademiia nauk, 1995.

Pustarnakov, V. F., and I. F. Khudushina, eds. *Liberalizm v Rossii*. Moscow: Rossiiskaia akademiia nauk, 1996.

Putnam, George F. *Russian Alternatives to Marxism: Christian Socialism and Idealistic Liberalism in Twentieth-Century Russia*. Knoxville: University of Tennessee Press, 1977.

Randall, Francis B. *N. G. Chernyshevskii*. New York: Twayne Publishers, 1967.

Riasanovsky, Nicholas. *A History of Russia*. New York: Oxford University Press, 1993.

Rimlinger, Gaston V. "Autocracy and the Factory Order in Early Russian Industrialization." *Journal of Economic History* 20, no. 1 (1960): 67–92.

Robbins, Richard, Jr. *Famine in Russia, 1891–1892: The Imperial Government Responds to a Crisis*. New York: Columbia University Press, 1975.

Roosevelt, Priscilla Reynolds. *Apostle of Russian Liberalism: Timofei Granovsky*. Newtonville, MA: Oriental Research Partners, 1986.

Rosenberg, William. *Liberals in the Russian Revolution: The Constitutional Democratic Party, 1917–1921*. Princeton: Princeton University Press, 1974.

———. "The Zemstvo in 1917 and Its Fate Under Bolshevik Rule." In *The Zemstvo in Russia: An Experiment in Local Self-Government*, edited by Terence Emmons and Wayne S. Vucinich, 383–423. Cambridge: Cambridge University Press, 1982.

Ruble, Blair. *Second Metropolis: Pragmatic Pluralism in Gilded Age Chicago, Silver Age Moscow, and Meiji Osaka*. Cambridge: Cambridge University Press, 2001.

Rudolph, Richard. "Agricultural Structure and Proto-Industrialization in Russia: Economic Development with Unfree Labor." *Journal of Economic History* 44, no. 1 (March 1985): 47–69.

Ruud, Charles. *Fighting Words: Imperial Censorship and the Russian Press, 1804–1906*. Toronto: University of Toronto Press, 1982.

Salov, O. A. *Zemstvo: Pervyi real'nyi institut mestnogo samoupravleniia v Rossii*. Moscow: Ekonomika, 2004.

Sanders, John Thomas. "'Once More Into the Breach, Dear Friends': A Closer Look at Indirect Tax Receipts and the Condition of the Russian Peasantry, 1881–1899." *Slavic Review* 43, no. 4 (Winter 1984): 657–666.

Sarbei, V. G. et al., eds. *Istoriia Kieva*. Vol. 2, *Kiev perioda pozdnego feodalizma i kapitalizma*. Kiev: Naukova Dumka, 1982.

Savenkov, A. A. "Vestnik Evropy." In *Ocherki po istorii russkoi zhurnalistiki i kritiki*. Vol. 2, *Vtoraia polovina XIX veka*, edited by V. E. Evgen'ev-Maksimov, 367–376. Leningrad: LGU, 1965.

Schumpeter, Joseph. *History of Economic Analysis*. New York: Oxford University Press, 1954.

Semanov, S. N. *Aleksandr II: Istoriia tsaria-osvoboditelia, ego ottsa i ego syna*. Moscow: Algoritm, Eksmo, 2003.

Seton-Watson, Hugh. *The Russian Empire, 1801–1917*. Oxford: Clarendon Press, 1967.

Shaginian, M. S. *Chelovek i vremia: Istoriia chelovecheskogo stanovleniia*. Moscow: Khudozhestvennaia literatura, 1980.

Shatsillo, K. F. *Russkii liberalizm nakanune revoliutsii, 1905–1907 gg.: Organizatsiia, programmy, taktika*. Moscow: Nauka, 1985.

Sheehan, James. *German Liberalism in the Nineteenth Century*. Chicago: University of Chicago Press, 1978.

Shelokhaev, V. V. *Kadety—Glavnaia partiia liberal'noi burzhuazii v bor'be s revoliutsiei, 1905–1907 gg.* Moscow: Nauka, 1983.

———. "Russkii liberalizm kak istoriograficheskaia i istoriosofskaia problema." *Voprosy istorii* 4 (1998): 36.

Shepelev, L. E. *Tsarizm i burzhuaziia vo vtoroi polovine XIX veka: Problemy torgovo-promyshlennoi politiki*. Leningrad: Nauka, 1981.

Simms, James Y., Jr. "The Crisis in Russian Agriculture at the End of the Nineteenth Century: A Different View." *Slavic Review* 36, no. 3 (September 1977): 377–398.

———. "The Crop Failure of 1891: Soil Exhaustion, Technological Backwardness, and Russia's 'Agrarian Crisis'." *Slavic Review* 41, no. 2 (Summer 1982): 236–250.

———. "More Grist for the Mill: A Further Look at the Crisis of Russian Agriculture at the End of the Nineteenth Century." *Slavic Review* 50, no. 4 (Winter 1991): 999–1009.

———. "On Missing the Point: A Rejoinder." *Slavic Review* 37, no. 3 (September 1978): 487–490.

———. "'Once More Into the Breach, Dear Friends': A Closer Look at Indirect Tax Receipts and the Condition of the Russian Peasantry, 1881–1899: Reply." *Slavic Review* 43, no. 4 (Winter 1984): 236–250.

Simonova, M. S. *Krizis agrarnoi politiki tsarizma nakanune pervoi rossiiskoi revoliutsii*. Moscow: Nauka, 1987.

Sinel, Allen A. "The Socialization of the Russian Bureaucratic Elite, 1811–1917: Life at the Tsarskoe Selo Lyceum and the School of Jurisprudence." *Russian History* 3, no. 1 (1976): 1–31.

Smirnov, V. B. *"Otechestvennye zapiski" i russkaia literatura 70–80-kh godov XIX veka*. Volgograd: Izd-vo Volgogradskogo gos. universiteta, 1998.

Smith-Peter, Susan. "Defining the Russian People: Konstantin Arsen'ev and Russian Statistics before 1861." *History of Science* 45, no. 1 (March 2007): 47–64.

"Sochineniia Karla Marksa v russkoi tsenzure (Arkhivnaia spravka)." *Dela i dni* 1 (1920): 315–331.

Solomon, Peter H., Jr., ed. *Reforming Justice in Russia, 1864–1996: Power, Culture, and the Limits of Legal Order*. Armonk, NY: M. E. Sharpe, 1997.

Starr, S. Frederick. *Decentralization and Self-Government in Russia, 1830–1870*. Princeton: Princeton University Press, 1972.

Stepanov, V. L. "Nikolai Khristoforovich Bunge." *Istoriia SSSR* 1 (1991): 19–35.
———. *N. Kh. Bunge: Sud'ba reformatora.* Moscow: Rosspen, 1998.
———. "Rabochii vopros v sotsial'no-ekonomicheskikh vozzreniiakh N. Kh. Bunge." *Vestnik MGU, Istoriia* 3 (1987): 17–25.
Stepanskii, A. D. *Obshchestvennye organizatsii v Rossii na rubezhe XIX–XX vv.* Moscow: Moskovskii gosudarstvennyi istoriko-arkhivnyk institute, 1982.
Stites, Richard. *Serfdom, Society, and the Arts in Imperial Russia: The Pleasure and the Power.* New Haven: Yale University Press, 2005.
Stockdale, Melissa. *Paul Miliukov and the Quest for a Liberal Russia, 1880–1918.* Ithaca: Cornell University Press, 1996.
Stocking, George W. *Victorian Anthropology.* New York: Free Press, 1987.
Tarnovskii, K. N. *Sotsial'no-ekonomicheskaia istoriia Rossii: Nachalo XX v.* Moscow: Nauka, 1990.
Thurston, Robert W. *Liberal City, Conservative State: Moscow and Russia's Urban Crisis, 1906–1914.* New York: Oxford University Press, 1987.
Timberlake, Charles, ed. "Introduction." In *Essays on Russian Liberalism,* 3–29. Columbia: University of Missouri Press, 1972.
Treadgold, Donald. "The Constitutional Democrats and the Russian Liberal Tradition." *American Slavic and East European Review* 10, no. 2 (1951): 85–94.
Tumanova, A. S. *Obshchestvennye organizatsii i russkaia publika v nachale XX veka.* Moscow: Novyi khronograf, 2008.
Utevskii, L. S. *Zhizn' Goncharova: Vospominaniia, pis'ma, dnevniki.* Moscow: Agraf, 2000.
Venturi, Franco. *Roots of Revolution: A History of the Populist and Socialist Movements in Nineteenth-Century Russia,* translated by Francis Haskell. New York: Grosset & Dunlap, 1966.
Vinnikova, G. E. *Turgenev i Rossiia.* Moscow: Sovetskaia Rossiia, 1986.
Vital, David. *The Origins of Zionism.* Oxford: Clarendon Press, 1975.
Vizetelly, Ernest Alfred. *Émile Zola, Novelist and Reformer: An Account of His Life and Work.* London: John Lane, 1904.
Volin, Lazar. *A Century of Russian Agriculture: From Alexander II to Khrushchev.* Cambridge: Harvard University Press, 1970.
Von Laue, Theodore. "Factory Inspection under the 'Witte System': 1892–1903." *American Slavic and East European Review* 19, no. 3 (1960): 347–362.
———. "The Fate of Capitalism in Russia: The Narodnik Version." *American Slavic and East European Review* 13, no. 1 (1954): 11–28.
———. "The High Cost and Gamble of the Witte System: A Chapter in the Industrialization of Russia." *Journal of Economic History* 13, no. 4 (Autumn 1953): 425–448.
———. "Russian Peasants in the Factory, 1892–1904." *Journal of Economic History* 21, no. 1 (1961): 61–80.
———. "*Struve: Liberal on the Left, 1870–1905,* Richard Pipes." *The American Historical Review* 77, no. 4 (1972): 1162–1163.

———. "Tsarist Labor Policy, 1895–1903." *Journal of Modern History* 34, no. 2 (1962): 135–145.

Vucinich, Alexander. *Darwin in Russian Thought.* Berkeley: University of California Press, 1988.

Walicki, Andrzej. *The Controversy Over Capitalism: Studies in the Social Philosophy of the Russian Populists.* Notre Dame, IN: University of Notre Dame Press, 1969.

———. *Legal Philosophies of Russian Liberalism.* Notre Dame: University of Notre Dame Press, 1992.

———. "Russian Social Thought: An Introduction to the Intellectual History of Nineteenth-Century Russia." *Russian Review* 36, no. 1 (1977): 1–45.

Walkin, Jacob. "The Attitude of the Tsarist Government toward the Labor Problem." *American Slavic and East European Review* 13, no. 2 (1954): 163–184.

———. *The Rise of Democracy in Pre-Revolutionary Russia.* New York: Praeger, 1962.

Weeks, Theodore R. *Nation and State in Late Imperial Russia: Nationalism and Russification on the Western Frontier, 1863–1914.* DeKalb: Northern Illinois University Press, 1996.

Wheatcroft, S. G. "Crises and the Condition of the Peasantry in Late Imperial Russia." In *Peasant Economy, Culture, and Politics of European Russia, 1800–1921,* edited by Esther Kingston-Mann and Timothy Mixter, 128–175. Princeton: Princeton University Press, 1991.

———. "Grain Production and Utilization in Russia and the USSR before Collectivization." PhD diss., University of Birmingham, 1980.

Whittaker, Cynthia H. *The Origins of Modern Russian Education: An Intellectual Biography of Count Sergei Uvarov, 1786–1855.* DeKalb: Northern Illinois University Press, 1984.

Wirtschafter, Elise Kimerling. *Structures of Society: Imperial Russia's "People of Various Ranks."* DeKalb: Northern Illinois University Press, 1994.

Woehrlin, William F. *Chernyshevskii: The Man and the Journalist.* Cambridge: Harvard University Press, 1971.

Wolfe, Bertram D. "Backwardness and Industrialization in Russian History and Thought." *Slavic Review* 26, no. 2 (1967): 177–203.

Wortman, Richard. *The Crisis of Russian Populism.* London: Cambridge University Press, 1967.

———. *The Development of a Russian Legal Consciousness.* Chicago: University of Chicago Press, 1976.

Zaitseva, Tatiana, and Raisa Slonimskaia, eds. *Volnye mysli: K iubileiu Sergeia Slonimskogo.* St. Petersburg: Kompozitor, 2003.

Zelnik, Reginald. *Labor and Society in Tsarist Russia: The Factory Workers of St. Petersburg, 1855–1870.* Stanford: Stanford University Press, 1971.

Zyrianov, P. N., and V. V. Shelokhaev. *Pervaia russkaia revoliutsiia v amerikanskoi i angliiskoi burzhuaznoi istoriografii.* Moscow: Mysl', 1976.

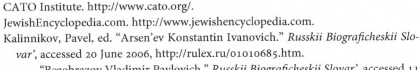

WEBSITES

CATO Institute. http://www.cato.org/.

JewishEncyclopedia.com. http://www.jewishencyclopedia.com.

Kalinnikov, Pavel, ed. "Arsen'ev Konstantin Ivanovich." *Russkii Biograficheskii Slovar'*, accessed 20 June 2006, http://rulex.ru/01010685.htm.

———. "Bezobrazov Vladimir Pavlovich." *Russkii Biograficheskii Slovar'*, accessed 11 May 2006, http://www.rulex.ru/01021112.htm.

———. "Chervinskii Petr Petrovich (Chirvinskii)." *Russkii Biograficheskii Slovar'*, accessed 27 September 2006, http://rulex.ru/01240132.htm.

———. "Chuprov Aleksandr Aleksandrovich." *Russkii Biograficheskii Slovar'*, accessed 11 May 2007, http://www.rulex.ru/01240025.htm.

———. "Engelgardt Anna Nikolaevna." *Russkii Biograficheskii Slovar'*, accessed 17 May 2006, http://www.rulex.ru/01300035.htm.

———. "Ermolov Aleksei Sergeevich." *Russkii Biograficheskii Slovar'*, accessed 10 July 2006, http://www.rulex.ru/01060183.htm.

———. "Gagarin Andrei Grigor'evich, kniaz." *Russkii Biograficheskii Slovar'*, accessed 11 May 2007, http://www.rulex.ru/01040781.htm.

———. "Ivaniukov Ivan Ivanovich." *Russkii Biograficheskii Slovar'*, accessed 11 May 2007, http://www.rulex.ru/01090088.htm.

———. "Kablits Iosif Ivanovich (Iuzov)." *Russkii Biograficheskii Slovar'*, accessed 12 March 2007, http://rulex.ru/011110371.htm.

———. "Kakhanov Mikhail Semenovich." *Russkii Biograficheskii Slovar'*, accessed 7 March 2007, http://rulex.ru/01110741.htm.

———. "Karamzin Nikolai Mikhailovich." *Russkii Biograficheskii Slovar'*, accessed 20 November 2006, http://www.rulex.ru/01110594.htm.

———. "Klements Dmitriii Aleksandrovich." *Russkii Biograficheskii Slovar'*, accessed 11 September 2006, http://rulex.ru/01111304.htm.

———. "Kruze Nikolai Fedorovich (fon)." *Russkii Biograficheskii Slovar'*, accessed 11 May 2006, http://www.rulex.ru/01110346.htm.

———. "Miklashevskii Aleksandr Nikolaevich." *Russkii Biograficheskii Slovar'*, accessed 19 July 2006, http://www.rulex.ru/01130472.htm.

———. "Posnikov Aleksandr Sergeevich." *Russkii Biograficheskii Slovar'*, accessed 11 May 2007, http://www.rulex.ru/01160497.htm.

———. "Rafalovich Artur Germanovich." *Russkii Biograficheskii Slovar'*, accessed 19 July 2006, http://www.rulex.ru/01170282.htm.

———. "Slonimskii Zinovii." *Russkii Biograficheskii Slovar'*, accessed 22 June 2006, http://rulex.ru/01181123.htm.

———. "Slonimskii Leonid-Liudvig Zinov'evich." *Russkii Biograficheskii Slovar'*, accessed 23 June 2006, http://rulex.ru/01181124.htm.

———. "Sol'skii Dmitriii Martynovich." *Russkii Biograficheskii Slovar'*, accessed 11 May 2006, http://www.rulex.ru/01180858.htm.

———. "Stasiulevich Mikhail Matveevich." *Russkii Biograficheskii Slovar'*, Studiia Kolibri, accessed 23 June 2006, http://rulex.ru/01181219.htm.

———. "Tsion Il'ia Faddeich." *Russkii Biograficheskii Slovar'*, accessed 18 July 2006, http://rulex.ru/01230085.htm.

———. "Valuev Petr Aleksandrovich." *Russkii Biograficheskii Slovar'*, accessed 11 May 2006, http://www.rulex.ru/01030018.htm.

———. "Vasil'chikov Aleksandr Illarionovich." *Russkii Biograficheskii Slovar'*, accessed 30 August 2006, http://rulex.ru/01030446.htm.

———. "Vorontsov Vasilii Petrovich." *Russkii Biograficheskii Slovar'*, accessed 5 March 2007, http://rulex.ru/01030853.htm.

———. "Voroponov Fedor Fedorovich." *Russkii Biograficheskii Slovar'*, accessed 29 August 2006, http://rulex.ru/01030861.htm.

Oxford Dictionary of National Biography. http://www.oxforddnb.com/.

Russkii Biograficheskii Slovar'. http://www.rulex.ru/

Zhurnal'nyi Zal: Vestnik Evropy. http://www.magazines.russ.ru/vestnik/.

Index

Made in the USA
Monee, IL
08 October 2021